TENSE/ASPECT
and the Development of Auxiliaries
in
KRU LANGUAGES

SUMMER INSTITUTE OF LINGUISTICS
PUBLICATIONS IN LINGUISTICS

Publication Number 78

EDITORS

Virgil L. Poulter
University of Texas
at Arlington

Desmond C. Derbyshire
Summer Institute
of Linguistics

ASSISTANT EDITORS

Alan C. Wares

Iris M. Wares

CONSULTING EDITORS

Doris A. Bartholomew
Pamela M. Bendor-Samuel
Robert A. Dooley
Jerold A. Edmonson
Austin Hale

Phyllis Healey
Robert E. Longacre
Eugene E. Loos
William R. Merrifield
Viola G. Waterhouse

TENSE/ASPECT

and the Development of Auxiliaries

in

KRU LANGUAGES

Lynell Marchese

A Publication of
The Summer Institute of Linguistics
and
The University of Texas at Arlington
1986

© 1986 by Summer Institute of Linguistics, Inc.
Library of Congress Catalog Card. No.: 86-060586
ISBN: 0-88312-097-6

ALL RIGHTS RESERVED

No part of this publication may be reproduced, stored in a retrieval system, or transmitted in any form by any means--electronic, mechanical, photocopy, recording, or otherwise--without the express permission of the Summer Institute of Linguistics, with the exception of brief excerpts in magazine articles and/or reviews.

Cover design by Lynne Fiore

Copies of this publication and other publications of the Summer Institute of Linguistics may be obtained from:

Bookstore
Summer Institute of Linguistics
7500 W. Camp Wisdom Road
Dallas, TX 75236

CONTENTS

Preface ix

Abbreviations xi

1 Introductory Remarks for a Diachronic Study 1
  1.1 Theoretical Outlook and Subject of Study 1
  1.2 Geographic Situation and Classification of the Kru Language Family 2
  1.3 The Data Base 11
  1.4 Phonological and Grammatical Overview 12
    1.4.1 Phonology 12
    1.4.2 Word order 16
  1.5 Verbal Categories 23
    1.5.1 Morphological expressions of verbal categories 23
    1.5.2 Definition of terms 25
  1.6 Conclusion 28

2 Basic Aspectual Categories in Kru 29
  2.1 Introduction 29
  2.2 The Perfective/Imperfective Distinction 30
    2.2.1 The factative 30
    2.2.2 The imperfective 39
  2.3 The Progressive Aspect 63
    2.3.1 Basic structure of the periphrastic progressive 63
    2.3.2 The progressive vs. the imperfective 66

2.3.3 The universality of the locative-progressive connection	67
2.3.4 Relative age of the progressive construction	68
2.4 The Perfect Aspect	68
2.5 Conclusion	70
3 The Emergence of Three Future Auxiliaries	**72**
3.1 Futures in Kru	72
3.2 Etymological Links between Auxiliaries and Full Verbs	73
3.3 Are Auxiliaries Main Verbs?	77
3.4 How Do Full Verbs Become Auxiliaries?	82
3.4.1 Hyman's proposal	83
3.4.2 Objections to the serialization hypothesis	84
3.4.3 The alternative	93
3.4.4 The verb-->auxiliary continuum	95
3.5 'Go': a Case History	96
3.5.1 The verb 'go'	96
3.5.2 Semantic shift	98
3.5.3 Phonological changes	104
3.5.4 Interaction of semantic shift and phonological change	109
3.5.5 Grammaticalization	114
3.5.6 Double reanalysis	117
3.6 The 'Come'-related Future Auxiliary	120
3.6.1 Semantic shift	121
3.6.2 Phonological change	126
3.6.3 Reanalysis	127
3.6.4 Relative age of the 'go'- and 'come'-derived future auxiliaries	127
3.7 The 'Have'-related Future Auxiliary	133
3.7.1 The development of the 'have' auxiliaries	133
3.7.2 Semantic shifts	137
3.7.3 Phonological change in the auxiliary	141
3.8 Further Innovations	142
3.8.1 Discourse functions of the innovated future auxiliaries	142
3.8.2 "Double" auxiliaries	146

3.8.3 Future auxiliaries and the conditional	153
3.8.4 The auxiliary **ye**	163
3.9 Conclusion	166

4 Negation: Strategies and Innovation — 167

4.1 The Two Negative Strategies	167
4.1.1 Negative auxiliaries	170
4.1.2 Negative particles	193
4.2 Elaborative Innovation in the Negative System	204
4.3 Interaction of Negation with the Tense/Aspect System	208
4.3.1 The negative future	208
4.3.2 Negative progressives	213
4.3.3 Negative conditionals	214
4.4 Conclusion	216

5 Exbraciation: the Breakdown of the S AUX (O) V Construction — 218

5.1 Introduction	218
5.2 Synchronic Variation: Evidence for Historical Change	218
5.2.1 Temporal adverbs	219
5.2.2 Manner adverbs	221
5.2.3 Reason phrases	222
5.2.4 Locatives	224
5.2.5 Summary of elements which vary with respect to their position within the verb brace	225
5.2.6 Implications of the variation in word order	226
5.3 Factors Motivating Exbraciation	227
5.3.1 Basic word order	228
5.3.2 Rightward movement rules	228
5.3.3 Placement of sentential objects	232
5.3.4 Auxiliary-->verb "attraction"	233
5.3.5 Summary: Motivation for exbraciation	234
5.4 Actualization of the Change	235
5.4.1 The stages of exbraciation: From optional to obligatory movement	235
5.4.2 "Valence" as a determining factor in exbraciation	242
5.4.3 Exbraciation and individual lexical items	245
5.4.4 The hierarchy of exbraciated elements	250

5.5 Alternative Proposals	241
5.5.1 Proposal I: Inbraciation	252
5.5.2 Proposal II: No exbraciation or inbraciation took place	252
5.6 Tense Innovation and Exbraciation	254
5.6.1 The data	254
5.6.2 Arguments for a time adverb-->tense marker reanalysis	255
5.6.3 Proposed scenario for tense innovation	262
5.6.4 The interaction between tense innovation and exbraciation	265
5.7 Conclusion	267
6 On the Nature of Syntactic Change: Concluding Remarks	**268**
6.1 Implications of This Study for Word Order in Proto-Kru	268
6.2 Observations on the Nature of Syntactic Change	269
6.2.1 Reanalysis	269
6.2.2 On the role of variation and competing systems	275
6.3 Conclusion	277

List of Maps

1	Kru Language Family	4
2	Eastern Kru	6
3	Western Kru	8
4	Distribution of *e	50
5	Remnants of *a	56
6	Conditional Auxiliaries	157
7	Distribution of Negative Auxiliaries	178
8	Distribution of **nī**	200
9	Tense Innovation	274

PREFACE

Working on a single language is an exciting task, but an even more exciting one is working on several at a time. The structure of one language becomes clear against the backdrop of another. In this book I have presented material from over fourteen Kru languages, focussing on the areas of tense, aspect, negation, modality, and word order. While I hope a good overview of these systems within this language family has been given, my real goal is to describe the nature of syntactic change in this restricted context. The various syntactic and semantic changes described here are very much in line with wider universal tendencies. Hopefully, then, this study will be of interest not only to Africanists but also to anyone who is interested in the general nature of linguistic change.

My work on Kru began in 1972 when I moved into a warm Godié village in southwest Ivory Coast. Four years later, on the other side of the world, my interest in comparative syntax was sparked in a diachronic seminar taught by Sandra Thompson. So my debts of gratitude go back a long way.

I would like to thank my friends and colleagues in Ivory Coast and Liberia for giving me access to their field notes and for sharing their ideas so freely: Thomas Bearth, Julie Bentinck, Keith Dawson, John Duitsman, Claire Grah, Carol Gratrix, Vreni Hofer, Pascal Kokora, Jim Laesch, Christa Link, Sharon Poellet, Peter Thalmann, Hans-Martin Werle, and Raymond Zogbo, as well as my language consultants who gave of their time so generously: Adou Roger, Ahipe Gbogia Celestin, Bori Gnaly Joachim, Dable Arsène, Dago Truŋwɔ Hélène, Dakouri Celestin, Gnina Bernard, Jacob Mephisto, 'Roger', Wohi Felix, Zadi Sassi Michel, Zondet Paul, Bob Jacobs, Bai Boikai, Victor Chumbe, Daniel Myers, Edward Payne, Peter Toby, Elizabeth Wah, and Daniel S. Wilson. I would also like to thank the Institut de Linguistique Appliquée (ILA), the Société Internationale de Linguistique (SIL), and The Institute of Liberian Languages (TILL) for their cooperation in making this study possible. Thanks are also due to the agencies which supported this project through two grants: Fulbright-Hays research abroad (1977-78) and the National Defense Education Act, Title vi (1978-79).

I would also like to thank those people at UCLA who helped guide my thinking and writing: Pamela Munro, a good teacher and demanding reader who supplied me with excellent comments and suggestions, William Welmers, whose background in African languages provided me with a unique opportunity for discussion and learning, and Sandra Thompson, who continues to be one of the most inspirational people I know, both personally and linguistically. A. Faltz and Larry Hyman gave helpful suggestions on chapters 2 and 3, and I am grateful.

I must also thank two dear friends and fellow Kru people: Inge Egner and John Singler for providing data, giving suggestions, and reading this draft most meticulously. Their humor and encouragement have been much appreciated.

Finally, to those who surrounded me with love and support while I was working on this project, I wish to express my thanks: Père, Mère and Bob, Grandma and Uncle Bud, Diana and John, Carol and Lynne, Keith and Diana, and Yero, who in a very special way helped me believe in myself.

ABBREVIATIONS

Abbreviation	Meaning	Abbreviation	Meaning
ACT	actuel	INST	instrumental
ADJ	adjective	INTR/	
ADV	adverb	INTRANS	intransitive
AF	assertive focus	IO	indirect object
AS	agent seul (agent only)	LOC	locative
		LTA	long time ago
ASP	aspect	M/MOD	modal
ASSOC	associative	MS	manuscript
AUX	auxiliary	N	noun
BEN	benefactive	NAR	narrative
C	consonant	NEG	negative
COMP	complement	NF	nonfinal
COND	conditional	NOM	nominalizer
CONJ	conjunction	NP	noun phrase
COP	copula	NUM	number
CR	current relevance	O/OBJ	object
D/DEF	definite	OE	Old English
DAT	dative	PART	particle
DBY	day before yesterday	PASS	passive
DEC/DECL	declarative	PER	perfective
DEM	demonstrative	PERF	perfect
DO	direct object	PERM	permansif
ET	earlier today	PL	plural
EMPH	emphatic	PN	pronoun
FACT	factative	POSS	possessive
FOC	focus	POST	postposition
FUT	future	POT	potential
GEN	genitive	PREF	preferred
GER	gerund	PR/PRES	presumptive
GRAM	grammar	PROJ	projective
HORT	hortative	PROH	prohibitive
IMP	imperfective	PURP	purpose
IMPER	imperative	Q	question
INCH	inchoative	REAS	reason
INF	infinitive	REC	recent past

Abbreviation	Meaning	Abbreviation	Meaning
REL	relative	SYL	syllable
REM	remote past	T	tense
S/SUBJ	subject	TR/TRANS	transitive
SEQ	sequential	V	vowel
SING	singular	V	verb
SUB	subordinating marker	VOL	volitive
SUF	suffix	VP	verb phrase
SUP	supportive element		

1 INTRODUCTORY REMARKS FOR A DIACHRONIC STUDY

1.1 Theoretical Outlook and Subject of Study

Diachronic syntax, once a neglected subject, is now a flourishing field of research. In the past two decades, efforts have increased to determine how and why syntactic structures change. Quite naturally, most work in historical syntax has been done in language families where a large data base is available. Thus, work has been done in families such as Romance and Germanic, and in languages like Chinese. Recently, however, studies with a historical perspective have been carried out on languages for which little or no historical documentation is available. Starting with only comparative synchronic data, linguistics have attempted to reconstruct the basic structures of a mother language and to sketch out the lines of linguistic change. Examples of such studies can be found in the works of Jacobs (1975), Langacker (1976), and Munro (1973) on American Indian languages, Chung (1976) on Polynesian languages, and Givón (1971a and b, 1975b), Hyman (1975), and Lord (1973) on the Niger-Congo family. These studies have provoked some criticism, however, by linguists who maintain that historical work cannot be done without historical documents. David Lightfoot (1979:7) notes:

> There are very few languages, apart from Chinese, Tamil, Kannada and those of the Indo-European and Semitic families, which have a rich attestation over a long enough period of time. In order to write a grammar of an early stage of a language, one needs many texts covering many literary genres, and in order to discuss subsequent changes one needs a grammar of a later stage and usually some attestation of a substantial intervening period. The Bantu and Iroquoian languages, for example, do not fulfil this requirement and therefore will not be an appropriate basis for work on syntactic change. ... This limits the number of language-types which can be examined from the viewpoint of syntactic change.

The stipulation proposed by Lightfoot, that historical documentation is a prerequisite for a study in diachronic syntax, is explicitly rejected in this study. It is assumed, rather, that with the growing body of knowledge concerning the mechanisms and motivation of syntactic change, it is possible to begin with comparative synchronic data to reconstruct protostructures and to infer what change or changes have taken place. This follows from reasoning principles which are basic to scientific study: Given a result and a law, a case may be inferred; or given a result and a case, a law may be inferred. Thus in this study, documented cases of syntactic change will be used to support parallel cases of syntactic change in languages where historical documents are unavailable. Benveniste (1968) uses this method in his study of the development of tense and auxiliaries in some well-documented Indo-European languages. When he finds parallel developments in certain American Indian languages, he considers this evidence as a confirmation of his own proposals for Greek and Latin. He also concludes (p. 94): "Conversely, where languages without recorded history exhibit auxiliary structures comparable to those of the Indo-European languages, we should feel free to make use of the Indo-European model in genetic explanations."

This study follows this basic approach. Though Kru languages have little historical documentation, synchronic variation is studied both within and between languages. Protoconstructions are posited and historic developments are proposed. In large part, confirmation of these proposals comes from documented cases of syntactic change around the world. Thus, this is not just a book about Kru; it is first a book about language change. Particular attention will be given to changes affecting verbal categories, especially tense, aspect, and polarity. Another area of study will be the effect certain innovations have had on general word order.

This book is divided into six chapters, with the remainder of this chapter presenting background information on the classification of the family, the data base, unifying characteristics of the group, and a general definition of terms used in this study. Chapter two treats the basic aspectual distinctions found in the family as a whole. Chapter three describes the development of an auxiliary construction S AUX O V, with special attention given to features, conditionals, and sequential markers. Chapter four first describes strategies of negation with Kru and then discusses the development of negative morphemes. Chapter five discusses the changes which the S AUX O V construction is undergoing at the present time and suggests a mechanism for the innovation of tenses. Finally, chapter six provides an overview of the changes discussed in this study. There is a general discussion on the nature of reanalysis and the role of variation in language change.

1.2 Geographic Situation and Internal Classification of the Kru Language Family

Kru languages are spoken primarily in southwest Ivory Coast and southern Liberia. Many Kru, however, began leaving the area as early as the sixteenth century to serve as crewmen on European

Introductory Remarks for a Diachronic Study

ships (this, according to some, gave rise to their name). These early travels led to the establishment of Kru or, more particularly, Klao and Bassa settlements in major seaports all along the coast of West Africa--from Dakar to Libreville. The larger groups, including the Bêtés, Guérés, and Didas, remained in their own territory. Despite the wide distribution of the Kru peoples, their population is still quite small, numbering no more than approximately 1.8 million (Lafage 1977).

Because little has been known about the Kru peoples or their languages, the classification of the group within its larger family, Niger-Kordofanian, as well as its internal classification, has remained undefined. In 1952, Westermann and Bryan listed Kru as an isolate within the languages of West Africa. Later, in 1966, Greenberg (1966b) tentatively included Kru in the Kwa group, which neighbors the Krus on the east. More recently (Vogler 1974; Bennett and Sterk 1977; Welmers 1977a; Marchese 1979) this classification has been questioned. Vogler attempts to show that Kru is closer to the Voltaic (Gur) and Mandé families (situated to the north and west of Kru) than to Kwa. Bennett and Sterk also try to bring the Gur and Kru languages together into one sub-group in Niger-Kordofanian. Like Westermann and Bryan, Welmers lists Kru as a separate branch in Niger-Kordofanian without saying anything about its relative closeness to other branches. For the moment, more research needs to be done before the exact status of Kru can be determined. However, the present tendency is to place it outside the Kwa group.

Delafosse (1904) was the first to point out that the Sassandra River forms a natural boundary, dividing the family into two parts (see map 1). Exceptionally, Nyabwa, a Western language, is spoken in a region to the east of the Sassandra River. He labelled the Eastern group 'Bêté' and the Western group 'Bakwê'. While this basic subdivision is certainly justified, it seems wiser to refer to Eastern Kru and Western Kru, since Bêté and Bakwê are names of individual languages within each group. The east/west division is confirmed by numerous phonological, lexical, and grammatical facts. There are phonological correspondences between t and s, and n and ŋ as seen below:

	western languages	eastern languages	
t/s	tu	su	'tree'
	tu	sū	'push'
ɲ/ŋ	ɲlɔ́	ŋ(w)lɔ́	'wife, woman'
	ɲne	ŋlɩ	'name'

Isoglosses abound, confirming the east/west division:

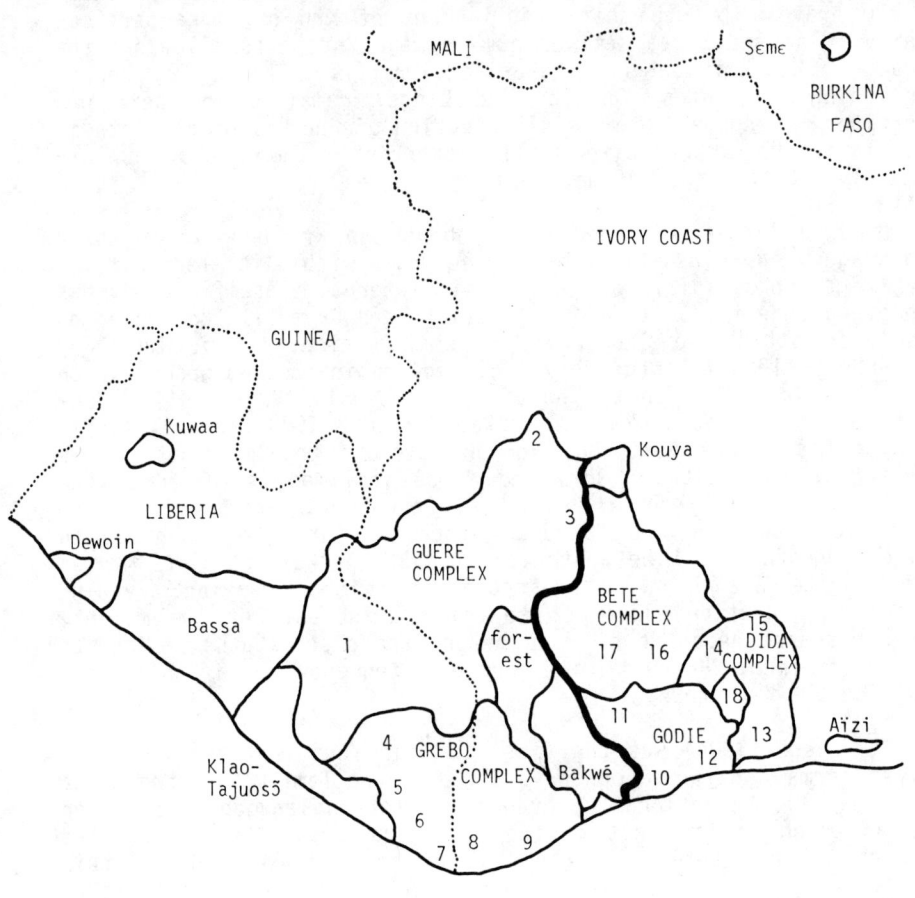

KRU LANGUAGE FAMILY

adapted from Marchese 1979

━━━ division between Eastern and Western Kru

─── division between complexes or unaffiliated languages

..... division between countries

1. Krahn
2. Wobé
3. Nyabwa
4. Cedepo
5. Borobo
6. Nyabo
7. Grebo
8. Tepo
9. Bereby Kru
10. Neyo
11. Kwadia
12. Koyo
13. Lozoua Dida
14. Lakota Dida
15. Vata
16. Bété (Gagnoa)
17. Bété Soubré-Daloa-Guibéroua)
18. Ega (non-Kru)

Map 1. The Kru Languages

Introductory Remarks for a Diachronic Study

	western languages	eastern languages
'ten'	bue/pue	kʊgba
'fire'	nɛ/na	kosu
'blood'	nemo	dlu
'tooth'	nene/ŋɛ	gle/gla

The distribution of grammatical markers and certain word order properties (to be discussed in detail in this work) also provide evidence of an east/west split.

The internal classification of both the Eastern and Western groups is far from resolved. One major problem is the presence of dialect chains where a series of speech forms are intercomprehensible along a continuum, with speech at the ends of the continuum being quite divergent. Other problems in classification are due to sociological and historical factors. Dating from colonial times, there have been divisions which may have obscured linguistic realities. Nevertheless, some progress in classification is now being made.

1.2.1 Eastern Kru

Eastern Kru (map 2), spoken exclusively in Ivory Coast, is the more homogeneous of the two groups. There appears to be at least one important subdivision between the Bété complex and the Dida complex. (The term **complex** will be used in this study to refer to a group of related languages, while **cluster** will refer to groups of mutually intelligible dialects.) One distinguishing characteristic between the two complexes is the presence of innovative central vowels in the Bété region. Though Bété is viewed as a sociological unit, it is made up of what appears to be two distinct languages: one spoken in the region of Gagnoa (known as Gbadié or Gbadi), the other over a wider region (Soubré, Guibéroua, Issia, and Daloa). Most examples in this study will come from the latter group which is itself subdivided into two major dialects (Werle, Zogbo, Hook 1977). The Dida complex contains at least two separate groups. Kaye (1982) describes these two groups as Dida-k^w and Dida-f, based on this sound correspondence. Dida-f is made up of six different varieties, including Vata (once believed to be isolated from the other Dida dialects). Dida-k^w is spoken over the rest of the Dida region. Brief surveys in this region (Gratrix and Marchese, MS) suggest that this latter group should be subdivided into two, with dialects around Lakota forming one group, and those around Yokoboué, another. In this study, data will be presented from Lozoua (or Yokoboué) Dida and Lakota Dida, as well as from Vata. Within the Dida complex, there is a non-Kru isolate, Ega or Diès, which is probably related to Kwa (Marchese 1979:9).

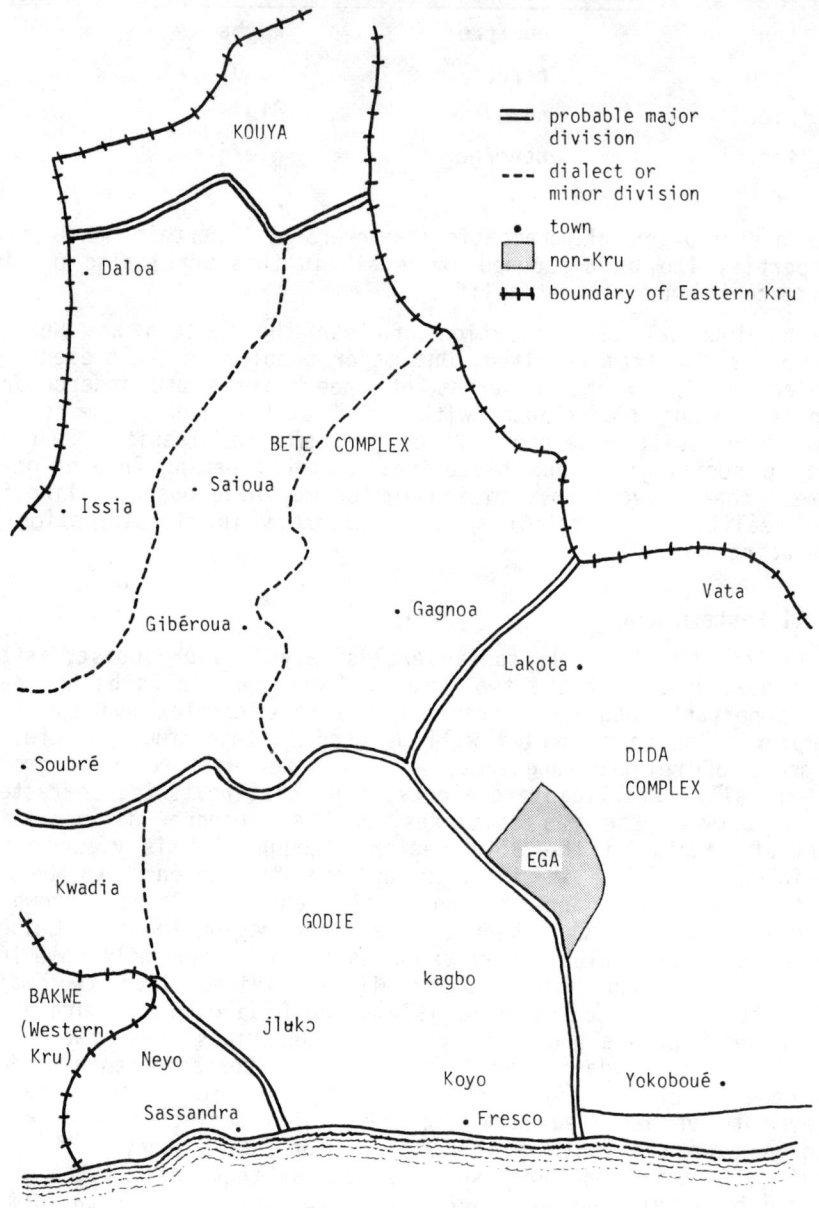

Map 2. Eastern Kru

Introductory Remarks for a Diachronic Study

Other Eastern languages include Louya, Godié, Neyo, and Kwadia. The Kouya are surrounded by Bété on the south, Nyabwa (a Western Kru language) on the west, and Gouro (a Mandé language) on the east and north. Limited contact with this language has revealed a close connection between Kouya and eastern Bété (Gbadi; Werle, pers. com.). Because of lack of data, no further reference to Kouya will be made in this study.

Godié, spoken to the south of Bété, is made up of nine separate but mutually intelligible dialects. Intercomprehension tests have shown that the Godiés living near the Bété region also understand up to 90 percent of spoken Bété. However, Godiés living near the Dida region have a low comprehension of this language (55-63%), but a very high comprehension of Lakota Dida (90%; Gratrix and Marchese, MS). Though from colonial days speakers of these dialects have been grouped together into a unit, it is hard to tell, linguistically, whether they constitute a unit or whether they are actually part of the Bété and Dida complexes. The full set of central vowels in most Godié dialects, however, points to a closer connection between Bété and Godié. Data will be given from two Godié dialects: ɟlʊkɔ and kagbo, as well as from koyo, whose status as a dialect of Godié has not been completely determined (Kokora 1976:212-16).

Neyo, though it is situated on the east-west border next to Bakwé, is clearly an Eastern language, intercomprehensible with at least some dialects of Godié. Its exact status within Eastern Kru has not been established, but its vowel system and other features seem to link it to the Dida complex.

Kwadia is wedged between Godié, Bété, and Bakwé. From limited contacts I have had with speakers of this language, I would say that it is close to Western Godié. Again, however, due to lack of data, no further reference will be made to this language.

1.2.2 Western Kru

The Western group is much larger than the Eastern one, extending from the Sassandra River across the Liberian border, and covering over half of the Liberian territory (see map III). There is a major subdivision within this group between the Guéré complex and the Grebo complex. The status of the other Western languages such as Bakwé, Bassa, Dewoin, and Klao (traditionally called Kru) has not yet been determined (in parts of this study these languages are referred to as the "unaffiliated" Western languages).

Bakwé poses a problem because although it has traditionally been called Western, it does exhibit many features of Eastern Kru. As far as Dewoin is concerned, it is generally accepted that its nearest neighbor is Bassa. Little is known, however, about the relationship of these languages to the Grebo and Guéré complexes.

Within the Guéré complex, there are thirty-five dialects which appear to constitute a dialect chain. Neighboring dialects on the chain understand each other, but dialects at both extremes of the

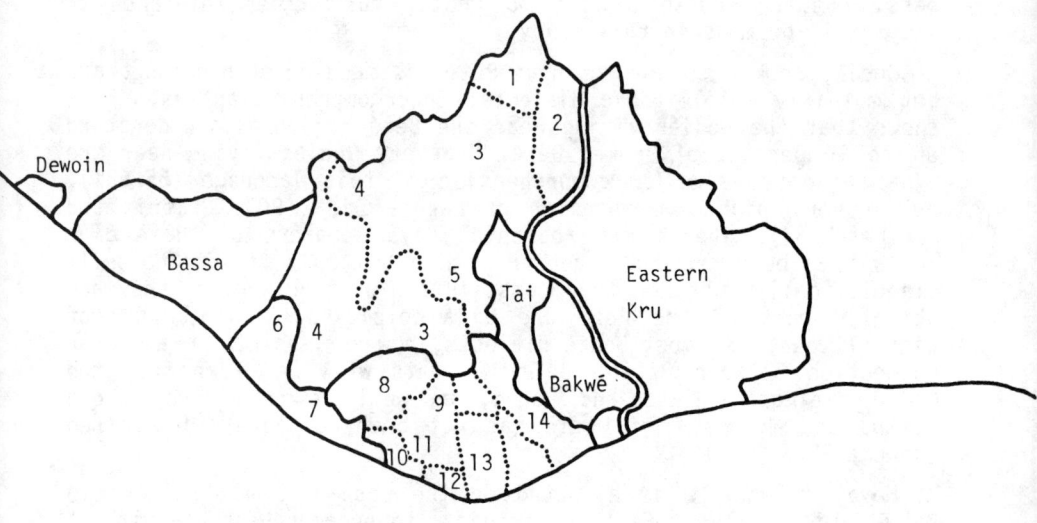

Guere complex
1. Wobé
2. Nyabwa
3. Central Guere
4. Western Guere (Krahn)
5. Glio-Oubi

Unaffiliated
6. Tajuos
7. Klao

Grebo complex
8. Chedepo
9. Webo
10. Kplebo
11. Borobo
12. Glebo
13. Tepo
14. Dougbo

⎯⎯ Division between Eastern and Western Kru

Map 3. Western Kru

(Adapted from Marchese 1979)

Introductory Remarks for a Diachronic Study 9

chain do not (Duitsman, Campbell, Kwejige, MS). This group is subdivided into Western and Central Guérē (known as Krahn in Liberia), and what could be called Eastern Guérē: Wobē and Nyabwa. In this study, data will be presented from Tchien Krahn, Gbaeson Krahn, Nyabwa, and Sapo, and two types of Wobē spoken in the Tao and Pēomē regions.

Like the Guérē complex, the Grebo complex also straddles the Liberian-Ivorian border. The group is made up of several clusters of dialects which constitute separate languages. According to a survey done by Maire and Thalmann (1980), there are two major clusters in Ivory Coast--one comprised of Tepo, Plapo, and a few small neighboring dialects; the other of Piē, Dougbo, Trepo, and Oubi. In Liberia, there are seven clusters made up of the following dialects (Ingemann and Duitsman 1978):

1. Wedebo and Kplebo
2. Glebo
3. Jabo, Nyabo, Wrelpo
4. Gedebo, Gbolo, Nyenebo, Dorobo, Borobo, Trembo
5. Nitiabo, Sabo, Tuobo, Kitiapo, Webo
6. Fopo and Bua
7. Palipo, Gbepo, Cedepo, Jedebo, Tiempo, Klepo

Grebo data come from the dialects underlined above, as well as from Tepo and Piē (Bereby Kru). Data are also available from the following Western languages--from Liberia: Grand and River Cess Bassa, Dewoin, and Klao (Nifu, Betu, and Settra dialects), and from Ivory Coast: Bakwē.

1.2.3 Kru isolates: Kuwaa, Aīzi, Seme

There are three languages which can be called Kru isolates.[1] Each of these is spoken in a different country. Kuwaa (or Belle) is spoken in Liberia, but is separated from the main Kru region and is surrounded by Mandē and West Atlantic languages. According to a cognate count done by Thompson (1976:2), Kuwaa shares 33 percent of its common vocabulary with other Kru languages. This is possibly a conservative count, however. The similarities of syntactic patterns and grammatical morphemes strongly reinforce Kuwaa's relationship to the other Kru languages.

Another Kru isolate is Aīzi, situated on the Ebrie Lagoon in Ivory Coast, to the east of the Eastern group. There are three dialects known as Aīzi; however, only two of these, spoken in Tiegba and Abrako, appear to be Kru related (Marchese and Hook 1982b). The people of Tiegba have oral traditions linking them to

---

1 Though Dewoin is separated from Kru territory, it is not considered a Kru isolate. According to Welmers (pers. com.), before the arrival of the Americo-Liberians and the subsequent development of the capital, Monrovia, Bassa and Dewoin speakers were within a few miles of each other. Furthermore, the cognate count between Dewoin and its closest neighbor, Bassa, is more than that of an isolate.

the Didas. Cognate counts reveal only 22-25 percent of vocabulary in common, however, thus confirming Aïzi's status as an isolate. The third dialect (spoken mostly on the seaside of the Lagoon) certainly belongs to another family, possibly Lagoon or Kwa. Data in this study come from both Kru-related dialects.

Sɛmɛ, or Siamou, is spoken in Burkina Faso (formerly Upper Volta) in the region of Orodara and was recently identified as a Kru language. Person (1966) suggests that in earlier times, Kru territory was situated to the north of the present location. Mandé invasions caused the majority of them to move south. According to this theory, the Sɛmɛ probably fled to the north at this time, rather than to the south with the rest of the Kru groups. While this classification should be viewed as tentative, the hypothesis warrants closer examination. This language could prove to be a key to the Kru-Gur connection.

For quick reference, the classification of the languages referred to in this study is summarized below:

Eastern Kru

    Dida complex: Dida-k^w (Lakota Dida, Lozoua Dida)
    Bété complex: Kosseoa Bété
                     Daloa Bété
                     Gagnoa Bété
    others: Godié (jlʉkɔ, kagbo)
                     Koyo
                     Neyo

Western Kru

    Guéré complex: Wobé
                     Nyabwa
                     Guéré (Central)
                     Krahn (Tchien, Gbaeson)
    Grebo complex: Grebo
                     Tepo
                     Bereby Kru
                     Cedepo
                     Nyabo
                     Borobo
    others: Bassa (Grand, River Cess)
                     Dewoin
                     Klao (Nifu, Betu, Settra)
                     Bakwé
                     Sapo

Isolates

                     Kuwaa (Liberia)
                     Aïzi (Ivory Coast)
                     Sɛmɛ (Upper Volta)

For a more detailed presentation of Kru classification, see Marchese (forthcoming).

1.3 The Data Base

As was mentioned earlier, there is little historical documentation on the Kru family. The lack of source material may be due to the inaccessibility of the Kru area, which is, for the most part, covered with thick rain forest. The earliest set of word lists comes from Koelle (1854) who worked in Freetown with Kru speakers who had travelled from their home regions (probably as sailors). Koelle provided word lists and some verbal paradigms from five Kru languages: Dewoin, Klao, Bassa, Grebo, and Gbe (possibly Guêrê), all of the Western group. At about the same time, missionaries working in Liberia began publishing the first grammatical descriptions of Grebo (Payne 1860, 1864, 1867; Wilson 1838, 1839, 1849; Auer 1870) and Bassa (Crocker 1844). Work on Ivorian, and in particular Eastern Kru, languages was not begun until some decades later. In 1905 Thomann, a French colonial administrator working in Sassandra (see map 2), published a grammar and a vocabulary of Nyo entitled Essai de manuel de la langue néoulé. Meanwhile, Delafosse (1904) devoted thirty pages of his Vocabulaires comparatifs de plus de 60 langues ou dialectes parlés a la Cote d'Ivoire to word lists and a certain number of grammatical observations on the Kru group. The next major work on Kru did not appear until 1966 when Gordon Innes produced an Introduction to Grebo along with a Grebo-English dictionary. Since that time, articles have appeared in both English and French. (These later works on Kru languages can be found in the list of references at the end of this volume.) Most of the data come, however, from unpublished material such as field notes from (and/or discussions with) researchers who are presently investigating various Kru languages. These include:

Kru Languages	Researchers
Bété (Kosséoa)	Hans-Martin Werle
Cedepo	Jim Laesch
Dewoin	William Welmers and Mortvedt
Gbaeson Krahn	John Duitsman
Klao (Talo Kru)	John Singler, Sharon Poellot
Kuwaa	Francis Howard (transcribed texts)
Lozoua Dida	Carol Gratrix
Nyo	Claire Grah and Carol Gratrix
Nyabwa	Julie Bentinck
Tchien Krahn	Herb Tisher
Tepo	Keith Dawson and Peter Thalmann
Wobé	Thomas Bearth, Inge Egner, Vreni Hofer, and Christa Link

When examples are cited from languages where many linguists are doing research, such as in Wobé and Tepo, the source of the example will be cited. However, if the data come from one person alone, as is the case for Cedepo or Lozoua Dida, the sources will not be stated in the text.

Data also come from my own personal research with the following language consultants who aided me during short periods between November 1978 and August 1979:

Language Consultants

name	age	origin	language
Liberia			
Bai Boikai	20	John Town (Bomi territory)	Dewoin
Victor Chumbe	19	Wissiken (Barrobo Chiefdom)	Borobo
Bob Jacobs	43	Nifu	Klao (Talo)
Daniel Myers	23	Kanya	Grand Bassa
Edward Payne	26	Golita	Kuwaa
Peter Toby	20	Nyarn Teewleh Town	Sapo
Elizabeth Wah	18	Pleebo	Nyabo
Daniel S. Wilson	37	Gbodo-bo	Nyabo
Ivory Coast			
Adou Roger	32	Abrako	Aïzi
Ahipe Gbobia Celestin		Soubré	Bakwé
Bori Gnaly Joachim	25	Zegreboué	Godié (kagbo)
Dable Arsène	21	Batlébré II	Neyo
Dago Truŋwɔ Hélène	23	Guigéboua	Dida (Lakota)
Dakouri Celestin	20	Ligrohoin	Dida (Lakota)
Gnina Bernard	23	Sarékoragué	Bakwé
Jacob Mephisto	18	Gazolilié	Dida (Lakota)
Roger			Tepo
Wohi Felix	20	Kebly	Wobé (Péomé)
Zadi Sassi Michel	35	Dakpadou	Godié (jlukɔ)
Zondet Paul	30	Kouibly	Wobé (Tao)

In addition, I worked on Klao with Bob Jacobs in Los Angeles during the fall of 1976, and with Zadi Michel on Godié since 1972.

Thus, it can be seen that the data base in this study is essentially synchronic and for the most part unpublished.

1.4 Phonological and Grammatical Overview

Because few readers will be familiar with the Kru group, a rough typology of the phonological and grammatical systems is given below.

1.4.1 Phonology. The phonological systems in Kru languages resemble those of many West African languages. Syllable structure is restricted, except in a few rare cases, to open syllables:

$$([-syl])\ ([-syl])\ [+syl]\ ([+syl])$$

In general, words are mono- or disyllabic, though words containing more syllables are possible:

Introductory Remarks for a Diachronic Study

ɔ́	'he'	Bété
gɛ̃	'antelope'	
nʌ́mɛ	'animal'	
nyī6ɛ̃lū	'man'	

Vowel sequences are common in many Kru languages, though in some there are restrictions as to which type of vowels can cooccur:

zīá̰	'today'	Nyabwa
pēī⁻	'grass'	Krahn
kɔ̃ũ̀	'medicine'	Dewoin
mí ɔ́	'tear'	Godié

Many Kru languages have a **ClV** syllable structure which is realized as longer than CV but shorter than a disyllabic CVCV. The realization of /l/ is determined by the preceding consonant (typically [ř] after alveolars and palatals, [ñ] after nasals). This syllable usually contains a predictable transition vowel:

/klṹ/	[kᵘlṹ]	'face'	Godié
/tlɔ/	[třɔ]	'broom'	Nyabwa
/ŋlɔ/	[ŋᵓñɔ]	'woman'	Bété

Some languages have another syllable structure **CbV**, which is syncopated (Link 1975; Kokora 1979):

/dbū/	[dᵊɓū]	'rope'	Wobé
/nybɔ́/	[nyᵓmɔ]	'blood'	Krahn

In Eastern Kru, the set of consonants typically includes the following (Marchese 1979):

```
p   t   c   k   kp   cʷ
b   d   ɉ   g   gb
f   s
v   z
ɓ   l   y   ɠ   w
m   n   ny  ŋ
```

where /c/ and /ɉ/ are palatal stops, /kp/ and /gb/ coarticulated stops, /ɓ/ a bilabial implosive stop, and /ɠ/ a velar approximant. /l/ has an implosive variant /ɗ/ in many Eastern languages. Note that **ɓ, l, y, ɠ, w** is a series of resonants found in many West African languages (Bearth 1971, LeSaout 1974). Labialized consonants (**cʷ**) are interpreted by many researchers as systematic phonemes.

Western Kru languages lack some of the above consonants. Usually the velar approximant /ɠ/ and sometimes voiced fricatives /v/ and /z/ do not occur. In Wobé, Krahn, Grebo, and Tepo no implosive

/6/ has been reported. However, Western languages often have an extra phoneme /ŋm/ (a coarticulated nasal) and sometimes an /h/, which has developed in most cases from a proto- *s (Marchese 1979). Another interesting feature of Western Kru is that voiced consonants and nasals are typically in complementary distribution: nasals occurring only before nasalized vowels and voiced stops only before oral vowels, as seen in these Tepo examples from Dawson:

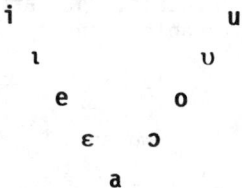

/gbĩ/	[gbĩ]	'dog'
/gbĩ́/	[ŋmʷĩ]	'intestines'
/dĩ/	[dĩ]	'mother'
/dũ/	[nṹ]	'rain'

With the exception of four languages (Bassa, Dewoin, Kuwaa, and Sɛmɛ), all Kru languages have four front and four back vowels and a central vowel /a/:

```
    i           u
      ɪ       ʊ
      e     o
        ɛ ɔ
          a
```

The vowels ɪ, ʊ, ɛ, and ɔ are usually retracted (pronounced with the tongue root retracted and the neck muscles tightened). According to researchers, Bassa, Dewoin, Kuwaa, and Sɛmɛ lack the high retracted vowels ɪ and ʊ.

Besides the standard inventory, several Eastern languages have an additional set of central vowels. Below is the vowel chart for some dialects of Bété and Godié (Marchese 1975; Werle and Gbalehi 1976; Werle et al. 1977):

```
    i   ɨ   u
    ɪ   ʉ   ʊ
    e   ə   o
    ɛ   ʌ   ɔ
        a
```

Bakwé, bordering Neyo, Kwadia, and Bété, is the only Western language known to have central vowels. Most Western languages, however, have distinctive nasalized vowels which do not occur in most Eastern Kru languages.

Vowel harmony is common. In the Eastern group and in Nyabwa, vowels are divided into two sets: one advanced and one retracted. A typical system can be seen in Godié:

Introductory Remarks for a Diachronic Study

	advanced			retracted	
i	ɨ	u	ɪ	ʉ	ʊ
e	ə	o	ɛ	ʌ	ɔ

Within any given morpheme, only vowels of one set will occur:

advanced		retracted	
sísĩõ	'quickly'	**6ʉ́tɛ́**	'winnowing fan'
ɓíɓĩẽ	'to beg'	**tʉ́tɔ́**	'ashes'
nɨ̃nə́	'story'	**pɪ̃ʌ̃**	'to buy'

The low central vowel /a/, however, cooccurs with both sets:

        sīkā   'gold'   (advanced)
        dʊ̄ānʊ̄ 'machete' (retracted)

Vowel harmony rules often cause changes across morpheme boundaries (Marchese 1975; Werle and Gbalehi 1976). This can be seen in Godié:

/ ɔ ni + ɛ /   (he see:IMP it)   'He sees it.'
[ɔ ni + e]
/ ɔ ni + ɔ /   (he see:IMP him) 'He sees him.'
[ɔ ni + o]

In Tepo, Grebo, and Krahn, another type of vowel harmony exists. Vowels are divided into three groups (Innes 1966:16):

        A   B   C
   i   u   ɛ   a   ɔ   ɪ   ʊ

Vowels of any one group may cooccur in a morpheme. Also vowels in adjacent sets may cooccur. Thus A + B and B + C can cooccur, but never vowels from A + C. The following examples are taken from Tepo:

      A + A: **yíẽ**   'eye'
      A + B: **yíŋɔ́**   'egg'
      B + C: **tɔ́tʊ̄**   'bat, SP.'
      C + C: **tʊ̄tʊ̄**   'earth'
      B + B: **yákɔ́**   'sky'
     *A + C

Vowel harmony of this type may also cause vocalic changes across morpheme boundaries.

Kru has both lexical and grammatical tone. Languages have either three or four register tones, which in this study will usually be marked in the following way: in a four-tone system, high tone will be marked by ´, mid-high tone by ', mid tone by ¯, and low tone by ˋ. In three-tone systems, the symbol ´ will mark high, - mid, and ¯ low. In both three-tone and four-tone languages, mid tone is often unmarked.

Nyabwa	(four tones)	Godié	(three tones)
kpá	'beaten earth'	sú	'push'
kpa'	'bone'	sū	'tree'
kpā	'marry'	sù	'be hot'
kpà	'help'		

What appear to be contour or modulated tones also occur in several languages. These are interpreted as a combination of two register tones, except in the case of the low falling tone in Wobé which is marked as ˬ (examples from Bearth and Link 1980):

sǒ	'jaundice'
sō̋	'arm'
ső́	'chicken'
sɔ̋̀	'day'
sō̋ˋ	'year'
sɔ̀̋	'under'

Tone plays an extremely important role in the grammatical systems of the Kru family, making such distinctions as perfective/imperfective aspect, possessive/relative/subject pronouns, definite/indefinite, and sometimes singular/plural.

1.4.2 Word order. From the viewpoint of Greenberg's universals (1966a) and other typological word order studies, Kru would be described as a mixed system, since it has both OV and VO characteristics.

1.4.2.1 OV characteristics of the noun phrase. Kru languages are exclusively suffixing (a typical feature of OV syntax), and in the noun phrase, many distinctions are made by nominal suffixes. For example, nonmass, countable plurals are always marked by a suffix, which in most Kru languages has the underlying form /ɪ/. Suffixes often coalesce with or replace the final vowel of the stem and may be affected by vowel harmony:

| Tepo | pu | pui | 'gun/guns' |
| | plɛ́ | plí | 'machete/machetes' |

Introductory Remarks for a Diachronic Study

Sɛmɛ	sõ	sõe	'horse/horses'
	flɔ̃	flɛ̃	'Fulani/Fulanis'
Wobé	gbū̀	gbī̀	'house/houses'
	mlá̰	mlḭ́	'nose/noses'
Godié	sū̀	sī̀	'tree/trees'
	gū̀	gwī̀	'stomach/stomachs'

In many languages, definite nouns are also marked by suffix:

<u>Neyo</u> (Gratrix, pers.com.)

cʋ́	+ ɔ	→ cʋ́ɔ́	'the moon'
moon	+ <u>DEF</u>		
jí	+ ɛ	→ jíɛ́	'the panther'
panther	+ <u>DEF</u>		
ŋá̰	+ á̰	→ ŋá̰á̰	'the gizzard'
gizzard	+ <u>DEF</u>		

Several Kru languages have remnants of noun class suffixes. In the following examples from Godié, the nouns are apparently made up of a noun stem and a class suffix. Each of the following liquids ends in a back vowel. The suffix is probably ʋ, the pronoun and concord marker for these words. In most cases, the original final vowel of the stem has been lost.

nyū[2]	'water'	nū̄	'alcoholic drink'
ɓlʋ́	'milk'	dlù	'blood'
nyɔ̂ɔ̂nū	'soup'	mɪ́ɔ́	'tear'
ɓúɓú	'sweat'	zɔ̃	'sauce, SP'

Nouns may also carry suffixes indicating aspect or negation (as seen in chapters 2 and 4.).

Another OV characteristic of the noun phrase is the order Genitive-Noun. Possessive pronouns and genitives both precede the nouns they modify:

<u>Godié</u>	**ná̰**	**ɓùtū**	'my house'
	my	house	
	POSS	N	

---

[2] The Proto-Kru word for water was ***nɪ**. Apparently in Godié and in some other Eastern Kru languages, the combination **nɪ** + noun class suffix ʋ gave rise to the form **nyú**.

ɔ́	wū̄tɔ̄ŋlɔ̄	'his mother-in-law'
his	mother-in-law	
POSS	N	
6ū̀tū̀ū́	kplū	'a door of a house'
house:ASSOC	door	
GEN	N	

An associative marker **a** (reduced to a high tone in Godié) usually separates two nouns:

Grebo	ke <u>a</u> kae	'the chief's house'
	chief ASSOC house	
Neyo	no <u>a</u> lōkwe	'the man's cloth'
	man ASSOC cloth	
Nyabwa	gbe <u>a</u> kpa	'the dog's bone
	dog ASSOC bone	

Body parts are used to indicate directions, such as 'up', 'under', 'inside', etc. In some languages these constructions can still be analyzed as <u>noun + ASSOC + noun</u>.

There is evidence that the associative marker combines with personal pronouns to form possessive pronouns (see Marchese 1979). The Godié form **na** 'my' is probably a combination of Ā̃ 'I' and **a** (ASSOC).

Welmers (1963) suggests that **a** is the protoform of the associative in Niger-Kordofanian.

The structure <u>noun + postposition</u> also exists, another common OV pattern:

Neyo (Thomann)	**nezo**	**ko**	'on the road'
	road	on	(**kólő** = 'face')
Vata	**kɔlá**	**mlé**	'in the forest'
	forest	in	(**mlé** = 'stomach')
Godié	**tlo**	**wlú**	'on the hill'
	hill	on	(**wúlú** = 'head')
Tepo (Dawson)	**Sɛpɛtu**	**lú**	'at Sɛpɛtu'
	Sɛpɛtu	at	(**lú** = 'head')

Introductory Remarks for a Diachronic Study

Note the following distinction in Grebo between the structures <u>noun + ASSOC + noun</u> and <u>noun + postposition</u>:

   kḗ + fɛ   'next to the chief'
   chief + next
   <u>nou</u> + <u>POST</u>

   kḗ + à   + fɛ 'the chief's skin'
   chief + ASSOC + skin
   <u>noun</u> + <u>ASSOC</u> + <u>noun</u>

OV word order can also be seen in compounds in all Kru languages:

<u>Godié</u> **mesi-pʌ-nyɔ** 'fetisher'
     fetish-throw-person
      O   V

<u>Wobé</u> **jã̄ē-m̄aã̄-ī**   'potter'
     pot-make-agent
     O V

<u>Klao</u>   **dɛ̃-dɔ́-yɔ́**   'farmer'
     thing-plant-person
     O V

<u>Aïzi</u>   **kɔsɔ-go-nyɔ** 'chicken-farmer'
     chicken-raise-person
     O   V

The morpheme 'person' in the above examples signals an agent.

1.4.2.2 VO characteristics of the noun phrase. Contrary to the typical OV pattern, most modifiers in Kru follow their heads. This is usually true of demonstratives, definite markers, numbers, adjectives, and relative clauses:

Klao   **kugbi pri gbi na** 'the little white cats'
(Settra) cats white little DEF
     N ADJ ADJ DEF

Godié   **6iti kʌdi nī sɔ́** 'these two big houses'
    houses big these two
     N ADJ DEM NUM

Tchien Krahn

    jṹ ó̰ jè-ā̰   'the boy I saw'
    boy I saw-SUB
    N   REL

In the Godié example above, there is noun class concord within the noun phrase; both the adjective and the demonstrative agree in number and class (inanimate) with the modified noun. There is also at least number agreement in the Klao example (**Kugbi̱ pri̱ gbi̱**).

1.4.2.3 OV characteristics of the verb phrase. The Kru verb phrase is also characterized by a mixture of OV and VO features. Suffixes are very common in the verbal system, and inflectional suffixes include tense and aspectual markers.

<u>tense</u>   **nḗ dū-dá̰ blā̰**   'I pounded rice the
  Grebo   I pound-<u>T</u> rice   day before yesterday.'

<u>aspect</u>   **ɔ ci-e**   'He's coming.'
  Lozoua/Dida he come-<u>imperfective</u>

Verbs may also be marked with the following derivational suffixes:

causative
  Godié   **ŋwi/ŋwie**   'cry/cause to cry'
               mlʌ/mlʌ-a   'drink/cause to drink'
  Grebo   **te/teɛ**   'go down/make go down'
               punu/punie   'boil (INTR)/cause to boil (TRANS)

benefactive/dative
  Grebo   **duie   do bla**   'Pound rice for Doe.'
               pound-<u>BEN</u> Doe rice

  Klao (Singler)
               dō prō +le tītī kɔ bō 'Doe sold rice to Titi.'
               Doe sell+<u>DAT</u> Titi rice PART

passive
  Wobé   **ko dii-ɛ́**   'The rice is eaten.'
           rice eat-<u>PASS</u>

  Godié   **mlɛ-ɛ lɨ-ʊ**   'The meat is eaten.'
           meat-DEF eat-<u>PASS</u>

Introductory Remarks for a Diachronic Study

inchoative
Godié	ā zʌ̄ / a zʌ-mʌ	
	it red it red-INCH	
	'It is red./It is getting red.'	

instrumental
Bassa (Hobley)	ɔ ɓaɗaa-in wa cu	'He's hitting them
	he hit-INST them stick	with a stick.'

1.4.2.4 VO characteristics of the verb phrase. The above suffixes are, of course, consistent with OV syntax. When we consider the verb phrase as a whole, however, there are many VO characteristics. First of all, with the exception of auxiliary constructions, the order of the verb and complement is always VO:

Wobé	ɔ pō-ɛ̄ gbṳ̀	'He built a house.'
	he build-DEC house	
	S V O	
Godié	ɔ lɨ̄ sʉ̄kʌ̄	'He ate some rice.'
	he eat:FACT rice	
	S V O	

When an indirect object is present, it normally precedes the direct object and occurs closest to the verb. Thus VO word order is still maintained:

Neyo	kɔkɔ la gla té	'Kɔkɔ is bringing
	Kɔkɔ bring Gla yams	yams to Gla.'
	S V IO DO	
Tepo	a nye nyesʋa wio	'We thank God.'
	we give God thanks	
	S V IO DO	

Conforming to the basic order, sentences containing copulas have the form NP copula NP:

Dyabo (Walker et al.)	ɔ mɔ dawe	'He is a stranger.'
	he be stranger	
	NP COP NP	
Godié	ɔ gṳ̀lṳ̀ mōkōsíyī	'He is a Mossi.'
	he be Mossi-child	
	NP COP NP	

As is the case in most SVO languages, adverbs follow, rather than precede, the verb:

Bassa	ɔ	se-ɛ	nyu	kpɛ́kpɛ́	'He doesn't do it
	he	NEG-it	do	frequently	frequently.'

Tchien Krahn	nī-ā		duba	zūāzūā	'The rain is pouring down.'
(Hansell)	water-IMP		fall	a-lot	

In Kru, auxiliaries precede the main verb in the clause, as is the case in typical SVO languages (Greenberg 1966; Canale 1975):

Godié	ɔ	yī	mū		'He will leave.'
	he	FUT	go		
	S	AUX	V		
Dewoin	ɔ	nā	sāyɛ̄	pī	'He has cooked meat.'
	he	PERF	meat	cook	
	S	AUX	O	V	

Note, however, in this last example, that objects occur between auxiliaries and main verbs, suggesting an OV word order. (This subject will be discussed in detail in chapter 3.)

1.4.2.5 Other OV characteristics. Finally, in Kru languages, yes-no questions are marked by sentence-final suffixes. This is known to be a common OV characteristic (Greenberg 1966).

Neyo	ò	ko	dè	a	'Is he there?'
(Thomann)	he	is	there	Q	
Wobé	ɔ	mūɛ̄	ŋmɛ̄ī-ī		'Did he go to the
(Egner, Hofer)	he	go	concession-Q		concession?'

1.4.2.6 The implications of the mixed system. It has been shown that Kru languages are typologically mixed, exhibiting both OV and VO characteristics. These can be summarized in the following chart:

OV	VO
suffixing (both noun and verb)	N ADJ DEM NUM
Gen N	VO
OV word order in compounds	AUX V
position of question particles	V ADV

The chart shows that, as far as morphology is concerned, OV characteristics are dominant since Kru languages are exclusively suffixing. In terms of word order, however, the chart indicates that VO word order is predominant. What do these facts tell us about the history of Kru?

The mixed system may be explained by the fact that Kru languages, as part of the larger Niger-Congo family, have developed from a proto-word order SOV. This viewpoint is held by the majority of Africanists[3] (Givón 1975b; Hyman 1975), and it accounts for the data just presented. That is, one could say that suffixing morphology as well as noun phrase orders Gen-N and OV-nominalizer are remnants of a previous SOV word order, while the predominant word order reflects an innovative SVO word order. It is not assumed, however, (cf. Venneman 1974) that languages are on a direct path from SOV to SVO and will at some point reach a "pure" SVO stage. As several have pointed out (Hawkins, MS; D. Lightfoot 1979; Langdon 1977), mixed systems exist and are perfectly viable. English, for example, has apparently undergone an SOV-->SVO shift, all the while maintaining some basic OV characteristics. It will be shown, in fact, that the SVO word order has given rise to a new construction S AUX O V (chaps. 3 and 4), apparently "recreating" an OV word order. This swing to SOV is then counteracted by another change, a shift back to a basic SVO structure: S AUX V X (chap. 5).

There appears to be no reason to reject the SOV origin of the Kru language family. Indeed, the data support such a hypothesis. On the other hand, it is assumed that while the general tendency has been, and is, towards a predominantly SVO order, this tendency is not absolute.

1.5 Verbal Categories

In Kru, there is no one-to-one correspondence between verbal categories and the morphological expression of such categories. This is the case in many languages of the world. In English, for example, tense may be expressed by inflections on the verb (past and nonpast) or by a modal (future 'will') (Traugott 1978; Schachter 1985). The morphological expression of Kru verbal categories will be discussed first; then the verbal categories will be defined and illustrated.

1.5.1 Morphological expressions of verbal categories. In Kru languages, notions such as aspect, tense, negation, and mood are generally expressed in one of the following ways:

1.5.1.1 Suffixes may be attached to either a noun or a verb and form a phonological word with that entity. They are typically subject to rules of vowel harmony.

Godié (verbal suffix indicating tense)

>   ɔ̃ mɯ̀-ā̰   sūkú   'He went to school.'
>   he go:FACT-REC school

---
[3] Heine (1975) maintains that Proto-Kru had an SVO word order.

Klao (nominal suffix indicating aspect)

    ɔ-ɔ̄   di   dɛ   'He's eating.'

    he-<u>IMP</u> eat thing

1.5.1.2 Sentence-second particles occur in sentences where the basic word order is SVO. Unlike suffixes, particles are independent words.

<u>Dewoin</u> (sentence-second particle indicating negation; Welmers 1977b)

    ɔ nī pī sã̄yɛ̀   'He doesn't usually cook meat.'

    he <u>NEG</u> cook meat

    S   PART V   O

<u>Bassa</u> (particle, obviously borrowed from English, indicating a modal; Hobley 1965)

    m̄ mɛ nyu kṹã̀   'You may work.'

    you <u>may</u> do work

    S   PART V   O

In chapters 2 and 4, it will be shown that particles often reduce and become attached to the preceding subject of the clause. In this way, sentence-second particles may develop into nominal suffixes (strategy (a)).

1.5.1.3 Auxiliaries also occur in sentence-second position, but they differ from sentence-second particles in that they always occur in sentences with the word order S AUX O V.

<u>Wobé</u> (auxiliary indicating negation)

    ɔ sɛ̄ gbǔ pō   'He didn't build a house.'

    he <u>NEG</u> house build

    S   AUX O   V

<u>Godié</u> (auxiliary indicating future tense)

    ɔ yi-ɛ wʌ lɨ   'He was going to eat it.'

    he <u>FUT</u>-it PAST eat

    S   AUX O T   V

As will be argued in chapters 3 and 4, auxiliaries are historically derived from main verbs. Synchronically they maintain a certain degree of verbal behavior in that they host object clitics and tense suffixes as seen in the Godié example above.

1.5.1.4 Sentence-initial markers may occur in sentences with any type word order (SVO OR S AUX O V). They precede the subject and,

Introductory Remarks for a Diachronic Study 25

like particles, may coalesce with adjacent elements such as the subject pronoun.

Grebo (sentence-initial marker indicating the subjunctive; Innes 1966)

<u>b</u>-a   du   nɛ̄   'Let us pound it.'
SUBJ-we pound it

Gbaeson Krahn (marker indicating a conditional)

<u>pō</u>   ɨ̃   nú-ɛ́   nɛ̀   ã̌ mú   ɨ̃   blā   'If you do it,
COND you do-it then I FUT you hit   I will hit you.'

1.5.1.5 Periphrastic verbal constructions may express progressives or futures, as well as other tense/aspect categories. Usually periphrastic constructions are made up of a main verb followed by a complex complement (nominalized verb).

Godié (periphrasis expressing a progressive)

ɔ́   kʋ̀   nā̀ā̀   dʌ̄ ,...   'He is walking.'
he be-at walk NOM
(literally: he is at walking-place)

Cedepo (periphrasis expressing a future)

ɔ́   mĩ́   tulubɔ́   mú ma   'He will go to Monrovia.'
he go:IMP Monrovia go NOM
(literally: he is going to go to Monrovia)

1.5.2 Definition of terms. Since this study is primarily concerned with tense, aspect, and negation, these verbal categories will now be defined, discussed, and illustrated.

1.5.2.1 Aspects are generally defined as "different ways of viewing the internal temporal constituency of a situation" (Comrie 1976). More specifically, "aspect marking indicates whether the action of the verb is regarded as complete or incomplete, durative or momentaneous, a single act or a repeated one..." (Schachter, forthcoming, p. 12). Within the Kru family, most languages make four aspectual distinctions (to be discussed in detail in chapter 2):

>   perfective
>   imperfective
>   progressive
>   perfect

These aspectual categories are marked by suffixing (imperfective, perfective, perfect), by auxiliary (perfect), or by periphrasis (progressive). In some languages the perfective is unmarked (Dewoin, Klao, Wobé).

1.5.2.2 Tense is described as relating "the time of the situation referred to, to some other time, usually the time of speaking" (Comrie 1976:1,2). In Kru, there is usually a basic division between past, present, and future. The present tense is never overtly marked. Past and future tenses may be expressed by verbal suffix, auxiliary, or periphrasis.

<u>suffix</u>   Lakota Dida

ɔ   **ble-wa**   saka   'She was pounding rice.'
she pound:IMP-PAST rice

<u>auxiliary</u>   Godié

ɔ̃   **yī**   mɔ́   mɐ̃   'He will go there.'
he FUT there go

<u>periphrasis</u>   Wobé

ɔ̃ɔ̃   mū gbŭ   pō-à̱   'He is going to build
he:IMP go house build-NOM   a house.'

While aspectual categories are generally uniform throughout the family, tense varies from language to language. Many languages, such as Godié, Dewoin, Kuwaa, and Tepo, have a distinction between recent and remote past tense. Some languages, like Wobé, have no tense suffixes and apparently contrast only future and nonfuture tenses. Other languages, like Grebo, Tepo, and Klao, have extensive tense suffix systems, indicating specific past and future times such as 'day after tomorrow' and 'day before yesterday'. As will be seen in chapter 5, these complex tense systems are innovative.

Tense combines with mood in certain instances. For example, future auxiliaries often express more than just temporal information. They also express potentiality, obligation, and desire, as seen in Godié:

<u>potential</u>

ɔ̃   **yī**   mɐ̃   'He will/may/can go.'
he FUT-AUX go

<u>obligation</u>

ʌ̀   **yī**   nɔnʊ zlɪ   'You will/ must work.'
you FUT-AUX work do

<u>volitive</u>

ɔ̃   **kʌ̃**   mɐ̃   'He will/wants to go.'
he FUT-AUX go

This being the case, future auxiliaries could be called modals. According to Comrie (1976:2): "The so-called future tense of many languages has modal as well as tense value." In this study, however, the term **future auxiliary** will be used. In languages with more than one future auxiliary, auxiliaries will be referred to by their individual names. For example, in Godié there are two future auxiliaries: **yi**, the potential future (POT), and **kʌ**, the volitive future (VOL).

1.5.2.3 Negation in Kru may be expressed by nominal or verbal suffix, by auxiliary or sentence-second particle, or by periphrasis.

suffix (Bété)

ɔ-ɔ́   nīmʌ̀   'He doesn't drink.'
he-NEG drink

sentence-second particle (Dewoin)

ɔ   nī   pī   sāyɛ̄   'She doesn't usually
she NEG cook meat   cook meat.'

auxiliary (Krahn)

ɔ   se   dɛ   di   'He didn't eat anything.'
he NEG thing eat

periphrasis (Klao)

bɔ   mu-mu-ɛ   'Don't go.'
stop go-go-NOM

Chapter 4 will include a discussion of the factors determining the negation strategies illustrated here.

1.5.2.4 Mood has to do with the actuality of an event, though it may also be concerned with speaker involvement, subject involvement, and evidence of the reliability of the message (Chung and Timberlake 1985:33-35). Traditionally, grammarians speak of indicative, interrogative, imperative, and subjunctive moods. It is not at all clear what moods should be distinguished in Kru. As will be seen in chapter 4, there may be reasons for distinguishing imperatives and nonactual actions (like habituals) from other actual events, since these two categories are often negated in contrasting ways. Innes (1966:61-62) proposes the following moods in Grebo:

indicative   ɔ   du   nɛ ne   'He has pounded it.'
               he pound it BE[4]

subjunctive   b-ɔ   du   nɛ   'Let him pound it.'
               SUBJ-he pound it

---

[4] This BE-related particle signals assertion (Marchese 1963b).

conditional	b-ɔ	du	nɛ	'If he pounds it,'
	COND-he	pound	it	
result	ɔ	du	nɛ	'and he pounded it.'
	he	pound	it	
imperative		du	nɛ	'Pound it!'
		pound	it	

In some languages, like Godié, the division between subjunctive and imperative does not exist. In Godié, the imperative mood (marked by the base tone of the verb stem) is used not only for second person but also for all persons. It expresses the desire on the part of the speaker that an act be carried out:

mū	(go:IMPER)	'Go!'
ɔ mū	(he go:IMPER)	'He should go' or 'Oh, that he would go.'

1.6 Conclusion

The above sections have shown that in Kru there are a number of ways of expressing tense, aspect, polarity, and mood. These verbal categories will be the main focus here. The goal is not to present an exhaustive study of each one, since each in itself constitutes a large enough area for an independent study. Instead, I have tried to describe, and in some cases reconstruct, the basic aspectual distinctions in both affirmative and negative clauses, and to propose possible developments in each of the various verbal categories: aspect, tense, polarity, and to a lesser extent, mood. It is well known that one change may provoke changes in other parts of the same system. Thus, changes affecting these verbal categories will be seen to also affect basic word order in the family.

Now, the discussion will turn to the basic aspectual categories found within the Kru family.

2 BASIC ASPECTUAL CATEGORIES IN KRU

2.1 Introduction

Within the Kru family, there are four aspectual categories: the perfective, the imperfective, the progressive, and the perfect. Briefly, the perfective refers to punctiliar action, though it will later be seen that this definition needs to be considerably broadened. The imperfective aspect indicates durative or ongoing action and is often used to indicate habitual action. Progressives are very close semantically to imperfectives in that they too express ongoing actions. They are only rarely used to express habituals, however. Finally, the perfect aspect refers to a past action whose result is still relevant at the time of speaking. Examples of these four aspectual categories can be seen in sentences 1-4 taken from Godié, an Eastern Kru language:

(1) perfective
    ɔ kú̃   'He died.'
    he die:PER

(2) imperfective
    ɔ kṹ   'He is dying.'
    he die:IMP

(3) progressive
    ɔ kʊ̀ kú dʌ̃   'He is in the process of dying.'
    he be-at die place

(4) perfect
    ɔ yʌ̃ kú   'He is dead' or
    he PERF die   'He has died.'

Not every Kru language has all four aspectual distinctions. With the possible exception of one language, however, the perfective and imperfective aspects have been found in every Kru language examined in this study. For this reason, these two aspects are considered to be basic to the Kru system and will be the major focus of this chapter. Each of the aspects will be viewed in turn. The synchronically attested morphological markers will be presented, and an attempt will be made to reconstruct the protoforms of each aspect. Essentially, it will be claimed that the perfective was unmarked in Proto-Kru, while the imperfective was marked by two separate suffixes. The discussion will cover cases of semantic shift, reanalysis, and phonological reduction (leading to the formation of new pronoun sets). Following this detailed presentation of the perfective and imperfective aspects, the perfect auxiliary and the periphrastic progressive construction will be briefly discussed.

2.2 The Perfective/Imperfective Distinction

At first glance, the major aspectual distinction within the Kru family appears to be between perfective/completive and imperfective/incompletive actions. According to Comrie (1976:25), this is a common subdivision in languages of the world. Perfective actions are typically punctiliar and refer to events which have already occurred. Imperfective actions, on the other hand, are actions viewed as taking place over an extended period of time, whether in reference to present, past, or future. The following from Klao, a Western Kru language, shows a typical perfective/imperfective distinction (N. Lightfoot 1974):

(5) ɔ́ blɛ̄   'He sang.'
    he sing

(6) ɔ́ɔ́ blɛ̄   'He is singing' or
    he:IMP sing   'He sings habitually.'

Actually, the term **perfective** does not seem to adequately express the semantic range of this aspect. In the next sections, a new term **factative** will be introduced and described in detail.

2.2.1 The factative

2.2.1.1 Defining the category factative. Within Kru, the aspect designating punctiliar action is expressed in one of two ways. It may be indicated by a bare verb stem, as seen in 5, or it may be expressed by a low tone on the verb stem, as seen in Koyo:

(7) á lɨ̀   'They ate.'
    they eat:LOW TONE

(The verb stem 'eat' normally has mid tone: lɨ̄)

When the distribution of these markers is examined, however, it becomes obvious that they do not signal only completive action. Stative verbs like 'have', 'be at', or 'be red' also occur with either zero or low-tone marking. When this is the case, the verbs have a present reading. This can be seen in Krahn (a Western language) and Godié (an Eastern language):

(8) Krahn (bare verb stem)

   ō   jūbō dɛ   'They know something.'
   they know thing

   ō   kɔ   dɛ   'They have something.'
   they have thing

(9) Godié (low tone on the verb stem)

   ɔ̄   kʋ̀   sūkú   'He is at school.'
   he be-at school

   ɛ̄   zʌ̀   'It is red.'
   it red

Zero marking and low-tone marking sometimes designate past punctiliar actions, as seen in 5 and 7, but they give a present reading if the verb is stative, as in 8 and 9. Thus the terms **completive** or **perfective** do not seem to adequately describe this aspectual category.

In 1968, Welmers first used the term **factative** to describe an aspect in Igbo which refers to "past time for verbs expressing action" and to "present or undefined time for verbs expressing state or situation" (1973:311). For active verbs like 'eat', 'hit', 'walk', or 'sing', the aspect designates a past perfective action: 'I ate rice', 'I walked to the market', etc. But for stative verbs like 'have', the verb has a stative reading: 'I have a thousand francs', 'The car is red', etc. In the following examples from Igbo, the factative aspect is marked by an **rṼ** suffix (Welmers 1973:346-47):

(10) ó **byàrà**   'He came.'
     he come-FACT

    ó **ŋwèrè** é'gó   'He has money.'
     he have-FACT money

    ó **tòrò** ùtó   'It's delicious.'
     it

Welmers (1977b) noted the existence of the same aspectual category in Dewoin, a Western Kru language. In this language, the factative is expressed by a bare verb stem:

(11) ɔ̄ pī sāyɛ   'He cooked meat.' (example from
    he cook meat   Welmers

   ī́ ɓélé bélé   'I have a towel.' (example from
   I have towel   Mortvedt)

Indeed, with one exception (see sect. 2.4), virtually every Kru language examined in this study has an aspectual category that falls under Welmers' definition of factative.

As already noted, one proof of the existence of the factative category is the distribution of certain morphological markers. Whether a language expresses this aspect by zero (i.e., by a bare verb stem) or by low tone (as in Godié 1 and 9, and Koyo 7), the marker always has two readings: a past punctiliar reading for action verbs and a present reading for stative verbs. Further support for the factative aspectual category comes from data involving negation. As will be seen in detail in chapter 4, every Kru language has at least two negation strategies: one for imperfectives and one for factatives. Verbs marked in the affirmative by the zero or low-tone factative marker are always negated in the same way--by a negative auxiliary. This is true whether the verbs have a punctiliar or a stative reading. Imperfective actions, on the other hand, are negated by sentence-second particles. (See section 1.5 for a description of the differences between auxiliaries and sentence-second particles.) In the Neyo sentences, 12 shows the negative of an active factative clause, while 13 shows the negative of a stative factative clause. Note that both are negated by auxiliary with the expected S AUX O V word order.

(12) ma **ne** wa yo la
    but I:NEG[1] PAST child bring
    S-AUX   O   V
    'But I didn't bring the child.'

(13) e **ne** fe ka
    I NEG strength have
    S AUX O   V
    'I don't have any strength.'

In contrast, imperfective (habitual) clauses are negated by sentence-second particles which cause no change in the basic SVO word order:

(14) nē mla dili-no
    I:NEG[1] drink raphia-wine
    S:PART V   O
    'I don't drink wine from the raphia palm.'

These examples show that factatives are negated by one strategy and imperfectives by another. Thus, the grammar of Kru formally groups past punctiliar actions and present states and contrasts them with the imperfective (or habitual). This formal distinction

---

[1] Often, first and second person pronouns coalesce with auxiliaries (see sect. 3.8.2).

in negation strategies provides further evidence in favor of the factative category.

A similar, though not exactly parallel, aspectual category is attested in other language families in the world. D. Lightfoot (1979:101, 103) notes the existence of a class in Old English, which he calls **preterite-presents**. These verbs were marked like past (preterite) forms, but had a present reading. He also notes a similar situation in Greek with verbs like 'know' and in Latin with verbs like 'hate'. Thus, the Kru factative category is in no way unusual from a typological point of view.

To briefly summarize, then, the factative indicates past punctiliar action when referring to action verbs, but indicates present or undefined time for stative verbs. The category division is based on the distribution of morphological marking and on certain facts about negation. A similar semantic grouping occurs in related Niger-Congo languages such as Igbo and Yorube (Welmers 1973) and certain Bantu languages (Stucky, pers.com.). It is also attested in completely unrelated languages. In this study, the term **factative** has been adopted because it has been used in the description of African languages. **Perfective** could, however, be used to designate this category if it is defined as suggested by Comrie (1976:16, 22). He defines this aspect as:

> The view of a situation as a single whole, without distinction of the various separate phases that make up that situation ... we may consider that the perfective represents the action pure and simple, without any additional overtones ....

Now that the factative (or perfective) category has been defined, its marking in Proto-Kru will be discussed.

2.2.1.2 Reconstruction of the factative marker. In the preceding section, it was noted that the factative aspect may be signalled in one of two ways: by a bare verb stem or by a low tone on the verb stem. In Western Kru, it is typically expressed by a bare stem, which is the form found in the imperative or in the auxiliary construction S AUX ... V. The unmarked factative occurs in Dewoin, Grebo, Nyabwa, Klao, Krahn, and Wobé. In these languages, tonal differences on the verb have nothing to do with aspect; they merely reflect the lexical tone of the verb, as in Krahn:

(15) ō   bā   dōbō   'They whittled a mortar.'
      they whittle mortar

      ō   bá   dōbō   'They grabbed a mortar.'
      they grab mortar

      ɔ   dī   dɛ̄   'He ate something.'
      he eat thing

In most languages in Eastern Kru, the factative is overtly marked. A factative verb differs from the basic verb stem (indicated by the imperative) by its tone. All factative verbs in this group of languages have a low tone or a related variant, irrespective of the inherent lexical tone. In Godié, verbs have inherently high, mid, or low tone. In the factative, however, the final syllable of the verb stem always carries a low tone. High stem verbs are realized high-low, mid-tone verbs are realized as low, and low-tone verbs are realized as low:

stem	factative	
nú	nǔ	'hear'
yī	yì	'come'
6à	6à	'leave'

If the verb has two syllables, the last syllable is always low in the factative:

fétē	fétè	'pierce'
6ʌ́lʌ́	6ʌ́lʌ̀	'hit'

In Vata, the situation appears to be similar.[2] Verb stems in the factative are realized as mid-low, low, or descending (Vogler 1976: 396-99):

stem	factative	
gbā	gbà	'speak'
nú	nǔ	'understand'
pálá	pálà	'show'
lō̌	lō̌	'to make mounds (for yams)'

Other Eastern Kru languages (e.g., Koyo) show a similar pattern:[3]

stem	factative	
lɨ̄	lɨ̀	'eat'
ḿlá	ḿlà	'drink'
vé	vè	'fight'
gōlū	gòlù	'plant'
wɔ̄lū	wɔ̄lù	'wash'

---

2 Vogler (1976:396-99) calls this aspect **accompli** and states that it "confère au verbe une valeur perfective telle que le procès est envisagé dans sa finitude, sans considération du maintenu de ses conséquences." This corresponds to the punctiliar past reading of the factative. It is not known if the low tone also marks stative verbs.

3 Note that in what appears to be disyllabic verb stems, both syllables have a lowered tone in the factative (**gòlù** 'plant'), while in others just the last syllable is lowered (**ḿlà** 'drink', **wɔ̄lù** 'wash'). This seems to give evidence that **gòlù** is functioning as one syllable unit (**ClV**), while **wɔ̄lù** is functioning as two (**CVlV**).

The low-tone factative is also found in Lakota Dida. From preliminary work in Lozoua Dida, however, it appears that the factative is replaced in these languages by an auxiliary indicating both completive and perfect actions (Gratrix, pers.com.; see sect. 2.4).

To summarize up to this point: In Western Kru the factative is expressed by a bare verb stem, while in Eastern Kru the factative is expressed by low tone on the verb stem. This leaves us with two possibilities in Proto-Kru. The factative could have been marked by low tone, a low tone suffix, or a vowel suffix with low tone (which was subsequently lost in all Western languages). It would have been retained in certain Eastern languages like Godié, Koyo, Lakota Dida, and Vata. The other possibility is that the factative was expressed by a bare verb stem in Proto-Kru. Given this assumption, those Eastern languages with low-tone factatives would have acquired this marker through some innovative process. Data from Bété, an Eastern language bordering the Western group, sheds some light on the problem. Werle (field notes) points out the existence of two past-related aspects, which he labels the passé accompli ponctuel and the permansif. The passé accompli ponctuel describes a punctiliar event, without consideration of its length or its effect in the present. The permansif, on the other hand, apparently insists on the effect of a past action in the present:

(16) passé accompli ponctuel

    ɔ́ glɔ̄ˋ   'He got tired' or
    he tire   'He tired himself out.'

permansif

    ɔ́ glɔ̄   'He got tired out and
    he tire   is worn out.'

What Werle calls passé accompli ponctuel certainly corresponds to the factative we have seen in both Eastern and Western Kru. The permansif, on the other hand, apparently conveys some kind of perfect meaning. In some Bété dialects, the permansif has a passive-like reading:

(17) Soubré Bété

    ɔ lɩ6ã   'He has been hit.'
    he hit-PERM

(18) Kosséoa Bété

    ɔ lɩ6ʌ̃   'He has been hit.'
    he hit-PERM

What is interesting about the permansif is that it is marked by low tone, which in other Eastern languages marks the factative. The Bété factative, on the other hand, is unmarked, even though it is an Eastern language.

factative	permansif	
pʌ́	pʌ́ʌ̀	'throw'
cɛ́lĩ	cɛ̋lĩ	'write'
ŋʌ́mʉ̀	ŋʌ́mʉ̀	'sleep'
lĩ́	lĩ́	'eat'
dĩ̀	dĩ̋ĩ̀	'cut'
mɛ́	mɛ́ɛ̀	'stick'
kʉ6ʌ́	kʉ6ʌ̀	'grab'
wʌ́zĩ̀	wʌ́zĩ̀	'call'
lĩ́6ɨ́	lĩ́6ɨ́	'pick up'

There is some evidence that the low-tone <u>permansif</u> suffix had the shape **a**. In a few of the forms supplied by Werle, there are apparently remnants of a low-tone **a** suffix when the final vowel of the verb stem is ɛ or ɔ:

factative	permansif	
nyɛ̋	nyáa̋	'give'
sɛ̀	sáa̋	'pick'
sɔ̀	sɔ́ɔ̋a̋	'get up'
6ɛ̀	6ɛ̀ɛ̀/6ɛ̀a̋	'make, fabricate'

These paradigms from Bété are significant for two reasons. First, they provide evidence of an unmarked factative in Eastern Kru. Taken together with evidence from Western Kru, this would tend to suggest that the factative in Proto-Kru was unmarked. Second, the examples seem to provide a source for the low-tone factative found in the majority of Eastern Kru languages.

If the factative in Proto-Kru was indeed unmarked, then the low-tone marker found in the majority of Eastern languages must be an innovation. Where, then, did the low-tone factative marker come from? The Bété paradigms provide evidence that in at least one Eastern language, low tone indicates some type of perfect aspect. It is possible, then, that Proto-Eastern Kru had a low-tone suffix **à** which indicated the perfect. This aspect would have been conserved in Bété, but reanalyzed as a factative in languages such as Vata, Godié, Koyo, and Lakota Dida. There are several arguments in favor of this scenario.

First, the shift which is being proposed is semantically plausible. Factative and perfect aspects both refer to realized actions. Perfects contrast with factatives in that they express realized actions which have some relevance to the present situation. However, we have already seen that when used with stative verbs, the factative also refers to a state or situation, much as a perfect aspect does. Thus the semantic shift from a perfect (or permansif) to a factative is slight.

Basic Aspectual Categories in Kru

Second, the shift is attested in other language groups. Comrie (1976:61) notes that in many Romance languages a perfect aspect was reanalyzed as a simple (punctiliar) past. In French, for example, the passé composé 'compound past' used to have a perfect reading. In modern French, however, it expresses the simple past (punctiliar action in the past).

Third, besides the semantic closeness of the two aspects and the fact that such a shift occurs elsewhere, there is another possible motivation for the change. Many Kru languages have developed a perfect auxiliary (this will be discussed in section 2.4).

(19) Godié

ɔ yʌ̄ mū   'He has gone.'
he PERF go

(20) Bété (Kosséoa)

ɔ yɛ mū   'He has gone.'
he PERF go

It is not known at what stage the development of the perfect auxiliary took place, but it is quite likely that at some point, there were two ways to express the perfect aspect: by the low-tone perfect suffix *ā̀ and by the auxiliary *ya (see sect. 2.4). This proposal can be seen schematically in the following chart:

Proto-Eastern Kru

aspect	factative	perfect	
marker	unmarked	verbal suffix **ā̀**	auxiliary **ya**

It appears that the auxiliary perfect eventually dominated over the suffixal form, leaving the latter to be reanalyzed as the factative marker in most Eastern languages. Thus, Modern Eastern Kru developed the following system:

Modern Eastern Kru

aspect	factative	perfect
marker	verbal suffix (or its remnant)	auxiliary **ya**

Exceptionally, some dialects of Bété (including the one spoken at Kosséoa) conserved both marks of the perfect,[4] leaving the factative unmarked.

Again, this type of scenario is not unheard of. A similar change is attested in Latin. Benveniste (1968:88) notes that the emergence of a periphrastic perfect involving the verb habēre 'have' (audītum habeō) had the end result of weakening the synthetic perfect (audīvī). This eventually led to its reanalysis as an aorist (corresponding to a punctiliar aspect).

The proposal, then, is that in Eastern Kru there were two past-related aspects: the factative, expressed by an unmarked verb stem, and a perfect, expressed by the verbal suffix ā. At some point in time, a perfect auxiliary emerged and eventually dominated over the suffix, resulting in the reanalysis of the perfect suffix as a factative marker in many Eastern Kru languages.

It is interesting to note, along these lines, that in the Kru isolate Kuwaa, there is a perfect suffix **ya**, which occurs on the main verb of the clause. There is a shift in word order when the marker is present.

(21) **wɔ́ ji-ō wá**   'He ate rice.'
    he eat-PAST rice

(22) **wɔ́ ō wá jī-yā̄**   'He has eaten rice.'
    he PAST rice eat-PERF

Despite the unusual word order in Kuwaa, there is a noticeable similarity between the phonological shape and the semantic content of the perfect suffix **ya** and the permansif suffix **ā** in Bété. While not conclusive evidence, these data at least suggest that a perfect suffix of the same shape may eventually be reconstructed for a stage earlier than Proto-Eastern Kru.

If the above scenario is correct, then, it is quite likely that the factative in Proto-Kru was essentially unmarked, consisting of an unmarked verb stem (typically found in imperatives and auxiliary constructions). This basic form would have been conserved in the majority of Western languages and in Bété. In a subset of

---

4 Some slight semantic difference has apparently developed between the two. Werle (field notes) provides the following examples:

  ɔ́ yɛ́ ŋʌ́mʉ̀   'Il s'est endormi.'
  he PERF sleep   (Il dort encore)

  ɔ́ ŋʌ́mʉ̀   'Il s'est endormi.'
  he sleep-PERM   (et est maintenant quelqu'un qui dort)

Basic Aspectual Categories in Kru   39

Eastern languages, a perfect-like low-tone suffix would have replaced the unmarked stem as the mark of the factative aspect.

2.2.2 The imperfective aspect contrasts with the factative (or perfective) in that it indicates an ongoing or durative action. It is also used in most Kru languages to express habitual or customary actions.

(23) Godié

    ɔ   lɨ̄   tlɛ̄   'He ate a snake.'
    he eat:FACT snake

    ɔ   lɨ̄   tlɛ̄   'He eats snakes' or
    he eat:IMP snake   'He's eating a snake.'

(24) Klao (Monu, p.30)

    ɔɔ   du   kɔ̀   'She pounds rice every day' or
    she:IMP pound rice   'She is pounding rice.'

(25) Grebo (Innes 1966:74)

    ne du-i   nɛ ne   'I am pounding it' or
    I pound-IMP it BE[5]   'I pound it habitually.'

The use of the imperfective to signal both continuousness and habituality is quite common in languages of the world (Comrie 1976:26). However, it is worth noting that Kru languages differ from most languages in the Niger-Congo family in this respect since, according to Welmers (1973:39), they often formally distinguish habitual and continuative action.

It must be noted that the imperfective aspect in Kru is not a present tense. It may, for example, cooccur with past tenses, indicating ongoing or habitual actions in the past.

(26) Koyo

    n mlɛ -a   suklu   'I used to go to school.'
    I go:IMP-REC school

(27) Grebo

    nɛ́ dū -ī -dá̄ nɛ̄ ne   'I was pounding it.'
    I pound-IMP-T it BE

Because the action is viewed as unrealized, the imperfective aspect in some languages must occur with future tenses or in future constructions.

---

[5] The **ne** morpheme comes from a locative 'BE' and marks assertive focus (Marchese 1983b).

(28) Klao (Rickard:35)

ɔ̄ɔ̄   mú ká   'She will go tomorrow.'
she:IMP go one-day-removed

(29) Krahn

ã̌   mú dɛ   dī   'I will eat (something).'
I:IMP FUT thing eat

As these examples show, not all Kru languages indicate the imperfective aspect in the same way. There are basically two means of expressing this aspect--either by a verbal suffix (27) or a nominal suffix occurring on the subject of the sentence (28). Of these two strategies, verbal suffixation is more common.

2.2.2.1 The imperfective verbal suffix in the majority of Kru languages has the same form: a front vowel which typically agrees in vowel height and vowel harmony with the verb stem. Often the imperfective suffix completely replaces the final vowel of the verb stem or it may cause morphophonological changes within the verb stem itself. In the following examples from Koyo, an Eastern language, the factative is contrasted with the imperfective (Kokora 1976):

(30) á   lù   á   lē
      they eat:FACT   they eat:IMP
      'They ate.'   'They are eating.'

(31) á   gòlù   á   gòlē
      they plant:FACT   they plant:IMP

Similar paradigms are found in both Eastern and Western Kru.

EASTERN

Neyo (examples from Thomann, pp. 82-83, 190)

verb stem	imperfective	
li	lye	'eat'
i	ye	'come'
ka	kɛ	'have'
ku	kue	'die'
dodo	dodoe	'study'

Lakota Dida

ɓlū	ɓlḛ̄	'pound'
pi	pe	'cook'
lĩ	lḛ̄	'eat'

Lozoua Dida

ci	cié	'come'

Vata (Vogler, pp. 393-95)

si	sié	'laugh'
i	ié	'come'

WESTERN

Bakwé

pi	pie	'cook'
su	suə	'buy'
bli	ble	'pound'
mi	mə or mʉ	'go'

Grebo (Innes 1966:28)[6]

du	dui	'pound'
ko	ko	'have'
sɔ̃	sõẽ	'rot'
to	toe	'string'
wɔ	wɛ	'fatigue'
po	pe	'throw'
mʉ	mi	'go'

Nyabo

nu	ni	'do'
mu	mi	'go'
di	di	'eat'
wɔ	wɛ	'finish'

Cedepo

tɔ̃́	tṍḛ́	'buy'

---

[6] Auer (1870) reports the same alternation: **ha/he** 'take out', **nwõ/nwẽ** 'hear', **po/pe** 'place', **mu/mi** 'go', **pa/pe** 'lie down'.

Borobo

    nu   **ni**   'do'

In all languages, the suffix agrees with the vowel harmony class of the verb stem. Besides this, the suffix may also agree with vowel height, as is normally the case in Grebo (Innes 1966).

stem	imperfective	
mu	**mi**	'go'
po	**pe**	'throw'
wɔ	**wɛ**	'finish'

Not all forms are regular, however. For example, within the same language the suffix may be merely attached to the verb stem in some forms, but may replace the final vowel of the verb stem in others. Again in Grebo:

mu	**mi**	'go'
du	**dui**	'pound'

In several languages, the final vowel of the verb stem may be raised[7] when preceding the imperfective, as can be seen in Cedepo and Grebo.

Grebo

    sɔ̃   **sõẽ**   'rot'

Cedepo

    tɔ̀   **tòẽ̀**   'buy'

In Bakwé, the addition of the imperfective suffix yields centralized vowels in some cases:

su	**suə**	'buy'
mi	**mə** (or **mu**)	'go'

Though it is not always possible to state the rules of regular phonological change that are involved in the formation of each imperfective stem, there still seems to be adequate evidence for positing a proto-imperfective marker ***e**. This hypothesis gains further support from Sɛmɛ, a Kru isolate spoken in Burkina Faso. Here, what Prost designates as the <u>présent</u> is also indicated by a vowel change in the verb stem. Though there is a lot of irregularity in the system, the following stems contain a front vowel in the présent (Prost 1964:365-66):

---

[7] Raising of the first vowel in a sequence of two vowels is common in many Kru languages. It occurs in Godié, Tepo, and Klao (Dawson 1975, Marchese 1975, Singler 1979).

radical	présent	
di (_)	le (—)	'eat'
ko (_)	klɛ (—)	'do'
fe (_)	fɛ (—)	'throw'
wo (⁻)	wɛ (—)	'fall'
kul (_)	kwel (—)	'sew'
ti (_)	hlẽ (—)	'dig'

Certainly, when the imperfective suffix is attached to an unmarked verb stem, it usually refers to a continuing action in the present. From Prost's data, it is not possible to tell whether what he calls the présent is not actually the imperfective aspect. If Sɛmɛ acts at all like other Kru languages, it is likely that the **e** form may also occur with a past tense, indicating an ongoing action in the past.

Up to this point in the discussion, we have seen overt **e** imperfective suffixes in both Eastern and Western Kru and in the Kru isolate Sɛmɛ. In the next two sections, tonal remnants of ***e** will be discussed.

(1) Reduction of the ***e** imperfective. In several languages where the **e** suffix appears, there is evidence that it is being assimilated to the vowel quality of the final vowel of the verb stem. Often, when the stem already contains a front vowel, the distinction between the factative and imperfective may be neutralized. In Bakwẽ, the verb **ble** 'sing' has the same shape whether it is imperfective or not. In Koyo, when the verb stem ends in an **a**, the **e** suffix assimilates completely (Kokora 1976).

verb stem	incompletive	
mɨlá	mɨlá	'drink'
pa	pã	'run'

The same kind of assimilation apparently occurs in Lozoua Dida where Gratrix (pers.com.) reports that the **e** suffix occurs on some stems but not on others.

cī	cīé	'come'
būdō	būdō	'bathe-INTRANS'

In Vata (Vogler, pp. 393-95), the **e** suffix is retained when the verb stem ends in a high front vowel:

si	sié	'laugh'

but apparently becomes a back vowel when the final vowel of the verb stem is a high back vowel:

nǫ	nɔ́	'do'
fu	fṍ	'die'
gu	guó	'run'

When the stem ends in **a**, **o**, or **ɔ**, the suffix is completely assimilated and the forms are apparently neutralized.

stem	imperfective	
pɔ	pɔ	'shine'
go	go	'put up a fence'
ila	**ilá**	'taste'

A similar assimilation apparently occurred in Grebo. In an early work (Auer 1870:24-25), it was reported that verbs ending in front vowels show no perfective/imperfective alternation.

| bi | bi | 'beat' |
| **lede** | **lede** | 'tell' |

Certain verbs with back vowels also show no distinction.

| kũ | kũ | 'grow' |
| ho | ho | 'be plentiful' |

When vocalic assimilation does take place, the distinction between the factative and the imperfective may be maintained by tone. In Koyo, the factative is realized as a low tone on the verb stem. The imperfective suffix, which typically has the shape **e**, carries a mid tone (Kokora 1976).

factative	imperfective	
lù	lē	'eat'
gōlù	gōlē	'plant'
wɔ̄lù	wɔ̄lū	'wash'
yì	yē	'come'

When the suffix is completely assimilated to the final vowel of the verb stem, the mid tone of the imperfective remains, maintaining the distinction between the imperfective and the factative.

(32) Koyo

ɔ́ pà̀	ɔ́ pā̄
he run:FACT	he run:IMP
'He ran.'	'He's running.'

Basic Aspectual Categories in Kru

The same is true in Lakota Dida, where similar assimilations occur.

(33) Lakota Dida

ɔ mlɛ̃	ɔ mlɛ̃
he go:FACT	he GO:IMP
'He left.'	'He's going.'

In Grebo also, the imperfective is usually signalled by a vowel suffix. However, when the verb stem has the shape CV̀CV̀, CV́CV̀, or CV̀, Innes (1966:72) reports that the imperfective is indicated by a change in tone. In the following examples, the difference between the factative and the imperfective is marked on the first and second syllable of the verb word. The imperfective is realized on a high mid /'/ rather than a low mid /-/ tone. (Note: Grebo has four tones rather than three, as in Koyo or Dida.)

(34) **nē gādē-dá   nɛ̀ nē   né gáde-dá   nɛ̀ nē**
  I deny:FACT-T it BE   I deny:IMP-T it BE
  'I denied it.'   'I was denying it.'

In Godié, the imperfective vowel suffix **e** has completely disappeared, leaving only a mid tone on the verb stem to indicate this aspect. To my ears, the final vowel of the imperfective verb form sounds slightly lengthened, but it is certainly not as long as a phonetically long vowel. Thus verbs have three tones in Godié: their inherent tone (high, mid, or low), which appears in the imperative form and in the auxiliary construction frame S AUX ... V, the factative form, always realized on low tone, and the imperfective tone, which always ends on a mid tone.

stem	factative	imperfective	
yī	**yì**	**yī**	'come'
ɓā	**ɓà**	**ɓā**	'leave'
nú	**nù⁻**	**nū⁻**	'hear'
būdō	**būdò**	**būdō**	'bathe'
ɓʌ̄lʌ̄	**ɓʌ̄lʌ̀**	**ɓʌ̄lʌ̄**	'hit'

In Bété, the **e** suffix has also been reduced, but the form of the imperfective is not quite as regular as in Godié. Bété has four lexical tones (rather than three as found in Godié): high ´, mid-high ', mid ⁻, and low ˋ. The imperfective in Bété is always in the middle range, never high or low. It has already been mentioned that, unlike the rest of the Eastern languages, Bété does not mark the factative with low tone. Rather, the factative is expressed by the unmarked verb stem (i.e., by the inherent tone of the verb). Thus the distinction between factative and imperfective is also tonal in Bété. Verbs which are inherently high or low are either mid or mid-high in the imperfective (Werle, field notes).

stem (factative)	imperfective	
pʌ́	pʌ́	'throw'
sɛ̂	sɛ̂	'pick (fruit)'
6ɛ̂	6ɛ̂	'make'
bídã̄	bídã̄	'bathe'
cɛ́lí	cɛ́lí	'write'

Verbs that are inherently mid-high or mid retain the same tone in the imperfective.

lī	lī	'eat'
mɛ́	mɛ́	'stick'
kü6ʌ̄	kü6ʌ̄	'grab'
ŋʌmʉ́	ŋʌmʉ́	'sleep'

Thus, the factative/imperfective distinction is neutralized in this case.

It has been seen, then, that in several languages the imperfective verbal suffix *e is reduced in certain environments. In Bété and Godié, *e has virtually disappeared. However, when such reductions occur, the factative/imperfective distinction is maintained by tone. The imperfective is always, in this case, realized on mid tone. It is interesting to note that even in the Kru isolate Sɛmɛ, the imperfective is realized on mid tone. This suggests that the protoimperfective verbal suffix had mid tone: *ē.

(2) Other remnants of the *e suffix. In at least two languages where the imperfective is marked by a nominal suffix, there are remnants of the imperfective verbal suffix. In both Krahn and Klao, there are vocalic remnants as well as tonal ones.

(a) Vocalic remnants. Singler (pers.com.) reports that in Klao, an e suffix sometimes appears on the verb when an action is ongoing in the past. He calls this the "past incompletive":

(35) ɔ̄ɔ̄ plō-é kɔ́   ɔ̄ɔ̄ dī-í kɔ́
      he:IMP sell-e rice   he:IMP eat-e rice
      'He was selling rice.'   'He was eating rice.'

The e does not appear in the present, and it does not appear if a tense marker is present. Given this distribution, it could be argued that e is a past tense marker rather than an aspect. However, tense markers may occur in either perfective or imperfective sentences, and, as the following example shows, this particular suffix may not occur in an otherwise factative sentence.

(36) *ɔ plṓ-ḛ   kɔ̄   'He sold rice.'[8]
    he sell:FACT-e rice

Thus the **e** does not qualify as a tense marker and is probably a reflex of the imperfective *e, which somehow became restricted to past action.

In Krahn as well there is at least one overt suffix that looks very much like the **e** imperfective marker. In Gbaeson Krahn, the **i** suffix apparently indicates an imperfective action.

(37) ǎ   mū-ḭ̄   Ø[9] yĕ   dɛ́   dī   'I'm going in order
     I-INC go-SUF Ø   SEQ thing eat   to eat.'

(38) ḭ̄ mū Ø yĕ dɛ́ dī   'I went in order to eat.'
     I go Ø SEQ thing eat

The exact distribution of this suffix is not known, but according to John Duitsman (pers.com.) it is not very common. It is not referred to in any other Krahn field notes (such as those from Hansell or Tisher).

(b) <u>Tonal remnants</u>. In both Klao and Krahn, there are what appear to be tonal remnants of the **e** suffix. As mentioned earlier, both these languages make predominant use of the nominal suffix **a** (see sect. 2.2.2.2). However, in both these languages, tone on the verb seems also to signal the imperfective. In fact, as in languages where tone is the only signal of the imperfective, it is <u>mid tone</u> which is primarily associated with this aspect. In Klao, <u>verbs that</u> are inherently mid-low in the factative are realized as mid in the imperfective (N. Lightfoot 1974:433).

---

[8] There is a homophonous tense marker in Klao, which designates recent tense (Singler, pers.com.):

   ī   dū-ī̄   gblā̰-nā̄   'They pounded the rice
   they pound-REC   rice DEF   earlier today.'

   yiɛ̄   fɔ̰̄-ɛ̄̄   'They were fighting
   they-INC   fight-REC   earlier today.'

The two particles are clearly distinct, however, since they differ in distribution. In subordinate clauses, the past incompletive marker occurs before the subordinating particle (and is not subject to deletion), while the recent tense marker comes after the subordinating marker and is subject to deletion. Thus sentence 36 is grammatical if **e** is interpreted as a recent tense marker:

   ɔ   plo-ḗ   kɔ̄   'He sold rice earlier today.'
   he   sell-REC   rice

[9] In many Kru languages, first and second person singular subject pronouns may be deleted before an auxiliary (see sect. 3.8.2). The abbreviation <u>SEQ</u> refers to a sequential auxiliary.

(39) dō nā̄˜   dó-ā̄   nā̄
    Doe walk   Doe-IMP walk
    'Doe walked.'   'Doe is walking.'

Verbs that are high-low in the factative divide into two sets. In one set, verbs are realized as mid-low or mid in the imperfective.

(40) dō pí̋ī̋   dó-ā̄ pi̋ī̋   dó-ā̄ pī̄ī̄
    Doe lift   Doe-IMP lift   Doe-IMP lift
    'Doe lifted.'   'Doe is lifting.'

In the other set of verbs high-low in the factative (presumably with a different underlying tone), verbs are realized as mid-low in the imperfective.

(41) dō fí̋ˆ   dó-ā̄ fī̄˜
    Doe cry   Doe-IMP cry
    'Doe cried.'   'Doe is crying.'

As was the case in Bété, verbs that are inherently mid have mid tone in both the factative and the imperfective.

(42) dō blē̄   dó-ā̄ blē̄
    Doe sing   Doe-IMP sing
    'Doe sang.'   'Doe is singing.'

In the data presented so far, the tonal behavior of imperfective verbs in Klao looks like that of the other languages already discussed. Evidence has already been given that the protoimperfective suffix had mid tone. However, there are two important exceptions in Klao which must be noted. First, with low tone verbs there is no tonal distinction between the factative and the imperfective.

(43) dō slɛ̀   dó-ā̄ slɛ̀
    Doe read   Doe-IMP read
    'Doe read.'   'Doe is reading.'

And second, in a class of verbs that is realized as mid in the factative (Lightfoot claims an underlying mid-high tone in this group), the imperfective verb stem is realized as mid-low.

(44) dō cɛ̄̄   dó-a cɛ̄̄˜
    Doe learn   Doe-IMP learn
    'Doe learned.' 'Doe is learning.'

Basic Aspectual Categories in Kru

Thus the parallelism with other Kru languages is not complete. Nevertheless, it can still be claimed that in this dialect of Klao, the imperfective verb stem tends to be realized on mid tone. It must be added that the tone system in Klao is complex, and it may be that some tonal rules may account for these two exceptions. Despite these exceptions, it could very well be that the mid tone in Klao is a remnant of the **e** imperfective suffix found throughout the rest of the Kru family.

Finally, in both Gbaeson and Tchien Krahn, there is some evidence that a mid-tone suffix was once part of the imperfective verb stem. Tisher (field notes) reports that in the majority of cases the imperfective aspect is indicated solely by the nominal suffix. This is true when the verb stem has an inherent tone which is high, mid-high, or mid. However, when the verb has an inherent low tone, the verb stem carries a mid tone in the imperfective. Again, this mid tone is probably derived from the proto-*e suffix.

In Gbaeson Krahn, there is even more evidence of a tonal remnant of the imperfective verbal suffix. In this dialect, when the verb stem is low in the factative, it is realized as a rising tone in the imperfective.

(45) ɔ́ tɛ̀ dbū̄˙   ɔ́ tɛ̌ dbū̄´
      he buy rope   he buy:IMP rope
      'He bought rope.'   'He is buying rope.'

When the verb stem is high in the factative, there is a glide from high to mid tone in the imperfective.

(46) ɔ́ cɛ́ dbū̄˙   ɔ́ cɛ̂ dbū̄˙
      he cut rope   he cut:IMP rope
      'He cut rope.'   'He is cutting rope.'

The imperfective form in both these cases could be explained by a mid-tone imperfective marker. Exceptionally, however, verbs with an inherent mid tone are realized as high in the imperfective.

(47) ǐ sɔ́ tlūgbɔ́   ǎ sɔ́ tlūgbɔ́
      I come-from Monrovia   I:IMP come-from Monrovia
      'I came from Monrovia.'   'I'm coming from Monrovia.'

This last form is more difficult to explain. The high tone in the imperfective may be due to dissimilation. In any case, the tonal changes on imperfective stems in Klao and in two dialects of Krahn (Gbaeson and Tchien) seem indicative of an earlier suffix, which in all likelihood was the proto-*e suffix.

In summary, map 4 shows the distribution of the reflexes of the imperfective verbal suffix *e (in unbroken lines) and the areas where remnants remain (in broken lines). Thus, reflexes of

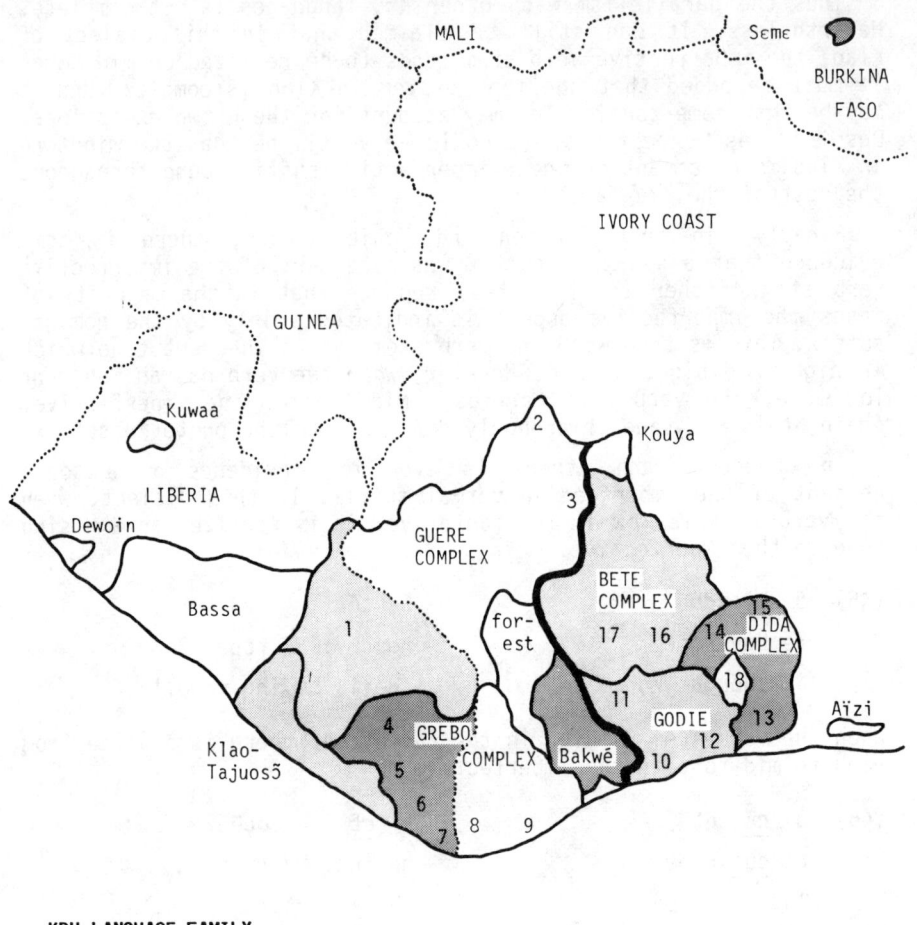

KRU LANGUAGE FAMILY
adapted from Marchese 1979

▬ division between Eastern and Western Kru

— division between complexes or unaffiliated languages

····· division between countries

▓ reflexes of *e

☐ remnants of *e

1. Krahn
2. Wobé
3. Nyabwa
4. Cedepo
5. Borobo
6. Nyabo
7. Grebo
8. Tepo
9. Bereby Kru
10. Neyo
11. Kwadia
12. Koyo
13. Lozoua Dida
14. Lakota Dida
15. Vata
16. Bété (Gagnoa)
17. Bété Soubré-Daloa-Guibéroua
18. Ega (non-Kru)

Map 4. Distribution of *e

the suffix are found in major parts of Eastern and Western Kru, as well as in the Kru isolate, Sɛmɛ.

(3) <u>Possible form of proto</u> ***e**. Up to this point, much evidence has been given in support of the reconstruction of ***e** as the imperfective verbal suffix in Proto-Kru. Actually, the suffix may have had a slightly different shape. In his dissertation on Vata, Vogler attempts to explain why the form for 'go' in Vata is different from the form in Bété. He notes (1976:297):

> En Kra, on oppose nàgi/nàgre 'je viens' où le duratif est de signifiant **-re** (S.W. Koelle, p. 158). Dans cette optique il est possible de comparer bété **mo** 'aller'/vata **mle** où la forme ancienne **le** du duratif (?) [question mark his, L.M.] semble avoir fusionné avec le monème verbal.

Evidence from Neyo points in the same direction. A **lɛ** suffix also occurs with some verbs in the imperfective (Grah, pers.com.).

stem	imperfective	
zɛ	zɛlɛ	'read'
mʊ	mʊlɛ	'go'

Something similar occurs in Koyo (**mlɛ̄** 'go:IMP', **mū̄** 'go:FACT').

There are a few other cases of an lV morpheme carrying an imperfective meaning. Vogler also points out the following irregular imperfective forms (p. 395):

stem	imperfective 'duratif'	
ká	kálá	'have'
gālɛ̄	glālɛ̄	'follow'

Along with this, in Sɛmɛ, the Kru isolate examined earlier, an **l** sometimes cooccurs with the **e** imperfective form.

(Prost 1964:366):

stem	imperfective	
to	tɛl	'hunt'
ko	klɛ	'do'
di	le	'eat'
duko	duklɔ	'raise'

This is hardly enough evidence to posit a ***le** as the imperfective aspect marker for all of Kru, but it is suggestive that it might have been the case, given the widespread distribution of **e** and the commonness of l-reduction in the family (Marchese 1979).

It is also interesting to note that if ***le** is eventually reconstructed, it may be linked to the existential verb BE **ne** or **ni**.[10]

2.2.2.2 The imperfective nominal suffix. The nominal suffix which has been alluded to in the previous discussions occurs primarily in Western Kru. Throughout the family, it has the form **a** and is always suffixed onto the last element of the noun phrase which functions as subject.

(48) Klao (N. Lightfoot)

    dō blē   dō-ā blē

    Doe sing   Doe-IMP sing

    'Doe sang.'   'Doe is singing.'

  (Rickard)

    slā ná wā   slā ná-ā wā

    house DEF burn   house DEF-IMP burn

    'The house burnt.'   'The house is burning.'

(49) Tichien Krahn (Hansell)

    nī-ā duba   'It is raining.'

    water-IMP fall

    gōō-ā nā pēpē   'The chameleon walks slowly.'

    chameleon-IMP walk slowly

When a subject pronoun occurs, **a** is suffixed directly onto this element. However, since the vowel **a** is very susceptible to assimilation, the combination pronoun + **a** often reduces to a lengthened form of the pronoun.

(50) Klao

    / ɔ̄ + ā blē   'He is singing.'

    he + IMP sing

    [ɔ̄ɔ̄ blē]

(51) Nyabwa

    ī + a poōo   'I am planting.'

    I + IMP plant

    [īī poōo]

---

10 This form appears to be cognate with copulas and existential verbs in other branches of Niger-Congo. Compare Ewe **lè** 'be located at', Bantu **li**, Fanti **nĭ**, Yoruba **ni**, Igbo **di**, all 'BE' verbs or particles of identification.

Basic Aspectual Categories in Kru   53

Note that in Nyabwa, the prolonged vowel has a low tone.

Given that pronouns are frequent subjects in both narratives and conversations, the reduction of the combination pronoun + **a** is a very common occurrence. In many languages, the coalescence of **a** with pronouns has led to the emergence of new pronoun sets. In Tepo, most pronouns have an imperfective form which consists of a lengthened form of the pronoun (Thalmann, field notes).

unmarked	imperfectiv	
ɔ́	ɔ́ɔ́	3 sing, human or non-human
ʊ̀	ʊ̀ʊ̀	3 sing, non-human, 3 pl, human
ɛ́	ɛ́ɛ́	3 sing, human, non-human
ɩ	ɩ́ɩ́	3 pl, non-human
nɩ̀	nɩ̀ɩ̀	2 sing
á	áá	2 pl
à	àà	1 pl

In languages where the first and second pronouns are nasalized, the addition of **a** causes a change in the shape of the pronoun. This is the case in Wobé:

í + ā ⟶ má   1st person sing:IMP
ì̃ + ā ⟶ mà̃   2nd person sing:IMP

A similar phenomenon occurs in Dewoin (see discussion following). Again, the merging of the imperfective suffix **a** and the unmarked pronoun set has given rise to[11] what some researchers have termed an "imperfective" pronoun set.

In the present discussion, the **a** suffix has been seen to occur in Wobé, Krahn, Nyabwa, Klao, and Tepo, all Western languages. There is also evidence that an **a** subject suffix was once present in Dewoin, another Western language. According to Welmers, the imperfective in Dewoin is not signalled by suffixes, but rather by a periphrastic construction containing the locative verb 'be at' (see sects. 2.3.1 and 2.3.2).

(52) ɔ́ nɩ̀ sāyɛ̄ pi na   'She is cooking meat.'
     she be-at meat cook LOC

---
[11] Some researchers have differentiated between two sets of pronouns: completive and incompletive. While the merged set can and perhaps should be called incompletive, it is incorrect to call the unmarked set completive, since they are used in many contexts--including futures and progressives and other aspectual/temporal settings where an action is not necessarily viewed as completed.

However, in examining the Dewoin verbal system, we note that there is a set of pronouns which Welmers (1977b) describes as "presumptive." These pronouns, characterized by a lengthened low-tone vowel, are used to designate future and customary actions.

(53) Welmers

    ɔ̄ɔ̀   zà   kēlē   'She sells pepper (it's her job).'
    she:PRES sell pepper

    āà   tà   zīmī   'We eat fish (habitually).'
    we:PRES eat fish

    ɔ̄ɔ̀   mū   sāyɛ̀ pīī   mù   'He's going to cook meat.'
    he:PRES FUT meat cook-NOM FUT

It has already been mentioned that the imperfective marker in Kru (whether in the form of a verbal or nominal suffix) is used to indicate habitual actions. It was also shown that sometimes imperfective suffixes cooccur with futures. The common semantic feature between imperfective customary and future actions is that they are all unrealized. Thus it would appear that the presumptive set of pronouns in Dewoin is really a combination of an unmarked pronoun and an imperfective **a** suffix which has been totally assimilated. It becomes even clearer that we are dealing with the **a** imperfective marker when we examine the first and second person pronouns of the presumptive set. Evidence of the underlying **a** can be clearly seen.

    í + a ⟶ ná   1st person (PRES)
    ì + a ⟶ nà   2nd person (PRES)

In this language, then, the imperfective use of the **a** marker has been replaced by a periphrastic progressive construction, but is still used to refer to habitual and unrealized future actions.

To summarize up to this point, the imperfective nominal suffix **a** and its remnants are found in Klao, Krahn, Tepo, Nyabwa, Wobé, and Dewoin. Note that these languages represent the Grebo and Guéré complexes as well as the unaffiliated Western languages (Dewoin and Klao). There is, then, adequate evidence for positing a protoform ***a** for Western Kru. In Eastern Kru, the nominal suffix seems almost nonexistent. The only Eastern language where there is a clear remnant of ***a** functioning as an imperfective marker is in Nyo, a language which borders the Western group. According to Grah (pers.com.), there are two imperfective constructions: one with a reflex of both the ***e** verbal suffix and one with what appears to be reflexes of both the verbal suffix ***e** and the nominal suffix ***a**. Note the long-form pronoun in sentence (55):

(54)   ɔ́   61ī-ɛ̄   'He sings.' or
        he sing-IMP   'He can sing.'

Basic Aspectual Categories in Kru 55

(55) 5̄3̄ 6lɪ-ɛ   'He's in the act of singing.'
    he:IMP sing-IMP

The nominal suffix in Neyo is apparently also used in an innovative way in conditional statements marking the less real of two actions (Gratrix, pers.com.).

(56) 5 nī 6lī ā   5̄3̄ nī 6lī ā
    he when sing SUB   he:IMP if sing SUB
    'When he sings,...'   'If he sings,...'

Note that this corresponds with the general semantic domain of the imperfective aspect, i.e., unrealized actions such as ongoing, habitual, and future actions.

   In the rest of the Eastern languages, the imperfective is exclusively indicated by reflexes of *e (see sect. 2.2.2). However, there is also some evidence that the a suffix was at one time present in Eastern languages besides Neyo. If we compare the third person plural pronouns in both Eastern and Western Kru, it seems that the Eastern forms can be broken down into two morphemes: the Western form pronoun ʋ and the imperfective marker a.

Nyabwa	ʋ̄	Godié	wā
Wobé	ʋ̄ʋ̄	Bété	wá
Tepo	ʋ̄	Vata	ɔā
Grebo	ʋ̄	Neyo	aa

   It has already been shown that the nominal suffix a is highly susceptible to assimilation, especially when it occurs following a pronoun. In fact, in Nyabwa, when a is added to the ʋ pronoun, the form becomes wā-ā (Bentinck, pers.com.). The above data suggest that the a imperfective nominal suffix was, in fact, present in Eastern languages but disappeared in all contexts except the third person plural. These pronoun forms are now frozen. They in no way carry any aspectual information. If the above scenario is correct, then the a nominal suffix could be reconstructed not only for Proto-Western Kru but also for all of Proto-Kru (before the east/west split). The distribution of *a is summarized in map V. Unbroken lines indicate a sure remnant; broken lines a probable one.

2.2.2.3 The imperfective in Proto-Kru. In the preceding sections, evidence was given supporting the reconstruction of two imperfective markers: a verbal suffix *e and a nominal suffix *a. If these reconstructions are correct, this implies that at some stage of Proto-Kru the imperfective had the following form:

$$*S\text{-}a \quad V\text{-}e \quad (0)$$

There is, in fact, evidence that this structure did exist. It has already been mentioned that some languages have remnants of both

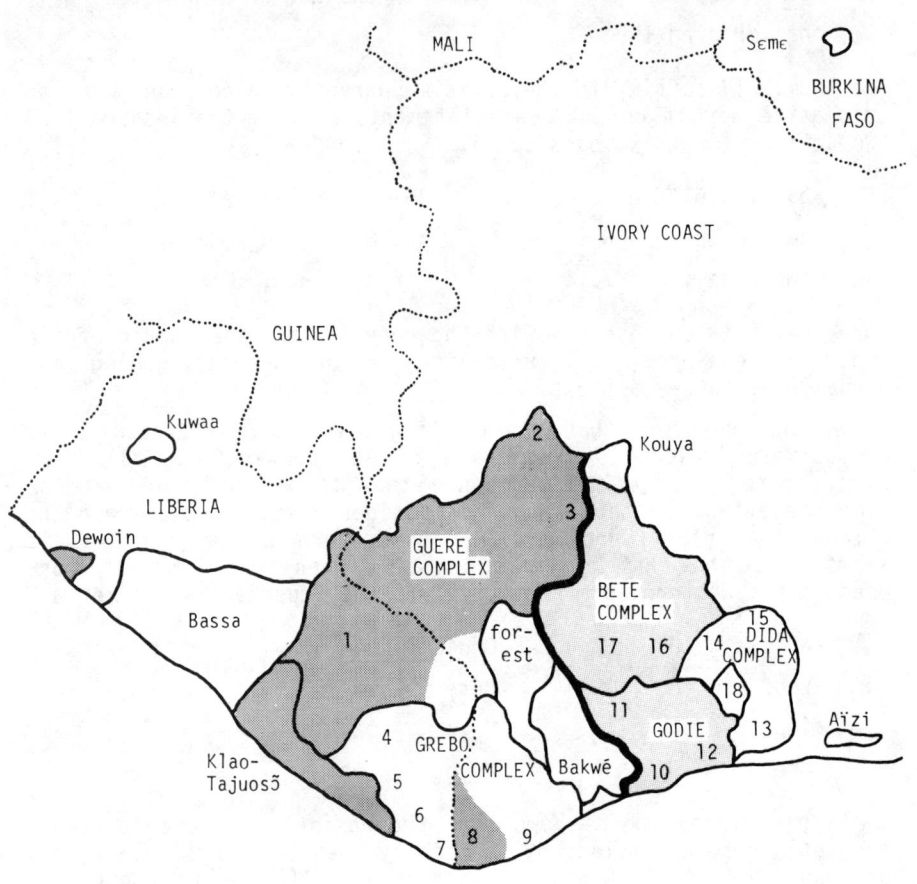

KRU LANGUAGE FAMILY

adapted from Marchese 1979

━━ division between Eastern and Western Kru

── division between complexes or unaffiliated languages

····· division between countries

▨ sure remnants of *a

▧ probable remnants of *a

1. Krahn
2. Wobé
3. Nyabwa
4. Cedepo
5. Borobo
6. Nyabo
7. Grebo
8. Tepo
9. Bereby Kru
10. Neyo
11. Kwadia
12. Koyo
13. Lozoua Dida
14. Lakota Dida
15. Vata
16. Bété (Gagnoa)
17. Bété Soubré-Daloa-Guibéroua)
18. Ega (non-Kru)

Map 5. Remnants of *a

Basic Aspectual Categories in Kru 57

the nominal and verbal imperfective suffixes. These include Neyo in the east and Klao and Krahn in the west.

The protostructure has undergone several changes in the daughter languages. These changes are represented here schematically:

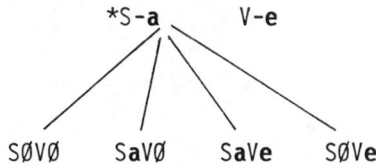

Each of these daughter structures is synchronically attested in the Kru family.

(1) S Ø V Ø. Bassa, Dewoin, and Kuwaa all seem to have lost both the verbal and nominal imperfective suffixes. These have been replaced by periphrastic constructions. It was noted, however, that the nominal suffix **a** in Dewoin remains to signal habitual and future actions. Imperfective actions are expressed by the periphrastic progressive construction containing the verb 'be at' (for details on the structure of this construction in Kru, see section 2.3.1).

(57) Welmers

    ɔ <u>nī</u> sāyɛ̄ pī nā   'He is cooking meat.'
    he <u>be-at</u> meat cook NOM

The periphrastic progressive seems to have also entirely supplanted the imperfective suffixes in Kuwaa. In this language, it is used to express both continuousness and habituality.

(58) wɔ́ dē⁻ nāmū nū⁻ sīā̰   'He's walking slowly.'
    he <u>be-at</u> walk LOC slowly

    ɟegbî̂ nū wɔ́ <u>dē⁻</u> wá jīī nū   'He's always eating rice.'
    always he <u>be-at</u> rice eat LOC

Finally, in Bassa, it seems there are two strategies for indicating ongoing action. Like Dewoin and Kuwaa, Bassa often makes use of the periphrastic progressive construction containing the locative verb 'be at':

(59) Hobley

    ɔ <u>nī</u> kùā nyuɛń   'He is working.'
    he <u>be-at</u> work do-NOM

Hobley reports that in another construction, her "present tense," a high tone **nī** occurs in sentence-final position.[12] This **nī**, however, is often omitted.

(60) ɔ **nyu kua nī**   'He works.'
    he do work BE

   ɔ **sã ni**   'He's tired.'
   he tire BE

Again, as in Dewoin and Kuwaa, there is no trace of an **e** verbal imperfective suffix in Bassa.

(2) S a V Ø. In many Western languages, the nominal suffix ***a** is the predominant signal of the imperfective. This is the case in Wobé and Nyabwa. If there was a verbal suffix in Proto-Kru, the question arises as to what became of it in these languages. It is interesting to note that in Wobé there is a front vowel verbal suffix. Because of its distribution (in affirmative indicative clauses but never in imperatives, interrogatives, or negative ones), it has been described as a declarative marker. A similar particle occurs in Nyabwa.

(61) Wobé

   ma   mū-ɛ̄   kwɛ́ɛ̄   tɛ̃-ã̄   kã̄ã̄   'I am going to buy
   I-INC go-DECL peanuts buy-NOM now   peanuts now.'

   aã̄   blɛ̃-ɛ̄   dʋ   due   'We are singing a
   we-INC sing-DECL song one   song.'

---

12 A sentence-final BE-related morpheme **ni** or **ne** is reported in several Western languages. Auer (1870:15) reports that in Grebo "the verb **ne** 'to be' is often added to a verb, especially in the present and perfect tense, to express the duration of an action; as: **o di ne**—he is coming."

J. Payne (1864) cites a similar form occurring with present ongoing or perfect actions. A hundred years later, Innes (1966) notes the particle occurs with both completive and incompletive actions. In the latter case, it cooccurs with the **i** incompletive suffix.

   ne du-da   bla ne   'I pounded rice.'
   I pound-PAST rice BE

   ne du-i-da   bla ne   'I was pounding rice.'
   I pound-INC-PAST rice BE

This **ne** does not seem to be related to proto ***e** since significant differences exist in distribution and meaning. In Marchese (1983b), it is argued that these **ni** or **ne** markers in Kru signal assertive focus.

(62) Nyabwa

    nyɔ́kpakpʋ̀ʋ̀ pɪ́eè   **kɔ̀bʋ̀**   'The woman is cooking rice.'
    woman:IMP   cook:DECL:SUF rice

At first glance, one is tempted to associate this front vowel suffix with the imperfective marker **e**. However, researchers working on these two languages (Bearth, Bentinck, Egner, Hofer, and Link) are quick to point out that the marker does not carry an imperfective meaning. In fact, it may occur in affirmative factative (or completive) clauses.

(63) Wobé

    ɔ́ dɪ́-ɛ̄   dɛ̄   'He ate.'
    he eat-DECL thing

(64) Nyabwa

    nyɔ́kpàkpʋ́ pɪ́eè   **kɔ̀bʋ̀**   'The woman cooked rice.'
    woman   cook:DECL:SUF rice

Though the ɛ suffix in Wobé and the low tone in Nyabwa definitely do not function synchronically as imperfective markers, it may well be that they are derived from this source. There are two pieces of evidence in favor of this hypothesis:

(i) the phonological similarity between the two verbal suffixes
(ii) the fact that the declarative marker in Wobé and Nyabwa and the imperfective marker in the rest of Kru have a similar distribution

The last point is particularly interesting. Like the declarative marker in Wobé and Nyabwa, the **e** imperfective marker never occurs in the negative (this fact was first observed by Kokora (1976) in his description of Koyo).

(65) Koyo

    à lʉ̄   à tá lʉ̄
    we eat   we NEG eat
    'We ate.'   'We did not eat.'

    à lē   à lʉ̄ tá
    we eat:IMP   we eat NEG
    'We are eating.' 'We are not eating.'

(66) Neyo

    ɔ 6lɪ-ɛ   ɔ ní 6lɪ
    he sing-IMP   he NEG sing
    'He is singing.' 'He is not singing.'

(67) Grebo (Innes 1966:72)

  nē du-i   nɛ̄ nē   nè du   nɛ̄
  I pound-IMP it BE   I-NEG pound it
  'I am pounding it.'   'I am not pounding it.'

Also, like the suffix in Nyabwa and Wobé, the imperfective suffix does not occur in the imperative. The similarities in distribution of the imperfective suffix and the declarative marker in Wobé and Nyabwa seem to suggest that the **e** imperfective suffix may have existed at one time in Wobé and Nyabwa. If this was the case, it apparently lost its imperfective meaning and was generalized to apply to all affirmative indicative actions.

(3) S Ø V e. With the exception of Neyo, the Eastern languages have lost the **a** nominal suffix. It was pointed out (in sect. 2.2.2.2) that *a was retained only in the forms of the third person plural subject pronouns. The verbal suffix *e or its tonal remnant is the only signal of the imperfective aspect at the present time.

(4) S a V e. Earlier, Klao, Krahn, and Neyo were mentioned as languages which have retained both imperfective suffixes. However, even in these languages, there is a tendency for one of the markers to disappear. It is interesting to note that each language is responding differently to the double set of markers.

In Klao, the nominal suffix has become dominant, with the tonal markings on the verb stem being only sometimes significant.

(68) **dó-ā   blē**   **dó   blē**
      Doe-IMP sing   Doe sing
      'Doe is singing.'   'Doe sang.'

but: **dó-ā   nā**   **dó   nā̀**
      Doe-IMP walk   Doe walk
      'Doe is walking.'   'Doe walked.'

In Neyo, the cooccurrence of both suffixes can be clearly seen.

(69) **na   po-e   sa**   'I'm lying down.'
      I:IMP lie-IMP down

cf.   **e a   sa   po**   'I have lain down.'
      I PERF down lie

The **na/e** pronoun distinction has apparently been weakening for some time, however, as seen in the following from Delafosse (1904:86):

(70) **nă mle / ĕ mle**   'Je vais.' (I'm going; I go.)

Basic Aspectual Categories in Kru

This can also be seen in forms where the ε apparently carries the imperfective meaning and the long form pronoun seems to emphasize the duration (or possibly the current relevance) of the action (Carol Gratrix, pers.com.).

(71) ɔ́ bɨ̄-ɛ   ɔ̄ɔ́ bɨ̄ɪ-ɛ
      he sing-IMP   he:IMP sing-IMP
      'He sings.' or 'He can sing.'   'He's singing.'

In Krahn, the nominal suffix **a** is also beginning to weaken. While **a** must occur on full nouns, it is disappearing on simple pronouns. In Gbaeson Krahn, Duitsman (pers.com.) reports that the factative/imperfective distinction is no longer made on pronouns of the third person singular or on the second person plural pronoun. Tisher (field notes) reports that in Tchien Krahn the neutralization has gone even further, also affecting the first person plural pronoun.

unmarked	imperfective	
ó	á	1 sg
ò	à	2 sg
ɔ́	ɔ́	3 sg
à	à	1 pl
ā	ā	2 pl
ō	ā	3 pl

When neutralization takes place, the distinction between factative and imperfective actions is expressed by the tone on the verb stem, as in 72-73 from Gbaeson Krahn:

(72) ɔ̀ cɛ́ dbū   ɔ cɛ̄ dbū
      he cut rope   he cut:IMP rope
      'He cut rope.'   'He is cutting rope.'

(73) ɔ pà tōō   ɔ pǎ tōō
      he carve mortar   he carve:IMP mortar
      'He carved a mortar.'   'He is carving a mortar.'

Thus in Krahn, the remnants of the **e** suffix are beginning to dominate as the signal of the imperfective.

The distribution of the reflexes of the protoimperfective structure can be seen in the following chart:

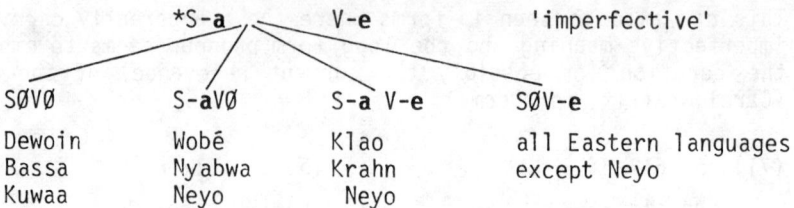

Dewoin / Wobé / Klao / all Eastern languages
Bassa / Nyabwa / Krahn / except Neyo
Kuwaa / Neyo / Neyo

It is interesting to note that except for the S-a V-e group, languages which are geographically close to one another have responded in the same way to the double set of markers found in Proto-Kru. The Western-like behavior of Neyo could possibly be explained through language contact, since slaves from both Eastern and Western Kru were kept in and shipped out from Neyo territory.

Before considering this section, it is worth noting that according to Welmers (1973:343), a typical pattern for verbal constructions in Niger-Congo is:

    Pronoun   Construction-marker   Verb base-Affix

He points out that this pattern emerges in the Bantu family, Mandē, and many other branches of Niger-Congo as well. If both the **a** and the **e** imperfective markers were present in Proto-Kru, then the imperfective clause would have had a shape quite similar to the one proposed by Welmers. Though there is no synchronically attested case of **a** occurring as an independent particle, it is very likely that **a** was, in fact, an independent word (as **e** could have been) that only later became affixed to the subject:

    S   **a**   V-e >
    S-**a**   V-e

In chapter 4, a similar scenario will be proposed for the negative particle **ní**, which acts as an independent word in some languages and as a subject affix in others. If this assumption is correct, then the imperfective structure in Proto-Kru would correspond exactly with the typical Niger-Congo pattern as proposed by Welmers.

Presumably, one of these imperfective suffixes is older than the other. At this stage, it is difficult to tell which, though it is likely that a BE-related *e, presently functioning in both Eastern and Western Kru, is a later innovation.

It has been suggested that in Kru the main aspectual distinction is between the perfective and imperfective. It was pointed out that the perfective category in Kru (also called factative) includes a present reading for stative verbs as well as a punctiliar (past) reading for active verbs. The imperfective expresses the idea of continuous, customary, and sometimes unrealized action. From the evidence available, it seems very likely that in Proto-Kru the perfective was unmarked, while the imperfective was marked by one, and at some stage, two markers.

Basic Aspectual Categories in Kru

Several linguists have tried to study the markedness features associated with tense-aspect systems. Despite some irregularities (Comrie 1976), there is a general consensus that imperfectives are more marked than perfectives, both by their morphological marking and their lower frequency (Friedrich 1974, Givón 1982). Despite the fact that historical changes have brought about a system in some Eastern Kru languages where both aspects are morphologically marked, these aspects can be traced back to a basic protosystem which is more in line with the universal prototype.

In the next two sections, two more aspects will be discussed—the progressive and the perfect.

2.3 The Progressive Aspect

In the preceding sections, it was seen that the imperfective/factative distinction is basic in every Kru language. Along with these aspectual categories, most languages have a periphrastic progressive construction containing the locative verb 'be at'. The only language that apparently does not have this construction is Klao. The progressive aspect is always used to designate durative or ongoing actions, which can be seen in Godié:

(74) mà, ŋʷɔdɪɔ kʊ kí dʌ,...   'Now as the man
      now man-DEF be-at speak place...   was speaking.'

In the following sections, the periphrastic progressive construction will be briefly described. First, its basic structure will be presented. Then, it will be briefly compared to the imperfective. The universality of the locative-progressive connection will then be discussed. Finally, it will be suggested that the periphrastic construction probably existed at some stage of Proto-Kru.

2.3.1 Basic structure of the periphrastic progressive.
All progressive constructions in Kru have basically the same structure. They all contain the locative verb 'be at' followed by a nominalized verb: S BE-AT (O) V-nom. (O) V-nom acts as the complement of the verb 'be at', as with any normal locative. Compare, for example, the following sentences from Godié:

(75) ɔ   kʊ   sūkú   'He is at school.'
      he be-at school

      ɔ   kʊ   lɔ   'He is there.'
      he be-at there

      ɔ   kʊ   6lɪ-dʌ   'He is singing.'
      he be-at sing-place

Thus the construction 'he is at VP-nom' is always interpreted as a progressive action. Though languages may differ in their forms for the verb 'be-at' and in their forms for the nominalizer, the structure is generally the same.

Western Kru

In Western Kru, the verb 'be at' generally has the shape n + front vowel. In many languages, the nominalizer has the shape <u>la</u>, <u>na</u>, or <u>a</u>.

(76) Krahn

    ɔ <u>nɛ</u> kɔɔ dǔ <u>lá</u>   'She is pounding rice.'
    she <u>be-at</u> rice pound <u>NOM</u>

(77) Wobé

    ḕ <u>ne-ɛ</u> dɛ di <u>á</u>   'I am eating.'
    I <u>be-at</u>-DECL thing eat <u>NOM</u>

(78) Dewoin (example from Welmers)

    ɔ́ <u>nĩ</u> sāyɛ̀ pī <u>ná</u>   'He is cooking meat.'
    he <u>be-at</u> meat cook <u>NOM</u>

(79) Nyabwa

    ɔ <u>nĩ-é-ẽ</u> kɔ́bʊ̀ po <u>namʊ</u>[13] 'He is planting rice.'
    he <u>be-at</u>-DECL-SUF rice throw <u>NOM</u>

(80) Bassa

    ɔ <u>nĩĩ</u> mɔ̃ di-<u>ɛ</u>   'He is eating.'
    he <u>be-at</u> rice eat-<u>NOM</u>

As a stative verb, 'be at' is usually in its factative form.

Typically, the form (O) V-nom functions as a regular NP in the language. It may designate a locative NP, as in Krahn:

(81) dě dle lá nmɔ-jiĩ 'The bathing place is good.'
    LOC bathe NOM good

or it may be used as a regular nominalized verb, as is the case in Wobé:

---

13 In Nyabwa, the nominalizer namʊ appears to be cognate with nominalizers in Krahn, Wobé, and Dewoin. However, another element mʊ has been interpreted as part of the marker. The origins of the morpheme mʊ are not known, but it does resemble Kru cognates ■u 'inside' and mʊ 'BE' (copula).

(82) gbǔ po a̓   'building a house'
      house build NOM

In Tepo, no nominalizer is present. As will be seen in the following chapter, the loss of nominalizers is a fairly common development.

(83) Tepo
     ɔ ne dɛ   di   'He is eating.'
     he be-at thing eat

The isolates

Two Kru isolates, Kuwaa and Aīzi, both have progressive constructions containing a verb which appears to be cognate with the Western n + front vowel. In Kuwaa, the verb 'be at' is **de,** and the nominalizer is **nu.**

(84) ā de-ó   bɛ̀ nú ...   'While we were going ...'
     we be-at-PAST go NOM

In Aīzi, the verb 'be at' is **nɛ.** This language has the most divergent progressive form, since the word order appears to be S V V O.

(85) e nɛ   ne ɟi saka   'He is eating rice.'
     he be-at ? eat rice

The role of the particle **ne** is not understood. The unusual word order is possibly due to language contact since this language is completely surrounded by non-Kru languages.

Eastern Kru

Progressives in Eastern Kru have exactly the same structure as those found in Western Kru. The nominalizer in Neyo and Godié (**dʌ̃** or **dã**) appears to be related to the Western nominalizer (**la/na/a**). The verbs for 'be at' (**kʊ/wʊ**) are quite distinct, however.

(86) **Neyo** (Grah)

  kɔkwιɛ 5 6la la   a,   'She had killed
  chicken she kill there SUB,   the chicken and
                                    was in the process
  ɛ́mɛ 5 kʊ   pii-da ...   of cooking it.'
  that she be-at cook-NOM

(87) Godié
     ɔ kʊ̀ sɨkʌ̃ dι   dʌ   'She is cutting rice.'
     she be-at rice cut place

(88) Bété (Werle and Gbalehi 1976:198)

    ń wʊ̀ mʌ̀   ji do   wʊ́   'I am coming.'
    I be there come state on

(The morpheme-by-morpheme translation in the last example was supplied by Werle and Gbalehi. I suspect that it is the morpheme **do** which is acting as the nominalizer.)

Thus, the progressive construction always has the shape S be-at (O) V-nom, both in Eastern and Western Kru, as well as in at least two of the isolates.

2.3.2 The progressive vs. the imperfective. It was already noted that the progressive aspect indicates ongoing or durative action. In section 2.2, it was seen that the primary function of the imperfective aspect is also to express durativity. This "semantic overlap" can be seen in Godié.

(89) ɔ   kʊ   sʉkʌ̄ 6lɨ   dʌ   'She is pounding rice.'
       she be-at rice pound place

(90) ɔ   6lɨ   sʉkʌ̄   'She is pounding rice.'
       she pound:IMP rice

This overlap is not uncommon in languages of the world (Comrie 1976). In French, the same question Qu'est-ce qu'il fait? 'What is he doing?' may be answered with an imperfective or a progressive.

(91) **Il lave   sa voiture**   'He's washing his car.'
       he wash:IMP his car

(92) **Il est en train   de laver sa voiture**   'He's washing his car.'
       he is in process of wash his car

The same phenomenon also occurs in Portuguese (Vroman 1977:131). Despite the semantic overlap, there are differences in the functions of the progressive and imperfective in Kru.

First, it was noted in section 2.2.2 that imperfectives in Kru may signal habitual actions. This is not the case with progressives. While sentence 90 can mean 'she pounds rice (habitually)' or 'she is pounding rice', sentence 89, containing a progressive, cannot have a habitual reading. The one exception to this is found in the Kuwaa isolate. Not much data is available on this language, but it appears that there is no remnant of an imperfective suffix, and the periphrastic progressive construction has been extended to express habitual as well as ongoing actions (cf. Comrie 1976:103; Traugott 1978:388).

(93) **wɔ de   namu nu sia**   'He is walking slowly.'
       he be-at walk NOM slowly

Basic Aspectual Categories in Kru

The second difference between imperfectives and progressives has to do with function in discourse. Though progressives are common in everyday conversations, they do not seem to occur frequently in narrative texts (except, of course, in Kuwaa, where they appear to be the only signal of the imperfective). Statistics are not available on most languages, but in Godié, in a collection of 135 pages of text (Marchese and Gratrix 1974), only 30 occurrences of the progressive were noted. When progressives do occur, they typically "frame" an event in the story. Given its locative connection, progressives often "set the scene" for an event which is about to happen. This can be seen in Godié:

(94) ɔ   ŋwɔnɔ ɔ   kʊ̃   budo dʌ,   'While his$_1$ wife was
      <u>his wife   she be-at bathe place</u>   taking a bath, he$_2$
                                          shot the arrow.'

      lé ɔ   pʌ̃   jɔlie
      and he throw-FACT arrow-DEF

Finally, progressives and imperfectives differ formally in that imperfectives are signalled by suffixes, while progressives are expressed by periphrasis. Because 'be at' is a stative verb, it usually occurs in the factative aspect. In chapter 4, it will be seen that negation strategies are determined by the aspect of the affirmative clause. Even though progressives are semantically imperfective, they negate as factatives. This point will be illustrated and discussed further in chapter 4.

To summarize these points, progressives differ from imperfectives in that they do not normally express habitual actions, they occur only rarely and have a special function in narrative text, and they are negated by a different negation strategy.

2.3.3 The universality of the locative-progressive connection.

The connection between locatives and progressives is well established. It occurs in innumerable languages throughout the world. It is found in Scottish and Welsh (Traugott 1978:388), Lakota (A. Faltz, pers.com.), Quechua (D. Weber, pers.com.), Japanese (N. Sugamoto, pers.com.), and Thai (Thompson, pers.com.). The English progressive is also derived from a locative expression (he's ahunting—> he's hunting). The locative-progressive is also found throughout Niger-Congo: in Yoruba and Ewe (Kwa languages), Kpelle (a Mandé language: Welmers 1973:314, 15, 17, 24), and Fula (a West Atlantic language: Sylla, pers.com.). In fact, Welmers (1973:324) makes the following statement:

> An underlying relationship and near identity between expressions of location and present action has been noted in a number of ... Niger-Congo languages; it would appear that the association has its roots in Proto-Niger-Congo, ...

Thus, it is not at all surprising from a universal or genetic viewpoint that the locative-progressive connection is found in Kru.

2.3.4 Relative age of the progressive construction. It has been shown that the progressive construction occurs in the majority of Kru languages. Similar, though not identical, constructions are found in many language families in Niger-Congo. These facts tend to suggest that the periphrastic progressive is very old, dating back to some stage of Proto-Kru. The problem with this proposal is that there is some diversity in the forms of both the verb 'be at' and the nominalizer. Rather than assuming that there were independent innovations in each language or in each group, it seems more reasonable to posit a Proto-Kru construction of the following type:

S **ne** (O) V **la**
be-at   NOM

This proposal is supported by the forms found in Western Kru and the Kru isolates. The Eastern forms for 'be at' **kʊ/wʊ** are probably innovative and could have been substituted into an already existing periphrastic progressive construction.

2.4 The Perfect Aspect

The perfect aspect is found in many Kru languages and is most often expressed by an auxiliary. It indicates a past action whose result is still effective at the time of speaking. The contrast between the factative and the perfect can be seen in Dewoin (Welmers 1977a).

(95) ɔ pī   sāyɛ̄   'He cooked meat.'
      he cook:FACT meat

      ɔ́ nà̄ sāyɛ̄ pī   'He has cooked meat.'
      he PERF meat cook

There is some controversy (Comrie 1976:52) as to whether the perfect is actually an aspect at all. However, it is quite clear that it is an aspect in Kru, since tense markers never cooccur and the perfect may occur with tense markers.

(96) Godié
     ɔ́ yʌ̄ -ā̄ zʌ̄   pʉ́lʉ́   'He had already passed
     he PERF REC already pass   (in front of them).'

(97) Dewoin (Mortvedt)
     ɔ́ nà̄ í̄ gbɔ̀ɔ̄ mú   jā̄
     he PERF PAST house inside enter
                 DEF

Perfect auxiliaries are found in Eastern Kru, the Guéré complex, and the nonaffiliated languages in Western Kru (Bassa,

Bakwé, and Dewoin). From the data available at this time, I know of no language in the Grebo complex which has a perfect auxiliary, however. The forms of the perfect auxiliary are:

Eastern Kru

Neyo	a/ya
Koyo	ya
Godié	yʌ
Dida (Lozoua)	ya
Bété (Gagnoa)	ya
Bété (Soubré)	yɛ

Western Kru

Bakwé	a
Wobé (Péomé)	ɟa
Guéré	náa
Dewoin	nã
Bassa	na/dã

The auxiliaries appear to be relatively similar. The forms in Eastern Kru and in Bakwé and Wobé suggest a reconstructed form *ɟa or *ya. As was noted earlier, in Kuwaa, a Kru isolate, the perfect is expressed by a verbal suffix. Its shape, interestingly enough, is **ya** (Welmers, pers.com.).

(98) **mã̀ o   bi-ya**   'I've gone today.'
     I PAST go-PERF
           (REC)

This suffix resembles the Bété permansif suffix **ã̀**, described on page 35. Given the similarity in shape and meaning, these two suffixes do appear to be related to the perfect auxiliaries seen above.

It is interesting to speculate on the origins of the perfect auxiliary. As will be seen in the following chapters, the future, conditional, sequential, and negative auxiliaries are all derived from verbs. It is assumed that perfect auxiliaries have a similar origin. Hyman (pers.com.) has suggested that a common verbal source of perfect markers is the verb 'take'. He notes the following construction in Gwari (1971:32):

(99) **wó kū nyágyī gyī**   'He has eaten food.'
     he take food   eat

The source of present auxiliaries in Kru is not nearly as clear as in the Gwari case, but it is worth noting that the perfect forms in Kru bear some resemblance to the verb 'bring'.

	'bring'	perfect auxiliary
Wobé	ɟa	ɟa/ɟa
Tepo	ya	(no perfect)
Nyabwa	yã	(no perfect)
Koyo	la	ya
Godié	lʌ̃	yʌ̃

No real conclusion can be drawn from this evidence, but it suggests the possibility of a verbal origin for the perfect auxiliary. In chapter 3, a mechanism will be proposed for the development of auxiliaries from main verbs.

According to the definition given in this section, perfects refer to past punctiliar actions whose result is still in effect at the time of speaking. Thus, as was noted in earlier sections, there is actually very little semantic difference between a factative and a perfect, since factatives also designate punctiliar actions in the past. Because of this semantic overlap, there is sometimes a tendency for the two aspects to collapse into one aspectual category.

In Lozoua Dida (Gratrix, pers.com.), what normally occurs as a perfect auxiliary in other Kru languages is used to designate both factative and perfect actions.

(100) ɔ ya   pãlṹ sla   'He built a house.' or
      he PERF house build   'He has built a house.'

This phenomenon parallels one described by Comrie (1976:61). He notes that in French the passé composé originally designated a recent perfect (occurring within the past twenty-four hours). Later, however, it replaced the simple past (referring to past punctiliar actions). In French, the perfect reading of the passé composé, completely disappeared. It now refers to punctiliar actions in the past. The same phenomenon was seen to occur in the reanalysis of perfect auxiliaries into factative ones (sect. 2.2.1.2). It appears that in Lozoua Dida, however, the perfect reading was not lost. The form **ya** is ambiguous, having both a factative and a perfect reading.

2.5 Conclusion

Four aspectual categories exist in Kru: the factative, the imperfective, the progressive, and the perfect. In this chapter, it was suggested that the factative/imperfective distinction goes back to Proto-Kru. The factative verb stem was unmarked, while the imperfective was marked by two suffixes--a nominal suffix *a and a verbal suffix *e.

S-a   V-e   (0)

Basic Aspectual Categories in Kru   71

This construction was probably derived from one in which **a** was an independent particle.

                    S   **a**   V-e   (O)

Along with the factative and imperfective, two other aspects, the progressive and the perfect, have coexisted over a long period of time. In several Eastern languages, a perfect marker was reanalyzed as factative aspect. And in at least two languages (Dewoin and Kuwaa), the progressive construction replaced the imperfective.

Now that the basic aspectual system in Kru has been described, the discussion will turn to the development of both future (chap. 3) and negative (chap. 4) auxiliaries.

3 THE EMERGENCE OF THREE FUTURE AUXILIARIES

3.1 Futures in Kru

In Kru, the future tense may be expressed in three different ways: by suffix, by periphrasis, or by auxiliary:

(1) <u>suffix</u>   Grebo (Innes 1966)

    nḗ dū-a̍   blā   'I shall pound rice tomorrow.'

    I pound-<u>T</u> rice

(2) <u>periphrasis</u>   Cedepo (Laesch)

    èh mī   e kou tɔ̄ ma   'I will buy rice'
                                          or
    I go-INC rice buy NOM   'I'm going to buy rice.'

(3) <u>auxiliary</u>   Gbaeson Krahn (Duitsman)

    ǎ <u>mú</u> dɛ́   dī   'I will eat.'

    I <u>FUT</u> thing eat

Future suffixes are highly specific in meaning, often referring to tomorrow or the day after tomorrow, as can be seen in sentence 1. Most of these suffixes are innovative. (They will be discussed in detail in chapter 5.) Periphrastic future constructions contain the verbs 'come' or 'go' (see 2) and they are usually ambiguous, referring to motion in both space and time. These constructions will be described in some detail in this chapter and will be seen to be the source for future auxiliaries. Future auxiliaries, such as the one seen in 3, are generally not temporally specific. Rather, they refer to an indefinite time in the future. They may also give information pertaining to the immediacy of an action or the participant's involvement in an action (his volition, desire, or capacity to carry out a given action in the future). Thus, future auxiliaries are in a certain sense modal elements.

Future systems vary considerably from one Kru language to another. In some languages, such as Klao, both auxiliaries and suffixes are used to express future actions.

(4) future suffix

    sḗtū-ā   dī́-lā̄mā́   tī̃   'Seto will eat
Seto-IMP eat-<u>day-after tomorrow</u> palm kernels palm kernels the
                                                   day after to-
                                                   morrow.'

(5) future auxiliary

    Dô-ā   **mū**   dɛ   dī̃   'Doe will eat.'
Doe-IMP <u>FUT</u> thing eat

In other languages, like Cedepo and Nyabo, the future is most often expressed by periphrasis or by a combination of periphrasis and a future suffix.

(6) Nyabo

    ɔ mi-<u>a</u>   naa   'He will walk tomorrow.'
    he go:IMP-<u>T</u> walk

In some languages, future action is expressed only by auxiliary. This is the case in Godié, where two separate future auxiliaries exist.

(7) ɔ **yi**   **mʉ**   'He will/can go.'
    he <u>FUT-POT</u> go

(8) ɔ **kʌ̄**   sʌ   pɩ   'He will/wants to go to lie down.'
    he <u>FUT-VOL</u> down lie

Except for the Kru isolates, future auxiliaries have been found to occur in all Kru languages examined in this study. At least three of them can be shown to be etymologically linked to the full verbs 'go', 'come', and 'have'.[1] In this chapter, these auxiliaries will be studied in detail. After the evidence linking them to full verbs has been presented, the mechanisms of reanalysis will be discussed. It will be shown that the full verbs 'go', 'have', and 'come' have undergone semantic and sometimes phonological change; they have lost some of their basic verbal characteristics; and in many cases they have been reanalyzed, emerging as members of a new syntactic category AUXILIARY.

3.2 Etymological Links between Auxiliaries and Full Verbs

In Western Kru, commonly there is a future auxiliary which resembles the verb 'go'. In chart I, the relation between the future auxiliary and the verb 'go' can be clearly seen.

---

[1] Other future auxiliaries such as **nya** in Bakwé and ŋwemʉ in Béréby Kru will not be discussed because not enough data are available.

Chart I

	Bassa	Dewoin	Tepo	Krahn	Klao
'go'	mu	mu	mu	mú	mu
FUT	mu	mu...mu	mʊ́	mú	mu

Below, examples are given of both the verbal and the auxiliary use of the related morphemes:

(9) Klao

ɔ̌ɔ   mū nī tó   'He is going to the store.'
he:IMP go LOC store

ɔ̌ɔ   mū nī kpa   'He will swim.'
he:IMP AUX water hit-low tone clitic

(10) Dewoin

ɨ́ mū   wa   'I went last time.'
I go:FACT last-time

ɔ̌ɔ mū sayɛ̄ piī mū   'He will cook meat.'
he AUX meat cook FUT

(The sentence-final **mu** will be discussed in a later section.)

(11) Tepo

ɔ̌ɔ   mū dáklɔ mʊ́   'He's going to the field.'
he:IMP go field to

yruwle mʊ́ kayú gbo pa̍   'The chameleon is about to enter the house.'
chameleon AUX house under enter

(12) Gbaeson Krahn

ǎ̰   mú nã̄-ɛ   'I'm going now.'
I:IMP go now

ɔ̌ mú dɛ́ dī   'He will eat.'
he AUX thing eat

(13) Bassa

ɔ mu ɔ kɛ́-ɛ nyu   'He goes to do it.'
he go he AUX-it do

ɔ mu kua nyu   'He will work.'
he AUX work do

The Emergence of Three Future Auxiliaries 75

While the 'go'-related future auxiliary occurs only in Western Kru, a 'come'-related auxiliary occurs in both Eastern and Western Kru. In most cases, this auxiliary indicates a distant or potential future. Chart II shows the relationship between the verb 'come' and the future auxiliary.

Chart II

	Neyo	Godié	Koyo	Bété	Dida	Tepo
'come'	i/yi	yi	yi	yi	cɩ	di
FUT	i/yi	yi	yi	yi	cɩ	di

Eastern Kru

(14) Neyo (Thomann)

    i   dẽ^2 'Come here.'
    come-IMPER here

    e i   mã   li   'I will eat bananas.'
    I AUX bananas eat

(15) Godié

    wā yī   'They are coming.'
    they come:IMP

    wa yi bʊkʊ pɔrtʉmʊnɛ́ɛ kʊ 6lɨ   'They will take the
    they AUX again pocketbook up take   pocketbook again.'

(16) Lakota Dida

    kúdū yī zīkī   yī   'Kudu will come tomorrow.'
    Kudu AUX tomorrow come

    ē yī mɔ̄ɔ̄ lɛ̄tɛ̄ nyɛ̄   'I will give you the knife.'
    I AUX you knife give

(17) Koyo

    A6i yī   du   'Abi came home.'
    Abi come:FACT town

    A6i yi du   mo   'Abi will go to town.'
    Abi AUX town go

---

2 Thomann's orthography differs from the symbols used in the rest of this study. Accents mark vowel quality and not tone. **ò**, for example, represents ɔ; è, ɛ.

(18) Bété

   ɔ yii ɓlie   yi   'He will come to play.'
   he AUX play-NOM come

   ɔ yi sɩka-a   li   'He will eat rice.'
   he AUX rice-DEF eat

(19) Lozoua Dida

   cī   'Come!'
   come-IMPER

   ɔ cī pàlʊ́ slā   'He will build a house.'
   he AUX house build

Western Kru

(20) Tepo (Dawson)

   ɔ lɛ-ne   di   'He's coming.'
   he PRESENT-PROG come

   a di a kle   hʊa   'We will ask for his strength.'
   we AUX his strength ask

Finally, chart III shows that several Eastern languages have a future auxiliary related to the verb 'have'. In one language, Neyo, the auxiliary indicates obligation as well as future action.

Chart III

	Neyo	Godié	Lakota Dida	Vata	Bété
'have'	ka	kʌ̃	kā	ka̋	kã
FUT	ka	kʌ̃	kā	kā	kã

(21) Godié (jlʉkɔ)

   ɔ kʌ̃ monii   'He has money.'
   he have money

   ɔ kʌ̃ sʌ pɩ   'He is going to lie down.'
   he AUX down lie

(22) Neyo (Thomann)

   õmo w̃lõ õ ka yo   sõ   'This woman has two children.'
   she woman she has children two

ne ka mã   li   'I'm starting to eat bananas.'
I AUX bananas eat

(23) Lakota Dida

ɔ́ kā dālā kā ...   'If he has money...'
he COND money have

ɔ́ wā gbā ɔ́ kā ānyē yōkū nī ...   'He wants to see us ...'
he wants that he AUX us   side see

(24) Vata

kɔ́ɔ́ ka̋ɔ́ tɛ́tɛ́   'The man has strength.'
man has strength

ń kā me gba   'I will say that.'
I AUX that say

(25) Bété (from Guiberoua)

ɔ́ɔ́ɔ́   kɔkɔ́   kʌ   'She doesn't have a chicken.'
she-NEG chicken have

ā kʌ́ sīka̋á lī   'Let's eat some rice.' or 'We're
we AUX rice eat   going to eat some rice.'

It has been shown that future auxiliaries in several Kru languages are related to the full verbs 'come', 'go', and 'have'. The question arises as to the status of these auxiliaries. Are we really justified in speaking of two separate categories?

3.3 Are Auxiliaries Main Verbs?

In his paper "Auxiliaries as Main Verbs," Ross (1967) argues that in English and German, auxiliaries and main verbs belong to the same lexical category. He notes that certain syntactic rules apply equally to verbs and auxiliaries and that considering auxiliaries as main verbs permits some basic generalizations. If this analysis were applied to Kru languages, then the future auxiliaries **mu**, **yi**, and **ka** would be analyzed as the verbs 'go', 'come', and 'have'. Kokora (1976:178-81) shows how this analysis could be applied to auxiliary constructions in Koyo, an Eastern Kru language.

Ross's proposal has met with several counterarguments, however (R.A. Hudson 1976; D. Lightfoot 1974). Probably the most relevant ones to this discussion were given by David Lightfoot in his paper "The diachronic analysis of English modals." Lightfoot (p. 233) argues that modals in English cannot be analyzed synchronically as main verbs. He states:

Modals simply do not have the syntactic properties of verbs: they do not undergo Number agreement or Do support but do undergo Subject-Auxiliary Inversion and Negative placement. They cannot appear in infinitives and gerunds, cannot occur adjacent to each other and cannot take normal complementation types.

He points out, however, that at a stage in their history, the precursors of present-day English modals actually were verbs, undergoing number agreement, occurring next to one another, occurring in gerunds and infinitives, and acting as all other verbs in regard to negative placement and inversion. He also notes that many of them even took direct objects. Lightfoot concludes that there was a historical change whereby full verbs were reanalyzed as a new category M (modal).

Though the documentation available on Kru cannot compare with the detailed documentation available on English verb forms, I will claim that similar reanalyses have occurred and, in fact, are occurring in the Kru language family. It will first be shown that, despite many similarities between auxiliaries and their related verbs and the fact that they can be shown to be historically related, auxiliaries in Kru must, in many cases, be analyzed synchronically as belonging to a category separate from their related verbs. For purposes of this discussion, data will be limited to future auxiliaries in the jlʉkɔ dialect of Godié and a closely related (and mutually intelligible dialect) Koyo, both in the Eastern group. The same kind of arguments could be given for other types of auxiliaries (including negatives, sequentials, and conditionals). Similar (though perhaps not identical) arguments could be given for auxiliaries in other Kru languages.

Auxiliaries in Kru languages act very much like full verbs. First, both auxiliaries and full verbs occupy sentence-second position. (Particles occupy the same position but bear no similarity to full verbs.) Second, when object clitics and tense suffixes occur, they normally occur on full verbs, but if auxiliaries are present, these clitics and suffixes attached to them instead. In the Godié example 26, the order is S V O ADV. No auxiliary is present, and the object clitic and tense suffix are attached to the verb.

(26) ɔ lɨ̄-ɛ-a   zıka   'He ate it yesterday.'
      he eat:FACT-it-REC yesterday
      S   V   OBJ-PN T ADV

In 27, however, an auxiliary **yi** is present. Consequently, the order is S AUX O ADV V. In this construction, the object clitic and tense suffix occur on the auxiliary, not on the verb.

(27) ɔ yi-ɛ-a   zιka   lɨ   'He was going to eat
    he FUT-it-REC yesterday eat   it yesterday.'
    S AUX-PN-T   ADV   V

Thus, full verbs and auxiliaries share the basic characteristic that both act as host to object and tense suffixes.

Another common feature of both auxiliaries and verbs is the placement of the negative. In some languages, a negative particle normally follows the verb, but follows the auxiliary if one is present. This is the case in Koyo.

(28) ɔ mʊ tā suklū   'He doesn't (habitually)
    he go NEG school   go to school.'

(29) ɔ yi tā sākā lɨ   'He won't eat rice.'
    he AUX NEG rice eat

Despite these similarities, there is much evidence showing that auxiliaries do not share all the characteristics of verbs. One of the main differences between auxiliaries and full verbs is that auxiliaries can take unmarked or simple verb stems as sisters while regular verbs cannot. In Godié, the future auxiliary derived from **yi** 'come' may be followed by a simple verb stem like **budō** 'bathe'. In contrast, a full verb like **6ā** 'come back from' must be followed by a nominalized verb (marked by the nominalizing particle **kʌ**).

(30) ɔ yi budō   'He will bathe.'
    he POT bathe
       AUX

(31) ɔ 6ā   budō kʌ   'He came back from bathing.'
    he come- bathe NOM
       back:
       FACT

The full verb **6ā** cannot occur with a simple verb stem.

(32) *ɔ 6ā   budō   'He came back from taking
    he come-back:FACT bathe   a bath.'

It is easy to show that the relationship between an auxiliary and the elements which follow it is not the same as the relationship between a verb and its object complement. Typically, a complement follows the main verb, but it may occur in initial position when focussed. Focus constructions are used in answer to specific questions or to correct a false impression. Thus 34 could be the answer to "Where did she come back from?" or it could be said if the hearer believes she came back from somewhere other than cutting rice.

(33) normal order

ɔ	6à	sʉkʌ̃	dɪ	kʌ̃	'She came back from cutting rice.'
she	come-back:FACT	rice	cut	NOM	
S	V		OBJ-COMP		

(34) focus order

sʉkʌ̃	dɪ	kʌ̃	ɔ	6à	'It's from cutting rice that she came back' (not, for example, from chopping trees).
rice	cut	NOM	she	come-back-FACT	
	OBJ-COMP		S	V	

However, elements following auxiliaries may not be focussed in this way.

(35) ɔ yi sukú mʉ   'He will go to school.'
    he POT school go

    *sukú mʉ ɔ yi

This shows that sukú mʉ is not an object complement of yi. sukú is, however, a complement of the main verb 'go', and as such, it may occur in initial position.

(36) sukú ɔ yi mʉ   'It's to school he will go.'
    school he POT go

Another difference between full verbs and auxiliaries is that while full verbs are typically inflected for aspect (the factative/imperfective distinction seen in chapter 2), auxiliaries are not. In Godié, full verbs are marked with low tone for the factative and with mid tone for the imperfective.

(37) ɔ̃ yì   'He came.'
    he come:FACT

    ɔ̃ yī   'He's coming.'
    he come:IMP

However, the 'come'-related auxiliary yi is invariant--it cannot be inflected for the factative/imperfective distinction.

(38) ɔ̃ yī mʉ̄   'He will/can go.'
    he POT go

The Emergence of Three Future Auxiliaries 81

(39) *ɔ́ yī mū
  he POT:FACT go

As was stated previously, both auxiliaries and full verbs occur in sentence-second position. However, unlike full verbs, auxiliaries must occur in this position. For example, auxiliaries cannot occur adjacent to each other.

(40) *ɔ yi kʌ́
  he POT VOL

Neither can they occur as a complement of another verb.

(41) *ɔ ɓā kʌ́ kʌ́
  he leave VOL NOM

Also, auxiliaries cannot be nominalized nor do they occur in compound words,³ even though verbs of all classes may occur in these contexts.

(42) kʌ́-nyɔ   'owner'
  have person

  *kʌ́-nyɔ   'person who wants'
  VOL (AUX)-person

(43) mlʌ-lɩ   'drinking'
  drink-NOM

  *yī-lɩ   'will (N)'
  POT (AUX)-NOM

Finally, auxiliaries serve a function in the sentence different from that of regular verbs. A sentence is never complete with just an auxiliary. In a clause with an auxiliary and a verb, semantic prominence is given to the verb, not to the auxiliary.⁴ For exam-

---

3 Auxiliaries do, of course, occur in full sentences which function as nouns. They occur in relative clauses and in 'that' clauses.

Godié
  yɩɔ   ɔ yi-a ɓɔtɔ nʌ   'The child he was going to hit ...'
  child:DEF he POT-REC hit NF

  ʌ́ ɓʊɓʊ mā   ɔ yi yi   'I think that he will come.
  I think that he POT come

4 Benveniste (1968:88) similarly notes for Latin: "habēre becomes the auxiliary charged with the syntactic relations proper to the utterance; the participle in turn serves as the auxiliate, conveying the semantic kernel of the verb." [underlining L.M.]

ple, in sentence 44 'going' is asserted. The auxiliary merely provides modal information about the main verb.

(44) ɔ yi mʉ   'He will go.'
    he POT go

Also, in the negative counterpart of 44, 'going' rather than the futurity of the action is being denied.

(45) ɔ náã̀ mʉ   'He will not go.'
    he NEG-FUT go

To sum up this section, it has been claimed that auxiliaries are derived historically from full verbs and share the following basic characteristics.

  (i) they carry object clitics
  (ii) they are marked for tense
  (iii) they occur in sentence-second position
  (iv) in some instances (as in Koyo), they precede the negative marker

It has also been suggested that in spite of these similarities, there are enough significant differences between auxiliaries and their related verb forms to warrant the claim that they belong to two distinct grammatical categories (that is, that full verbs have, in certain instances, been reanalyzed as a new category, AUX). The differences between auxiliaries and full verbs are listed below. Unlike full verbs, auxiliaries:

  (i) take unmarked verb stems as sister
  (ii) do not have the same relationship with the elements that follow it as a verb has with its complement
  (iii) never occur adjacent to one another
  (iv) cannot be the main predicate
  (v) never occur in nominalized verb forms or in compound words
  (vi) are not inflected for the factative/imperfective distinction
  (vii) do not carry semantic prominence in the sentence

It is interesting to note that some of the similarities and differences between auxiliaries and full verbs in Kru are the same ones that occur in English (i, iii, v, and vii). This parallelism suggests that D. Lightfoot's analysis does not apply only to English. The features mentioned above may be part of a universal definition of the category AUX (or at least AUX as it occurs in SVO languages).

3.4 How Do Full Verbs Become Auxiliaries?

In the preceding sections, it has been shown that future auxiliaries in Kru are closely linked to the verbs 'go', 'come', and 'have'. It has also been shown that though basic similarities exist, auxiliaries differ in fundamental ways from full verbs and, following D. Lightfoot's analysis of English modals, constitute a separate syntactic class. But what caused the reanalysis of verbs as auxiliaries and how has this change come about?

3.4.1 Hyman's proposal. As was stated in section 1.4.2.6, most Africanists (Migeod 1911; Givón 1975b; Hyman 1975) claim that languages in the Niger-Congo family (of which the Kru group is a part) developed from a protolanguage which had the basic order subject-object-verb (SOV). In his paper "Serial verbs and syntactic change: Niger-Congo," Givón (1975b:72-73) notes that in the Kru family (and more specifically in Klao) there are remnants of SOV order in "the complements of modality verbs, as well as in other modality-related environments...." He cites examples from Klao where the order is subject-modality-object-verb.[5]

(46) **nyeyu-na mu nyino-na bla** 'The man will beat the woman.'
 man-the go woman-the beat

(47) **nyeyu-na si nyino-na bla** 'The man did not beat the woman.'
 man-the NEG woman-the beat

He also notes (see sect. 1.4.2) that Klao has OV characteristics such as POSS-N word order and postpositions.

In an article in the same volume entitled "On the change from SOV to SVO: Evidence from Niger-Congo," Hyman (1975:125) suggests that auxiliaries in Klao first developed in a structure S V_1 O V_2, where the first verb was intransitive. Hyman does not say how this source construction could have evolved. Though Hyman does not explicitly state that serialization played a role in the development of the S V_1 O V_2 construction, he notes that "the resemblance

---

5 Givón (1975b:72, 73) also cites examples which do not seem to be properly analyzed. In the following sentences:

nyeyu-na jilá boy nyino-na bla 'The man wants to beat the woman.'
man-the want M woman-the beat

nyeyu-na bèé nyino-na bla 'The man may beat the woman.'
man-the M woman-the beat

Givón analyzes **boy** and **bèé** as modalities. Actually, there are three morphemes in these phonologically reduced forms:

 boy: b-ɔ ye that-he-SEQ

The string **bee** seems to represent the same combination. It these cases, it is the sequential marker which is the auxiliary, not the other parts. The incorrectness of the analysis does not actually do damage to Givón's point, however (cf. Hyman 1975:125). See also section 3.8.1 for a discussion on sequential auxiliaries.

of this reconstruction to present-day Ijo (Williamson 1965) is obvious." Note that Ijo is an SOV serializing language. One possibility is that the S V_1 O V_2 structure arose through a process of serialization (of the type found in many West African languages) when the basic order was still SOV. With a slight semantic shift, V_1 would become an auxiliary, giving rise to the present-day construction S AUX O V. It is easy to imagine that with time, object pronouns which were complements of the final verb (and thus occurring before it) would eventually come to be associated with (or cliticized onto) the first verb (Hyman, pers.com.).

                    he go it-eat   --->   he go-it eat

The serialization hypothesis is certainly appealing. It suggests that serial constructions, which seem to be a general characteristic of many West African languages, at one time did occur in the Kru family. It also provides an explanation for the word order difference found in all Kru languages between clauses with regular verbs (SVO) and clauses with auxiliaries (S AUX O V).

3.4.2 Objections to the serialization hypothesis. There are, however, several problems with the serialization hypothesis. First, there is little evidence that serialization existed, or exists, in the Kru language family. To my knowledge, with the exception of Givón, no researchers currently working in the family have reported any cases of serialization or remnants of such a process. In his discussion of Klao, Givón notes that serial constructions are not used to express locative, comitative, dative, benefactive, or accusative cases, but he does claim that serialization is used to express the instrumental or manner case. The following are examples of what he considers to be two types of serial verbs (1975b: 74):

(48) **o-nu   faka   o-cye   swa**   (Serial$_1$)   'He used the knife
     he use knife   he-cut meat   to cut the meat.'

(49) **o-nu   faka   o-ye swa   cye**   (Serial$_2$)   'He used a knife in
     he use knife   he-? meat   cut   order to cut meat.'
     (**ye** was not glossed by Givón.)

Admittedly, the task of defining serialization is not easy. However, if we consider examples from other languages of serial constructions which express the instrumental case, the differences between the Klao constructions and "traditional" serial constructions become clear. The following are from various languages within the Kwa family where extensive serialization occurs:

(50) Fante

    ɔ-dI   sI'kán   kwIá-ã   nám   nŪ   'He cut the meat
    he-take   knife   cut   meat   the   with a knife.'

(51) Yoruba

ó	ń	fi	òbe	ge	išu	'He's cutting the yam with a knife.'
he	is	using	knife	cut	yam	

(52) Igbo (Welmers and Welmers 1968)

ó	jì	ḿ'má	à	bèē	á'nū	'He cut the meat with this knife.'
he	have	knife	this	meat	cut	

Upon examination, it becomes evident that there are important syntactic distinctions between the constructions cited by Givón and those listed as 'traditional' cases of serialization. Hyman (1971:30) notes that the term "serialization" generally refers to "cases where two verbs occur within one sentence, but do not enter into any of the coordinate or subordinate relationships defined elsewhere in the language." Schachter (1974) proposes that serial constructions be viewed as a series of VPs dominated by a single S:

S   NP VP (VP)*

In the Kwa examples 50-52, it can be seen that there is only one overt subject, and the clause itself can only be analyzed as one complex sentence. In both Klao examples 48 and 49, on the other hand, there are two overt subjects and there is every evidence that the construction is made up of two independent sentences expressing consecutive action. Each of the sentences contains a subject, a finite verb, and an object. Sentence 49 differs from 48 only by the presence of a sequential auxiliary **ye** which causes a change in the word order of the second clause (see sect. 3.8.1). That we are really dealing with two clauses is supported by facts from another Kru language, Wobé, where a conjunction may optionally appear in similar environments:

(53)

ɔ	no-ɛ	cèē	ɔ	je	ko	cé	'He cut the rice with a knife.'
he	do-DEC	knife	he	SEQ	rice	cut	

(54)

ɔɔ	no-ɛ	gbŏpà	wèè	ɔɔ	ce	tu	'He's cutting the tree with an axe.'
he:IMP	do-DEC	axe	CONJ	he:IMP	cut	tree	

It seems clear from these facts that the serial constructions proposed by Givón are actually not cases of serialization at all, but rather examples of consecutive clauses.

Van Leynseele (1978) points out that even in a serializing language such as Anyi (a Kwa language spoken in Ivory Coast), there is an important distinction between serial verb constructions and consecutive constructions. She notes that in Anyi, true serials have only one subject pronoun (preceding V_1) and V_1 and V_2 must agree in polarity (they must both be either positive or negative).

In consecutive constructions, on the other hand, two subject pronouns are present, and the two clauses do not necessarily agree in polarity.

It is interesting to note that where Kwa languages have serialized constructions, Kru consistently has other means of expressing semantic case relations, be it through overt marking (such as postpositions or suffixes) or through series of sentences strung (or conjoined) together. For example, in serializing languages, benefactives are expressed through serialization. In Kru they are expressed by postposition or verbal suffix.

benefactive

Kwa

(55) Twi (Lord): serializing

    ɔ yɛ adwuma ma   me   'He works for me.'
    he do work   give me

Kru

(56) Godié: postposition

    ɔ zɪrɛ nənʊ nã zɛ   'He works for me.'
    he do work my cause

(57) Klao (Singler): suffixing

    ī   dī-e-mū   kɔ̃   'They ate rice for me.'
    they eat-BEN-me rice

In serializing languages, instrumentals are expressed by serial constructions, as seen in 50-52. In Kru languages, instrumentals are expressed by nominal (58) or verbal (59) suffixes or through conjoined or juxtaposed clauses (see 53 and 54).

Kru

(58) Godié: suffixing

    ɔ dɪ mlɛ bʌkã́   'He cuts meat with a knife.'
    he cut meat knife:ASSOC TONE

(59) Grebo: suffixing

    du-di   blã su   'pound rice with a pestle'
    pound-INST rice pestle

Again, in Kwa languages like Fante, serialization is used to express comparatives (60). In Kru, the same verb 'surpass' is used, but the construction consists of two complete sentences (61 and 62).

The Emergence of Three Future Auxiliaries

Kwa

(60) Fante: serializing (Welmers 1973)
mÚ hÚ yɛ̃ dIn kyIn nÙ   'I am stronger than
my body is strong surpass him   he is.'

Kru

(61) Godié: conjoined clauses
anomɛ dii   glʉ́ nʉ́ ɛ zi jəneti di   kʊ́
Anom plantation big and it pass Jeanette plantation on
'Anomé's field is bigger than Jeanette's.'

(62) Tchien Krahn: juxtaposed clauses
ɔ kmuū   ɔ zī   ɔ bā́ā́ā́   'He is stronger than
he strong he surpass his father   his father.'

While the comitative is expressed by serialization in most serializing languages (63), Kru typically uses conjunctions to express the same notions (64 and 65).

Kwa

(63) Yoruba: serializing
mo wà nibɛ̃ kpɛ̃lú   aki   'I was there
I be there be-included-with Akin   with Akin.'

Kru

(64) Godié: conjunction
ɔmɔ yʌ̄ gwʉjɛ sɔ́ wa mʉ̀ dakpadu   'He and Gwʉdɛ went
him and Gwʉdɛ two they go-FACT Dakpadou   to Dakpadou.'

(65) Tepo: conjunction (Dawson)
m bu kɔ́ hɛ̌ wɛ̌ mu   'My father and I were
my father have me-with earlier go   leaving earlier today.'

There is some evidence that the conjunctions in question come from verbs: **yʌ̄** in Godié seems cognate with the verb 'carry' in some other Kru languages. In Tepo, the conjunction has the same form as the verb 'have' (Dawson, pers.com.). There is no evidence, however, that these arose through serialization. In Godié, **yʌ̄** (the conjunction) is optionally preceded by an inanimate plural pronoun ɩ, suggesting a nonserial origin.

Given these facts, I think it is clear that the Kru language family does not have serial constructions at the present time. However, the serialization hypothesis does not depend on the present status of serialization but rather on its past status. Did serialization once exist (in particular, before the OV ---> VO shift)? Unfortunately, there is so little historical data available that it is difficult to determine if there ever was serialization. Also, there are very few documented cases of serializing SOV languages. However, an exception to this is Ijo, an SOV serializing language of West Africa. A general characteristic of this language type is the occurrence of tense and aspect markers in sentence-final position. In a well-known Ijo dialect, Kalabari, the basic word order is SOV-aspect (Jenewari).

(66)   **gogó ani okĩm̄**   'Gogo took it.'
      Gogo it take-FACT
      S   O   V-ASP

In serial verb constructions, whether involving a transitive or intransitive verb, the tense marker always occurs in sentence-final position.

(67)   **bila o nanga bãm̄**   'An elephant trampled
      elephant him trample kill-FACT him and killed him.'
      S   O   V   V-ASP

(68)   **gogó bó láātéē**   'Gogo has arrived.'
      Gogo come reach-ASP
      S   V   V-ASP

If the construction S V_1 O V_2 in Kru resulted from a serialization process which occurred while the language was still SOV, it would be expected that tense and aspect markers occur in final position (Williamson, pers.com.). However, as was shown in preceding discussions, it is the first verb V_1 and not V_2 which is inflected for tense and aspect.

Also, in other languages where serialization has begun and stopped at some point in time, there are still traces of the serialization process. In many Kwa languages, for example, serial verbs have given rise to prepositions (Lord 1973). Li and Thompson (1974) have shown that in Chinese, serial verbs have given rise to case markers. However, if there was any serialization in Kru at some point, there do not appear to be any traces of such a process.

Furthermore, Hyman (1971) gives convincing arguments that Proto-Niger-Kordofanian did not have serialization. In a later article (1975:141) he shows that serialization swept like a wave through Sub-Saharan Africa, hitting primarily those languages in the Kwa group, stopping short of the Kru and Mandé families bordering Kwa on the west, and the northeastern language, Gwari. Thus, this view of serialization as an areal feature provides a

The Emergence of Three Future Auxiliaries 89

natural explanation for why Kru does not currently, and did not in the past, have serial constructions.

It would appear, then, that there is no independent evidence that serialization did once occur in the Kru language family. If the construction S V_1 O V_2 did not develop through serialization, it must have arisen in another way. As noted earlier, Hyman suggested that V_1 was intransitive. OV_2 could have been a purpose clause. For example, a string like:

	I	go	in-order-to		you	see
	S	V_1			O	V_2

could have arisen at a time when Kru was still SOV and could have undergone deletion, giving rise to the following structure:

	I	go	∅		you	see
	S	V_1			O	V_2

This hypothesis poses some serious problems, however. First, no structure S V_1 in-order-to O V_2 is presently attested in any Kru language. In section 3.8.1, it will be shown that purpose clauses are normally expressed by full clauses containing auxiliaries. Furthermore, the claim that V_1 was intransitive is not supported. If we consider which verbs in Kru have given rise to auxiliaries, we come to the conclusion that they are not all intransitive. For example, the verb 'have' and verbs like 'leave' (discussed in the next chapter) are definitely transitive verbs.

(69) Godié

ɔ kà monɨɨ   'He has money.'
he has money

(70) Neyo (Thomann)

ōmo w̃lõ õ ka yo sõ   'This woman has two children.'
she woman she has children two

Besides, while the motion verbs 'go' and 'come' may be used intransitively in all Kru languages, in at least some cases they also seem to function as potentially transitive verbs. Welmers (1973:454) points out that this is often the case in Niger-Congo languages, where motion verbs "have meanings like 'go to', 'be from', 'arrive at', and the like, and nothing like a preposition [or any kind of case marker-L.M.] is used with them."

Stucky (1976) notes that in Tshiluba, locatives often function as objects of a 'strongly' transitive verb. It is well known that in many Niger-Congo languages, certain locatives may be passivized just like object NPs. (This is true in OluLuyia (Dalgish 1976), Chichewa (Trithart, pers.com.), and in Fula (Sylla, pers. com.).

Also in Yoruba, Awobuyuli (MS, 1974) notes that: "One finds so-called intransitive verbs also taking what can only be structurally analyzed as objects...." In the cases he describes, the object is a nominalized verb which is the same verb functioning as predicate in the clause. This can be seen with the verb 'go': **Adē kō līlō kānkan** (Ade not go going any) 'Ade didn't go at all.' Though these types of construction appear to be specific to Yoruba, they nevertheless illustrate the potential transitivity of normally intransitive verbs like 'go'.

Innes (1966:102-3) gives arguments for considering the NP following the verb 'go' in Grebo as a regular object. First, he points out that the complements of the verb **mu** 'go' are nothing more than unmarked NPs, identical to regular object NPs. He lists some typical complements of 'go'.

Kubli	'Europe'
Mena	'Kru-land'
bli	'home'
gye	'prison'
yu	'up (the direction)'

Second, there are also syntactic arguments for considering the complement of 'go' as an object rather than as an adjunct. Innes points out that in Grebo, adjuncts (nonterms) and objects occur in different positions in the sentence. Objects occur directly following the verb and precede the emphasis marker **ne**.

(71) nē dú-dà͎ blā̀ nḕ   'I pound rice!'
     I pound-T rice EMPH
                  O

Adjuncts (or nonterms) indicating both time and location occur after the **ne** marker.

(72) **ne yi-da nɔ ne ke sɔ**   'I saw him on the farm.'
     I see-T him EMPH farm on

(73) **ne du-da bla ne Mɔle**   'I pounded rice on Monday.'
     I pound-T rice EMPH Monday

However, complements of the verb **mu** 'go' occur before the emphatic marker **ne** (in the same position as objects):

(74) **ne mu-na London ne**   'I went to London.'
     I go-T London EMPH

Similarly, when there is an auxiliary, objects occur within the verb brace S AUX V (between the auxiliary and the main verb).

(75) **ne yi-da bla du**   'I did not pound rice.'
     I NEG-T rice pound

However, adjuncts occur outside the verb brace.

(76) **ne yi-da bla du   Mole**   'I didn't pound rice
     I NEG-T rice pound Monday   on Monday.'

Again, complements of **mu** 'go' behave as objects rather than adjuncts since they occur inside the verb brace.

(77) **ne yi-da London mu**   'I did not go to London.'
     I NEG-T London go

These show that Grebo makes the distinction between argument (term) and nonargument (nonterm) locatives. 'Go' takes an argument and thus could be described as a transitive verb.

Similar evidence of the transitive nature of the verb **go** is available in Wobē. In this language, there appear to be two kinds of locatives: those that are part of subcategorization of the verb, and those that are not. This latter type is similar to the nonterm or nonargument locative described above. When a verb is subcategorized for a locative, as is the case with 'go', the locative occurs within the verb brace (S AUX LOC V), just as an object does.

(78) object within the brace

     ɔ se dɛ   di   'He didn't eat anything.'
     he NEG thing eat

(79) locative within the brace

     ɔ se (e) dɔɔ   mu   'He didn't go to the market.'
     he NEG (to) market go

However, when the verb is not transitive, the locative is only a nonterm, and as such it occurs outside the verb brace. This is the case with the verb **na** 'walk'.

(80) ɔ se na   miablí   'He didn't walk to Kouibly.'
     he NEG walk Kouibly

     *ɔ se miablí na

Also, in Wobē, it is interesting to note that when verbs like 'go' or 'come' occur without an object complement, they have a special marker indicating this is the case. The researchers working on this language call the mark **agent seul** 'agent alone'.

(81) ɔ mu-ú   'He went.'
     he go-AS

(82) ɔ ɟi-í   'He came.'
     he come-AS

This would seem to indicate that these verbs are, in a sense, transitive, since they must occur with the special suffix whenever they occur without a complement.

These facts in Wobé suggest that there needs to be a distinction between two types of motion verbs--those such as 'go' which take locative complements that function like terms, and those like 'walk' which take only nonterm locatives.

In other Kru languages as well, complements of motion verbs like 'go' and 'come' act somewhat like object NPs. In Godié, locative NPs may be pronominalized by a special locative pronoun, just as regular direct objects may be.

(83) ɔ mʉ̀ sukú   'He went to school.'
     he go:FACT school

     ɔ mʉ̀ mɔ́   'He went there.'
     he go:FACT there

(84) ɔ lɨ̈ mlɛɛ   'He ate the meat.'
     he eat:FACT meat-DEF

     ɔ lɨ̈ -ɛ   'He ate it.'
     he eat:FACT it

However, NPs which function as complements of motion verbs do not have all the characteristics of objects. They cannot be passivized in the same way as direct objects.

(85) mlɛɛ lɨ̈-o   'The meat is eaten.'
     meat-DEF eat-PASS

(86) *sukúu mʉ-ɔ   'the school is gone to'
     school-DEF go-PASS

Thus, while complements of 'go' and 'come' act very much like direct objects, they do not share all the characteristics of objects. Nevertheless, the data suggest that motion verbs reflect some degree of transitivity.

According to a list of transitivity correlates established by Hopper and Thompson in their paper "Transitivity in grammar and discourse" (1980), Kru clauses containing motion verbs share with highly transitive clauses a goal-oriented directionality. However, unlike other highly transitive clauses, clauses containing motion verbs like 'go' and 'come' do not indicate an action that brings about a "change in state, substance, or condition in O." Also, the object in this case is not animate, nor is it "totally ... affected by the action of the verb." The object is, however, typically referential, and often definite.

To summarize this section, it was shown that two basic hypotheses about the origin of the S V_1 O V_2 construction are open to debate: one, that serialization was the process by which an S V_1 O V_2 was established (eventually leading to the S AUX O V construc-

The Emergence of Three Future Auxiliaries   93

tion of present-day Kru), and two, that the first verb in the series (V_1) was basically intransitive.

3.4.3 The alternative. These facts permit the formulation of a new hypothesis. If the first verb of the series was transitive or could take an object complement, then the following structure may have been the source of the present-day auxiliary construction:

$$S \quad V_1 \quad (O) \quad V_2 \text{ OBJ COMPLEMENT}$$

In this construction, the sequence (O)V_2 is functioning as the object complement of the first verb, V_1. There are, in fact, several arguments in favor of this hypothesis.

First, it has been shown that the S AUX O V construction is found in both Eastern and Western Kru. However, in some languages, there is a particle that occurs after the final verb, which seems to be functioning as a nominalizer.

$$S \quad V \quad (O) \quad V_{\text{particle}}$$

This is the case in Wobé and Sapo, where nominalizers occur in sentence-final position.

(87) Wobé

ɔɔ   mu-ɛ   gbŭ   po-á   'He will build a
he:IMP go-DECL house build-NOM   house.'

(88) Sapo

ɔ̃   mī̀   kò   tī-ɛ̃́   'He will buy rice' or
he   go:IMP rice buy-NOM   'He's going to buy rice.'

The nominalizing particles following the final verb in the above examples suggest that OV is functioning as a unit. The sequence (O)V-NOM is, in fact, a regular nominal, which may function (in these two languages) as a subject.

(89) Wobé

gbŭ   po   á   kmaí   'It is difficult to build a house'
house build NOM difficult   or 'House-building is difficult.'

(90) Sapo

ko   pi-ɛ̃́   kma-mo   'Cooking rice is hard.'
rice cook-NOM be-hard

While in some languages nominalizing particles do not presently occur in the S AUX O V construction, there are apparently remnants of such particles in other languages. In Klao, the auxiliary construction has a fall sentence final.

(91) dó-á   mū   dɛ̄   dī̄   'Doe will eat.'
     Do-IMP FUT thing eat-low tone clitic

In Krahn, verbs in the future auxiliary construction undergo some tonal changes. When the verb is inherently high, it becomes a mid in this environment (Duitsman, pers.com.).

(92) ɔ́ mú dɛ́   dī̀   'He will eat.'
     he AUX thing eat

This tends to suggest that a nominalizing particle was once present in Krahn. In other languages, no nominalizing particle occurs at all. This is the case in Tepo.

(93) **yruwle** mʊ́ kayú gbo pá̀   'Chameleon is about to enter the house.'
     chameleon AUX house under enter

More evidence is presented in later sections (see 3.5.3.1). For the moment, these data suggest that a nominalizer was once present and subsequently lost in some languages.

Further evidence that auxiliary constructions came from a structure

$$S\ V_1[(O)V_2\ nom]_{COMP}$$

is that present-day compounds, nominalized verbs, and complex complements have OV_{nom} word order.

(94) Klao
     dɛ̄- dī̄- ɛ̄   'eating'
     thing-eat-NOM
     O   V

(95) Godié
     lokwi-kpʌlʌ-nyɔ   'tailor'
     cloth-sew-person
     O   V

(96) Wobé
     gbū- pō- a   'house-building'
     house-build-NOM
     O   V

This would mean that the OV word order in the S AUX O V construction is not necessarily due to formation during an SOV stage. Rather, a structure with word order SVO (where O is a complex complement OV-nom of the type described above) could have given rise to the S AUX O V word order. It is not uncommon for a language which has developed from SOV to SVO (as is assumed to have occurred in Kru) to retain an OV word order in compounds. Such is the case in English. Thus, the SV_1OV_2 construction could have arisen from a structure

$$S\ V_1\ [O\ V_2\ nominalizer]$$

where $OV_{2\ nom}$ functioned as an object complement of V_1.

The Emergence of Three Future Auxiliaries

Another argument in favor of this hypothesis is that typically compounds and embedded complements take neither tense nor negative markers. Considering the OV as being derived from a nominalized verb phrase would explain why neither of these markers occurs on the second or main verb.

Finally, it can be noted that the complex-complement or nominalized verb hypothesis proposed in this section is a known route of syntactic change. That is, in languages of the world, it is often the case that periphrastic constructions containing main verbs followed by some sort of nominalized verb or infinitive give rise to auxiliaries or to aspectual readings (Binnick 1976:43; Traugott 1965; Vroman 1976).

French:

> **Je vais chanter**   'I'm going to sing.'
> I   go   sing-INF

> **Je viens de chanter**   'I just finished singing.'
> I   come from sing-INF

Furthermore, and more importantly, in section 2.3 it was shown that such notions as the progressive aspect are expressed in Kru by a periphrastic construction with the structure:

$$S\ V_1\ [(O)\ V_{2\ nom}]$$

Thus, there is an existing pattern for the source construction which has been proposed.

To sum up, the proposal that the construction

$$S\ V_1\ [(O)V_{2\ nom}]$$

object complement is the origin of the S AUX O V structure is supported by the following:

(i) V_1 is potentially transitive, capable of taking a term complement
(ii) There is evidence in many languages that a nominalizer was present and was subsequently lost
(iii) Considering OV as a nominalized form would explain why it never carries tense or negation
(iv) In other languages the combination V + V-NOM has given rise to aspectual readings
(v) Other constructions in Kru, such as the progressive, make use of an identical structure to express aspectual/modal notions

3.4.4 The verb ---> auxiliary continuum. Accepting the hypothesis that auxiliaries first arose in a construction of the type

$$S\ V\ [(O)\ V_{nom}],$$

we can now ask how and why this construction became S AUX O V. As the data are examined, it becomes obvious that this was not an overnight shift. If we consider the future auxiliary related to 'go', for example, we will see that in some languages the form has almost exclusively verbal characteristics, while in others the form has almost exclusively auxiliary characteristics. Thus, it becomes clear that verbs like 'go' are on a kind of continuum, where they move away from their "verbal-ness" towards their new identity as auxiliaries.

$$\text{Verb} \dashrightarrow \text{AUX}$$

According to the progress of the verb 'go', languages can be placed along the continuum:

$$\text{Verb '----'----'----' -> AUX}$$
$$\text{Godié} \quad \text{Wobé} \quad \text{Dewoin} \quad \text{Krahn}$$

It is important to note, however, that when a verb takes on auxiliary characteristics, the verb from which it is derived does not cease to exist. Thus, in languages like Krahn, there are two entities: **mu**, the motion verb meaning 'go', and **mu**, the auxiliary.

While continua of the type mentioned above do, in a sense, reflect the development of a verb in a given language, they seem to be oversimplified. Many features are affected as a verb turns into an auxiliary, and the exact order of these changes may vary from language to language and from auxiliary to auxiliary.

Givón (1975b:86) notes that similarly in the verb preposition shift, different serial verbs within a given language may undergo reanalysis at different times and perhaps at a different pace (cf. Pike 1970).

In the next section, the development from the verb 'go' to a future auxiliary will be discussed in detail. In later sections, 'come'-related and 'have'-related auxiliaries will also be discussed.

3.5 'Go': a Case History

3.5.1 The verb 'go'. The ways in which verbs differ from auxiliaries have already been discussed (see sect. 3.3). While several Kru languages have a 'go'-related future auxiliary, in many other languages 'go' acts much like any other verb. Thus on the verbal end of the continuum 'go' begins its development in regular verbal constructions NP go (NP), where the second NP is the complement of the verb. Like all verbs, 'go' is inflected for tense and aspectual distinctions, as seen in Godié:

(97) ɔ̃ mɛ̈ sūkú   'He's going to school'
      he go:IMP school   or 'He goes to school.'

(98) ɔ̃ mɛ̈ sūkú   'He went to school.'
      he go:FACT school

The Emergence of Three Future Auxiliaries

The meaning of the verb in these contexts is totally literal, referring only to motion through space. Like most transitive verbs, 'go' may be followed by a complex complement of the type described earlier (sect. 3.4.3).

$$S \quad go \quad (O) \quad [V_{nominalizer}]$$

Despite the complex structure in this environment, 'go' still inflects for tense and aspect and still refers to a literal move through space. The sentence taken as a whole, however, has a purpose reading 'go in order to'. Every Kru language examined in this study has such a construction. Examples below come from Eastern and Western Kru.

Eastern

(99) Godié

ɔ mʉ̀   sʉkʌ́ dɪ kʌ̀   'She went to cut rice.'
she go:FACT rice cut NOM

(100) Neyo (Thomann)

le yo   mo   lagba sye ka   'Then the child went
then child go:FACT fields burn NOM to burn the fields.'

(101) Bété (Mahibouo)

ɔ mì   síká pīā ká   'He went to buy some rice.'
he go:FACT rice buy NOM

(102) Vata

ɔ mlḕ 6ū̀ 6lí ká   'He went to dig a hole.'
he go hole dig NOM

(103) Lakota Dida

ɔ̄ mlē   líkpā 6ā 6ɔ̄ɔ̄   'He's going to kill a monkey.'
he go:IMP monkey kill NOM

Western

(104) Bakwé

ɔ̄ mí   brē kālē   'He went to sing.'
he go:FACT sing NOM

(105) Borobo

ɔ̄ mū dɛ́ fī   à   'He went to cook.'
he go thing cook NOM

(106) Wobé

āā   mū-ɛ̄   káfé   sā   å̀   'We're going to pick coffee.'
we:IMP go-DECL coffee pick NOM

In regard to negation and other notions, such as focus, the S go (O) V nom construction acts just like any other clause. When the negative auxiliary occurs, the main verb 'go' occurs in sentence-final position, with the complement of 'go' occurring between the AUX and the main verb.

(107) Godié

ɔ́ɔ́   wʊ̀   sʉkʌ́   dɩ   kʌ̄   mʉ   'He didn't go to cut rice.'
he:NEG NEG rice cut NOM go
S   AUX   O   V

(108) Wobé

ɔ   se   gbǔ   po   å̀   mu   'He didn't go to build a house.'
he NEG house build NOM go
S AUX   O   V

The complex complement may be focussed in the same way as other complement NPs. In Godié it is fronted like regular postverbal NPs:

(109) ɔ   mʉ̀   sukú   sukú   ɔ   mʉ̀
      he go:FACT school   school he go:FACT
      'He went to school.'   'It's to school he went.'

(110) ɔ   mʉ̀   sʉkʌ́ dɩ kʌ̄   sʉkʌ́ dɩ kʌ̄   ɔ   mʉ̀
      he go:FACT rice cut NOM   rice cut NOM he go:FACT
      'He went to cut rice.'   'It's to cut rice
                                 that he went.'

Thus, initially, the verb 'go', even when followed by a complex complement NP, basically functions as does any other verb. From this setting, the verb 'go' may undergo several changes, affecting either its phonological shape or its basic meaning. As the verb moves toward the auxiliary side of the continuum, many subtle changes in meaning can be observed. These will be described in the following section.

3.5.2 Semantic shift

3.5.2.1 Loss of the feature intention. Apparently one of the first semantic shifts to take place has to do with the nature of the subject NP which occurs with the verb 'go'. Like all motion verbs,

The Emergence of Three Future Auxiliaries   99

such as 'come', 'run', 'jump', 'walk', etc., the verb 'go' usually takes a subject which is animate and a voluntary participant in the act. The subject of 'go' propels itself through space.

(111) Wobé

    ɔ na   miabli   'He walked to Kouibly.'
    he walk Kouibly

(112) Godié

    ɔ mʉ̀   magʉ̀tı kʋ́   'He went to the market.'
    he go:FACT market on

However, very early, this restriction on the subject may change. The verb may be used with inanimate subjects as well as animate ones (cf. Wald 1973:117). The element of volition or self-propulsion is lost.

The same point is made in Givón's 1973 article "The time-axis phenomenon," where he notes that a basic part in the shift from verb to modality in many cases is the loss of the intent presupposition. He notes (p. 916) that in three unrelated languages (English, Swahili, and Palestinian Arabic), a future modality meaning 'will' has come from an intentional verb meaning 'want'. According to Givón, the loss of the feature [+intent] has allowed for the semantic reanalysis of the verb. This is exactly what has occurred in the past and what is occurring now with the verb 'go' in Kru.

In Godié, the shift is only beginning to occur. In a collection of 135 pages of typed texts, 'go' occurred with inanimate, and thus nonvolitional, subjects approximately three percent of the time (13 out of 429 examples). Only one example was found with a noncomplex NP complement of the verb.

(113) nàa gɔlʋ́ nááà   mʉ   'Your canoe won't go.
    your canoe NEG-FUT go

In all the other examples of inanimate subjects, 'go' was followed by a complex nominal marked by kʌ. Five of the thirteen examples involved sun or sunlight.

(114) yʋ́lʋ́ mʉ̀   ɓɛ́lɪ̄ʌ́ kʌ, nʉ́   ɔ   yɪ̄ kʋ́ gʉ̄lʉ̀
    sun go:IMP lean NOM then he POT up get
    'As the sun was still coming up, he got up.

The preceding examples involve subjects which, though inanimate, actually move through space (though not of their own volition). In the following, however, 'go' combines with a complex nominal containing the verbs 'finish' or 'fall' with subjects which can in no way be interpreted as moving. In these contexts, 'go' seems to take on the meaning 'about to' or 'almost':

(115) **ɓūtùu**   mʉ yι lɔ́ dʉgāsa dʉgāsa zɔ́ ɓιʌ kʌ̄
      house-D go now there slowly slowly bottom finish NOM
      'The house was in the process of being finished.'
      (literally: the house was slowly going to finish)

(116) **sʉkáa**   kʌ̄ mɔ́ ɓιʌ kʌ̄ mʉ nʌ
      rice-DEF VOL there finish NOM go NF
      'When the rice was almost gone, ...' (literally:
      the rice was going to go to finish)

Thus in Godié, while the temporal use of the verb 'go' is fairly uncommon, it is beginning to appear.

The combination of the volitive auxiliary **kʌ** and the verb 'go' is often found in sentence-initial dependent clauses. Even with animate subjects, 'go' appears to have a kind of aspectual reading ('starting to') in this context.

(116a) **dʌ́bū kʌ̄ yī kʊ́ gʉ̄lʉ̀ kʌ̄ mʉ̄ nʌ̄ ɔ́ kʌ̄ yι kí**
       duck VOL now up get NOM go NF he VOL now talk

       kʌ̄ mʉ̄ nʌ, ʊʊ́   bàzʊ̀wā lī̄ kʌ̄
       NOM go NF he:NEG voice   have

       'As the duck started to get up, as he started to talk, he didn't have any voice' or 'As the duck was going to get up, as he was going to talk, he didn't have any voice.'

The same loss of the intent feature has occurred in other languages, like Wobé, but to a greater extent. As in Godié, however, the verb 'go' still retains its verbal characteristics. It is marked for aspectual distinction, and complex complements are also marked by a nominalizing particle (in this case **a**, which is possibly a reduction of Eastern **ka**):

(117) ɔ mu-ɛ gbǔ po-á   'He went to build a house.'
      he go-DEC house build-NOM

(118) ɔɔ́ mu-ɛ gbǔ po-á   'He's going to build
      he:IMP go-DEC house build-NOM   a house.'

In Krahn, however, the verb 'go' occurs commonly with inanimate subjects and gains a movement-in-time rather than a movement-in-space reading.

(119) **junu-a mʉ duba glae**   'Dew will fall tomorrow.'
      dew-IMP go fall tomorrow

3.5.2.2 Ambiguity. The loss of the intent feature may lead to ambiguity between movement-in-space and movement-in-time. This type of ambiguity is attested in several languages. As can be seen in the examples, sometimes the nominalizing particle is present, sometimes it is reduced to a tone, and sometimes it is absent altogether. This phonological change will be treated separately in section 3.5.3.1, and a discussion of the interaction of the two changes will follow (sect. 3.5.4).

(120) Bereby Kru

    ɛ mi dɛ di wɔ̃   'He will eat it' or 'He is
    he go:IMP thing eat NOM   going (somewhere) to eat it.'

(121) Sapo

    ɔ mi kō ti-ɛ   'He will buy rice' or 'He's
    he go:IMP rice eat-NOM   going (in order) to buy rice.'

(122) Cedepo

    èh mí e kou tɔ̃ ma   'I will buy rice' or 'I am going
    I go:IMP rice buy NOM   (in order) to buy rice.'

(123) Klao (N. Lightfoot)

    do-a mu dɛ diĩ
    Doe-IMP go thing eat-low tone clitic

    'Doe is going to eat' or 'Doe goes (in order) to eat.'

It is important to note that in all these cases it is the imperfective form of 'go' that gives rise to an ambiguous reading. The form of 'go' in the factative consistently gives a past-literal reading. This is, of course, due to the fact that the imperfective designates unrealized actions and thus may be associated with future as well as present unrealized actions. In a later section it will be shown that the presence of the imperfective marker may eventually affect the shape of the future auxiliary (see sect. 3.5.3.2).

3.5.2.3 Loss of ambiguity. It has been shown that even in languages where 'go' has remained quite verbal, in some contexts it may only be construed to refer to future tense (see 115-116). Through time, the verb occurs in more and more contexts where it is unambiguously a future marker. At this point it begins to occur in the consequent of conditionals; it may also cooccur with itself (another verb 'go'); and it may eventually be frozen into a form which is never ambiguous. These cases will now be discussed in more detail.

    (1) Cooccurrence of temporal 'go' and the verb 'go'. A main indication that 'go' is becoming more auxiliary-like is that it

may cooccur with itself. Hyman notes a similar phenomenon in Igbo and Fe?Fe? (1971:3). In Igbo, the verb 'take' often gets an instrumental reading.

  ó wèrè ḿmà bèé ánụ́ 'He cut the meat with a knife.'
  he take knife cut meat

Hyman also points out that in consecutive constructions, as the verb 'take' is bleached, a new verb 'take' must be introduced if the physical act of taking is to be conveyed. In the following sentence, the first 'take' is used in its literal sense, while the second 'take' is used to convey an instrumental reading (p. 37):

  ó wèrè ḿmà, wèré (yà) bèé ánụ́ 'He took a knife and
  he take knife and-take (it) cut meat cut the meat with it.'

Similarly, in the following Kru examples the verb 'go' appears twice. In this case, the first 'go' cannot possibly refer to motion. It clearly gives an unambiguous future reading to the sentence.

(124) Grand Bassa

  ɔ mu múù̀ ɔ ké mɔ̀ɔ dɔ̀ 'He will go and buy rice.'
  he FUT go:NOM he AUX rice buy

(125) Nyabo

  ɔ mi gbla pi-ɛ mu-ɛ 'He will go to cook rice.'
  he go:IMP rice cook-NOM go-NOM

(126) Cedepo

  ɔ́ mí tulubɔ́ mú ma 'He will go to Monrovia.'
  he go:IMP Monrovia go NOM

(127) Tchien Krahn

  ɔ mū gw̄lɔ̄ mū 'He will go to town.'
  he go town go

(128) Tepo

  yruwle mū mumu 'Chameleon is about to leave.'
  chameleon AUX go-go

(129) Dewoin

  ɔ mu mūù̄ mū wɔ̀ ɔ má ziɛ pi
  she go go:NOM FUT that she SEQ rice cook
  'She will go in order to cook rice.'
  (The third **mu** will be dealt with in section 3.5.6.)

(2) Use in the consequent of conditions. One of the tests of how far the verb 'go' has moved toward the auxiliary side of the continuum is whether it may occur in the consequent of conditionals. For example, Binnick (1976:42) notes that the periphrastic 'going to' in English is only marginally acceptable in this environment:

    I'll kill Sam if you ask me to

    (?) I'm going to kill Sam if you ask me to

Similarly, Innes (1966:74) notes that in Grebo the 'go'-related future may not occur in the consequent of a conditional. Rather, suffix-marked futures occur in this context. However, in several Kru languages the 'go'-related future may occur in the consequent of conditionals, showing the extent of its reanalysis.

(130) Sapo
ɔ dībɛ̄ kō dī, ɔ mī kmā̄
he COND rice eat he go:IMP sick
'If he eats rice, he will be sick.'

(131) Gbaeson Krahn
pɔ̀ ī nū-ɛ nɛ̀ ā̀ mú ī blā̀
COND you do-it then I:IMP go you hit
'If you do it, I'll hit you.'

(132) Grand Bassa
ɔ jī mɔ́ɔ dɔɛ ɔ mū-ɛ pīī̀
he COND rice buy he go-it cook-NOM
'If he buys rice, he'll cook it.'

(3) Complete semantic shift. In some languages the future construction containing 'go' is totally unambiguous, irrespective of environment. In these languages, the construction may refer only to future actions and never to motion. This is a case of total semantic bleaching, which is not common in the Kru family. It is the case, however, in Gbaeson and Tchien Krahn, as well as in Dewoin.

(133a) Gbaeson Krahn
ɔ mu dɛ di
he go thing eat
'He will eat' or 'He is going to eat.'

The bleaching of the verb 'go' in certain contexts does not mean, however, that it is no longer used elsewhere in its literal (motion) sense. In other constructions, 'go' refers unambiguously to motion in space, as seen below:

(133b) ɔ mu dɛ di la
      he go thing eat NOM
'He is going in order to eat.'

It is obvious that 133a has undergone phonological reduction. The interaction between semantic bleaching and phonological reduction will be discussed in section 3.5.4.

3.5.2.4 Further semantic extensions. Once 'go' has achieved the status of a future marker, it may extend to cover other areas typically expressed by modals.

(1) The 'go' future > potential. In most languages, 'go' usually develops an immediate future reading 'is about to' or a definite future reading 'will'. However, in some cases, the meaning of 'go' is extended to cover potential actions. As we will see later, it is much more common for the 'come'-related auxiliary to express potential action. In Grand Bassa, however, there is apparently only one future, which is the 'go'-related one. It is used to cover potential as well as immediate and definite futures.

(134) ɔ   mu yi   kpaa   'He may fall down.'
       he go down fall

(2) The 'go' future > obligation. In at least one language, Grebo, the 'go'-related auxiliary occurs in clauses expressing obligation. In a later section, it will be shown that in other languages a 'come'-derived future may also give rise to a hortative. In the Grebo examples 135, 136, it is again the imperfective form of the verb stem which has been reanalyzed as a future modality.

(135) nè̌ mi   nɛ̃ du   'that I should pound it' or
      I go:IMP it pound

(136) bɛ̃   mi   nɛ̃ du
      that-I go:IMP it pound

3.5.3 Phonological changes. Along with the various semantic shifts discussed in section 3.5.2, the construction S go [(O) V nom] may undergo various phonological changes as the verb 'go' moves along the verb--->auxiliary continuum. One change which can occur is in the shape of the verb stem itself, that is, in its tone or vowel quality. It will be shown that in some cases one form of the verb "freezes" to emerge eventually as an auxiliary distinct from the verb 'go'. Another important change which may occur is the reduction of the sentence-final nominalizing particle.

3.5.3.1 Reduction or loss of the nominalizing particle. There are several attested cases of reduction of the nominalizing particle in the S go [(O) V nominalizer] construction. In Eastern Kru, the reduction is reported to occur in several Bété dialects. Werle et al. (1977:17) have reported that Bété dialects often differ in their **ka** nominalization marker. Of the ten Bété dialects surveyed, four had a **ka** marker on either mid or low tone. But in six dialects the **ka** had been reduced to a vowel.

The Emergence of Three Future Auxiliaries   105

(137) Mahibouo
ɔ mì síká pīā ká   'He went to buy some rice.'
he go rice buy NOM

(138) Tagoura
ɔ mʉ̃ síká pīā-ā̃   'He went to buy some rice.'
he go rice buy-NOM

(139) Kosséoa
ń ɔ̃ ɟīɛ bídò-ō̰ mʉ̃   'And she went to bathe.'
and she SEQ bathe-NOM go

It is interesting to note that the six dialects where the reduction has taken place are geographically close together. The dialects that have a single vowel as a nominalizer are those closest to Nyabwa territory, which is the border that separates Eastern and Western Kru. Note that in Wobé, a Western language, the marker occurring with **mu** 'go' is **a**.

(140) ɔ̃ mū̃-ɛ̃ gbǒ pō a̋   'He went to build a house.'
he go-DECL house build NOM

Thus, this Western nominalizer could be a reduction of **ka**, the form the Eastern languages, other than Bété, retain in full.

       Neyo   ká
       Vata   ká
       Godié   ká / ká̃

As has been suggested, in Western Kru there are cases of reduction of the nominalizing particle. In Grand Bassa, though the full nominalizing suffix ɛ̃ appears in the negative future forms, it is being assimilated in the affirmative forms, leaving a lengthened nasalized vowel (of identical vowel quality) realized on low tone.

(141) NEG with nominalizer
ɔ séè mɔ́ɔ pi-ɛ̰̀ mu   ɔ séè mɔ́ɔ di-ɛ̰̀ mu
he NEG rice cook-NOM go   he NEG rice eat-NOM go
'He will not cook rice.'   'He will not eat rice.'

(142) AFFIRM with assimilated nominalizer
ɔ mu-ɛ pi-ḭ̀   ɔ mu mɔɔ dɔ-ɔ̰̀
he go-it cook-NOM   he go rice buy-NOM
'He will cook it.'   'He will buy rice.'

The above data support Givón's (1975a) claim that affirmative clauses (containing more new information) are more innovative, while negative clauses (containing less new information) tend to conserve earlier forms. While this claim is certainly true (more examples of the conservative nature of negative constructions are given in section 3.6.4), there may be a simpler explanation in this case--namely, that in the negative clauses in 141 the nominalized verb occurs in sentence-final position and is more susceptible to phonological reduction than it is in non-final position, as in 142.

In Dewoin there is evidence that a nominalizer was once present. In the future construction containing 'go', the main verb always has a low tone vowel suffix with the same phonological shape as the preceding vowel. (The second **mu** (glossed as FUT) is discussed in section 3.5.6.)

(143) (Mortvedt)

    ná   mū ɟīi̱   mū là   'I will come here.'
    I-PR go come:TONE FUT here

(144) (Welmers)

    ɔ́ɔ̄   mū sāyɛ̄ pīi̱   mū   'He will cook meat.'
    he-PR go meat cook:TONE FUT

This low-tone suffix is more likely the remnant of a vowel nominalizing suffix.

In Klao, the nominalizer appears to have been reduced to a tonal clitic. N. Lightfoot (1974:435) notes that whether a clause is referring to literal motion or to a future action, there is a low-tone clitic which typically occurs on the main verb stem.

(145) **dó á mū cɛ̄--**   'Doe is going to learn' or
     Doe IMP go learn-TONE   'Doe will learn.'

(146) **dó á mū dɛ̄ dī͂**   'Doe will eat' or 'Doe is
     Doe IMP go thing eat-TONE going in order to eat.'

The tonal clitic is, in all probability, a remnant of a nominalizing suffix. Rickard (1970:7) notes that all nominalizing suffixes in Klao have low tone.

        trá   'to appoint'   **trátrɛ̄**   'appointment'
        ɟipo   'to know'   **ɟipoɛ̄**   'knowing'
        drá   'to kill'   **dráyɛ̄**   'killing'

Now, however, the low-tone clitic has come to be associated with sentence-final position. Lightfoot reports that it may occur on the final element in the sentence whether it is the main verb or not. Compare:

(147) dó á mū dɛ̄ dī tīwɛ̄⁻   'Doe goes to eat all
      Doe IMP go thing eat always-TONE   the time.'

(148) dó á mū kó dī⁻ ⁻   'Doe will eat bananas.'
      Doe IMP go bananas eat-TONE

This generalization can be attributed to the fact that the low-tone clitic is no longer viewed by speakers as a nominalizer.

It has already been mentioned that in Krahn there is also evidence that a nominalizing particle was present and subsequently lost. In the future construction, if the main verb is inherently non-high, no marker occurs; if the verb is inherently high, however, it is realized on a mid tone.

(149) ɔ́ mu sùkúú mū   'He will go to school.'
      he go school go   (go = mū)

Thus, in Krahn, the nominalizing particle has virtually disappeared, except for the tonal remnant affecting high tone verbs.

In other languages, there is no remnant left, and it is assumed that the nominalizing particle has been completely assimilated. In Tepo Kru, there is no change in the verb stem.

(150) ʊ mʊ́ n cré   'They're going to shave me.'
      they FUT me shave

(151) ɛ mʊ́ yruwle da   'He's going to call Chameleon.'
      he FUT chameleon call

Thus, it can be seen that there is a tendency for the sentence-final nominalizing particle to be reduced or lost. In the cases we have seen, a monosyllabic CV reduces to a vowel suffix, V, which eventually assimilates to the vowel quality of the preceding vowel of the verb stem. Tonal remnants then occur and may eventually disappear.

3.5.3.2 Change in the shape of the verb stem. Several cases of change in the shape of the verb stem are seen as the verb 'go' moves toward the auxiliary end of the continuum. One such change occurs in those languages where the verbal imperfective *e is overtly manifested (see sect. 2.2.2.1). In many languages of the Grebo complex, the imperfective form of the verb stem **mu** 'go' is **mi**. Because it is the imperfective use of 'go' which gets a future reading in the first place, it is this form that gets reinterpreted as a future auxiliary.

(152) Nyabo

ɔ mī   nīī tõ-ā   'He will buy fish.'
he go:IMP fish buy-NOM

(153) Sapo

ɔ mī   kò tī-ɛ̄   'He will buy rice' or
he go:IMP rice buy-NOM 'He is going to buy rice.'

(154) Grebo

ne mi   nɛ̄ du   'I should pound it.'
I go:IMP it pound

In languages, such as Dewoin and Krahn, where the dominant signal of the imperfective was apparently at one time the nominal suffix **a** (see sect. 2.2.2.2), the form used consistently for the future construction is **mu**. The connection between the imperfective and the future is still maintained, however, since the imperfective (or in the case of Dewoin presumptive) pronouns must occur in the future.

(155) Krahn

ā   mú dɛ́ dī   *ǐ mú dɛ́ dī
I:IMP go thing eat   I go thing eat
'I will eat.'

(156) Dewoin

ɔ̃ɔ̃   mū sāyɛ̄ pīī   mū   'He will cook meat.'
he-PR go meat cook-NOM FUT

Other changes may affect the verb stem as well. In Tepo, the verb stem for 'go' is **mu**. However, the future marker has the retracted high back vowel ʊ in place of the nonretracted high back vowel u: mʊ́. This raises an interesting question. Did the form of the verb change or did the emerging auxiliary diverge from the phonological shape of the verb? If we consider the form of 'go' in other, neighboring languages, it is clear that the original verb form was ***mu**. That is, it is the shape of the auxiliary (and not the verb) which has changed. Why this occurred in Tepo and not in other languages is not known.

However, a similar change in phonological shape occurs in another case of reanalysis. In most Kru languages, directionals are expressed by means of body parts (see page 18). Thus the word for 'back' may be used to express the notion 'behind'. The construction 'back of the house' or 'house-ASSOC back' refers to the position 'behind the house'. Peter Thalmann (pers.com.) reports that while in Tepo the word **ke** 'back' has the same phonological shape whether referring to a body part or to a direction, in Plapo, a closely related language, the same notions are expressed by two different forms. The word for 'back' is **ke**, while the word for 'behind' has a retracted ı: **kı**. The **kı** form has apparently been reanalyzed as a directional and can no longer refer to the body part 'back'. The parallels between the noun--->directional (or postposition) shift and the verb---->auxiliary shift are clear. In both cases, it is the morpheme with an innovative meaning (and a grammatical rather than a lexical function) which changes shape. In both these cases, the vowel in the innovated form is retracted. It is not known whether this is a general phonetic process affecting innovative words. (Usually retracted vowels make up the unmarked vowel set.)

Another case of phonological change has to do with the tone on the verb stem. In Tepo, **mu** has changed to high tone **mú**. In Grebo also, while the verb 'go' is realized on mid-high tone (**mu** is the stem and **mī** the imperfective form), the tone on the auxiliary is high: **mī**. It is not known why heightening of tone accompanies these reanalyses, since imperfective affixes are typically on mid or mid-high tone. Schachter (pers.com.) notes that in Twi, a related Kwa language, when 'come' is used as an auxiliary verb, it too occurs with a high tone. A parallel case of tone heightening will be seen when the 'have'-related auxiliaries are presented. In Godié, the future marker shifted from low to high (sect. 3.7.3).

3.5.4 Interaction of semantic shift and phonological change. Two parameters of change have been discussed in regard to the development of the verb 'go' into a future marker: semantic shift and phonological change. What can be said about their interaction?

In the literature, it has been suggested that phonological change may precede and precipitate changes in semantics or syntax. For example, Vennemann (1974:359) has proposed that the wearing down of case markers in certain languages has given rise to ambiguity which eventually leads to syntactic change. He suggests that if case markers in SOV languages are worn down, there are no signals to tell speakers which NP is the subject and which is the object. Vennemann suggests that in such a situation, if no other strategy emerges to distinguish the two, there may be a shift in word order from SOV to SVO, separating and thereby distinguishing the subject and object. The situation described by Vennemann is not similar to the one being described in Kru, but perhaps the basic principle can be applied to the Kru case. Has phonological reduction of the nominalizing particle, for example, opened the way for a change in the S go (O) V nom construction? Has phonological reduction triggered semantic or syntactic change?

First, it seems clear that the semantic shifts which affect the 'go' construction are not necessarily brought about by the phonological reduction of the nominalizing particle. Many examples of semantic shifts have occurred in the S go (O) V nom construction while the nominalizing particle was still present.

(157) Bereby Kru

ɛ mi dɛ di wɔ̃   'He will eat it' or 'He is going
he go:IMP thing eat NOM   in order to eat it.'

(158) Nyabo

ɔ mi lé mu-ɛ   'He will go there.'
he go:IMP there go-NOM

(159) Wobé

mä̀ me-ɛ dɔɔ mu-ä̀ klã̄ē˺   'I'm going to the
I:IMP go-DEC market go-NOM tomorrow   market tomorrow.'

In many cases, semantic shift is taking place without reduction of the nominalizing particle. Thus, phonological reduction cannot be considered as the motivating factor in the semantic changes outlined in the preceding section. What, then, accounts for the semantic shift? The only explanation appears to be the semantic makeup of the verb 'go' and the apparent universal tendency for languages to express time reference in terms of movement or distance through space (Givón 1973; Traugott 1978). The go--->future modality shift is attested in countless languages throughout the world. Traugott (1978:377) notes that cross-linguistically 'go'-related futures outnumber other verb-derived futures, though it does not appear to be especially common in the Niger-Congo family (Welmers 1973:354). Below are examples from several different language families in the world where 'go' is used to indicate future actions.

Indo-European family

Romance

French   je **vais** partir   'I'm going to leave.'
          I **go** leave-INF

Spanish   yo **voy** a vistarla mañana
          I **go** to visit-her tomorrow
          'I'm going to visit her tomorrow.'

Germanic

English   'I'm **going to (gʌnna)** see him tomorrow.'

Niger-Congo

Kwa

Igbo (Welmers 1973:354,405)

ō **gà** àbyá   'He's going to come.'
he **go** come-NOM

Bantu
  Kishamba (Givón 1973: Mould)
  sisi ma-ku-enda ko-ona yeye   'We will see him.'
            go

West Atlantic
  Dyola (Givón 1973)
  u-ja u-waloa di e-kolo-ŋ   'We will enter the well.'
  we-go we-enter LOC P-well-the

Quechua
  Ecuadorian Quechua (Muysken 1977:76)
  puñu-k   ri-ni   'I am going to sleep.'
  sleep-NOM go-I:SING

Creoles and Pidgins
  Haitian Creole
  li va vini   'He will come.'
  he go come

  West African Pidgin (Cameroun) (Shapira, MS)
  yú na mí, wí gow gów fo áftanún
  you and me we go go for afternoon
  'You and I will go in the afternoon.'

  Krio (Givón 1973: T. Peterson)
  wi go tray fo puš di trak
  'We will try to push the truck.'

As was already mentioned in 3.5.3.2, besides the naturalness of a go--->FUT shift, there is a definite link between the imperfective aspect and future action. In Hebrew (Gordon, MS), the early imperfect aspect was reanalyzed as a future tense. Benveniste (1968:90) notes that in Latin, it is the imperfect form of the verb 'have' which gives rise to an innovative future. In the Grassfields Bantu languages, futures are "redundantly and obligatorily marked as incompletive" (Hyman, pers.com.).

It has been shown, then, that the semantic shift from go--->FUT is a common one, occurring in languages throughout the world. It is also clear that in the Kru family this change takes place while the construction S go [(O) V nom] is intact, proving that phonological reduction does not in this case trigger the semantic shift. However, it is a fact that the nominalizing particle is sometimes phonologically reduced. Is this an independent change or is it in some way related to the semantic changes that have occurred?

First, it needs to be emphasized that the phonological processes in question are natural. There are many cases in Kru of the reduction of final morphemes or parts of final morphemes. One of the most striking examples is the loss of class suffixes which has affected most noun stems in the family. Another example is the reduction of sentence-final markers, which is widespread in the family. In Godié, sentence-final vowels are often reduced when following a nasal consonant.

(160) / ɔ yʌ bi kʌ̃ mʉ /   'He has gone for a walk.'
    he PERF walk NOM go
    [ɔ yʌ bi kʌ m̩]

Reductions such as ka→a→V→∅ seem possible, especially given the fact that nominalizing particles occur most frequently in sentence-final position.

Despite the fact that the processes being considered are natural, there is some evidence that semantic changes in a verb (in this case 'go') may set the scene for, or somehow precipitate, phonological change. In several Kru languages, the nominalizing particle has been conserved when 'go' retains its literal meaning, but is not present (and has presumably been lost) when 'go' has taken on a temporal reading.

(161) Tchien Krahn

literal use of 'go':   temporal use of 'go':

ɔ mu zĭmĭĭ flá-lá   ɔ mu gwlɔ mu ∅
he go fish catch-NOM   he go town to ∅
'He goes (in order) to   'He will go to town.'
catch a fish.'

(162) Tepo

literal use of 'go':   temporal use of 'go':

ɔ mu nã wɔ̃   ʊ mʊ n crẽ ∅
he go drink NOM   they FUT me shave ∅
'He went to drink.'   'They will shave (my head).'

It would appear that as the meaning of 'go' becomes less literal and more temporal, it is less recognizable as a motion verb. This means that the nominalized verbal complement no longer has the same function in the clause and that, therefore, the function of the nominalizer is obscured. This "upheaval" in the meanings of the component parts of the 'go' construction may make it susceptible to phonological change (that is, more susceptible than it would be on purely phonetic grounds). In other words, it would seem that semantic shift may create a situation where phonological change is likely.

A similar scenario is proposed by Carol Lord (1975) in her description of Igbo verbal compounds. She notes that once a compound is formed, the meanings of the individual components and the meaning of the compound as a whole may begin to differ: "As the meanings diverge ..., speakers begin to lose sight of historical relationship, and assimilatory phonological processes are allowed to apply, obscuring the relationship further."

In the case of Igbo, vowel harmony may change the phonological makeup of the compound. Lord concludes that "the semantic shift probably comes before the phonological assimilation; the shifted semantics are what allows the phonological assimilation to take place."

It seems that there is a similar phenomenon occurring in English which also affects the verb 'go'. As has been noted, in English the progressive form of 'go' may be used in a future sense.

> I'm going to buy a dress

The same set of morphemes can be used in a literal sense to indicate motion through space.

> I'm going to the store

Only in the nonliteral sentence may the sequence going to be phonologically reduced (Welmers, pers.com.; cf. Labov 1971):

> I'm gonna buy a new dress
>
> *I'm gonna the store

These data seem to suggest that speakers are somehow aware of the meaning divergence which has arisen and consequently treat the two forms separately.

Further support for this claim comes from data already presented. In all the cases of phonological change involving the verb, the form which undergoes semantic shift or reanalysis is the form which undergoes phonological change. This has been seen in Tepo, where the 'go'-related AUX has become retracted (**mu-->mʊ̄**), and in Grebo, where the go-related AUX is realized on higher tone than the verb 'go' (**mì-->mí**). It can also be noted that in Camerounian Pidgin as well, the form of 'go' used in a temporal sense differs from the verb used in the literal sense in that it is unstressed:

(163) **yū na mī wī gow gōw fo āftanūn**
 you and me we go go   for afternoon
 'You and I will go in the afternoon.'

To conclude this section, the data presented suggest that when the S go [(O) V nom] construction is used to express temporal notions, it is more open to phonological change than its literal counterpart. This does not exclude the possibility, however, that phonological changes based purely on phonetic grounds will occur whether or not semantic shifts occur. A case in point may be the nominalizing particle in the Bété dialects discussed earlier. No information is available at the present time to indicate whether semantic shift has occurred previous to the phonological reduction ka-->a--> V. It may be that these are cases of independent phonological change. Another possible case of independent sentence-final change may be in Kuwaa, where 'go' constructions of all types apparently do not take a nominalizer.

(163a) wɔ bɛ-ó   wá   fĩ   'He went to cook rice.'
        he go-PAST rice cook

3.5.5 Grammaticalization. This is perhaps a good time to come back to David Lightfoot's (1974) diachronic analysis of English modals. As was previously mentioned, Lightfoot claims that modals in English arose from full verbs, but must be synchronically analyzed as belonging to a new category. M. Lightfoot's explanation of the change is as follows: He claims that independent changes occurring within a given time span tended to isolate a particular set of verbs as "irregular." This class acquired a set of exception features which eventually became too burdensome for the grammar. Under pressure for "transparency," this set of verbs was reanalyzed, forming a new grammatical category, modal. In generative terms, the change is centered in the base component, affecting the basic phrase structure rules of the grammar.

In many cases, Kru facts can be viewed in much the same way. What are the effects of semantic shift and phonological reduction on Kru grammar as a whole? It must be remembered that specific verbs in individual Kru languages are at different stages on the verb-->auxiliary continuum. In many languages, such as Wobé, though the semantic shift has been great, the effects on the basic syntax have been almost negligible. In Wobé, the future containing the verb **mu** 'go' is still inflected like any other verb. The elements following 'go' clearly act as its object complement. The same is true in Klao, where the 'go' construction is inflected for the perfective/imperfective distinction.

(164) ɔ mu dɛ   di   'He went to eat.'
       he go thing eat

(165) ɔɔ   mu dɛ   di   'He's going to eat'
       he:IMP go thing eat   or 'He will eat.'

In the negative, the construction also acts like a regular verbal construction, with **mu** moving to sentence-final position like any regular verb (see sect. 4.3.1).

The Emergence of Three Future Auxiliaries

(166) ɔ   se   dɛ   di   <u>mu</u>   'He didn't go to eat'
       he NEG thing eat <u>go</u>   or 'He will not eat.'

These examples show that though there has been a semantic shift (and some phonological reduction), up to now **mu** has maintained its basic verbal characteristics. Though one might want to speak of semantic reanalysis (Givón 1973), it does not seem appropriate to speak of a formal syntactic reanalysis.

However, this is not the case in all the languages under study. If both semantic shift and phonological reduction occur, the structure of the 'go' construction may no longer be obvious. In Krahn, except for a tonal remnant that occurs some of the time, there is no nominalizer present. Thus what was once clearly

$$S\ V_1\ [(O)\ V_2\ NOM]\ OBJ\ COMP$$

is now simply $S\ V_1\ (O)\ V_2$. In the second construction, the prime signal of the complement nature of $(O)V_2$ is missing. The semantic shift of the verb 'go' has also obscured the role of V_1. It now gives temporal information about the clause, while V_2 is expressing the main action of the clause. Other factors may also detract from the verbal status of 'go'. In Krahn it was shown that the imperfective marker, which is typically needed for a future reading, has in a sense "frozen"--it has become an obligatory part of the 'go' future construction. In Gbaeson Krahn, the imperfective pronoun must occur in the 'go' future construction.

(167) ǎ   mú dɛ́   dī   *ī́ mú dɛ́   dī
      I:IMP go thing eat   I go thing eat
      'I will eat.'

Thus, in this specific construction, 'go' can no longer be inflected for the imperfective/factative in this context. These facts leave the 'go' construction with an ambiguous structure. It could be interpreted in the old way, namely:

$$S\ V_1\ [(O)\ V_2]\ OBJ\ COMP$$

But given the semantic readings of V_1 and V_2 and the inability of 'go' to undergo inflection, it could easily be interpreted in another way, namely,

$$S\ AUX\ (O)\ V$$

This situation parallels one described by Henning Andersen in his article "Abductive and deductive change" (1973). Though the paper deals with phonological change, its applicability to historical syntax has been well attested (Timberlake 1977; D. Lightfoot 1979). He points out that one output may correspond to two grammatical structures.

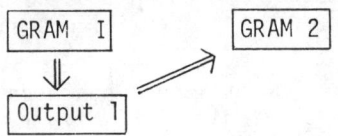

According to Andersen, a speaker observes a given output of another speaker's grammar and makes an abductive inference (he guesses what the grammar must be), thus constructing his own interpretation of the output. Once he has made his interpretation, his own grammar may lead him to produce a new sort of output different from the one he observed.

Coming back to the Krahn case, sentence 167:

ǎ   mū́ dɛ́   dī́   'I will eat.'
I:IMP go thing eat

may be interpreted in two ways. Older speakers may note the tone change on the final verb and interpret the sequence **dɛ di** as the complement of **mu**. Younger speakers will observe the same output and reinterpret the structure of the sentence as S AUX O V. On this basis, they may be led to produce a new output.

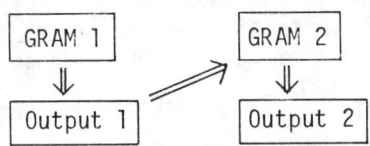

Most likely, the new interpretation would lead to the loss of tonal remnants which, it will be remembered, occur only on original high-tone verbs. Thus at this stage, reanalysis would be complete and subsequent generations would have only one interpretation of the construction: S AUX O V. It would appear that this is what has occurred in Tepo. The nominalizing particle has completely disappeared. The verb has lost its literal meaning and has even changed phonological shape. The construction as a whole may not be inflected for aspect. Given these changes, there appears to be only one possible interpretation of the structure (exemplified below) and that is S AUX O V.

(168) ɔ   mū́ sinema yé   **ɔɔ   mū́ sinema ye
       he FUT movie see   he:IMP
       'He'll see a movie.'

This kind of collapsing of complex structures into simpler ones has been attested in other language families (Li and Thompson 1974; Lord 1973; Givón 1975b).

The Emergence of Three Future Auxiliaries   117

Exceptionally in the Tepo case, the reanalysis of 'go' as a future marker has not been accompanied by the "freezing" of the imperfective marker as has occurred in Dewoin and Krahn.

It has already been noted that future auxiliaries in Kru carry modal as well as temporal information. Another factor which may have played a role in the verb-->auxiliary shift is the fact that second position is a very likely place for modal elements to appear. Steele (1975) notes that, cross-linguistically, modals typically appear in three positions: sentence-initial, sentence-second, and sentence-final (p.199). She notes that of these three, sentence-second position is the most common. She also points out that there is an overall "tendency for modals to occur toward the beginning of the sentence" (p. 215). Furthermore, the word order S MODAL O V is attested in several different language families in the world: Luiseno (Azteco-Tanoan), E. Ostyak (Ural-Ataic), Maidu (Penutian), Aranda and Walbiri (Australian). Thus, when in Kru, semantic bleaching of V_1, the reduction of NOM, and the consequent loss of the transparent structure

$$S\ V_1\ [O\ V_{2\ nom}]$$

complement led to a reinterpretation of S AUX O V (or S MOD O V), the reanalysis was a possible and natural change.

3.5.6 Double reanalysis. In Dewoin, it has been noted that there is an unusual form used to express the future. In this language, the future is indicated by two morphemes, both with the shape **mu** (Welmers 1977b).

(169) ɔ̄ɔ̄   mū   sāyɛ̀ pīī   mū   'He's going to cook meat.'
      he:PR FUT meat cook-NOM FUT

Though the structure looks somewhat different from the future constructions in the other Kru languages, there are several similarities. First, both future forms are homophonous with the verb 'go' as seen in its normal usage.

(170) ɔ nã̄   mu   'He has gone.'
      he PERF go

Second, it has been shown in chapter 2 that the long vowel pronominal form **ɔ̄ɔ̄** (labelled presumptive in 169) in Dewoin is actually a remnant of an unmarked pronoun and the Proto-Kru imperfective (IMP) marker ***a**. According to Welmers, this pronoun must be used in the future construction in Dewoin. This constraint parallels what has occurred in some Kru languages (such as Krahn), where the imperfective aspect has become an obligatory part of the future construction. Third, the construction parallels other Kru constructions in that the main verb appears to have been marked (at one time) as a nominalized verb. Thus, there is a low-tone remnant on the main verb (I have marked pronouns as IMP, conforming to my own analysis).

(171) nã   mu mɔ́ɔ gbuṵ̄   mu gàa
     I:IMP FUT rice pound-NOM FUT tomorrow
     'I will pound rice tomorrow.'

This analysis is confirmed when we consider the following sentence containing two nominalized verbs:

(172) ɔɔ   mu   ɔ   nuṵ̄   kpέὲ   mu
     he:IMP FUT it do-NOM learn-NOM FUT
     'He will learn to do it.'

In this construction, ɔ nuṵ̄ is the complement of kpε 'learn' while ɔ nuṵ̄ kpέὲ also appears to the complement of a verb. The question is--what verb?

This brings us to the main difference between the future construction in Dewoin and the 'go'-related future construction in other Kru languages. The striking difference, of course, is the fact that two **mu** forms occur. The sentence-second position **mu** appears to be playing the same role as in other languages. The presence of the second **mu** is, however, problematic. The **mu** could be, as Welmers suggests in his field notes, the noun 'inside', which often occurs with verbs as a kind of verbal particle in other Kru languages (see Marchese 1979:162-63). However, the noun 'inside' is usually realized on high tone: **mú**, and there is no reason, as far as I know, to consider this second **mu** as a tonal variation of the locative noun. The other possibility is that sentence-final **mu** is also the verb 'go'. Note, first, that it has the same tone as the verb **mu** 'go'. Besides this, there is other evidence lending support to this hypothesis.

In closely related Western languages, a similar construction exists. Hyman (1975:125) indicates the following construction in Klao:

(173) ɔ́ mú kɔ́ tὲ̃ mù   'He will go buy rice.'
      he FUT rice buy go

Note that with the exception of the low tone on the sentence-final **mu**, this example parallels the future construction in Dewoin. Another speaker of Klao, Bob Jacobs, offered the following as variants:

(174) ɔ **mu kɔ** na di mu   'He's going to eat the rice.'
      he go rice DEF eat go

(175) ɔ **mu kɔ** na di   'He's going to eat the rice.'
      he go rice DEF eat

I would claim that the future construction **mu...mu** in Dewoin arose from the expression 'going to go' rather than simply 'going to', as was the case in other Kru languages.

The Emergence of Three Future Auxiliaries   119

This kind of "double" reanalysis is not unknown in other languages. Lord (1976) makes a good case for double reanalysis in her paper "Evidence for syntactic reanalysis: from verb to complementizer in Kwa." First, Lord shows that languages often reanalyzed the verb 'say' as a complementizer, as seen in Ewe:

(176) **megblɔ bé mewɔe**   'I said that I did it.'
     I-say <u>say</u> I-did-it

However, she then points out that:

> Once a language has developed a new category, like preposition, or complementizer, the process does not necessarily stop. Verbs continue to become defective; meaning and syntactic properties are gradually "bleached" from more verbs leaving them to serve as function words (p. 183).

What happens is that once 'say' has been reanalyzed as a complementizer there is a need to reintroduce another verb 'say' to maintain the same meaning. This can be seen in Efik (Lord; Welmers 1968).

(177) **tíŋ nɔ̃ ẽyẽ ẽtẽ ké ńyé'dí**   'Tell him that I'll come.'
     tell give him <u>say</u> <u>say</u> I'll come

In this case, Lord claims that **te** is a "second generation" 'say' complementizer since it retains its prefix, while **ke** developed into a complementizer at an earlier time. Another case can be seen in Yoruba (p. 184). The first 'say' is the main verb; the forms **kpé** and **wí** are derived from verbs meaning 'say' and are now used as complementizers.

(178) **ó sɔ wí-kpé adé lɔ**   'He said that Ade went.'
     he say say-say Ade go

According to Lord's data, the reanalysis of the verb 'say' affects only one verb at a time. In the case of Dewoin, also, it is assumed that first there was a shift from literal meaning to temporal meaning in the first 'go' (** indicates proposed states).

    **ɔ̃ɔ̃   mu pií   'He will cook.'
     he:IMP go cook-NOM

Then, once this reanalysis occurred, the verb 'go' could be introduced to indicate motion.

    **ɔɔ   mu pií   muù 'He will go to cook.'
     he:IMP go cook-NOM go-NOM

Finally, the whole construction was reanalyzed as a future.

    **ɔɔ mu pií mu
     he will cook

Because **muu** was usually in sentence-final position, the nominalizing remnant was lost and the present-day future construction emerged.

(179) ɔɔ   mu   pií   mu   'He will cook.'
      he:IMP FUT cook-NOM FUT

There is good evidence that the second reanalysis really took place, since the construction **mu...mu** may now cooccur with the verb 'go' used in its literal motion sense.

(180) ɔ   mū   lé   mūù   mū   'He will go there.'
      he FUT there go-NOM FUT

Because the nominalizing particle on the last **mu** is gone, the complement-within-a-complement analysis cannot really be upheld synchronically. The best synchronic analysis might treat **mu ... mu** as a discontinuous morpheme, as Welmers and Mortvedt suggest.

The verb 'go' and its development along the verb-->auxiliary continuum has been studied in detail in this section. Because the shift is apparently recent (there is evidence that it is a change-in-progress), data are more readily available for this change than for auxiliaries which developed at an earlier time. In the remaining parts of this chapter, two other verbs which have also given rise to future auxiliaries will be studied: 'come' and 'have'. Following this, further innovations affecting the Kru future auxiliaries will be discussed.

3.6 The 'Come'-related Future Auxiliary

The 'come'-related future auxiliary is more widespread than the 'go'-related auxiliary just discussed in that it occurs in both Eastern and Western Kru. Chart II, which is repeated below as Chart IV, shows the relationship between the future auxiliary and the verb 'come' in several Eastern languages and in Western Tepo. It will be suggested that the 'come'-related auxiliary is an earlier development than the 'go'-related future.

Chart IV

	Neyo	Godié	Koyo	Bété	Lozoua Dida	Lakota Dida	Tepo
'come'	yi	yi	yi	yi	ci	yi	di
AUX	yi	yi	yi	yi	cɩ	yi	di

For examples of these morphemes, see sentences 14-20 in the beginning of this chapter.

3.6.1 Semantic shift

3.6.1.1 The 'come' > future shift in Kru. Basically, the same scenario as was proposed for the development of the 'go'-related

The Emergence of Three Future Auxiliaries

auxiliary is proposed for the 'come'-related auxiliary. Like 'go', 'come' also occurs in the S V_1 O V_2 nom COMPLEMENT construction. The same semantic shifts which were seen to affect the verb 'go' also affect the verb 'come'. To begin with, 'come' typically gets a literal reading. If there is a complex complement, it gets a purpose reading.

(181) Tchien Krahn

ɔ gi tɔ̃ dè̃ nā   'He comes (in order) to buy salt.'
he come salt buy NOM

(182) Wobé

ē jī-ɛ̄ kafé ple-a   'I came to sell coffee.'
I come-DEC coffee sell-NOM

As was the case with 'go', 'come' may be used with inanimate subjects. Thus, it may begin to take on a temporal/modal meaning, even while the nominalizing particle is still present. In the examples from Hansell (MS, p. 42) the subjects are inanimate and the verb itself does not refer to literal motion towards the speaker.

(183) pidɛ̄ gi kwɔ la   'The plantain is almost spoiled.'
plantain come spoil NOM

kòã gīi gwɛ̃ lā   'The work is almost finished.'
work come finish NOM

In Wobé, even though the subjects are animate, the reading is totally temporal.

(184) má dyī-ɛ̄ bia mū-a   'I will go to Abidjan.'
I:IMP come-DEC Abidjan go-NOM

(185) ɔ̃ɔ̃ dyī-ɛ̄ néá pō-a   'He is going to tell a story.'
he:IMP come-DEC story tell-NOM

Note that in each of these, the subject is in the imperfective form.

The construction may go through a period of ambiguity, where it refers either to literal motion or to inceptive action.

(186) Klao (Singler)

ɔɔ ji dɛ di   'He's coming to eat' or
he:IMP come thing eat   'He's about to eat.'

(187) Nyabwa

ī yī-e-ē   pō   kɔ̄bṵ nāmṵ́   'I have come in order to
I come-DECL-SUF plant rice NOM   plant rice' or 'I am
                                   about to plant rice.'

(188) Gbaeson Krahn

ɔ́ ɟí lá dɛ́   dí ā̄   'He's coming to eat' or
he come LOC thing eat NOM   'He's about to eat.'

(189) Sapo

ɔ ⁿdī kōō pī-ɛ̰̀   'She's coming to cook rice' or
she come rice cook-NOM 'She's about to cook rice.'

In example 189 I transcribed a prenasalized **d** in Sapo. I do not know the significance of this.

As was the case with 'go', the verb 'come' may eventually co-occur with itself, showing that at this point it is being used in a completely unambiguous way to indicate future actions.

(190) Borobo

ɔ́ dī gblà fí-á   dí-á 'She will come to cook rice.'
she come rice cook-NOM

(191) Kuwaa

ā dē ɟīi ɟī-nū   sana téí nū   'We will be coming
we be come come-NOM other time another day.'

In example 191 a 'come'-related future cooccurs with the periphrastic progressive construction (see sect. 2.3).

Again, as with 'go', 'come' may eventually appear in the consequent of conditions, with a nonambiguous future reading.

(192) Borobo

bɔ́   tɔ̂: gblà, ē dī lɔ́ fí-à   'If he buys rice,
COND-he buy rice I FUT it cook-NOM   I will cook it.'

3.6.1.2 The 'come' > future shift in other languages. In section 3.5.4, it was shown that the shift from 'go' to future marker has occurred in many nonrelated languages throughout the world. The same can be claimed for the verb 'come'. In fact, Welmers (1973: 354) notes that 'come'-related futures are more common in Niger-Congo languages than 'go'-related ones. The following languages also make use of 'come'-related futures.

The Emergence of Three Future Auxiliaries   123

Indo-European
  Romance
    Sursilvan Rhetian : come + INF > future (Reighard 1976:511)
Finno-Ugric
    Finnish : come > FUT   (Givón 1973; Anttila 1972)
Niger-Congo
  Mandé
    Malinke (Migeod 1911:217)
      a be <u>na</u> mita   'He will take.'
      he be <u>come</u> take

    Vai (Welmers, pers.com.)
      à bɛ̀ <u>ná</u> nà kéŋ sɔ́ nà   'He is going to
      he PROG <u>come</u> at house build at   build a house.'

    Kpelle (Welmers 1973:354)
      a <u>pâi</u> 'kêi   'He's going to do it.'
      he <u>came</u> it-do-NOM

  <u>Kwa</u>
    Akan (Welmers 1973:353-54)[6]
      ɔ́ -bɛ́-bá   ɔ́ -bɔ́-kɔ́
      he FUT come   he FUT go
    'He's going to come.' 'He's going to go.'

  Benue-Congo
    Wàpã (Jukun) (Welmers 1973:354)
      ku ri bi ya   'He's going to go.'
      he PROG <u>come</u> go

    Efik (Welmers 1973:354-55)
      ń-dî-dêp m̀bōrō   'I'm going to buy bananas.'
      I-<u>come</u>-buy bananas

---

[6] When the Akan verb **ba** 'come' is used to indicate future actions, it undergoes vowel harmony and a rounded-unrounded agreement. Thus, there are four variants: bɛ́, bé, bɔ́, and bó (Welmers, pers.com.). This parallels the findings discussed in section 3.5.3.2, where it was noted that it is the innovated form which tends to undergo phonological change.

Bantu

Luganda (Welmers 1973:355)

<u>àjjá</u>   kúgéndá   'He is going to go (sometime).'
he-<u>come</u> INF-go   (indefinite future)

Pidgins and Creoles

Liberian English (J. Singler, pers.com.)
it's coming to rain   she's coming to eat
'It's about to rain.'   'She's about to eat.'

3.6.1.3 'Come'-derived past and future tenses. Interestingly enough, Givón (1973:917) suggests that it is more common for 'come' to give rise to past tense markers than to future markers. In French, the verb 'come' is used to indicate a just-completed action.

il <u>vient</u> de partir   'He just left.'
he <u>come</u> from leave-INF

He notes the following correlation between motion in space and progress in time:

come -----> speaker's place -----> go
past -----> speaker's place -----> future

Indeed, in Kru, some languages do make use of a verb meaning 'come' to express past action.

(193) Klao (Singler)

ɔ <u>dɛ</u>   dɛ   di   'He just ate.' (literally:
he <u>come</u> thing eat   he came from eating)

(194) Nyabo

ɔ <u>wɔ</u> gblà pi-ɛ   'She's been cooking rice.'
she <u>come</u> rice cook-NOM

(195) Lakota Dida

ɔ̃ <u>wlɛ́</u> pɔ̃tɔ̃   yóonyu pi-dʌ̃ʌ̃   'She just fixed
she <u>come</u> just-now soup   fix-place   the sauce.'

However, it is important to note that typically in Kru, there are two lexical items: 'come to' and 'come from'.

	Klao	Godié	Nyabo	Sapo	Lakota Dida
'come from'	dɛ	6à	wɔ	suɛ̀	wlɛ́
'come to'	ɟi	yi	yi	dĩ	yĩ

The Emergence of Three Future Auxiliaries   125

(196) Godié

    ɔ yī   sukú   ɔ 6ā   sukú
    'He came to school.'   'He came from school.'
    he come-to:FACT school   he come-from: school
                                              FACT

In Kru, it is the verb 'come to' which typically gives rise to
a future auxiliary, while the verb 'come from' gives rise to a
past auxiliary. Note that both 'come'-related auxiliaries indicate
nonpresent action. Thus, in many Kru languages, the expression
"come to X" (motion with a purpose) has been reinterpreted as a
simple immediate future 'is about to'.

3.6.1.4 The correlation between the 'come'-related future and the imperfective. It was noted in the section on 'go' that there is a correlation between the imperfective aspect and the future. The correlation is not so regular for the verb 'come'. It is most often the case that the verb 'come' is interpreted as a future modal when it is imperfective. This can be seen by comparing the following two sentences from Gbaeson Krahn. It is only the imperfective form which can be interpreted both in a future and in a literal sense, while the factative may only be interpreted literally. Note that since the imperfective/perfective distinction has been neutralized on the third person pronouns in Krahn, the only indication of aspect is the sequential auxiliary in 198. The presence of this auxiliary forces a completive (perfective) reading in this example.

(197) ɔ jī̀ lá dɛ́   dī ā   'He's coming to eat.' or
      he come LOC thing eat NOM   'He's about to eat.'

(198) ɔ jī̀ ɔ yě dɛ́   dī   'He came in order to eat.'
      he come he SEQ thing eat

Note that this is also the case in Wobé:

(199) mà̀ jī̄-ɛ̄   bia   mū-à̀   'I am going to Abidjan.'
      I:IMP come-DEC Abidjan go-NOM

(200) ế jī̄-ɛ̄   káfé   plḗ-à̀   'I came to sell coffee.'
      I come-DEC coffee sell-NOM

The same correlation can be noted in Godié, where the future marker has the imperfective rather than the factative form.

(201) ɔ yī̀   'He's coming.'
      he come:IMP

(202) ɔ yi   'He came.'
       he come:FACT

(203) ɔ yī lɨ   'He will eat.'
       he AUX eat

Exceptionally in Nyabwa, it is apparently the factative form which is giving rise to a future reading, as seen in 187 repeated here.

(187) ı̋ yī-e̋-e̋   kɔ̀bū pō   nām̋ʋ   'I have come in order to plant rice' or 'I am about to plant rice.'
       I come-DECL-SUF rice plant NOM

3.6.1.5 'Come' future > obligation.

As the 'go'-related future auxiliary underwent semantic extension to express obligation, so the 'come'-related future also extends beyond reference to immediate future actions. In Godié, the 'come'-related auxiliary is often used to express capacity (thus its label POTENTIAL). It may also have a kind of hortative (obligatory) flavor, as seen in sentence 206.

(204) ɔ yi dú   mʉ   'He will go to town.'
       he POT town go

(205) ɔ yi nā̀ā̀   'He can walk.'
       he POT walk

(206) ʌ̃̋ yi nɔnʋ zlɛ   'You will work!'
       you POT work do   (i.e., you must)

The same shift from future to a sort of hortative occurs in Tepo.

(207) ā̰ di gblā nḭ̄ di   'We should eat rice.'
       we FUT rice PART eat

3.6.2 Phonological change

3.6.2.1 Phonological reduction.

In regard to the reduction of the nominalizing particle, the same scenario that was proposed for 'go' is proposed for 'come'. I have argued that the nominalizing particle has a tendency to reduce, especially when the semantic shift has been great. It may, however, remain intact when it refers to literal motion. This appears to have been the case in Tepo and Godié. In these languages, the nominalizing particle is not present when 'come' has a future reading, but it is obligatory when it has a literal reading.

(208) Godié

   ɔ yi lɨ   ɔ yi lɨ kʌ̃
   he AUX eat   he come eat NOM
   'He will eat.'   'He's coming to eat.'

(209) Tepo

ɔ́ dī ŋa ní nyrē   ń dayú   ń di yē wɔ̄
he AUX T PART arrive my brother(FOC) I come see NOM
'He will arrive tomorrow.'   'It's my brother I came to see.'

There is not as much evidence as was presented for 'go' that there was a nominalizing particle following the verb 'come'. The lack of remnants is believed to be a result of the early development of the auxiliary, however (cf. 3.6.4).

3.6.2.2 Change of phonological shape. There is only one attested case of a 'come'-related AUX which has a different shape from the verb 'come'. According to data supplied by Gratrix, the potential future marker in Lozoua Dida is **cɪ** while the verb 'come' is **ci**. This change in shape parallels what was seen in the 'go'-derived futures—it is the element which has undergone semantic shift and/or grammaticalization which changes shape rather than the source verb. Also it is interesting to note that when there is a shift, again it is a shift to the unmarked retracted form of the vowel (i--->ɪ).

3.6.3 Reanalysis. In languages where the semantic shift has been great and phonological reduction or change has caused a contrast to arise between the future construction and the purpose-oriented 'come' construction, 'come' has been reanalyzed as belonging to a new category, AUX. Except for Vata, this appears to have occurred in all the Eastern languages for which data is available: Godié, Neyo, Lozoua Dida, and Bété, as well as Western Tepo. In Nyabwa and Tchien, it appears that in spite of the semantic shifts which have occurred, 'come' is still functioning primarily as a verb.

3.6.4 Relative age of the 'go'- and 'come'-derived future auxiliaries. It has been shown that a 'come'-related future has a widespread distribution, occurring in almost all Eastern languages and in some Western languages. Further, there is some evidence of a 'come'-related future in Kuwaa, one of the Kru isolates (see example 191). On the other hand, 'go'-related futures occur only in Western Kru. Also, in Niger-Congo as a whole, 'come'-related futures are more common than 'go'-related ones (Welmers 1973:354). These facts suggest that the 'come'-related future is much older than the one related to 'go'. Crucial evidence comes from the negative future forms.

In Kru, one typical way to negate a sentence is by auxiliary (see chapter 4 for more discussion of negation strategies). Thus, a sentence with the basic order SVO will be negated by a clause S NEG-AUX O V. This can be seen in:

(210) ɔ di dɛ   'He ate something.'
     he eat thing

(211) ɔ se dɛ   di   'He didn't eat anything.'
      he NEG thing eat

In some languages where 'go'-related morphemes indicate future action, the clause is negated in the same way; that is, the verb 'go' appears at the end of the clause, a negative auxiliary occurs in sentence-second position, and the object complement of 'go' (OV) occurs between the negative auxiliary and 'go'.

(212) affirmative

    ɔ mu dɛ   di   'He will eat.'
    he go thing eat
    S AUX O   V
    S V   O

(213) negative

    ɔ se dɛ   di   mu   'He will not eat.'
    he NEG thing eat go
    S AUX   O   V

Negative future constructions have the same shape in both Bassa and Gbaeson Krahn. Compare:

(214) Bassa

    ɔ nyu kṹã̀   ɔ se kṹã̀ nyu
    he do work   he NEG work do
    'He worked.'   'He didn't work.'

    ɔ mu kṹã̀ nyu-ɛ   ɔ se kṹã́ nyu-ɛ mu
    he go work do-NOM   he NEG work do-NOM go
    'He will work.'   'He will not work.'

(215) Krahn

    ɔ di dɛ   ɔ se dɛ   di
    he eat thing   he NEG thing eat
    'He ate.'   'He didn't eat.'

    ɔ mu dbū̄́ cɛ̃   ɔ́ sé dbū̄́ cɛ̃ ḿ
    he FUT rope cut   he NEG rope cut FUT
    'He will cut rope.'   'He will not cut rope.'

Note that in Krahn **mú** (FUT) reduces to **ḿ** in sentence-final position.

The Emergence of Three Future Auxiliaries   129

Thus in Klao, Bassa, and Gbaeson Krahn, 'go'-related futures are negated by the following structure:

S se O V mu

Though **mu** is giving temporal information, it is being negated like a full verb. However, in several Western languages where **mu** is found in the affirmative future, it is not found in the negative form. Instead, a morpheme **i** or **yi** occurs in its place. This is the case in Wobé, Dewoin, Tchien Krahn, and Nyabwa.

(216) Wobé

    ɔ sē dɛ̄ dī ī   ɔ sē gbǒ pō ī
    he NEG thing eat FUT   he NEG house build FUT
    'He will not eat.'   'He will not build a house.'

(217) Dewoin

    ná sē jī ī là   'I will not come here.'
    I-INC NEG come FUT here

(218) Tchien (Hansell)

    ɔ sēē plè-ī   'He will not run.'
    he NEG run-FUT

(219) Nyabwa

    ɔ sēé súkō lī yī   'He will not eat fufu.'
    he NEG fufu eat FUT

In the preceding examples, the **i** or **yi** morpheme has been glossed FUTURE since it is the only part of the sentence which differentiates it from the negative factative. Compare the following sentences from Wobé:

(220) ɔ sē dɛ̄ dī   'He didn't eat.'
    he NEG thing eat

(221) ɔ sē dɛ̄ dī ī   'He will not eat.'
    he NEG thing eat FUT

Given the position of the **i** marker, **i** could be either a remnant of a nominalizing particle which occurred in the structure

$$S\ V_1[OV_2\ _{nom}]$$

or as a verb with a complex complement OV: S AUX OV V.

The latter interpretation seems to be the correct one. This becomes clear when sentences containing **i** or **yi** are compared with negative sentences containing the 'go' morpheme.

(222) Klao
    ɔ se dɛ cɛ́ **mu**   'He won't learn anything.'
    he NEG thing learn <u>FUT(go)</u>

(223) Wobé
    ɔ̃ sē dɛ̄ dī ī   'He won't eat anything.'
    he NEG thing eat <u>FUT</u>

Furthermore, the form of the future marker **i/yi** indicates that it may be related to the verb 'come'.

	NEG FUT	COME
Wobé	i	ji
Tchien Krahn	i or ī	gi
Dewoin	i	ji
Nyabwa	yi	yi

The reduction of **ji**, **gi**, or **yi** to **i** is, of course, not surprising, given its position in the clause. Note that in Krahn negatives (see example 215), the morpheme **mú** reduces to **ḿ** in this position. Furthermore, cases of CV morphemes reducing to V in sentence-final position have been attested elsewhere in Kru (see sect. 3.5.3.1).

Given this evidence, it seems very likely that the negative future construction in Wobé, Tchien Krahn, Nyabwa, and Dewoin actually comes from this construction:

    S   NEG   (O)   V   <u>come</u>

    'S is not coming to V' or
    'S does not come to V'

If this proposal is correct, it means that Wobé, Tchien Krahn, Nyabwa, and Dewoin all had 'come'-related futures at one time. At present, however, the 'go'-related auxiliary is the primary means of expressing the future in these languages (except in Wobé, where there is what appears to be a 'come'-related future; see section 3.8.4). How did this situation develop? It would appear that at an earlier stage, all Kru languages had a 'come'-related future auxiliary. At some point in time, however, a 'go'-related auxiliary emerged. The two types of futures coexisted over a period of time. This situation is presently attested in Tepo, where both 'come'-related and 'go'-related futures exist. Not much is known about the semantic difference between the two, but the glosses suggest that 'go' signals a more immediate action while 'come' signals a more potential future (examples from Dawson).

The Emergence of Three Future Auxiliaries   131

(224) Tepo

yruwle   mṹ   kayú gbo   pa   'Chameleon is about
chameleon AUX(go) house under enter   to enter the house.'

a   di   a   kle   hʋa   'We will ask for his strength.'
we AUX his strength ask

This type of coexistence of competing forms has been attested in other language families in the world (Li and Thompson 1974 [Chinese]; Vroman 1977 [Latin, Portuguese]; Labov 1971 [Pidgin]), as well as in other contexts in the Kru family (see sects. 2.2.2.3 and 6.2.2). While the coexistence of the two forms continued in Tepo, it would appear that in Wobé, Tchien Krahn, Dewoin, and Bassa, the 'go'-related future "won out" over the 'come'-related one. This is evident from the fact that in the affirmative, the main signal of future action is the auxiliary **mu** (< 'go'). However, the 'come'-related future was retained in the negative construction. This means that the 'go'-related future has not yet begun to affect negative clauses. These data confirm Givón's (1975a) claim that negative structures are the most conservative, in that innovations reach them only after having affected affirmative clauses. It is interesting to note that in Gbaeson Krahn, where **mu** has really achieved full auxiliary status, it does occur in the negative.

(225) ɔ̃   sẽ   dɛ́   dĩ   mú/m̃   'He will not eat.'
      he NEG thing eat   FUT

It was shown that in Dewoin, the future is 'go'-related, while the negative form seems to retain a 'come'-related morpheme. Interestingly enough, there is apparently a change currently under way which may eventually lead to the loss of the 'come'-related negative future. Bai Boikai, the young consultant with whom Welmers and Mortvedt worked, volunteered two negative future constructions while working with me: the 'come'-related one (noted by Welmers and Mortvedt) and another, containing the morpheme 'go'.

(226) ɔ   se   sayɛ̃   pi   yi   'He will not cook meat.'
      he NEG meat cook FUT(come)

(227) ɔ   se   sayɛ   pi   mu   'He will not cook meat.'
      he NEG meat cook FUT(go)

It is the second construction that is clearly innovative. Unlike Wobé, the construction cannot be misconstrued as having a literal meaning since in Dewoin a **na** nominalizer must be present for this to be the case:

(228) ɔ   se   sayɛ̃ pi   nã̄   mu yi   'He will not go in order
      he NEG meat cook NOM go FUT   to cook meat.'

The Dewoin case is particularly interesting because it too shows two coexisting forms: a conservative 'come'-related future negative and an innovative 'go'-related future negative. It is expected that with time, the negative form which makes use of the "old" negative marker **i/yi** will eventually give way to the more transparently relatable forms containing the 'go'-derived morpheme.

(229) affirmative

    ɔ mu sayɛ̄ pi-ī   mu   'He will cook meat.'
    he FUT meat cook-NOM FUT

(230) negative

    ɔ se sayɛ̄ pi   mu   'He will not cook meat.'
    he NEG meat cook FUT

I do not have an explanation for why the nominalizing marker on the main verb is gone, nor why only one **mu** occurs in this form.

What became of the 'come'-related futures in the other Western languages? In a later discussion (3.8.3) it will be shown that in some languages, the 'come'-related future was reanalyzed as a conditional and/or sequential auxiliary. In some languages (like Tchien Krahn), it appears to be the case that a new 'come'-related future is being reintroduced through periphrasis. This can be seen in the following examples:

(231) 'go'-related future in the affirmative

    ɔ mu gw̃lɔ̃ mu   'He will go to town.'
    he FUT town go

(232) 'come'-related remnant in the negative

    ɔ se gw̃lɔ̃ mui   'He will not go to town.'
    he NEG town go-FUT

(233) 'come'-related future is reintroduced through periphrasis

    nī gī plṹ-ā   'The water is about to boil.'
    water come boil-NOM

To sum up, it has been suggested that the 'come'-related future auxiliary is older than the 'go'-related one. Evidence includes the fact that the 'come'-related auxiliary is found in both Eastern and Western Kru, while the 'go'-related auxiliary occurs as a full auxiliary only in Western Kru. It was also shown that there are remnants of a 'come' morpheme in the negative futures of several languages. In section 3.8.3.3, more evidence will be given supporting the fact that 'come' was used as an auxiliary long before the 'go'-related future arose.

3.7 The 'Have'-related Future Auxiliary

The 'have'-related auxiliary is found mainly in Eastern Kru. It typically has the shape **ka** or **kʌ**, with low or mid tone as a verb, and high tone as an auxiliary. Chart V repeats the forms for 'have' and its related auxiliary:

Chart V

	Neyo	Godié	Lakota Dida	Vata	Bété	Koyo
AUX	ká	kʌ́	ká	ká	kʌ́	ka
'have'	ka	kʌ	kā	ka	kʌ	ka

Examples of both the auxiliary and verbal use of these morphemes can be seen in sentences 21-25 in the beginning of this chapter.

3.7.1 The development of the 'have' auxiliaries. It is assumed that the 'have'-related auxiliaries developed in much the same way as the 'come'- and 'go'-related auxiliaries, though there is one striking difference: in the development of the 'go' and 'come' auxiliaries, there was always a stage when the source construction had a literal (motion) sense. Then the construction passed through an ambiguous stage, where it had both a literal and an aspectual-modal reading. In the case of 'have', however, it seems that the initial construction had a nonliteral meaning right from the beginning. In the typical "S have [(O) V$_{nom}$]" structure of the following examples, the construction as a whole means 'be obliged to' and never 'to be in possession of'.[7]

---

[7] Paralleling these nominalized constructions are structures containing sentential complements. They get the same reading 'to be obligated to'. The structures vary from language to language. In Tepo, Klao, and Grebo, the embedded clause is introduced by the particle **b-**.

Tepo

ā kɔ́ b-ā pō kayū
we have that-we build house
'We have to build a house.'

Klao

ɔ kɔ b-ɔ mú nī tó ná
he has that-he go LOC store DEF
'He has to go to the store.'

In Godié, Dewoin, Koyo, and Bassa, there is no **b-** particle present. The verb 'have' is directly followed by the embedded sentence. Typically, the second sentence has an auxiliary in it, indicating purpose.

Bassa

ɔ 6édé ɔ kē-ɛ nyu
he has he AUX-it do
'He has to do it.'

Koyo (Kokora)

Abi ka o ka bɔgɔ ciya
Abi has he AUX book learn
'Abi must learn to read and write.'

In all languages with these constructions, there is never EQUI-NP deletion.

(234) Tepo
 ã **kɔ̃** kayū a pupué   'We have to
 we have house ASSOC build-NOM   build a house.'

(235) Grebo
 ne **kɔ** London mu-ɛ   'I have to go to London.'
 I have London go-NOM

(236) Klao (Nifu)
 ɔ **kɔ̃** dɛ pipiɛ sɔnati   'It's her turn to
 she has thing cook-NOM today   cook today.'

The verb used in the following constructions does designate possession, however, when followed by a simple NP:

(237) Grebo
 ne **kɔ** bla   'I have rice.'
 I have rice

(238) Tepo
 yū **kɔ** tɔ   'The child has wisdom.'
 child has wisdom

(239) Klao (Nifu)
 ɔ **kɔ̃** fãkã   'He owns a knife.'
 he own knife

In some of the languages mentioned, there are two verbs translated as 'have'. One verb means 'to own (permanently)', and the other, an innovative form, means 'to have in one's possession (for a time)'. The form 'have in one's possession' is probably innovative, coming from the verb 'to seize' and 'take'. It appears to be a Western innovation, occurring in Klao, Tchien Krahn, Gbaeson Krahn, and Guéré. It seems that the **kV** stem has been lost in Nyabwa, Wobé, and Grand Bassa, and the innovative **ble** stem has been adopted for all forms of 'have' (compare Givón (1971a:175) who notes that 'grab' or 'hold' often develops into the verb 'have'). The contrast can be seen in the following examples:

(240) Klao (Nifu)
 ɔ **kɔ̃** fãkã   ɔ **ble** fãkã
 he own knife   he has knife
 'He owns a knife.'   'He has a knife.'

(241) Gbaeson Krahn

ɔ kɔ̃ tṹ   ɔ blɛ́ ã́ tṹ
he own hammer   he has my hammer
'He owns a hammer.'   'He has my hammer.'

In such languages, it is the verb kɔ, meaning 'own' or 'possess', which is typically used to express obligation in these periphrastic constructions. As will be seen later, however, in languages where the kɔ form has been lost, the innovative verb **ble** may itself take on an obligation reading.

In the Western languages discussed, though 'have' does indicate obligation (and has shifted away from its literal meaning), it still acts very much like a verb. It takes a nominalized complement as would any other verb. These same nominalized constructions may occur in subject position, as in sentence 242 from Grebo.

(242) **du-ɛ**   yakla ne   'Pounding is difficult.'
      pound-NOM hard is

In contrast, in Eastern Kru, 'have'-related forms appear to be completely reanalyzed as auxiliaries. They do not inflect for aspect, and in most cases there is no nominalizing suffix, as can be seen in an earlier example from Godié.

(21) ɔ kʌ̃ sʌ pɩ   'He is going to lie down.'
     he AUX down lie

There is at least one Eastern language, however, with forms suggesting that a nominalizing particle was once present in the Eastern group. In Vata, the **ka** nominalizing particle typically follows complex complements of such verbs as 'come' and 'go'.

(243) ń mlɛ pó   ka   'I am going to lie down.'
      I go lie-down NOM

Interestingly enough, it may also optionally follow clauses containing the 'have'-related auxiliary.

(244) ɔ́ ká-ua nyli   ka   'When she arrived at
      she AUX-T arrive ka   the village ...'

(245) ɔ́ na gúgué ɔ́ ká ɔ́ dĕ-bi ka   'Running, he went
      he run   he AUX her embrace ka   to embrace her.'

(The past tense reading of these future auxiliaries will be discussed in 3.8.1.) Thus, it would appear that though the development of the 'have' source construction differed slightly from the 'go' and 'come' sources (by not having an ambiguous stage), the other stages were essentially the same: semantic shift, loss of nominalizer, and loss of verbal characteristics of the main (second position) verb.

It is interesting to note that in Bassa and Nyabwa, where the 'have' morpheme **kV** has apparently disappeared and been replaced by the innovative **6le**, a morpheme similar to the older 'have' morpheme **ka** is found in temporal clauses.

In Nyabwa, **kā** behaves just like an auxiliary.

(246) ē **kā** kɔ̄bō-ō̄ pō,   nī-ī̄   16ā-à-ō̄
    you AUX rice-DEF plant, water-IMP fall-SUF
    'When you plant the rice, the rain falls.'

In Bassa, however, the **ka** morpheme is followed by a nominalized verb and thus looks as if it is functioning syntactically as a full verb (Hobley 1965:43).

(247) ɔ **kàà** dyi-ɛ   'When he came, ...'
    he   come-NOM

While at first glance these forms do not appear to be future auxiliaries, it will later be seen (3.8.1) that occurrence in temporal clauses is one of the discourse functions of **ka** 'have'-related future auxiliaries. It would appear, then, that the morpheme **ka** 'have' was used in both Nyabwa and Bassa in a nonliteral way before it disappeared from use as a regular verb meaning 'to possess'. This form was conserved in subordinate clauses, while another verb, **ble** 'have', was innovated for use in main clauses.

Another form in both of these languages also looks as if it could have been 'have'-derived. In both Bassa and Nyabwa, there is an auxiliary **ke** which expresses unrealized action. In Nyabwa, the auxiliary clearly expresses a projective future (Bentinck, field notes).

(248) ī̄ **ke** kɔ̄bū̄ pū̄   'I will plant rice.'
    I PROJ rice plant

The same auxiliary occurs in Bassa, but is apparently restricted to occurring in the second of two clauses. It is sometimes used to indicate purpose, and it sometimes occurs in clauses functioning as sentential complements (examples from Hobley).

(249) ɔ mu ɔ **kḗ-ɛ**   nyu   'He goes to do it.'
    he go he AUX-it   do

(250) ɔ 6édē ɔ **kḗ-ɛ** nyu   'He has to do it.'
    he has   he AUX-it   do

In the Kru language isolate Sɛmɛ, there is also a **ke** auxiliary which has a distribution strikingly similar to Bassa **ke**.

    n ši   **n ke dɛ**   'I lay down in order to sleep.'
    I lie-down I AUX sleep

The **ke** auxiliary in Sɛmɛ also is used to indicate sequential action:

    n ši   **n ke dɛɛ**   'I lay down and went to sleep.'
    I lie-down I <u>ke</u> sleep

The details of the development of such a **ke** auxiliary have not been worked out, but it seems quite possible that a verb **ka** or **kɔ** 'have', in combination with an **e** imperfective marker, could have given rise to a **kē** future auxiliary. The fact that both 'have' and the imperfective marker (designating unrealized actions) have been linked to futures would lend support to such a hypothesis.

Now the naturalness of the have > obligation shift will be discussed.

3.7.2 Semantic shifts

3.7.2.1 'Have' as an expression of obligation. It has been seen that from the beginning the construction containing 'have' indicates obligation rather than physical possession (examples 234-236). This metaphoric use of the verb 'have' is very common in languages of the world.

Indo-European

    Romance

        French   **Qu'est-ce que tu <u>as</u> à faire?**
                           what-is-it that you <u>have</u> to do-INF
                           'What do you have to do today?'

        Spanish   **Tengo que pagar-la**   'I have to pay her.'
                           I-have that pay-her

        Latin   **venir <u>habes</u>**   'You have to come.'
                           come <u>have</u>

    Germanic

        English   I <u>have</u> to wash my hair today.'
                         (have + INF = must)

Niger-Congo

Kwa

Yoruba (Welmers 1973:341-42)

mo ní l'átí lọ	cf.	mo ní bàtà
<u>have</u>		I <u>have</u> shoes
'I have to go.'		'I have shoes.'

Benue-Congo

Efik (Welmers 1973:342)

ḿmé'yéné ńdíkǎ   'I have to go.'
I-<u>get</u>   INF-go

Quechua

Ecuadorian Quechua (Muysken 1977:69)

rura-na ka-ni   'I have to work.'
work-NOM be-I:SING

As in many languages in the world, Quechua expresses possession by the expression Y be-at X (X has Y). Thus, though there is not a single morpheme 'have' or 'possess', the concept of possession is still used to express obligation.

3.7.2.2 'Have' > future. It has been suggested that it is fairly common for a verb denoting possession to be used to express obligation. However, in examples 21-25 we see that the 'have'-related auxiliary most often refers to future actions. This suggests that the following shifts have occurred: possession > obligation > future. Evidence for this shift comes from Neyo where 'have'-related auxiliaries have both a hortative reading and an inceptive reading (at least at the time Thomann was writing in 1905).

(251) ō **ka** li   'He should eat' (<u>qu'il mange</u>) or 'He's be-
    he <u>AUX</u> eat   ginning to eat' (<u>il commence à manger</u>).

The development from obligation to a future appears to be fairly common.[8] Similar shifts supposedly occurred as Latin changed into its daughter languages (Givón 1973; Vroman 1977).

---

[8] This claim contrasts sharply with the stand taken by Benveniste. In his discussion of the have-->future shift which occurred in Latin, he notes (1968:90):

> It follows from this construction that habēre did not mean 'have to', as in Fr. **j'ai à travailler**, Eng. <u>I have to work</u>, a meaning which would never have yielded the future **je travaillerai** and which in fact clashes so sharply with it that, now as before, **j'ai à travailler** is never confused with **je travaillerai**, ...

The Emergence of Three Future Auxiliaries

Latin > French

venire habes	>	**(tu) viendras**
come have		(you) come FUT
'You have to come.'		'You will come.'

Latin > Portuguese

cantare habeo	>	**cantarei**
sing INF FUT I		
'I will sing.'		

Sardinian (Reighard 1976)

must + INF > FUTURE

The same semantic extension occurs in Nyabo. For the English sentence 'He will go to Pleebo', two clauses were offered: one using the periphrastic 'go' and the other using 'have' followed by a sentential complement.

(252) ɔ mī plìibō mū-ɛ   'He will go to Pleebo.'
      he go:IMP Pleebo go-NOM

(253) ɔ kɔ̀ b-ɔ mū plìibō   'He will go to Pleebo.'
      he has that-he go Pleebo

Thus what presumably began as an expression of obligation is now being used as a future. Furthermore, it is the 'have'-related, rather than the 'go'-related future which is preferred in the consequent of conditionals.

(254) PREF bɛnɔ b-ɔ   mu plìibō ɔ kɔ̀ b-ɔ tɔ̀ɔ̄ nī
            if that-he go Pleebo he has that-he buy-me fish
            'If he goes to Pleebo, he will buy me fish.'

   ACCEPTED ... ɔ mī   nīi tõã
             he go:IMP fish buy-NOM

This viewpoint does not seem to hold, given the Kru facts (e.g., Neyo just seen) where 'have' does give rise to both an obligation 'should' and an inceptive future 'beginning to'. The data show that have + V very clearly gives rise to an expression of obligation. This may eventually give rise to the future. What appears to have occurred in the Latin case is that the construction verb + have did give rise to a future. The later construction J'ai a V-INF appears to be a recent periphrastic innovation.

Further evidence that 'have' has been reanalyzed (at least from a semantic point of view) into a future is that another construction has developed to express obligation.

(255) ɔ 6lê yē̄ b-ɔ   tɔ̀ɔ̄ nī   'He must/is supposed
    he have ? that-he buy fish   to buy fish.'

The language consultant could not readily identify the verb 6lɛ, but it is obviously a cognate with **ble** which, we have seen, means 'to have in one's immediate possession for a time' in many other Western languages. It appears that once the **kɔ** form of 'have' was reanalyzed as a future, a void was left in the system. Therefore, another periphrastic construction with a new 'have' morpheme came into being. This development parallels Lord's (1976) examples from Ewe and Efik, where reanalysis of the verb 'say' into a complementizer has caused the introduction of a new lexical item.

3.7.2.3 'Have' > volitional. In Godié, the 'have'-related morpheme has a volitional or desiderative meaning as well as a future reading.

(256) ɔ kʌ̄ sʌ pι   'He's going to/wants to lie
    he VOL down lie   down.'

Also, in Neyo, the 'have'-related future is often translatable as 'want'. (The following sentences were translated by Claire Grah, a native speaker of Neyo and herself a linguist):

(257) Gla slo kɔkɔ mã   ɔ kã klã koklo mo
    Gla tell kɔkɔ that he AUX bush far go
    'Gla told Kɔkɔ that he wants to go far into the bush.'

(258) ɔ kã sã po   'She wants to lie down.'
    she VOL down lie

It is not known exactly how this shift took place. The ordering could have been (1) have > obligation > future > volitive or (2) have > obligation > volitive > future. Sequence (1) seems more likely, however, since there is evidence from Neyo that the 'have'-related auxiliary first had obligatory and inceptive meaning (as reported by Thomann 1905), and seems to have developed a volitive reading only recently (as seen in examples 255-256).

Godié seems to have taken the semantic shift one step farther. In Godié, the 'have'-related auxiliary carries no meaning of obligation whatsoever. It now expresses only desire, volition, and the future.

This shift in meaning has left a gap in the system, and the verb 'have' has been reintroduced in a periphrastic construction to fill this gap. This can be seen in the following examples from the Kagbo dialect:

The Emergence of Three Future Auxiliaries   141

(259) ɔ **ká** ɔ **ká** sáká 6lɨ   'He has to pound rice.'
      he has he FUT rice pound

(260) ɔ **ká** sáká 6lɨ-lɪ   'He has to pound rice.'
      he has rice pound-NOM

It is interesting to note that in these examples, the sentential complement of the verb 'have' contains the original 'have'-derived auxiliary **ká**.

The reanalysis is complete, then, since the reanalyzed element cooccurs with itself. A similar phenomenon has occurred in Koyo.

(261) **A6i ha** o **ka** bɔgʊ ciya   'Abi must learn to read
      Abi has he AUX book learn   and write.'

Thus, where reanalysis has been complete, languages may either "reinvent" a periphrastic construction with the old verb 'have', as has occurred in Kagbo and Koyo, or they may develop a new verb for the construction, as was the case in Nyabo.

3.7.2.4 'Have' > customary. Another semantic shift has been observed in Kuwaa, the Kru language isolate in Liberia, where a **ka** morpheme expresses customary action (Welmers, field notes).

(262) mà **ka** bɛ̀   'I usually go.'
      I   go

Evidently this morpheme behaves like an auxiliary. More research may reveal that 'have' may have developed a reading expressing 'customary' in other Kru languages.[9]

3.7.3 Phonological change in the auxiliary. It has been shown that there is a link between 'have' and future auxiliaries in several languages. In at least five of the cases of reanalysis (Godié, Lakota Dida, Vata, Neyo, and Bété), the future auxiliary is realized on a different tone from that of the main verb:

	AUX	VERB
Godié	kʌ́	kʌ̄ or kʌ̀
Dida	ká	kā
Vata	ká	kā�
Bété	kʌ́	kʌ̄
Neyo	ká	kā

---

9 Compare the following idiomatic expression from Bakwé:

   ɔ ka yeyejlʉpa   'He is always dancing.'
   he has dance-dance-work
   (French translation given to me: Il ne fait que danser.)

Note that all auxiliaries have high tone. If we consider forms from other Kru languages, it becomes clear that the verb 'have' never has a high tone. Compare:

Gbaeson Krahn	kɔ̀
Tchien Krahn	kɔ̀
Dewoin	kɔ̀
Nyabo	kɔ̀
Guéré	kɔ̀

Thus, it would appear that the protoform has a non-high tone: kv̀. This indicates, then, that it is the auxiliary which has changed tone, rather than the verb. This is in keeping with what has been found in other cases of verb-->auxiliary reanalysis. In both Tepo and Grebo, it was seen that the 'go'-related auxiliary is realized on a higher tone than the corresponding verbal form 'go'. As previously mentioned, however, there is no known reason for this high-tone correlation. Nevertheless, one generalization holds: it is always the innovative form that undergoes change. Similarly, in English, it is the modal-like use of 'have' that undergoes phonological change: I hafta see him.

To sum up, evidence has been given showing that three future auxiliaries are related to the verbs 'go', 'come', and 'have'. It was suggested that all three arose from the same construction--

$$S\ V_1 [O\ V_2\ _{nom}]$$

--when V_1 underwent semantic change and the nominalizer was lost or reduced. In the next section, the same auxiliaries will be discussed in light of further innovations which they have undergone.

3.8 Further Innovations

The development of future auxiliaries from the three verbs 'come', 'go', and 'have' has been described in detail. Once this reanalysis takes place, other changes may affect these future auxiliaries. In some cases, verb-derived futures have been modified by the addition of other verbal elements. In other cases, future auxiliaries have been reanalyzed as conditional or sequential markers. These developments will be outlined in detail in the last section of this chapter. First, as a background to the discussion, there will be a brief presentation of some of the discourse uses of the 'go'-, 'come'-, and 'have'-related futures.

3.8.1 Discourse functions of the innovated future auxiliaries.
In the discussion of the origin and development of the 'go'-, 'come'-, and 'have'-related auxiliaries, most of the data came from single clauses. However, the three future auxiliaries often occur in conjunction with other clauses and may serve to indicate purpose or sequential actions. In Godié, the 'have'-related auxiliary is used to express purpose, while the 'come'-related future auxiliary is used to express sequential actions.

The Emergence of Three Future Auxiliaries   143

(263) ɔ gbʌlʌ su   ɔ kʌ̃ sugbie sʌ   'He climbed a tree in
      he climb tree he AUX fruit pick   order to pick fruit.'

(264) ɔ gbʌlʌ su   nũ ɔ yi sugbie sʌ
      he climb tree and he SEQ fruit pick
      'He climbed the tree and he picked some fruit.'

3.8.1.1 Purpose clauses. All the verb-related future auxiliaries discussed in this chapter occur in purpose clauses. In Eastern Kru, it is the 'have'-related auxiliary which typically occurs in this environment. This can be seen in examples 263, 265, and 266.

(265) <u>Vata</u> (Vogler:410)
      pé à tāglēā ká-uá́ɔ́ ulɔ́ se ɔ́ā ká-uá́ɔ́ mɛ̀ ii ...
      when our ancestors FUT-T leave that they FUT-T here come
      'When our ancestors were leaving (in order) to come here...'

(266) <u>Neyo</u>
      é ylā ká   la ɉie gɔ̃ mʊ ká   la zaasi   zɔ̃   po
      I want I:AUX T ocean ? go I:FUT T palm-tree under lie
      'I want to go to the beach in order to lie under the palm trees.'

In Western Kru, it is primarily the 'go'-related auxiliary which occurs in purpose clauses:

(267) <u>Tepo</u>
      ɔ dḗ le ɔ mú ó yé   'He came in order to
      he come LOC he AUX him see   see him.'

(268) <u>Cedepo</u>
      ɔ̃ mḯ   tulubɔ̃ mú ma ɔ mḯ kokwa nú
      he go:IMP Monrovia go NOM he AUX work do
      'He's going to go to Monrovia in order to work.'

(269) <u>Grebo</u>
      nɛ́ dḯ ne bɛ̀ mi kḗ yḯ   'I came to see the
      I come BE that:I AUX chief see chief.'

(270) <u>Bakwé</u>
      ʌ̃ nye Dali monii ɔ mʊ na lʊ̃ʊ sù
      I gave Dali money he AUX my cloth buy
      'I gave Dali money so he would buy my cloth.'

While 'have'- and 'go'-related auxiliaries occur most often in purpose clauses, there is at least one language where a 'come'-related auxiliary occurs in a similar environment, but as the complement of a verb such as 'want'.

(271) Sapo

ɔ pẽ ɔ di kò di   'He wants to eat rice.'
he want he AUX rice eat
        (come)

Compare this sentence with the following ones from Bakwé and Neyo where 'go'- and 'have'-related auxiliaries function in the same way:

(272) Bakwé

ɔ̄ bātā ɔ̄ mɔ̄ pùlù   'He wants to jump.'
he want he AUX jump
        (go)

(273) Neyo

ō yra Able ka kè i   'He wants Able to come.'
he want Able AUX T come
            (have)

3.8.1.2 Sequential clauses. In Eastern languages, the 'come'-related auxiliary is used to express sequential action. Sequential auxiliaries occur in every one but the first of a series. In Godié, if the first clause of a series contains a factative aspect, the following clauses, containing the 'come'-related auxiliary **yi**, will have a factative or punctiliar past reading.

(274) ɔ yĩ nʉ ɔ yi lɨ   'He came and ate.'
he come: then he AUX eat
FACT   (come)

If, however, the first clause itself contains the **yi** auxiliary and has a future reading, the following clauses also have a future reading.

(275) ɔ yi Dakpadou mʉ nʉ ɔ yi mɔ́ gʉ
he AUX Dakpadou go and he AUX there spend-the-night

'He will go to Dakpadou and he will spend the night there.'

In Bété, the 'come'-related future is also used in a sequential sense. Werle (field notes) observes that when this is the case, **yi** is followed by an ɛ suffix which he calls a narrative marker.

(276) ... ń ɔ̄ yī-ɛ̀ sɛ́ pʉ   'Then he went to bed.'
then he AUX-SUF down lie

The Emergence of Three Future Auxiliaries   145

Sequential auxiliaries are not present in all Eastern languages. Though limited texts are available in Neyo and Lakota Dida, no examples of a sequential use of the 'come'-related future auxiliary were found. In a series of clauses, the factative was used in each one.

'Come'-related sequential markers are known to occur in non-Kru languages as well. This is apparently the case in Crioula of Guinea (Traugott 1978:384) and Hebrew (Poythress, pers.com.). Welmers (1973:415) notes that the Swahili verb **kuja** 'come' "is used as an auxiliary before the future, hortative, or infinitive to convey the idea of 'then', or 'later' in the future." A similar phenomenon is reported to occur in Kasem, a language spoken in Ghana. In this language a consecutive tense is used for either future or past reference (Callow 1974:40).

3.8.1.3 Future auxiliaries in temporal clauses. Within narratives, future auxiliaries may occur in sentence-initial clauses and serve to "set the scene" for an upcoming event. The future is used with a past tense reference (explicit or implicit) as a means of bringing a past action to life.

(277) wa   kʌ̱   gbi kʌ   mʉ nʌ, kʉ-wa   6lɨ̄˜ zɔ̄
      they AUX run NOM go NF   CR-they fall down
      'As they were going to run, they fell down.'

The 'have'-related future auxiliary is used in this way in at least two Eastern languages: Godié (277) and Vata (278).

(278) pé   à   taglea   ká-uáɔ́ ulɔ́   se   ɔá   ká-uáɔ́ mɛ̀
      when our ancestors AUX-T   leave that they AUX-T here
      íí, pókú dlá uá kɔa
      come Poku kill T people
      'When our ancestors were leaving to come here,
       Poku was killing people.'

The 'go'-related future is used in a similar way in Wobé.

(279) ɔ   mu-ɛ   jrī-á   de   su satao je ɔ kpo
      he go-DEC steal-NOM then policeman SEQ him catch
      'He was going to steal (on the point of stealing)
       when the policeman caught him.'

To briefly summarize, then, the 'go'-, 'come'-, and 'have'-related auxiliaries play special roles in discourse. Both 'have'- and 'go'related auxiliaries may occur in the second of two clauses where they indicate purpose. In Eastern Kru, it is usually the 'have'-related auxiliary which plays this role, while in Western

Kru, it is the 'go'-related auxiliary which occurs in purpose clauses. In at least one language, Sapo, the 'come'-related auxiliary may also occur in a purpose clause. 'Come'-related future auxiliaries frequently occur in the second of two clauses (or in any subsequent clause) where they signal sequential action. Finally, the 'go'- and 'have'-related futures often occur in the first of two clauses where they set the scene for an upcoming event.

Now, several innovations will be described, including the development of double (bimorphemic) auxiliaries and the reanalysis of future auxiliaries into conditionals. In the last section, an auxiliary whose origin is unknown will be briefly discussed.

3.8.2 "Double" auxiliaries. In certain Eastern Kru languages, there are auxiliaries which appear to consist of two morphemes. In Lozoua Dida, there are two futures: a 'come'-related c_I and a complex form **cikā**.

(280) ɔ cɪ pàlʊ́ sla   ɔ cɪkã́ pàlʊ́ sla
       he AUX house build   he AUX house build
       'He will/can build a house.' 'He will build a house.'

The **cɪkã́** form is interesting in that it appears to be a combination of the 'come'-related auxiliary c_I and a 'have'-related auxiliary **kã́** (which apparently does not exist independently in this language). From the data available, it appears that the sequence **cɪkã́** is acting as one unit. This can be seen in the following sentence where it occurs in sentence-second position, causes the verb to occur in sentence-final position, and carries a tense marker like a regular simplex auxiliary.

(281) ɔ cɪkã́ a budō   'He was going to bathe.'
       he AUX REC bathe

Similar "double" future auxiliaries occur in Vata, Godié, and Neyo, but in these languages the auxiliary has the shape **nèkā** (Vata), **naka** (Neyo), and **nʌkã́/lʌkã́** (Godié).

(282) n̄ nekā tɛ̄⁻ ilé zèkā mlȩ́   'Maybe I will go to
       I AUX   maybe Hire tomorrow go   Hire tomorrow.'

(283) Neyo
      dū   a   nyʊaa nakā lu6o   'The villagers will
      town ASSOC men   AUX   have-fun have fun.'

(284) Godié
      zekī̵   ɔ   lʌkã́ lɔ́ɔ   kʊ   'Tomorrow he will be here.'
      tomorrow he AUX   here   be

(285) ʌ̃ nʌkʌ̃ zlɩ nɔnʋ   'I am going to work.'
     I AUX   work do

The forms in Godié are phonologically conditioned: nʌkʌ̃ occurs only following nasalized vowels, while lʌkʌ̃ occurs elsewhere.

All of the languages just mentioned have a 'have'-related future **ka**, and this is apparently the second element of the combined auxiliary.

(286) Vata
     ń ká mé gbā   'I will say that.'
     I FUT that say

(287) Neyo
     ɔ̌ ká 6lī   'He wants to sing.'
     he FUT sing

(288) Godié
     n kʌ̃ sʌ pɩ   'I'm going to/want to
     I FUT down lie   lie down.'

The first element in the complex auxiliary is harder to identify. In Godié, it is homophonous with the verb 'say' (used to report direct speech), which has the underlying form lʌ. (/l/ is realized as [n] when following nasalized vowels.)

     ɔ̌ lʌ̃   'He says ...'
     ʌ̃́ nʌ̃   'I say ...'
     ʌ̃̀ nʌ̃   'you say ...'

This rule applies only to the verb 'say' and does not affect other verbs or morphemes beginning with /l/. This can be seen with the verb lʌ 'bring'.

(289) ɔ̌ lʌ̃   bɛ̄ɛ̄   ʌ̃́ lʌ̃   bɛ̄ɛ̄
     he bring:IMP peanuts   I bring:IMP peanuts
     'He's bringing peanuts.'   'I'm bringing peanuts.'

The fact that the complex auxiliary undergoes the l--->n shift strongly suggests that the first element is, in fact, the verb 'say'. Further support of this hypothesis is that lʌ 'say' is the only verb which undergoes a tone change when preceded by a low-tone pronoun: /ʌ̃̀ lʌ/ (you say)--->[ʌ̃̀ nʌ̃]. The double auxiliary behaves in the same way.

The first element in the Neyo double auxiliary is not immediately identifiable. It has the shape **na**. In contrast, the verb form used for reporting direct speech is **anee**.

(290) dakɔ <u>anee</u>   : Lale, nɔnoɔ   é zle a , ó tɛ́   mó
      Dake <u>says/said</u> Lale, work-DEF I do SUB it hard inside
      'Dako said: Lale, the work that I do, it's hard.'

The two forms may be related, however, since **anee** is obviously a frozen form (no verbs have the structure <u>VCV(V)</u>). It could be made up of the **a** imperfective nominal suffix and the **e** imperfective suffix. Thus **na** could very well be the underlying form of 'say' in Neyo.

In Vata, the first element in the double auxiliary has the same form as the future auxiliary **ne**. (As was mentioned earlier, this is the only known Kru language with a future auxiliary of this shape.)[10]

---

10 The study of the use of future auxiliaries in sequential clauses reveals an interesting fact. In Cedepo, Grebo, and Sapo, single clauses containing the verb 'go' or 'come' always have a nominalizer following the sentence-final verb. They have an ambiguous reading, referring to either literal motion or future action.

Cedepo

ėh mĩ e kou tɔ̃ ma   'I am going to buy rice' or
I go ? rice buy NOM   'I will buy rice.'

However, when these verb-related future auxiliaries occur in the second of two clauses (in purpose clauses or as complements of a verb such as 'want'), the nominalizer does not occur.

Cedepo

ɔ̃ mĩ tlubɔ̃   mṹ ma ɔ mĩ kokwa nṹ
he go Monrovia go NOM he AUX   work do
'He will go to Monrovia in order to work.'

Another environment where the nominalizer may disappear is in imperative constructions, as in Bassa.

dyi nĩ mɔ̃ɔ̃ dɔ̃   'Come buy my rice.'
come my rice buy

Unfortunately, there is not enough data available at this time to determine just how widespread this phenomenon may be. The data in hand suggest that the nominalizer is being deleted when the verb-related auxiliary occurs in the second of two clauses. It could be that the use in this environment is totally unambiguous (temporal and not literal), and thus the semantic shift of the verb can be seen to affect the presence of the nominalizer. If this is the case, it confirms the proposal made in section 3.5.4 that semantic shift of the verb may permit the reduction and, in this case, the deletion of the nominalizing particle.

(291) glanlɛ̃ nɛ́ aɔ nlɛple li 'The leopard will eat
      leopard FUT T antelope eat   the antelope.'

The origin of the **ne** future auxiliary is not known. However, since all other future auxiliaries can be linked to full verbs, the **ne** is probably also verbal in origin. It could be the copula **ne**--the Bantu copula **li** developed into a future marker in Luganda (Givón 1971b:71). The trouble with this hypothesis is that the **ne** copula is primarily a Western Kru form. It is not known if **ne** in Vata is cognate with the verb **nʌ/lʌ** 'say' in Godié.

It is also difficult to determine what the exact semantic difference is between simplex auxiliaries and the complex one. In Godié, **kã** often expresses volition, but emphasizes the speaker's desire to carry out a given action. The complex **lʌkʌ̃** seems to express either certainty that an action will be realized in the future or the determination of the speaker to accomplish the act.

(292) ʌ̃ kʌ̃ zʉkʌ nyʌmʊ sʌ, mã zekɨ̃   ʌ̃ nʌkʌ̃ le6e no
      I VOL today rest   but tomorrow I FUT work do
      'Today, I'm going to rest, but tomorrow I'll work.'

One language consultant noted that the **lʌkʌ̃** future seemed interchangeable with the **yi** 'come'-related potential future, at least in certain contexts. In answer to the question, "Will the chief be here tonight?" the response could be either of the following:

(293) ʌ̃ʌ̃, zekɨ̃ ɔ lʌkʌ̃ lɔɔ kʊ̄   'No, tomorrow he'll be
      no tomorrow he AUX here be   here.'

(294) ʌ̃ʌ̃, zekɨ̃ ɔ yi lɔɔ kʊ̄   'No, tomorrow he will be
      no tomorrow he AUX here be   here.'

In this context, **lʌkʌ̃** seems to be linked more to prediction than to volition. This appears to be the case in Neyo, where **ka** expresses desire to carry out an action, while **naka** gets a more undefined future reading.

(295) ɔ kã blı   'He wants/intends to sing.'
      he AUX sing

(296) ɔ nakã blı   'He is going to sing.'
      he AUX sing

Vogler calls the **nɛ́ka** form in Vata "projective" and states that it emphasizes the certainty that a future action will actually take place. This coincides with the readings in Neyo and Godié. Thus the semantic difference between **ka** and **laka** could be related to the fact that the double auxiliary is a combination of the verb 'say' (expressing intention) and the volitive aspect (expressing desire). Thus I say - I want to sing is somehow more emphatic than simply stating 'I want to sing', showing that the subject is more determined that the action will be carried out.

The question now arises as to how these complex forms came into being. First, it is important to notice that in all cases the second member of the complex future auxiliary is the 'have'-related auxiliary **ka**. It was noted in section 3.8.1 that in Eastern Kru especially, this auxiliary is typically found in purpose clauses.

(297) Godié

    ɔ gbʌlʌ su   ɔ kʌ́ sugbie sʌ   'He climbed the tree in
    he climb tree he VOL fruit pick   order to pick fruit.'

(298) Neyo (Thomann)

    a toa gbosu a ka wlo ba   'It set a trap so it
    it set trap it AUX woman marry could marry a woman.'

(299) Vata

    glālɛ̄ āmé sḕ ā ká̄ dū́ɔ̀ có peɛ́ mlẹ̀
    follow me that we AUX village chief at go
    'Follow me so we can go to the chief's house.'

These same purpose clauses also occur following verbs like 'want', 'go', and 'have', and behave like a complement of that verb.

(300) Neyo

    ɔ yra ɔ ká si   'He wants to get married.'
    he want he AUX marry
    ɔ mīɛ ɔ ká̄ li   'He is going to eat.'
    he go he AUX eat

This looks like a proper environment for EQUI to apply, leaving the string S V-AUX (O) V, which eventually would collapse into S COMPLEX-AUX (O) V. However, there is one basic problem with such an explanation, and that is that EQUI does not apply in this environment in Neyo.

(301) * ɔ yra ∅ ká si
      he want ∅ AUX marry

The Emergence of Three Future Auxiliaries   151

    * ɔ mlê Ø kā li
      he go Ø AUX eat

There are some environments, however, where pronouns may be deleted. For example, in many Kru languages, first and second person singular pronouns may be deleted when they precede auxiliaries (Marchese 1979).[11] Note that when a pronoun is deleted in Kru, the tone of the auxiliary may be affected.

(302) Klao

    sḗ   klɔ   mú   'I didn't go to the village.'
    I:neg village go

    sḕ   klɔ   mú   'You didn't go to the village.'
    you:NEG village go

(303) Tepo

    mʋ́   cinéma yé   'I will see the movie.'
    I:FUT movie see

    mʋ   cinema ye   'You will see the movie.'
    you:FUT movie see

This also occurs in Neyo:

(304) yà   flí   'You are free (literally:
    you:PERF free   have been freed).'

    yáa   sıa   'I am tired out.'
    I:PERF tire

In Godié, a subject pronoun of first or second person singular may be omitted in certain environments without even leaving a tonal trace on the auxiliary verb. (The following was taken from a recorded story.)

(305) ... yʌ́ (ʌ̀) kʌ́ lɔ́   nyū   ŋwʋ́   'And you will put
    and (you) AUX there water put   the water there.'

---

[11] Bolinger (1977:515) notes a similar phenomenon in English, where first person singular is often dropped before auxiliaries.

    Don't mind saying that hers is almost as pretty as yours.

    Might as well tell you that I never did get along with him.

In Neyo a similar phenomenon occurs. First and second person singular subject pronouns may be deleted in the second of two classes if they are coreferent. The following examples from Thomann (1905) are not marked for tone, so it is not known if the deletion in this case leaves a tonal remnant on the auxiliary or not.

(306) e yra Ø ka se   'I want to marry.'
      I want Ø AUX marry

(307) mo Ø k'ō   bla   'Go kill him.'
      go Ø AUX-him kill

Compare the following sentence where the subjects are not identical and therefore no deletion is allowed:

(308) ī a ka bei   li   'Come, let's be friends.'
      come we AUX friendship eat

These deletions, which are a restricted kind of EQUI-NP deletion (applying only to first and second persons) provide an environment where verbs without single NP objects may be directly followed by the ka/kʌ marker. I believe this is the pattern that led to the emergence of the combined auxiliary. Presumably, at first the environment of the combination was restricted to first and second person, but eventually spread to all persons.

Thus in Lozoua Dida, I propose that the auxiliary cıkā started out in a construction such as the following:

**ı cı   ı kā pàlʊ́ sla   'I am coming to
   I come I AUX house build   build a house.'

Because the subjects were first (or second) person and identical, the second in the series was optionally deleted, leaving the following:

**ı cı   Ø kā pàlʊ́ sla
   I come Ø AUX house build

This string has two possible structural interpretations. It could be viewed as two juxtaposed clauses with deletion of the subject of the second clause.

$$\begin{bmatrix} \text{ı cı} \\ \text{S V} \end{bmatrix} \begin{bmatrix} \text{Ø kā pàlʊ́ sla} \\ \text{S AUX O V} \end{bmatrix}$$

Or, with V and AUX side by side, the two clauses could be interpreted as making up a single clause.

$$\begin{bmatrix} \text{ɩ} & \underbrace{\text{cɩ} \quad \emptyset \quad \text{ká}} & \text{pālʊ̃} & \text{sla} \\ \text{S} & \text{AUX} & \text{O} & \text{V} \end{bmatrix}$$

Again, in this case, a complex structure collapsed into a simplex one. As cɩ Ø ká was interpreted as AUX, it presumably became generalized, occurring in environments with persons other than first and second person singular. The same scenario is proposed for Godié (and if the analysis of the forms in Neyo and Vata is correct, for them as well). The sentence

Ã nʌ Ã kʌ̃ kʌ̃lʌ̃ mʉ	'I say I'm going to
I say I AUX bush go	the bush.'

would undergo deletion of the second subject:

Ã nʌ Ø kʌ̃ kʌ̃lʌ̃ mʉ

to be eventually reanalized as

Ã nʌkʌ̃ kʌ̃lʌ̃ mʉ	'I will go to the bush.'
I AUX bush go	

Here again, the deletion is allowed because first and second person singular are involved. Presumably, the frozen form then spread to other persons. This parallels the claim of many (Li and Thompson 1974, for example) that surface strings with ambiguous structures may be reanalyzed without any basic shift in word order.

3.8.3 Future auxiliaries and the conditional

3.8.3.1 General strategies for the conditional. There appears to be a distinct link between verb-derived future auxiliaries and conditional auxiliaries. In Kru the antecedent of the condition usually precedes the consequent and is typically expressed as a dependent clause. The antecedent is marked as a conditional in one of several ways (depending on the language): by conjunction, a special pronoun, a nonauxiliary marker occurring between the subject and the verb, or by auxiliary. Before we discuss the conditional auxiliaries, the other conditional strategies will be briefly described.

(1) <u>Conjunction or special pronoun</u>. In the two large Western complexes, Guéré and Grebo, the conditional is usually expressed by an introductory particle of the shape <u>bilabial stop (or nasal) + non-high back rounded vowel</u> which precedes the subject occurring in the antecedent.

(309) Wobé

    bō̰ í blḛ̄ kwɛ̄ɛ́ ɛ̄   'If I have a canoe, ...'
    COND I have canoe SUB

(310) Nyabwa

    ɓō̰ í yè ɛ̄   'If I see it, ...'
    COND I see it

(311) Gbaeson Krahn[12]

    pō̰ ī nú-ɛ́   'If you do it, ...'
    COND you do-it

(312) Tchien Krahn

    mɔ̰̄ ó dū lōō̄   'If I pound rice, ...'
    COND I pound rice

    The particle BO[13] often coalesces with the subject pronoun, so that in some languages one can speak of a new series of "conditional pronouns." This is Thalmann's analysis for Tepo. The same analysis seems valid for closely related Cedepo, Grebo, and Borobo, all of the Grebo complex.

(313) Tepo

    bɔ   nye mʊ́ didiɗɛ   'If he gives me food, ...'
    COND:he give me food

---

12 In Krahn (Duitsman, pers.com.), the conditional clause can only occur with an unmarked pronoun. The imperfective marker **a** never occurs in this environment. In Tepo, however, the conditionally marked pronoun may be optionally followed by the imperfective marker.

    b-ɔ́   nā   'If he drinks, ...'
    COND-he drink

    bɔ́-ɔ́ nā   'If he is drinking, ...'
    COND-he-INC drink

Such restrictions in other languages have not been studied in detail and will not concern the discussion here.

13 In some languages, the **b-V** conditional particle appears to be closely similar to a complementizer **b** which marks sentential complements.

    Tepo ā nḭ̄ hʊ̀à b-ā   kɔ̄   'We don't want to die.'
         we NEG want that-we die

Similar examples could be given from Grebo and Klao. More research needs to be done to determine if there is, in fact, a connection between 'that' complementizers and particles which introduce conditionals.

(314) Grebo
 bɔ̃   nū-a̍ nɛ̂   'If he does it tomorrow, ...'
 COND:he do-T it

(315) Cedepo (tones missing)
 bɔ   deba kwɛlɛ   'If he kills an antelope, ...'
 COND:he kill antelope

(316) Borobo
 bɔ̃   tɔ̂: gblã   'If he buys rice, ...'
 COND:he buy rice

The conditional pronoun must occur even when a full noun or a conditional conjunction is present.

(317) Tepo
 bɛ̃á yū **bɔ́ɔ̍** wɛ́ nyɛ̀ nɔ̍ mrɛ́kɛ̍
 COND child COND:he cry give him milk
 'If the baby cries, give him milk.'

(318) Grebo
 plɛ̍ **bɔ** hĩ́   'If a rat passes, ...'
 rat COND:he pass

Where conditional pronouns have developed, topics have become grammaticized. Note the topic-comment structure of this conditional:

rat	if he passes
TOPIC	COMMENT

Thus, topic in this case is no longer subject to the speaker's choice as to how he encodes his message. He is obligated to use a topic construction if he wishes to express a full noun referent.

(2) Other nonauxiliary markers. In a few languages, the conditional is expressed by a sentence-second particle. As was seen in section 1.5, particles do not cause a shift in word order. The markers are **ne** in Neyo (Eastern Kru) and **ma** in Bakwé (Western Kru).[14]

---

14 Interestingly enough, in two Kru isolates, Sɛmɛ and Kuwaa, there are homophonous conditional markers with Neyo **ne** and Bakwé **ma**. In Sɛmɛ, **ne** occurs in sentence-second position and does not cause a shift in word order (Sɛmɛ is already SOV). In Kuwaa, a particle **ma** suffixes onto the verb in the antecedent, also causing no change in word order.

(319) Neyo
 e ne wa ma   'If you like bananas, ...'
 you COND like bananas

(320) Bakwé
 ɔ mā klá mōnīī 'If he has money, ...'
 he COND have money

 The conditional markers described so far (a sentence-initial marker and a sentence-second particle) occur primarily in Western languages. However, the most common way of indicating conditionals is by auxiliary. In the following discussion it will be claimed that these auxiliaries are innovative, having evolved from 'come'- and 'have'-related future auxiliaries.

 (3) Conditional auxiliaries. Conditional auxiliaries occur on either side of the Guéré and Grebo complexes, in most Eastern languages (Bété, Godié, Koyo, Dida, and Vata), and in the nonaffiliated Western languages including Dewoin, Bassa, and Klao (see map VI). The conditional auxiliary occurs in the antecedent of the condition, which is usually marked as a dependent clause.

(321) Godié
 ɔ ku yi nʌ, ā yi lɨ 'If he comes, we will eat.'
 he COND come NF we FUT eat

(322) River Cess Bassa
 ɔ ji smi-ɔ kpɔ ni ā mu ɔ di
 he COND fish-DEF catch SUB we FUT it eat
 'If he catches the fish, we will eat it.'

The analysis of the marker ni is unsure. It appears to be a subordinate marker or a consecutive conjunction.

 There is no doubt as to the auxiliary status of these markers, since they cause a shift in word order: S COND (O) V, and act as host to tense suffixes and object clitics (cf. sect. 1.5).

 Sɛmɛ
  a ne bar klɛ̄ 'If you work, ...'
  you COND work do

  Kuwaa (example from a text by Francis Howard)
  wō jɛ̄ɛ̄-mā nà, wò java ve nà
  they meet-COND us they kill FUT us
  'If they meet us, they will kill us.'

The Emergence of Three Future Auxiliaries

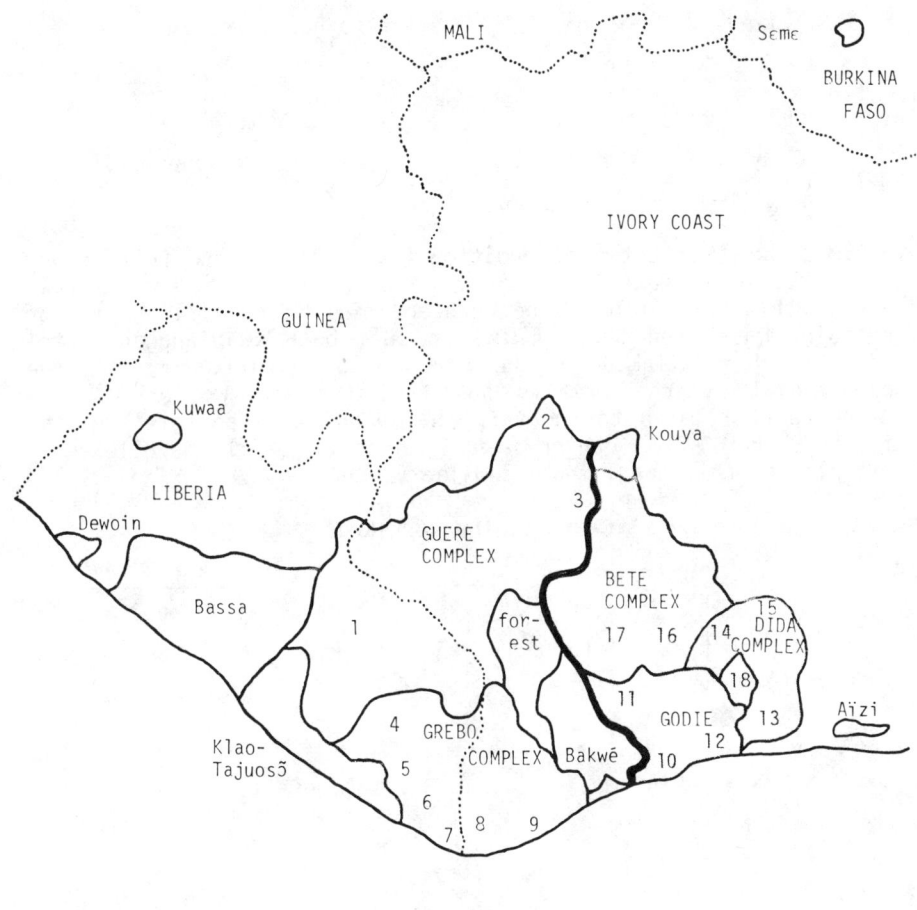

KRU LANGUAGE FAMILY
adapted from Marchese 1979

— division between Eastern and Western Kru

— division between complexes or unaffiliated languages

····· division between countries

☐ conditional auxiliaries

1. Krahn
2. Wobé
3. Nyabwa
4. Cedepo
5. Borobo
6. Nyabo
7. Grebo
8. Tepo
9. Bereby Kru
10. Neyo
11. Kwadia
12. Koyo
13. Lozoua Dida
14. Lakota Dida
15. Vata
16. Bété (Gagnoa)
17. Bété Soubré-Daloa-Guibéroua)
18. Ega (non-Kru)

Map 6. Conditional Auxiliaries

(323) Godié (tense suffix)

    ɔ kʉ-a   yi nʌ   'If he had come, ...'
    he COND-REC come NF

(324) Bassa (Hobley)

    ɔ dyi-ɛ nyu nĭ, nĭĭ   'If he does it, then ...'
    he COND-it do SUB, then

3.8.3.2 The link between conditional auxiliaries and full verbs.

All conditional auxiliaries in Kru appear to be linked to full verbs. This connection is not unheard of. Migeod (1911:201), for example, has noted that in Twi and Gã, both Kwa languages, the conditional is linked to the verb 'allow'. In Eastern Kru the conditional, which normally has the shape **ka** (**kʌ** or **kʉ**), is undoubtedly related to the verb 'have' and to the 'have'-related future markers. This can be seen in chart VI, which is followed by examples of this conditional auxiliary.

Chart VI (Eastern Kru)

	Koyo	Godié	Bété	Vata	Lakota Dida
COND	kã	kʉ̃	kʌ̃	ká!	ka
'have'	kã	kʌ̃	kʌ̃	kla	kã
FUT AUX	ka	kʌ̃	kʌ̃	kã	kã

(325) Koyo

    ɔ kã   suklŭ mʋ   'If he goes to school, ...'
    he COND school go

(326) Godié

    ɔ kʉ   yi nʌ,   'If he comes, ...'
    he COND come NF

(327) Bété

    ɔ kʌ̃ si li   'When he eats yams, ...'
    he COND yam eat

(328) Vata

    ń ká! tãklɛ́ ēfluaá 6áté 'If I had read the letter, ...'
    I COND PAST letter read

(329) Lakota Dida

    ɔ́ kã bɔ́ mñɛ   'If he goes there, ...'
    he COND there go

The Emergence of Three Future Auxiliaries

Note that conditional auxiliaries are not limited to signalling conditions. In the Bété example and also in the following from Godié, it can be seen that conditional clauses also express unrealized actions. Thus they can have either of two readings: 'if' or 'when'.

(330) Godié

    ɅÌ kʉ mʉ nʌ, sʉ nɔ̄ āyó   'If/when you go, tell
    you <u>if</u> go NF tell him hello him hello.'

On the Western side, conditional auxiliaries are linked to the verb 'come'. They have the shape **ɟi**, and often clauses containing these auxiliaries end in a **ni** particle. The forms of the Western conditional auxiliary and the verb 'come' are given in chart VII. Unlike the Eastern case, there is not a matching 'come'-related future.

              Chart VII (Western Kru)

	Dewoin	Bassa	Sapo	Klao
COND	ɟi...nī	ɟi	di	ɟi (pa)[15]
'come'	ɟi	ɟi	di (bɛ)	ɟi

(331) Dewoin

    ɔ̄ **ɟī** kṳ̀ã̀ nū ná-nī nī   'If he is working, ...'
    he <u>COND</u> work do PROG SUB

(332) Bassa (Hobley)

    ɔ **ɟi**-ɛ   nyu nī,
    he <u>COND</u>-it do SUB

(333) Klao (Rickard)

    ɔ **ɟi**-pa kōkwā na nú   'If he does the work, ...'
    he <u>COND</u> work DEF do

---

[15] The particles following the conditional auxiliaries in Klao and Sapo apparently indicate present tense. Other particles occur in the same position giving a past tense (counterfactual) reading.

    Klao

    ɔ ɟi-ye   kōkwā na nú   'If he had done the work, ...'
    he COND-past work DEF do

The particles **pa** (Klao) and **bɛ** (Sapo) only occur in a conditional environment, however.

(334) Sapo
  ɔ dībē kō dī   'If he eats rice, ...'
  he COND rice eat

3.8.3.3 The development of the conditional auxiliary.

It has been shown that there is an obvious connection between the verbs 'have' in the East and 'come' in the West and conditional auxiliaries. The fact that other strategies (conjunction, conditional pronoun, and nonauxiliary particles) exist to express the conditional seems to suggest that the auxiliary itself is an innovation. Further evidence of the innovation is the fact that two completely different morphemes are used as conditional auxiliaries—**ka** primarily in Eastern Kru and **ji** in Western Kru.

In section 3.8.1, it was shown that in Eastern Kru the 'have'-related future auxiliaries often occur in narratives in subordinate clauses before the main clause, where they provide a temporal setting. The construction is similar to the antecedent-consequent construction seen in clauses containing auxiliary conditionals. Compare:

(335) Godié temporal clause
  wa kʌ́ gbi kʌ́ mʉ nʌ, kʉ-wa 6lɨ zɔ
  they FUT run NOM go NF CR-they fall down
  'As they were going to run, they fell down.'

  conditional clause
  ɔ kʉ nyɩɛ nʌ   'If he laughs, ...'
  he COND laugh NF

It was also pointed out that conditionals may be analyzed as a type of dependent temporal clause, referring both to simultaneous ('when') and to conditional ('if') events, i.e., unrealized actions. This suggests that the conditional auxiliaries may have developed from clauses containing verb-derived future auxiliaries.

The semantic connection between futures and conditionals is not completely unheard of. It is well known that in Latin a periphrastic construction containing the infinitive and the verb 'have' gave rise to future constructions in most of the daughter languages. Bailard (pers.com.) notes that the verb in Latin also gave rise to an imaginative mood marker (cf. Anderson and Jones 1974:162). She notes that the French derivative of the INF + have construction can occur in the antecedent of conditionals without the normally occurring introductory particle **si** 'if'.

Viendrait-il que nous le recevrions   les bras ouverts
would:come-he that we   him receive-would the arms open
'If he would come, we would receive him with open arms.'

The Emergence of Three Future Auxiliaries   161

The more frequent French equivalent would be:

    S'il venait, nous le recevrions les bras ouverts
    If he come-   we   him receive-   the arms open
          INC   COND

If the assumption of a future--->conditional shift is valid, conditionals would have originally been expressed merely by their subordinate relationship to the main clause:

    'He will come; we will eat.'
    'He will have money; he will buy a car.'

This is not so surprising since the basic information structure in Kru is <u>given</u>, <u>new</u> (Marchese 1979; Werle 1976), and conditionals are known to contain given information (Marchese 1976; Haiman 1978; T. Payne, MS). In fact, the difference in tone between future auxiliaries and conditional auxiliaries may be related to the status of the clause in which they occur. In Daloa Bété, the future auxiliary has a high tone and occurs in independent clauses, but the conditional auxiliary, occurring in sentence-initial dependent clauses, has a low tone.

(336) (Zogbo 1975)

    ñ   jɛ́[16] ná   gú   jē-mʉ̄   'You will go look
    you <u>FUT</u> my child go-look-for   for my child.'

    ñ   jɛ̀   pɛ́rʊ   mʉ̄, pīā na bàna
    you <u>COND</u> market go   buy my clothes

    'If you go to the market, buy some clothes for me.'

The low tone may, in fact, be a remnant of a subordinate particle. These occur as verbal suffixes in Krahn, Wobé, and Klao.

(337) <u>Tchien Krahn</u>

    ti à mū ā   gwlɔ   'When we went to town, ...'
    time we go <u>SUB</u> town

---

[16] I have not been able to identify the origin of the auxiliary jɛ. It may be related to the potential marker **yi** (found in Kosséoa Bété and Godié). Zogbo (1975) calls the auxiliary a **futur immediat**.

    gi   ñ   jɛ́ lā nā   go   sʌ   zʊ
    come you AUX here your haunch down set
    'Come sit down here.'

It is apparently used in purpose clauses, but it does not appear to be related to **ka**, which also occurs in this dialect.

    gi   ñ   kʌ́   lagblɛ́ kwa   'Come, take me to the field.'
    come you AUX-me fields take

The difference in form found in the conditional auxiliary **kʉ** and the future auxiliary **kʌ́** in Godié may be yet another case of the phonological change that may affect the innovative member of a set of related forms.

In a previous discussion, it was noted that the Nyabwa auxiliary **kà** (presumably linked to 'have') is restricted to dependent temporal clauses. One interesting fact emerges in regard to conditionals, which is that this auxiliary cooccurs with the conditional conjunction in the antecedent of a conditional statement.

(338) <u>6ò</u> ẽ <u>kà</u> kɔbō-ò pō, nī-ī yé˜ lóà mʊ̀
     <u>COND</u> you <u>AUX</u> rice-DEF plant rain-INC FUT fall FUT
     'If you plant rice, the rain will fall.'

This appears to be another case in which the temporal 'have'-related auxiliary is linked to a conditional. Apparently, due to the presence of the conditional conjunction, **kà** was not singled out as the morpheme indicating the condition.

3.8.3.4 'Come'-related conditionals.

From similarity in shape and meaning (chart VII), it is assumed that there is a link between conditional auxiliaries in Western Kru and the verb 'come'. The difference between Eastern and Western Kru is not just that the East has a 'have'-related conditional and the West a 'come'-related one. A crucial difference is that in the East, there are 'have'-related futures, while in the West most languages have corresponding 'come'-related futures. This could pose a problem for the scenario:

     verb > future AUX > conditional AUX

However, it must be remembered that there is ample evidence for a 'come'-related future AUX at one stage of Western Kru. In section 3.6.5 it was seen that while affirmative futures use the innovative 'go'-related auxiliaries, negative futures conserve remnants of 'come'. Furthermore, considering evidence from Dewoin, one can see that sequentials also retain a 'come'-related AUX (it will be remembered that indicating sequential action is a discourse function of future auxiliaries).

(339) ...ɔ́ <u>ɟi</u> wuli jē   'And then he saw a goat.'
     he <u>SEQ</u> goat see

(340) ī sè la ɔ <u>ɟi</u> ɟi   'I stayed here until he came.'
     I stay here he <u>SEQ</u> come

In fact, since subordinate clauses (and therefore conditional clauses) are known to be conservative, it is no surprise that the older 'come'-related auxiliary is retained in this environment, having been "pushed out" of main affirmative clauses by the 'go'-related AUX. Thus, there is little doubt that there really was this development:

'come' > future AUX > conditional AUX

in several Western Kru languages.

3.8.4 The auxiliary ye.
In the preceding sections, it has been shown that future auxiliaries are often used to express purpose and sequential actions. In several Western languages, there is an additional auxiliary with the shape palatal consonant + front vowel, which seems to have the same function. In the next section, examples of **ye** will be given and the possible origin of this auxiliary will be briefly discussed.

3.8.4.1 Functions of ye.
The **ye** auxiliary is used to indicate sequential action.

(341) Nyabwa

lé í yé kɔ̄bū pō   'Then I planted rice.'
then I SEQ¹⁷ rice plant

(342) Tchien Krahn

a pi dɛ lɩ o ye dɛ di
they prepare thing then they SEQ thing eat
'They cooked something and ate it.'

(343) Klao

ɔ nu pɛpɛ ɔ yɛ nīgbà ná táà   'He crossed the river
he do slowly he SEQ river DEF cross   slowly.'

(344) Wobé

mari crɛ̄ɛ̄ kpéī ū jē jèī ī kpá
Mary hurry on she SEQ road on enter
'Mary hurried and started out on her journey.'

Besides expressing sequential actions, the **ye** auxiliary may also occur in a clause which functions as the complement of a cognitive/emotive verb.

(345) Klao

sɛ̄ jla bi yi klɔ mū   'I don't want to go
I-NEG want that-I SEQ town go   to town.'

---

17 In Nyabwa, **ye** apparently combines with a sentence-final particle mʊ or ∎ (> go?) to express a future.

ɔ̄ yéè sūkō lī mū   'He'll eat fufu.'
he:IMP AUX:SUF fufu eat mʊ

(346) Tchien Krahn (Hansell)
 ā   bɔ̄̃   ō̃   ye   tū   fá   'I want them to whittle
 I-INC want they SEQ gun whittle   a gun.'

(347) Gbaeson Krahn
 ɔ́   kɔ̄̃   ɔ́   yĕ   ɛ   nú   'He's supposed to do it.'
 he has   he SEQ it do

(348) Wobé
 ɔ   bɩ́ɩ   ɛ   ɔ   jé   ji   'He can come.'
 he can   DEC he SEQ come

In some languages, the **ye** auxiliary also expresses purpose.

(349) Gbaeson Krahn
 ɔ́   jí   ɔ́   yĕ   dɛ́   dī   'He came in order to eat.'
 he come he SEQ thing eat

(350) Wobé
 ʋʋa   pɔ̀   yesu   á   kɔ́ī   de   ʋʋ   jé   ɔ
 they:IMP look Jesus his footsteps then they SEQ   him

 tɩkpēī nɛ́ɛ̄   'They are observing Jesus
 affair stick   in order to accuse him.'

(351) Klao (Kru data book, p. 7)
 ɔ   mu cɔcɛti bɔyi   jruti   na
 he go church that:he:SEQ   children DEF
 'He goes to church to teach the children.'

In at least three languages, Dyabo, Wobé, and Gbaeson Krahn, the **ye** may be used in the second of two clauses, but express simultaneity.

(352) Dyabo (Walker et al.)
 ɔ   di   dɛ   ɔ   yé   na   'He is eating and drinking.'
 he eat thing   he SEQ drink

(353) Gbaeson Krahn
 ā̌   mú-i   Ø   yĕ   dɛ́   dī   'I am in the process of
 I-INC go-INC   Ø   AUX thing eat   going to eat.'

The Emergence of Three Future Auxiliaries   165

(354) Wobé

    ɔɔ   too   ɔɔ   ɟé-a   na   'He limps as he walks.'
    he:IMP limp he:IMP SEQ-? walk

It would appear that the interpretation of the clause containing **ye** depends to a certain extent on the aspect in the first clause. When the first clause is imperfective, the sentence will have a purpose or simultaneous reading. If the first clause is completive, the second would have a completive or sequential reading.

In Wobé, a clause containing **ɟe** can stand on its own and express obligation when followed by the identification particle **o**:

(355) ɔ ɟe gbei mu o   'He should go to the field.'
    he AUX field go IDENT

To briefly summarize, then, in many Western Kru languages, an auxiliary **ye** is used to express purpose and consecutive or sequential action. In some languages it is also used to express simultaneity and obligation.

3.8.4.2 Origin of the ye auxiliary. The origin of the **ye** auxiliary is not known. Its distribution and function make it look similar to certain future auxiliaries. It could be related to the verb 'come' (as was the case with sequential auxiliaries in the East), but this is not sure. Chart VIII shows the **ye** forms and those for the verb 'come'.

Chart VIII

	Nyabwa	Tchien	Gbaeson	Klao	Wobé
AUX	yé	ye	yĕ	yi/ye	ɟé
come	yi	ɟi	gi	ɟi	ɟi

The **e** present in the auxiliary forms above could possibly come from the imperfective. This chart, however, is not as convincing as the others (I-VI) in establishing a link between this particular auxiliary and verb. It may also be possible that instead of being related to the verb 'come', the **ye** auxiliary is actually related to the verb 'see'. Chart IX compares the form of the **ye** auxiliary and the verb for 'see'.

Chart IX

	Nyabwa	Tchien	Gbaeson	Klao	Wobé
AUX	ye	ye	ye	yɛ/yi	ɟe
'see'	ye	?	?	ɟe	ɟe

Though the forms of the verb 'see' for Tchien and Gbaeson Krahn are not immediately available, the form in Konobo Krahn is **je**. Further support of this verb-auxiliary connection comes from Grebo, where the auxiliary **yi** may be used in perfect sentences. It is homophonous with the verb 'see' (Innes 1966).

(356) **nē yī nɛ̄ dū-ī**   'I have been pounding it.'
   I   AUX it pound-NOM   [morpheme-by-morpheme
                                translation, L.M.]

If the link between the verb 'see' and the auxiliary **ye/je/yi** can really be established, it would mean that a sentence like the one above originally came from a sentence like 'I saw it-pounding.' It can be noted that in Bambara, a language distantly related to the Kru family, the particle **ye** is used to indicate a past action and is also homophonous with the verb 'see' (Bimson, pers.com.). It could be, then, that the connection between the verb 'see' and a past marker (and by extension in Kru a sequential marker) goes further back than Proto-Kru. More research needs to be done in this area before the 'see'-past-sequential connection could actually be demonstrated.

3.9 Conclusion

In this chapter, I have described the emergence of three future auxiliaries coming from the full verbs 'go', 'come', and 'have'. It was suggested that the auxiliaries arose in a construction of the following type:

$$S\ V_1\ [(O)\ V_{2\ nom}]\ \text{OBJECT COMPLEMENT}$$

V_1 was seen to have undergone various semantic shifts which seemed to reinforce the already natural tendency of the sentence-final nominalizing particle to reduce. With these changes, the structure of the original construction is obscured, and the construction as a whole may be reanalyzed as S AUX O V. In the next chapter, negation and, in particular, negative auxiliaries, will be examined. It will be claimed that the same types of changes affecting the future constructions in Kru also play a role in the emergence of certain negative morphemes.

4 NEGATION: STRATEGIES AND INNOVATIONS

In this chapter, a general description of negation in the Kru family will be given. Two strategies of negation will be discussed: negation by negative particle, and negation by negative auxiliary. In the first section, it will be shown that aspect or mood generally determines negation type. A negative particle **nī** will be reconstructed for the entire family, and the development of various negative auxiliaries will be described. In later sections, other innovations in the negative system will be presented, along with a brief discussion of the interaction of negation with futures, conditionals, and progressives.

4.1 The Two Negative Strategies

In chapter 2 it was noted that in Kru there are two basic aspectual categories--the imperfective aspect, indicating ongoing or habitual action, and the factative, usually indicating past punctiliar action. This aspectual distinction plays a major part in determining the type of negative strategy to be used in a given context. Every Kru language has at least two negation strategies, and sometimes three. In Borobo there are two main signals of negation: a negative auxiliary **i** and a negative particle **ne**. The negative auxiliary is used primarily to negate factative sentences (1), while the negative particle is used to negate imperfective sentences (2).

(1) ɔ **i** kùã nu   'He didn't do work.'
    he NEG work do

(2) ɔ **ne** nu kùã   'He is not working.'
    he NEG do work
       PART

---

[1] Dawson (MS, 1973) was the first to notice the two basic negation strategies and their correlation with aspect in Tepo Kru.

As it turns out, the same distribution of negation strategies occurs in every Kru language examined in this study. Factative clauses are always negated by auxiliary where the basic word order is S NEG O V.

(3) Dewoin (Welmers) (Western Kru)

affirmative factative	negative factative
ɔ pi sayɛ̃	ɔ se sayɛ̃ pi
he cook meat	he NEG meat cook
S V O	S AUX O V
'He cooked meat.'	'He didn't cook meat.'

(4) Bassa (Hobley) (Western Kru)

affirmative factative	negative factative
ɔ nyu-ɛ zɔ̃ɔ	ɔ se-ɛ zɔ̃ɔ nyu
he do-it long-time-ago	he NEG-it long-time-ago do
S V O	S AUX O V
'He did it a long time ago.'	'He didn't do it a long time ago.'

(5) Neyo (Eastern Kru)

ne bu fa	'I didn't carry a gun.'
I:NEG gun carry	
S:AUX O V	

Note that negative auxiliaries behave like other auxiliaries, hosting object clitics and tense suffixes (as seen in 4; negative auxiliaries will be discussed in detail in section 4.1.1.)

In contrast to factatives, imperfective clauses are never negated by negative auxiliaries. Rather, they are negated by negative particles which occur between the subject and the verb. The crucial difference is one of word order. Negative imperfective (or habitual) clauses always have the basic order SVO, or more precisely S NEG V O. As will be seen in later sections, negative particles may develop into nominal suffixes (S-NEG V O). When this occurs, the same basic word order occurs.

(6) Dewoin

affirm.imperf.(habitual)	neg. imperf.(habitual)
ɔɔ na tawa	ɔ nĩ na tawa
he:IMP drink tobacco	he NEG drink tobacco
S V O	S NEG V O
'He smokes.'	'He doesn't smoke.'

(7) Klao
    jie ni nu m̀   'I don't have a sore.'
    sore NEG do me   (literally: a sore is
    S   NEG V O   not doing me)

(8) Wobé

    affirmative imperfective   negative imperfective
    ɔ̃ɔ̃   cɛ̄ɛ̄   ā ō̃   ɔ̃ɔ̃́   cɛ̄ɛ̄   ā ō̃
    he:IMP criticize you   he:NEG criticize you
    S   V   O   S:NEG V   O
    'He is criticizing.'   'He is not criticizing you.'

Note that unlike auxiliaries, particles never host object clitics. In 7 and 8 above, object pronouns occur following the verb, not the negative particle (see 4 where a negative auxiliary is present). Negative particles will be discussed in detail in section 4.1.2.

As noted previously, the division of negation strategies according to the factative/imperfective distinction has been found in every Kru language examined in this study. Such wide generalizations cannot be made about clauses containing other aspects or moods, however. The negation of imperative appears to be language-specific. In some languages, imperatives are negated by the same morpheme used to negate imperfectives, i.e., by particle. This is the case in Dewoin. Compare:

(9) imperfective/habitual
    ɔ nĩ na   tawa   'He doesn't smoke.'
    he NEG drink tobacco

(10) imperative
    nĩ nu ɔ   'Don't do it.'
    NEG do it

In other languages, the imperative is negated by auxiliary. This is true in Wobé. Note, however, that the negative auxiliary used to negate imperatives differs from the auxiliary used to negate factative clauses. This is the case in all languages which negate imperatives by auxiliary. Compare:

(11) negative factative   (12) negative imperative
    ɔ̃ sɛ̄ gbŭ pō̃   ā ō̃ bó mu-ɛ
    he NEG house build   you NEG go-NOM
    'He didn't build a house.'   'Don't go.'

To summarize up to this point, two basic generalizations can be made: (1) the imperfective/factative distinction is always maintained by a difference in negation strategy, and (2) the negative imperative always differs from the negative factative, either by strategy or by morphological shape of the negative auxiliary.

Generalizations (1) and (2) above appear to be common in West African languages. First, many Niger-Congo languages seem to use different strategies or different markers to distinguish habitual/imperfective negatives from perfective (or factative) ones. In Bambara, a Mandé language, there are morphologically distinct negative forms for the "accompli" (**mā**) and the "inaccompli" (**tɛ́**) (Dawson 1973; Houis 1969:45). In Fula, a West Atlantic language (Sylla 1977:73-82), as many as six tense/aspect distinctions are neutralized to a perfect/imperfect distinction in the negative.

In regard to generalization (2), J. Payne (1985) notes that it is typologically common for the negative imperative strategy to differ from the other negative strategies. This may be due to the fact that typically the imperative is a separate mood from the indicative, by virtue of its speaker involvement (Chung and Timberlake, MS). Payne notes that two distinct negative markers may be reconstructed for Proto-Indo-European: *ne to negate statements and *me to negate imperatives (p. 43). Welmers (1973:406) points out that in Niger-Congo languages the imperative and hortative are often negated differently from other clause types. This is the case in Kpelle (a Mandé language), and Igbo and Efik (both Kwa languages).

It was noted that in some Kru languages (Tepo, Dewoin, Godié), imperatives and habituals are negated in the same way. This also occurs in other Niger-Congo languages, notably Bariba, a Gur language (Welmers 1973:393), where habitual and hortative actions are negated similarly (**kū** for the hortative and **kù** for habitual), with other actions, such as incompletive, experiential, and past, being negated by a different marker, **n**. This common negative strategy may be because imperatives and habituals are to some extent semantically related. Both refer to unrealized (irrealis) actions.

Now that the distinction between negative auxiliaries and negative particles has been made, these two types of negation will be examined in detail.

4.1.1 Negative auxiliaries. As was mentioned earlier, every Kru language examined in this study has a negative auxiliary or a tonal remnant of such a form. Negative auxiliaries occur in sentences with the basic order S NEG O V. They are always used to negate factative clauses, and they may also appear in negative progressives, futures, perfects, and imperatives. In this section the forms and distribution of the factative negative auxiliaries will be described first. This will be followed by a brief discussion of imperative negative auxiliaries. In later sections, it will be claimed that negative auxiliaries are derived from full verbs. The interaction of the factative negative auxiliaries with

Negation: Strategies and Innovations

future progressives and other constructions will be discussed in the final part of this chapter.

4.1.1.1 Forms and distribution of the negative factative auxiliary.
In the Kru family, the negative factative auxiliary has three basic shapes: **se, nē,** and **tā**. **Se** is found exclusively in Western Kru (although there may possibly be a remnant of **se** in the Kru isolate Kuwaa), while **nē** and **tā** occur primarily in Eastern Kru.

(13) **se** Klao (N. Lightfoot)
   nā gbè s̄ē slɛ̄ dī   'My dog didn't eat a snake.'
   my dog NEG snake eat

(14) **ne** Neyo
   ne bu fa   'I didn't bring a gun.'
   I:NEG gun bring

(15) **ta** Lozoua Dida
   ɔ tā pálṹ sīa   'He did not build a house.'
   he NEG house build

All three auxiliaries have similar distribution (sentence second in S AUX O V clauses) and behave similarly (bearing object clitics and tense suffixes).

Negative auxiliaries with object clitics

(16) **se** Nyabwa
   ɔ sèé-ɛ sʋ̄ā   'He hasn't sharpened it.'
   he NEG-it sharpen

(17) **nē** Godié
   ɔ n-ɔ́ wʋ̀ yī   'I don't know him.'
   I NEG-him NEG know

(18) **tā** Koyo
   e ta-N mɨlɛ̄ kalʉ   'It didn't hurt me.'
   it NEG-me inside make-bitter

Negative auxiliaries with tenses

(19) **se** Bassa (Hobley:39-40)
   ɔ se zɔ̀ɔ kṹā nyu   'He didn't work yesterday or before.'
   he NEG T work do

(20) **ne** Vata (Vogler)

kɔ́ɔ́ **né** uá zɛ̌ íímɛ̄lɛ̄   'The man hadn't recognized
man NEG T thing recognize   the thing.'

(21) **ta** Lozoua Dida

ɔ́ **tá-ā** budo   'He didn't bathe.'
he NEG-REC bathe

As was noted earlier, the basic distinction between imperfective and factative aspects is maintained in the negative. In chapter 2, factatives were described as having a past tense reading for action verbs and a present or undefined reading for stative, cognitive, and emotive verbs. Thus stative and cognitive verbs like 'have', 'know', 'be at', and 'be red' are negated as factatives (by negative auxiliary), rather than by the negative particle **nī** used to negate imperfective and habitual statements. This is true throughout Kru whether the negative auxiliary is **se**, **né**, or **tá**.

se

(22) Bassa

ḿ **se** dō 6édē   'I don't have any.'
I NEG one have
S AUX O V

(23) Tchien[2]

ō̄ **sè** bɛ́ɛ̄ jībō   'They don't like pepper.'
they NEG pepper like
S AUX O V

né

(24) Bété

na dıba **nī** kɔkɔ kʌ   'My father doesn't have
my father NEG chicken have   any chickens.'
    S AUX O V

---

2 Exceptionally, in Tchien Krahn stative and cognitive verbs take a form of the auxiliary **se** different from that taken by other factative verbs.

ō **sèè** pī zèā   'I did not cook today.'
I NEG cook today

ō **sè** bɛ́ɛ̄ jībɛ̄   'They don't like peppers.'
they NEG peppers like

(25) Neyo
    o   ne   gōlo   ne sa   yi   'They didn't know how to use a
    they NEG canoe do way know   canoe.'
    S   AUX   O   V

ta
(26) Dida (Guitry)
    ɩ   ta   kɔdʋnyɔ   glɩ   'I am not a farmer.'
    I   NEG farmer   be
    S   AUX O   V

(27) Koyo
    o   ta   yoo-o   yi   'He doesn't know the boy.'
    he   NEG boy-DEF know
    S   AUX O   V

Now that some of the general characteristics of the negative factative auxiliaries have been described, the individual auxiliary forms **se**, **tá**, and **né** will be examined in detail. In later sections it will be shown that at least two of these auxiliaries, **se** and **tá**, can be shown to be derived from full verbs.

(1) The auxiliary **se**. The negative auxiliary **se** occurs in a majority of the languages in the Western group.

(28) Klao (N. Lightfoot)
    nā gbè sē   slɛ̄   dī   'My dog didn't eat a snake.'
    my dog NEG snake eat

(29) Wobé
    ɔ   sē   dɛ̄   dī   'He didn't eat.'
    he NEG thing eat

(30) Nyabwa
    ɔ   séè súkō lī   'He didn't eat fufu.'
    he NEG fufu eat

(31) Dewoin
    ɔ   sē   wuli jɛ́   'He didn't see a goat.'
    he NEG goat see

(32) Krahn (Gbaeson)

ɔ sé dʊɩ blé 'He didn't sing a song.'
he NEG song sing

(33) Bassa

ɔ se zɔ́ɔ kṹã̀ nyu 'He didn't work a long time ago.'
he NEG T work do

These examples provide evidence for positing a **se** negative auxiliary for some stage of Proto-Western Kru. In a few languages of the Grebo complex, the protoform **se** has undergone some phonological changes. In Nyabo, the negative auxiliary is **he**.

(34) ɔ he ma kòã nu 'He didn't work yesterday.'
he NEG T work do

The development of *s-->h is well established in the Grebo complex, and thus **he** can be seen as a direct reflex of **se**.³

Not every Western language has an unmistakable reflex of **se**. In Borobo, another language of the Grebo complex, the negative auxiliary is **ye** (also transcribed as **i** or **e**). Sound correspondences have not been studied in this language, so we cannot be sure that *s > y. However, it seems probable that **ye** is cognate with **se**.

(35) ɔ ye kũã nu dyĩnõwã̀nã̀ 'He didn't work today.'
he NEG work do today

In Tepo, the negative auxiliary has the form **dḗ**, which may be a reflex of **se** or, more likely, of the auxiliary **nḗ**.

(36) ń dḗ dɛ̄ nū 'I didn't do anything.'
I NEG thing do

---

3 Consider, for example, the following forms taken from Marchese 1979. Tepo, Trewi, and Oubi all belong to the Grebo complex.

	'two'	'arm'	'hot'
Godié	sɔ̄	sɔ	su/srʉ
Guéré	sō	sʋ	sua
Tepo	ho	--	hnɛ
Trewi	hoɔ̄	ho	hene
Oubi	hwɔ̄	ho	--

(Vowel correspondences are quite complicated. At present, I have no explanation for the variation in the forms for 'hot'.)

Negation: Strategies and Innovations   175

In Grebo, there is a rather problematic case. In this language, every negative factative sentence contains an auxiliary **yi**.

(37) **ne yi-da-o   mu**   'I didn't go there day
       I   AUX-T-there go   before yesterday.'

This auxiliary also occurs with factative verbs like 'have' and 'be at' and appears in clauses where the copula 'BE' has apparently been deleted.

(38) ɔ   **yi** kpe   kɔ   'She does not have power.'
      she AUX strength have

(39) **ne yi dɔdɛ London ne**   'I was not in London yesterday.'
       I AUX T   London be

(40) **ne yi   ke**   'I am not a chief.'
       I AUX   chief

Thus, in distribution, **yi** is very similar to the other negative factative auxiliaries. Given the fact that **se** is sometimes realized as **si** in neighboring languages (Singler, Poellet, pers.com.), it would seem very likely that **yi** is also a reflex of *se (*se > si > yi). There is one serious problem with this analysis, however, and that is that the auxiliary **yi** also occurs in affirmative clauses.[4]

(41) **nē yī-dà blà dui**   'I was pounding rice.'
       I AUX-T rice pound-NOM

From the data available (in Innes 1966), it is difficult to tell just what the signal of negation is. In the following, however, it would seem that tone is playing a major role:

(42) **nē yi˦ nɛ̀ du**   'I have not pounded it.'
       I AUX   it pound

No conclusion can be reached concerning Grebo at this time; however, the evidence from the rest of Western Kru strongly supports a proto-*se for that group.

(2) The auxiliary **nî**. The auxiliary **nî** occurs overtly in at least four Eastern languages, with remnants occurring in several others. The full forms occur in Neyo, Bété, Vata, and in a dialect of Dida spoken at Zokoliliē.

---

4 J. Payne (1864:23) identifies **yi** as an auxiliary meaning 'to be in the act of doing'. Innes (1966) notes that **yi** is homophonous with the verb 'see' and occurs in indicative, conditional, and subjunctive clauses (p. 81).

(43) Neyo (Thomann)
    e ne fe   ka   'I don't have any strength.'
    I NEG strength have

(44) Bété (Werle and Dagou)
    ná díbà ní kɔ́kɔ́ kʌ   'My father doesn't have
    my father NEG chicken have   any chickens.'

(45) Vata (Vogler)
    ɔ́ lá ń né kɔ̄ lɛ̄   'She says that I am not a man.'
    she says I NEG man be

(46) Dida (Zokolilié)
    e ne kwla ka   'I don't have a farm.'
    I NEG farm have

In several languages, the **ní** auxiliary is often phonologically reduced and appears as a tonal suffix (usually with high tone) on the noun or pronoun which functions as subject in the negative clause.

(47) Bété (Guibéroua)
    ɔ́ɔ́ɔ́ kɔ́kɔ́ kʌ   'He doesn't have a chicken.'
    he:NEG chicken have

(48) Godié
    ʌ̋ a Dàkpʌ dʌ yī   'I didn't know where
    I:NEG REC Dakpa place know   Dakpa lived.'

(49) Lakota Dida
    ɔ́ɔ́ líkpā 6áà   'He didn't kill a monkey.'
    he:NEG monkey kill

However, in Bété of Kosséoa, the consonant **n** is retained when there is a pronominal object affixed to the auxiliary (Werle and Gbalehi 1976).

(50) ná díbà nɔ́-ɔ̄ yī   'My father doesn't know him.'
    my father NEG-him know

The same is true in both the kagbo and jlʉkɔ dialects of Godié.

Negation: Strategies and Innovations 177

(51) ɟlʉkɔ
 Ā̰ n-í wʊ⁵ yī   'I don't know (it).'
 I NEG-it NEG know

(52) kagbo
 6ɛ̄ Laagɔ n-ɔ́ yɛ 6lāā   'On the contrary, God
 yet God   NEG-him now kill   didn't kill him.'

The retention of **n** could be explained on phonological grounds since, in 50-52, **n** separates a clitic with the shape V from a word ending in a vowel, thus blocking any potential assimilation. However in Godié, **n** is not retained when a tense marker of the same shape (a single vowel) occurs next to the subject.

(53) ɟlʉkɔ
 Ā̰   ā   lɔ́   kʉ̄   'I wasn't there.'
 I:NEG REC there be

(See also 48.)

This provides evidence that object pronouns are more closely bound to the verb than tense suffixes are. It may be that **n** is retained when the syllable V in question is a clitic rather than just a suffix.

In Lakota Dida, the **nī** auxiliary never surfaces, even when object pronouns are forced to occur directly next to subject pronouns.

(54) é   á   wà   'I don't like it.'
 I:NEG it like

(55) é   ɔ́   wà   'I don't like him.'
 I:NEG him like

In at least three non-Eastern languages, there appear to be remnants of the negative auxiliary **nī**. In the Kru isolate Kuwaa, a rising **nɛ̌** is used when negation is emphasized.

(56) we nɛ̌ wá jī   'He hasn't eaten rice at all.'
 he NEG rice eat

(57) we nɛ̌ wá fī   'He hasn't cooked rice at all.'
 he NEG rice cook

---

[5] The form **wʊ** in Godié is a recently innovated negative marker. Its development will be discussed in section 4.2.

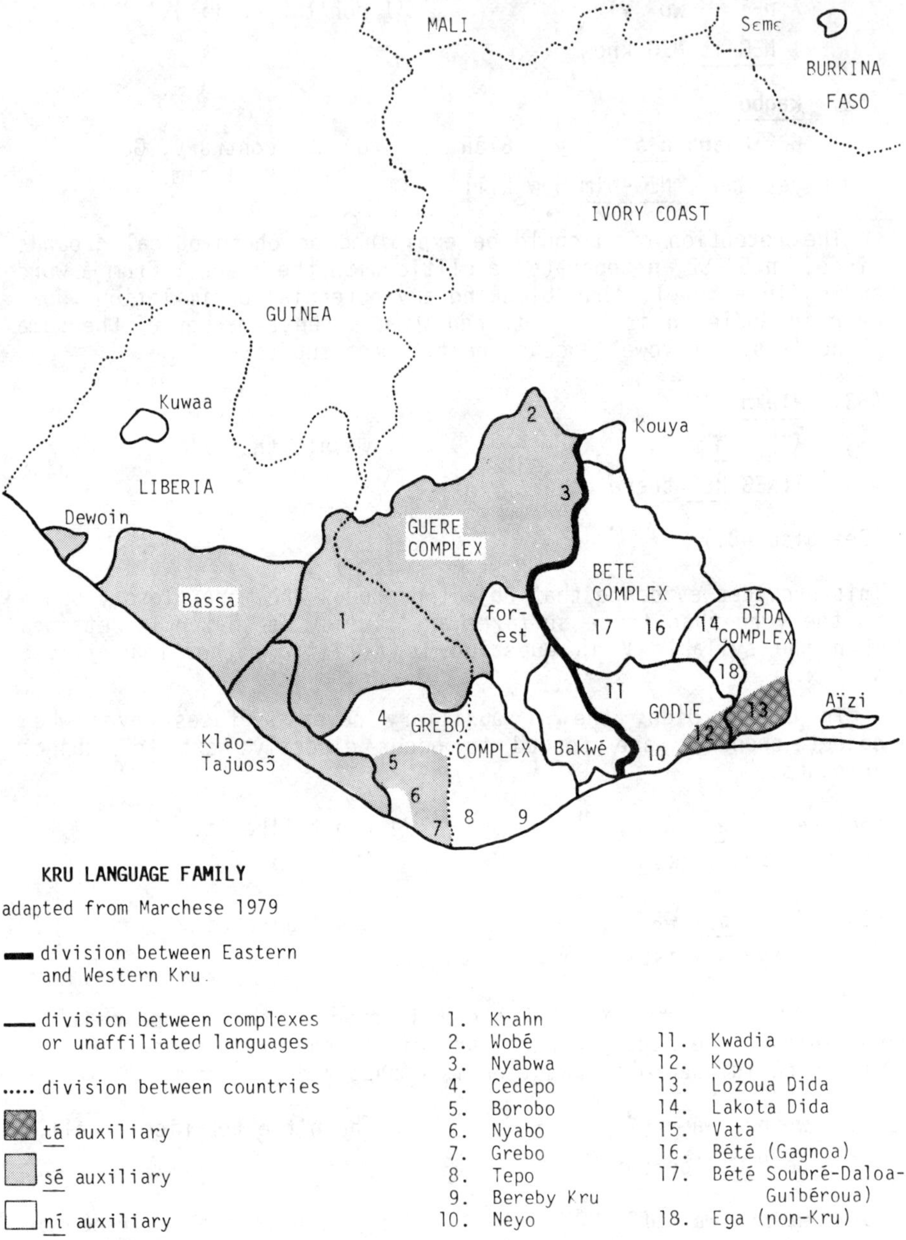

Tense/Aspect and Auxiliaries in Kru Languages

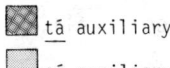

KRU LANGUAGE FAMILY
adapted from Marchese 1979

▬ division between Eastern and Western Kru

── division between complexes or unaffiliated languages

..... division between countries

▨ tá auxiliary

▧ sɛ́ auxiliary

☐ ní auxiliary

1. Krahn
2. Wobé
3. Nyabwa
4. Cedepo
5. Borobo
6. Nyabo
7. Grebo
8. Tepo
9. Bereby Kru
10. Neyo
11. Kwadia
12. Koyo
13. Lozoua Dida
14. Lakota Dida
15. Vata
16. Bété (Gagnoa)
17. Bété Soubré-Daloa-Guibéroua)
18. Ega (non-Kru)

Map 7. Distribution of Negative Auxiliaries

In Tchien Krahn, a negative **ne** auxiliary (which seems to be cognate with Eastern **nĩ**) occurs in negative subordinate clauses including reason, purpose, and complement clauses.

(58) ā bɔ̃ ō̃ ně bu ba   'I don't want them to
     I want they NEG gun whittle   whittle a gun.'

(59) ā̃ mū glē̌ mù, lɩ ō̃ ně gbɛ kpā
     they go farm inside so they NEG load carry
     'They went to farm so they will not (or will not have to) carry a load.'

(60) ā̃ mu kwla lɩ ō̃ ne dɛ pi
     they go bush so they NEG thing cook
     'They went to the bush, and therefore they didn't cook.'

Finally, in Bakwé, there is a negative auxiliary **nyə́** which may possibly be related to **nḗ**.

(61) ɔ nyə́ brekā́lēa mī̃   'He did not go to sing.'
     he NEG sing-NOM go

(3) The auxiliary **tá**. The negative factative auxiliary **ta** is very limited in distribution, occurring only in southeastern Kru.

(62) Koyo (Kokora)
     aɓi ta suklũ mu   'Abi did not go to school.'
     Abi NEG school go

(63) Godié (dialect spoken at Sago)
     ɔ tʌ́ yi   'He didn't come.'
     he NEG come

(64) Dida (spoken at Guitry)
     n ta kɔdʊnyɔ glɩ   'I am not a farmer.'
     I NEG farmer be

(65) Dida (spoken at Yokoboué)
     ɔ tā yi   'He didn't come.'
     he NEG come

The **tá** morpheme may be related to negative imperative auxiliaries **tɩ** (Bété) and **te** (Grebo) (discussed below). The distribution of the negative factative auxiliaries is shown in map 7.

4.1.1.2 The negative imperative auxiliary tī. Besides the negative factative auxiliaries just described, negative imperative auxiliaries also occur in both Eastern and Western Kru. It must be remembered (see sect. 1.5.2.4) that the term **imperative** is used in this study to refer to subjunctive or hortative actions, whether referring to second or non-second persons. In Eastern Kru, Werle (pers. com.) notes that Bété has a "prohibitive auxiliary" of the shape **tī**.

(66) tī ñ tuá wʌ̄zì   'Don't call your friend.'
     NEG your friend call

(67) ɔ tī-ʋ sí6ʎ   'He should not build it.'
     he NEG-it build

As 67 shows, **tɩ** acts as host for object clitics just as other auxiliaries do.

An apparent cognate form also occurs in Grebo (Innes 1966:112).

(68) né té nɛ̀ dū   'That I should not pound it.'
     I NEG it pound

(69) mú né té mó bí   'Go before I beat you.'
     go I NEG you beat

Later, it will be shown that another negative imperative auxiliary is being developed in some Western Kru languages.

4.1.1.3 Etymological links between negative auxiliaries and full verbs. In the previous sections, the forms and distribution of several negative auxiliaries were presented. Now we will turn to a discussion of the origin of these negative markers. According to Givón (1975a:36), "negative markers most often arise diachronically from erstwhile negative verbs, most commonly 'refuse', 'deny', 'reject', 'avoid', 'fail', or 'lack'." This appears to be true in Kru, where there is substantial evidence that the negative auxiliaries have developed from full verbs in much the same way that the verbs 'go', 'come', and 'have' have developed into future auxiliaries. In this section, evidence will be presented which links the negative auxiliaries **se, tā,** and **tī** to full verbs. Though the arguments are less convincing for the morpheme **ne**, it will be suggested that this negative auxiliary also developed from a full verb.

(1) The negative auxiliary **se**. The verbal nature of the negative auxiliary **se** was first noticed by E. Sapir in his short description of Gweabo, a language of the Grebo complex. He notes (1939:39) that "**se** 'not' is really a verb 'to be not' (class IIa) and is conjugated as such."

Negation: Strategies and Innovations   181

Again, in 1975, **se** was recognized as being verbal in origin. Luckau (Hyman 1975:143) suggests that the marker **se** may be derived historically from an intransitive verb meaning 'to tell a lie'. There is, in fact, evidence from several Kru languages which would seem to confirm that the morpheme **se** is related to a stem meaning 'lie'. In Grebo, **se** is a noun meaning 'lie'.

(70) **se be yia nɔ dida**   'If a lie never came, ...'
      lie if NEG   come-T

(71) **nu se**   'tell a lie' (Innes 1967:103)
      do lie

In Nyabwa as well, **se** means 'lie':

(72) **se á   gwló**   'the village of lies'
      lie ASSOC village

In Dewoin, a similar morpheme is a verb meaning 'to lie' (example from Mortvedt).

(73) **ɔ́ síá**   'He's lying.'
      he lie

Thus Luckau's suggested link between the stem 'lie' and the negative auxiliary **se** is plausible. However, there is another morpheme (perhaps coming from the same root as 'lie') which seems to have a more natural link to negation. It is the verb **se** which means 'leave', 'let go', 'miss', or 'stay'. A historical relationship between verbs with similar meanings and a negative modality has been attested in other Niger-Congo languages. In Chibemba, a Bantu language, the verb **-bul-** meaning 'to lack or miss' has recently become a negative modality prefix which occurs in negative conditionals and counterfactuals (Givón 1971b). Also, in the Fuuta Tooro dialect of Fula, a West Atlantic language, an auxiliary related to the verb 'miss' or 'lose' may be used to negate focus constructions (Sylla 1977:87, pers.com.).

(74) **ko miin waas-i am-de**   'It's me who did not dance.'
      FOC me   NEG-T dance-INF

In this language, **waas** functions as a full verb meaning 'lack' or 'lose'.

(75) **o waas-ii debbo makko**   'He has lost his wife.'
      he lose-T woman his

(76) **a waas-ii comci**   'You lack clothes.'
      you lack-T clothes

Thus a semantic link between verbs meaning 'lack', 'lose', or 'miss' and a mark of negation exists in other languages of the Niger-Congo family. It will, in fact, be claimed that negative auxiliaries **se**, occurring in Western Kru, and **ta**, occurring in Eastern Kru, are linked to such verbs.

According to Mortvedt's notes on Dewoin, the verb **se** may be used transitively or intransitively. In its intransitive usage, **se** means to 'stay'.

(77) i <u>se</u>   gee   kɔ   gaiya jisi   'I stayed at the feast
     I <u>stay</u> feast-the-on day break   until daybreak.'

But used transitively the verb means 'leave'. In Nyabwa, as well, the morpheme **si** is identifiable as the verb 'to leave'.

(78) (orthography)

   e <u>sie</u>   'bo   blii' loue 'treen   'He only left one
   he <u>leave</u> there cow   one only   cow there.'

Again, in Klao, the verb **si** means to 'let go' or 'leave' (Singler, pers.com.).

(79) nι <u>si</u>-le   nyakū́ ti   'I left Nyaku there.'
     I <u>leave</u>-LOC Nyakun PART

Besides etymological links, there is other evidence that the negative auxiliary **se** has verbal origins. Unlike most auxiliaries (see chapter 3), **se** may carry certain aspectual distinctions. In several languages, **se** is marked for the factative/perfect distinction.

(80) Dewoin

   ɔ <u>séē</u>   sāyɛ̀ pī   cf.   ɔ <u>se</u> sayɛ̀ pi
   he <u>NEG-PERF</u> meat cook   he <u>NEG</u> meat cook
   'He has not cooked meat.'   'He did not cook meat.'

(81) Bassa

   ɔ <u>séē</u>   kṹà nyu (ke)   cf.   ɔ <u>se</u> kṹà nyu
   he <u>NEG-PERF</u> work do (PART)   he <u>NEG</u> work do
   'He hasn't worked.'   'He didn't work.'

Similar examples occur in Krahn.

In contrast, the other two negative auxiliaries are not marked for the perfective/perfect distinction.

Negation: Strategies and Innovations   183

(82) ta Lozoua Dida
      ɔ **tá** pàlṹ slā   'He didn't build/hasn't
      he NEG house build   built a house.'

(83) ne Godié
      ɔ́ wṵ̀ lɨ   'He didn't eat/hasn't eaten.'
      he:NEG NEG eat

(2) The negative factative auxiliary **tá**. Like **se**, the negative auxiliary **tá** may also be linked to a verb meaning 'leave' or 'let go'. Unfortunately, data are not available on the Dida dialects where **tá** acts as a negative marker. However, in a neighboring Godié dialect, kagbo, the verb 'leave' is **tʌ̃**.

(84) **tʌ̃** nɔ̃ yí   'Let him alone' or 'Leave him
      leave him eyes   alone.' (literally: leave
                                  his eyes)

Kagbo territory is about half an hour away by car from Sago, where the negative auxiliary has the same shape, **tʌ̃**.

(85) ɔ **tʌ̃** yi   'He didn't come.'
      he NEG come

In the jluk̞ɔ dialect (where the negative marker is not related to **tá**), the verb **tu** is used transitively to mean 'leave' and intransitively or in its passive form to mean 'to be lost'.

(86) wa **tṳ** a mɔ́ nʌ   'When they had left there, ...'
      they leave REC there NF

(87) ɔ yʌ **tṳu**   'He is lost.'
      he PERF lose:PASS

The stem itself is also found in the Kru isolate Aīzi, meaning 'lack'.

(88) Aīzi (Herault 1971)
      saka a-ta   te   'There's no more rice.'
      rice it-lack ?   [morpheme-by-morpheme
                                 translation, L.M.]

In Bassa, a language of the Western group, the verb **tá** may be followed by a nominalized verb and express the meaning 'almost' (examples from Hobley; morpheme-by-morpheme translation, L.M.).

(89) ɔ **tá-à** nyu-ε   'He almost did it.'
      he lack-it do-NOM

(90) ɔ tá-á̱   hwɔ-ɔ   'He almost finished.'
      he lack-it finish-NOM

(3) The negative imperative auxiliary **tī**. The negative imperative auxiliary which occurs in Bété is also homophonous with the verb 'leave' or 'lose' (Werle, pers.com.).

(91) auxiliary
      ɔ tī-ʋ   sí6ʌ   'He should not build it.'
      he NEG-it build

(92) verb
      ɔ tī-ɔ   mʌ̃   'He left him there.'
      he leave-him there

In Grebo the negative auxiliary **te** is homophonous with the intransitive verb **te**, meaning 'stay'. Unfortunately, it is not known if this verb may also be used transitively, meaning 'leave'. (Remember that this was the case with the morpheme **se** in Dewoin.)

(93) auxiliary (Innes)
      ne tē nḕ du   'I should not pound it.'
      i NEG it pound

(94) verb (Innes 1967:112)
      ɔ te   ɔ ni   kōã   'He is still working.'
      he stay he do:IMP work

It has been shown that there is an etymological link between the auxiliaries **se, ta,** and **tɪ** and verbs meaning 'leave', 'let go', 'lose', or 'lack'. Now the question may be asked: Are these three auxiliaries related to each other? That is, do they all come from the same protostem? It seems safe to assume that the negative factative auxiliaries occurring in Southern Dida, Southern Godié, and Koyo (**tá** and **tʌ**) and the negative imperative auxiliary occurring in Bété (**tī**) are, in fact, cognate forms. It is interesting to note that in the ɟlʉkɔ dialect of Godié the form for 'leave' or 'let go' is **tátī**.

(95) **tátī nɔ̃ ylɨ**   'Leave him alone.'
      leave him eyes

It may be that the protostem was, in fact, ***tátī**, reducing in some languages to **tá** and in others to **tī**, as the following chart would seem to indicate.

Negation: Strategies and Innovations

Eastern Kru

	Bété	tī	V, tr	'leave'
	Vata	te	V, tr	'leave'
	Godié			
	jlʉkɔ	tātī	V, tr	'leave'
	kagbo	tʌ́	V, tr	'leave'

Western Kru

	Wobé	táī	V, tr	'leave'
	Bassa	tā	V, tr	'lack'
	Grebo	té	V, intr	'stay'

Isolate

	Aïzi	ta	V, ?	'lack'

The form in Wobé, **táī**,[6] seems to give further evidence that the protostem was originally *tātī. It is known that many intervocalic consonants in Wobé have reduced, giving rise to vowel sequences (Link 1975; Marchese 1979). Note that both the jlʉkɔ and Wobé forms have identical high-mid tones. Thus, there is evidence of a form *tātī which gave rise to **tā** in some of the languages and to **tī** in others.[7] This means that the negative factative auxiliaries **tā/tʌ́** and the imperative auxiliary **tī** are, in fact, related.

---

6 A similar verb **táī** appears in Wobé, which is used to mean 'leave' or 'permit'.

  kàá yesu sē sìì sàè̀ ī táī ī sē wlū
  but Jesus NEG spirits bad POST leave they NEG speak
  'But Jesus didn't allow the evil spirits to speak.'

It has also been brought to my attention that a particle **tà** occurs in sentence-initial position as a negative imperative marker (Egner, pers.com.).

  tà ī ji nɔ́ NEG you come here
  'Don't come here.'

It would appear that this **ta** is related to the negative imperative morphemes in Eastern Kru, but the exact connection has not yet been determined.

7 Another possible explanation for the variation in forms could be that the protostem tı was followed by a suffix, giving rise to a new form **ta**. Evidence for this scenario comes from Bété, where the auxiliary **tī** can apparently be followed by a suffix which Werle labels 'actuel'.

  tī-àá̀ sìkàá̀ jwī-dī sɛ́ 'Don't tell lies.'
  PROH-ACT now lie-message pick

The suffix may in fact be related to the negative postverbal particles discussed in section 4.2. This explanation cannot account, however, for the forms in Godié and Wobé.

Now that the forms **tá/tʌ́** and **tī** have been linked, can these forms be linked to Western **se**? Though no definite conclusion can be made at this time, evidence does suggest that there may be a link between the two forms. For one thing, they share the same semantic content and the same syntactic distribution. If there were to be such a connection, the most logical scenario would be that a morpheme **te** (coming from ***tātī** or just ***te**) would weaken to **se** in Western Kru. Though, admittedly, not a great deal of reconstruction has been done, most of the time ***t > t** (Marchese, 1977b).

	'three'	'father'
Dida (Guitry)	(mo)ta	to
Godié	ta	tʉ́
Neyo	ta	tʊ́
Bété (Daloa)	ta	to
Nyabwa	tā'	tītā
Bassa	ta	(no cognate)
Wobé	ta̰	
Kuwaa	tãã̀	tē˜

There are, however, two rather curious correspondences involving a ***t > s** shift that occurs in both Eastern and Western Kru, as seen in the following charts:

*t > s / __ u in Eastern Kru and Dewoin[8]

Eastern Kru

	'tree'	'push'
Dida (Guitry)	su	susuə
Godié	sū	sú
Neyo	sū	sú
Bété	sú	súni

Western Kru

Nyabwa	tu	túū
Wobé	tu	tu
Krahn (Konobo)	tu	tui
Kuwaa	ti	tō˜

and ***t > s / __ ɛ** in Western Kru.

Eastern Kru

	'snake'
Vata	tlɛ
Dida	[trɛ]
Godié	tlɛ
Neyo	tlɛ
Bété	tɪmɛ

---

[8] For the noun form, at least, it is highly probable that the original stem was **ti-u** (Welmers, pers.com.). Thus the actual conditioning of the t>s shift may have originally been **i** rather than **u**.

The Emergence of Three Future Auxiliaries 187

Western Kru

Niaboua	sẽ
Wobé	sẽ
Guéré	sẽ
Konobo Krahn	sɛrɛ
Klao	slɛ
Tepo	hre

Isolate

Aïzi	srɪ

Thus, it is very likely that *tatɪ or simply tɪ would have been related at some time to *se (given this last set of correspondences). It is not possible, however, at this point to link all three auxiliaries, tɪ, se, and nɪ.

(4) The negative auxiliary **nĩ**. The origin of the negative auxiliary **nĩ** is much more difficult to determine than the origin of the other negative auxiliaries. First, it must be noted that the auxiliary **nĩ** is homophonous with the negative particle **nĩ** (to be discussed in section 4.1.3), though its distribution in the family is much more limited. The difference between the negative auxiliary and the negative particle is, again, the fact that auxiliaries occur in S AUX O V structures, while particles appear in S PART V O structures. There is also a difference in semantic distribution in this case: **nĩ**, the auxiliary, is used primarily to negate factative clauses, while **nĩ**, the particle, is used to negate imperfectives and imperatives. Along these lines, J. Payne (1985) notes: "In many cases negative particles which are conditioned by the tense or mood of the predicate turn out to be reduced forms of negative verbs which have lost their person and number inflections."

This could suggest that the auxiliary **nĩ** and the particle **nĩ** may have the same origin. Are they, in effect, the same morpheme? Or, did **nĩ** become an auxiliary following some established pattern (for example, S **se** O V)? These questions must be left unanswered, since no data are available which could shed light on these problems.

Whatever the explanation of this homophony, it is interesting to note that both the **nĩ** particle and the **nĩ** auxiliary resemble the verb **ne (ni/nɪ/de)**, which functions as a locative verb 'be at' and as a copula in some languages.

(96) Tchien Krahn

gbú blĩnblĩn nè lé gwlɔ́   'A black house is in town.'
house black   is LOC town

(97) Wobé
  ḕ nē̄-ɛ̄ kẃlā̀ī   'I am a hunter.'
  I be-DEC hunter

(98) Bassa
  ɔ nĭ gedeɔ mú   'He's at the farm.'
  he be-at farm inside

(99) Dewoin
  ā̀ nĭ m̀m̀   'We are five.'
  we are five

(100) Grebo
  ɔ ne ku   'He is fierce.'
  he is demon

(101) Dyabo
  ɔ ne suɖu   'He's dirty.'
  he be dirty

(102) Aïzi
  cans na ɛ nɩ prɔ   'The cloth is white.'
  cloth DEF it be white

(103) Kuwaa
  ē̄ dē̄ gbāā   'It is big.'
  it be big

The connection between a negative marker and the verb 'be at' or 'be' seems odd indeed. However, J. Payne (1985:41) notes:

> The origin of negative verbs, both of the higher verb and auxiliary variety, is frequently obscure. Nevertheless, some evidence, both direct and circumstantial, exists that in at least some cases the negative verb is simply a negative form of the verb 'to be'.

For example, in Fijian, the higher negative **sega** may also be used to deny the existence of an object (J. Payne 1985). In Chukchi, the negative may contain a supportive BE element. Other linguists report similar findings. Munro (1976) notes that in Kuwaiisu, a Uto-Aztecan language, the negative morpheme, which is nominal in form, seems to include the morpheme BE.

Negation: Strategies and Innovations

(104) **yu-waa-tɨ** (negation marker)
 BE-negative suffix-participle

Yu is said to come from Proto-Uto-Aztecan ***yɨ** 'BE'. In Aymara (an American Indian language spoken in Bolivia), a particle **k**, derived from a copula, is obligatory in the negative (P. Landerman, pers. com.). In Toura, a Mandé language, the copula **nuu** also appears in certain negative clauses (Bearth 1971:279).

(105) máá nūū mɔɔ́ã ló-á   'I couldn't go there.'
 I:NEG COP can-GER go-GER

In Tiv (Arvanites: Abraham 1940:25), the negative may also include a negative copula.

(106) ŋ̀gù ə̀ hìdə̀ ga   'He hasn't returned.'
 NEG NEG return NEG
 COP

The problem with the connection between BE and the **nĭ** auxiliary in Kru is that there is no explanation why an affirmative element BE would have taken on a negative meaning. There is at least one possible explanation, however. It can be noted that while the copula and locative **nì** is always on low tone, the negative marker **nĭ** is always on high tone. This may indicate that the negative marker **nĭ** is really made up of two morphemes: the **nì** copula/locational verb and a negative element (whose remnant is high tone). Admittedly, this explanation is speculative.

4.1.1.4 On the development from verb to negative auxiliary. It has been noted that at least three negative auxiliaries, **se**, **ta**, and **tɩ**, are etymologically linked to full verbs meaning 'leave', 'let go', or 'lack'. It is believed that the shift verb-->negative auxiliary took place in much the same way as 'go', 'come', and 'have' developed into auxiliaries (as seen in chapter 3). That is, they arose from the construction:

$$S\ V_1\ [(O)\ V_{2\ nom}]$$

where OV_2 functioned as the complement of V_1.

There are two pieces of evidence in favor of this hypothesis. First of all, the verbs 'leave', 'let go', 'lack', or 'miss' imply that an action either did not occur or, at least, was not completed. Thus the semantic shift involved is plausible. A sentence meaning 'He left rice-eating' is easily reinterpreted as meaning 'He did not eat rice'. (Of course, the verb 'leave' implies that an action was begun and stopped, while the reinterpreted negative marker carries no such implication.) As was the case with the development of future auxiliaries, the semantic shift involves loss of the feature [+intent]. That is, in a statement like "Dago left rice-eating," Dago performed a volitional act, while in "Dago did not eat the rice," no such intent on the part of the subject is necessarily implied. The action merely did not take place. Second, the verbs which have given rise to negative auxiliaries are all potentially transitive verbs. This can be seen in 80, 86, and 97. As early as 1931, Sapir had noticed that the auxiliary **se** in Gweabo was transitive. Commenting on the sentences,

(107) ẽ nṹ   dɛ   ẽ sé   dɛ   nṹ
       I make thing   I NEG thing make
       'I make a thing.'   'I do not make a thing.'

he notes (1931:39): "Syntactically, the word group **dɛ nṹ** inverted from **nṹ dɛ**, acts as a sort of complementary absolute (or infinitive) following on the main verb ɛ **se** 'it negates' ...."

In Tepo, where the negative **dé** must be a reflex of **se** (or possibly **ne**), certain negative sentences have the structure SUBJ **dé** NP, indicating that **dé** may take sentential complements:

                    S
(108) ɔ **dé** b-ɔ   dī   lé   'He will not come.'
      he NEG that-he come PART

(109) ɔ **dé** b-ɔ̃   nylḗ   ŋa   'He will not arrive
      he NEG that-he arrive T   tomorrow.'

This same structure is found when full verbs like 'can' or 'want' take sentential complements.

(110) ɔ **wɛ̀rɛ́** b-ɔ   diré   le   'He can come.'
      he can   that-he come-PART LOC

(111) ń **hòà** b-ò   bi̋   m̀   'I want to hit you.'
      I want that-I hit you

Thus, the negative auxiliary **dé** in Tepo also appears to be transitive, that is, capable of taking object complements.

Lending support to the S V_1 [O $V_{2 \text{ nom}}$] $_{\text{COMP}}$ hypothesis is the transitivity of **se**, **tá**, and **tī**. Furthermore, there is evidence of a nominalizer in some Eastern languages where the negative auxiliary is **nī** or its remnant. Thus, in the Kagbo dialect of Godié, Lakota Dida, and Vata, the verb in the S NEG O V construction has a tonal fall, indicating there may have been a nominalizer present.

(112) Vata (data from Hilda Koopman)
      ǹ nī̀ sákā líì   'I did not eat rice.'
      I NEG rice eat-FALL

(113) Lakota Dida
    ɔ́   líkpā 6áà   'He didn't kill a monkey.'
    he:NEG monkey kill-FALL

(114) kagbo (Godié)
    Laagɔ n-ɔ́   yɛ 6láà   'God didn't kill him.'
    God   NEG-him now kill-FALL

There is, however, no evidence of a nominalizer remnant in the **se** and **tá** auxiliary constructions.

Another piece of evidence in support of the hypothesis that **se**, **tá**, and **tı** developed from full verbs is that there is a similar reanalysis presently going on in several Western languages. In Krahn, Bassa, Klao, and Sapo, the verb 'stop' is being used to negate imperatives. The structure of the negative imperative construction is exactly the same as the one proposed here and in chapter 3:

$$S\ V_1[(O)\ V_2\ _{nom}]$$

In these cases, V_1 is the verb 'stop'.

(115) Bassa (Hobley)
    6ɔ   kūà nyu-ɛ   'Don't work.'
    stop work do-NOM

(116) Klao
    bɔ   dɛ   di-di-dɛ   'Don't eat anything.'
    stop thing eat-eat-NOM

(117) Tchien Krahn
    ɔ́ **bɔ́**   dbū̄ tê-ɛ́   'He shouldn't buy a rope.'
    he stop rope buy-NOM

(118) Gbaeson Krahn
    bɔ dbu̱ cɛ́⁻   'Don't cut rope.'
    stop rope cut

In Sapo, the expression is preceded by a morpheme **b-**, a particle often used in hortative constructions.

(119) **b-ɔ   bɔ́ kō dī-ɛ̄**   'He mustn't eat rice.'
    that-he stop rice eat-NOM

(120) cf. ɔ bɔ   kō dī-ɛ̄   'He stopped eating rice.'
          he stop rice eat-NOM

Though the **bɔ** morpheme in each of the languages described above seems to have maintained all its verbal characteristics, there has been a semantic shift from 'stop' (as in 'stop eating') to NEG-IMPER (as in 'don't eat').[9] Again, the semantic shift involves a change from a verb implying that an action has begun to a negative marker without this implication. This particular shift does not appear to be very common in languages of the world, though it is attested in Welsh (J. Payne 1985).

(121) **paid â symud**   'Don't move.'
     (stop = **peidio**)

In Igbo, the verb 'refrain', which is similar to 'stop', is used in its affirmative hortative form as a negative imperative morpheme (Welmers 1973:406).

(122) **kà ọ̱ ghàrá í'rí ńrí**   'He shouldn't eat.'
     he refrain eat food

Despite the semantic shift in Bassa, Klao, and Krahn (examples 115-118), there has been no phonological change in the construction as a whole (neither in the shape of the verb or the form of the nominalizer). In Wobé, however, the verb 'stop' has presumably changed shape from **bɔ** to **bo**, as seen in the following examples. This confirms the general observation made in previous chapters, where it is shown that a verb which has undergone bleaching may be open to phonological change. Note, however, that the nominalizing particle is still present.

(123) 'stop'
    ɔ́ bɔ́ blé-à   'He stopped singing.'
    he stop sing-NOM

(124) negative imperative
    è̄ bō à blāā   'Don't hit us.'
    you NEG us hit-NOM

These Western languages show that, in this case at least, negative imperative markers are developing from the construction

$$S\ V_1[(O)\ V_{2\ nom}]$$

containing an overt nominalizer. This supports the hypothesis that other negative auxiliaries developed in a similar way.

---

9 In at least one Kru language, 'stop' is used with the negative to indicate past habitual actions:

Bassa
    nyɔ nà kɛɛ ɔ nī 6ɔ́àà nyuɛń wɛ̄
    man this ? he NEG stop-it do NOM ?
    'This man used to do it.'

Negation: Strategies and Innovations   193

It has been suggested that full verbs meaning 'leave', 'let go', and 'stop' have developed into negative auxiliaries. In her work Universal Grammar and Diachronic Syntax: The case of the Finnish Negative, Mulder notes that, in general, SVO languages shun the use of verbs as negative markers. She claims that if such a state exists, a "language will be under pressure to reorganize in such a way that the negative element loses whatever verbal properties it possesses" (1978, p. v). If her claim is valid, then there may be more pressure on the construction

$$S_{+NEG} \; V \; (O) \; V_{nom}$$

than on the other complex constructions such as futures (chapter 3) and progressives (chapter 2) to change into S AUX O V. Thus this "pressure" (to use Mulder's term) may perhaps account for the fact that verb-derived negative constructions often have no remnant of a nominalizing particle.

4.1.2 Negative particles. As was mentioned in section 4.1, negative particles are used to negate imperfective and habitual statements. In some languages, they negate imperatives as well. In this section, negative particles in both Eastern and Western Kru will be discussed. Evidence will be given for the reconstruction of a Proto-Kru negative marker *nĩ.

4.1.2.1 nĩ in Western Kru. The negative particle nĩ or a variant (n + high front vowel) is attested in several Western languages. It is found in the Grebo complex in Tepo, Grebo, and Borobo, and in nonaffiliated Western languages such as Klao, Bassa, and Dewoin. In the following, nĩ occurs between the subject and the verb. The word order is always S NEG V O.

(125) Grebo

    ɔ́ ně dú nὲ   'He is not pounding it.'
    he NEG pound it
     S NEG V O

(126) Tepo

    ʋ nɪ dī re bʋcʋ   'They don't eat pork.'
    they NEG eat PART pork

(127) Dewoin

    ɔ nĩ ná tàwa   'He doesn't smoke.'
    he NEG drink tobacco

(128) Klao (N. Lightfoot)

    Do nĩ slɛ tiwɛ̃   'Doe doesn't usually read.'
    Doe NEG read time-all

(129) Bassa (Hobley)

    ɔ **nĩ** sa   'He's never tired.'
    he **NEG** tire

Apparent cognates of the **nĩ** marker also occur in Bakwé, though this could be a combination of a BE verb and a negative marker.

(130) ɔ **ne** brē-brē-ã   'He's not singing.'
       he **NEG** sing-sing-NOM

The uses of the particle **nĩ** vary from language to language. Some generalizations can be made, however. In every language where **nĩ** occurs, it is always used to negate habitual and generic statements. In the majority of languages, it negates imperfective action. The particle also negates imperatives in some languages. In Tepo, for instance, the **nĩ** particle is used to negate all three categories. In 131-133 an additional element, **le** (or **re**), occurs in postverbal position. This morpheme may be an emphasizer.

(131) incompletive

    ɛ **nɩ** ŋla   lɩ   'She is not giving birth.'
    she **NEG** give-birth PART

(132) habitual

    ʋ   **nɩ** di re bʋcʋ   'They don't eat pork.'
    they **NEG** eat PART pork

(133) imperative

    nĩ[10] di re dɛ   'Don't eat anything.'
    NEG eat PART thing

The uses of **nĩ** in the Western languages are summarized in the chart on the next page. (***** means **nĩ** is not used to mark the mood or aspect in question; **?** means that information is not available on the use of **nĩ** in a given context.)

The summarizing chart shows that the **nĩ** particle occurs in several Western languages belonging to the Grebo complex and the non-affiliated group. No examples have been found in the Guéré complex.

4.1.2.2 nĩ in Eastern Kru. In Eastern Kru, the negative particle **nĩ** is not found in its full form in many languages. It does occur, however, in Neyo and Bété.

---

10 In the examples from Tepo and Dewoin, ni occurs with a low tone in the imperative. This is due to the deletion of the second person singular pronoun which is always on low tone (see also sect. 3.8.2).

Negation: Strategies and Innovations

language	form of NEG	habitual	imperfective	imperative
Tepo	ní...lɩ	x	x	x
Grebo	ne	?	x	?
Borobo	ne	?	x	?
Klao[11]	nɩ	x	x	x
Bakwé	nʉ, ne	?	x	x
Dewoin	nī	x	*	x
Bassa	ni	x	*	*

(134) Neyo

yuwliyo né ne saa   ɔ nī 6lɩ
man   NEG do like-that he NEG sing
'A man doesn't act like that.'   'He's not singing' or
                                  'He doesn't sing.'

(135) Bété (Kosséoa)

ná dībā nɪ́ lī kɔ̄kɔ́   'My father doesn't eat
my father NEG eat chicken   chicken.'

In the Bété spoken at Daloa, a similar particle **nʉ** is used to negate imperatives.

---

11 N. Lightfoot (1974:4) makes no mention of the fact that nɩ can be used to negate imperfective statements in Klao. She notes, in fact, that nɩ is used for habituals, while **se** is used for everything else. However, from her examples such as the following:

Wli nɩ je ni   'Wli doesn't see the water.'
Wli NEG see water

I infer that nɩ may also negate imperfectives. In other works on Klao (for example the Kru Data Book by the Catholic Sisters) nī also may negate imperfectives.

jie ni nu ḿ   'I don't have a sore' (literally:
sore NEG do me   "a sore is not doing me").

In another dialect (Sɛttra Kru), however, incompletive and habituals are apparently negated in two separate ways (Devlin et al.:248).

a nɛ pru sɔ̃   'We don't sell chickens.'
we NEG sell chickens

a sɛ sɔ̃ pru   'We're not selling chickens.'
we NEG chickens sell

This last form is quite divergent from all other Kru languages and cannot be explained at this point.

(136) (Zogbo, Raymond)

bɛ̀   nṹ   vlɛ   glɛ̀   'Nobody should insult a
person NEG insult mask   masked dancer.'

The evidence from both Eastern and Western Kru strongly suggests that a **nī** particle existed in Proto-Kru. In the following section, the remnants of the ***nī** marker as they occur in both Eastern and Western Kru will be described.

4.1.2.3 Remnants of **nī**.

Remnants of **nī** occur in both Eastern and Western Kru. As was the case with the imperfective particle **a** (see chapter 2), the second-position **nī** particle has a tendency to become affixed to the preceding word (the subject of the clause). In one description of Bassa (believed to be written by Clubvine), it is reported that habitual statements are negated by a special set of pronouns (p. 12).

	SING	PL
1	mɔ́n	ā̰n
2	mɔ̰n	6ḛ̀n
3	ɔ̰n	wà̰n

(137) ɔ̰́n   nyú kṵ̀à   'He never works.'
       he:NEG   do   work

(138) ā̰n   nyú kṵ̀à   'We never work.'
       we:NEG   do   work

The above forms appear to be reductions of pronouns followed by the imperfective negative marker **nī**.

(139) ɔ   nī   nyú kṵ̀à   'He doesn't work.'
      he NEG do   work

(140) ā   nī   nyú kṵ̀à   'We don't work.'
      we NEG do   work

According to the grammar, the two forms may cooccur, expressing a present emphatic (p. 15).

(141) mɔ́n   nī¹²   nyu kua   'I do not work' or
       I:NEG   NEG   do   work   'I am not working.'

---

12 The grammar states that **ni** may be omitted with first or second person singular. The **ni** is homophonous with a sentence-final **ni** which expresses aspectual notions and which is probably linked to the verb BE. The negative marker **ni**, however, does not function in any way like a verb. For example, tense markers occur after the main verb, never after **ni**.

   ɔ   nī   nyú ma   kua   'He never worked.'
   he NEG do   T   work

Negation: Strategies and Innovations

Thus, there are now three constructions:

    the source construction: S nī V O
    and two innovated ones: S-n   V O
                                  S-n nī V O

The new pronoun set has a syllable structure which is extremely unusual in the Kru family (Marchese 1979). It seems that the structure VN does occur elsewhere in Bassa where it contrasts with nasalized vowels.

(142) **badyōma mu Goozɔ̃̄ sɔ̃ñ**   'Badyoma will come
     Badyoma FUT Goozɔ̃ come-from from Goozo.'

Similar phenomena occur in Eastern Kru. In Bété, for example, **nī** occurs when there is a full noun functioning as subject (see 136 repeated here as 143). When the subject is a pronoun, however, **nī** reduces to a high tone, realized on the subject of the clause (Werle and Gbalehi 1976:176). Compare:

(143) **nā dībā nɨ̀ lī kɔ́kɔ́**   'My father doesn't eat
     my father NEG eat chicken   chickens.'

(144) **ɔ́ɔ̀   nímʌ́**   'He doesn't drink.'
     he:NEG drink

(145) **ǹń   nímʌ́**   'I don't drink.'
     I:NEG drink

Note that when **nī** reduces, the vowel of the pronoun is lengthened to carry high tone. This phenomenon parallels a development discussed in chapter 2. There it was seen that in Tchien Krahn the imperfective particle **a** was realized in its full form when it followed a full noun subject, but was reduced and often neutralized when following a pronoun subject (see sect. 2.2.2). Thus, the sequence <u>pronoun + particle</u> is much more likely to undergo phonological reduction than the sequence <u>full noun + particle</u>.

Other remnants of **nī** apparently occur in Godié, Lakota Dida, and Vata. In each of these languages, imperfective and habitual sentences are negated by high tone on the noun or pronoun functioning as subject in the clause.

(146) <u>Godié</u>

    Laagɔ́ɔ́ 6lā wʋ̀   **ɔ́ɔ́   mɛ̄wʋ̀**
    God:NEG kill NEG   he:NEG go NEG
    'God doesn't kill.'   'He doesn't go' or 'He's
                                      not going.'

(147) Vata

    ɔ́ɔ̱   lā   uā   kɔ̄⁻   'He wasn't calling anyone.'
    he:NEG call T   person

(148) Lakota Dida

    wobeŋwa wā́   li   trɛ   'Wobés don't eat snakes.'
    Wobés[13] they:NEG eat snake

Though data are not available on Vata and Lakota Dida, in Godié the high tone negator is also used to negate imperatives. An additional supportive element (SUP) occurs in both dialects of Godié cited below. (These elements will be briefly discussed in 4.2.)

(149) **jluko**

    ɔ́ɔ̱   pā-ā̀ā̀ā̀   kʉ̄lī   ʌ̄̀ʌ̄̀   ki   ā̀ā̀ā̀
    he:NEG throw-SUP anger   you:NEG speak SUP
    'He shouldn't get mad.'   'Don't speak.'

(150) **kagbo**

    ɔ́ɔ̱   lɨ   lʌ̄   sákā   'He shouldn't eat rice.'
    he:NEG eat SUP rice

There may also be remnants of the high tone **nī** in the Kru isolate Kuwaa. Note that high tone marks the negative in the following habitual sentence:

(151) **wɔ́ɔ̱   jɨ   wā**   'He doesn't eat rice.'
      he:NEG eat rice

---

[13] Though my data on Lakota Dida are not complete, it is worth mentioning that in what I do have, every time there is a full noun subject in a negative clause, the sentence has a topic-comment construction, as seen in the sentence just cited.

    wobeŋwa waā   li   trɛ   'Wobés don't eat snakes' or more literally,
    Wobés   they:NEG eat snake   'Wobés they don't eat snakes.'

The use of the topic-comment strategy in negatives is not surprising since negative statements tend to contain a great deal of presupposed information. In particular, the subject is virtually always presupposed. Givón (1979) notes:

Negative clauses are not used for introducing new referential arguments into the discourse, but rather, they are used in contexts in which a referential argument has already been mentioned in the preceding discourse (103) ... only a relatively small increment--namely the denial by the speaker of the hearer's belief, constitutes the new communicative contribution of the negative-assertion speech act... (112).

Negation: Strategies and Innovations

Up to this point, the negative particle **ní** has been found in its full form in both Eastern and Western Kru, with possible tonal remnants occurring in Eastern Dida, Vata, Godié, and the Kru isolate Kuwaa. These findings are summarized on map VIII, where cross-hatching indicates the presence of a full **ní** marker, and slanting lines, the presence of a tonal remnant.

In studying the map, one can see that **ní** is conspicuously absent in parts of the Grebo complex and in the entire Guéré complex. Lack of data is probably responsible for the gaps in the Grebo complex. In the Guéré complex, however, imperfective, habitual, and generic statements are negated by a vocalic suffix **a** which is attached to the subject of the sentence.

(152) Nyabwa
    Grace-a̍ pō kɔ̄bū   'Grace does not plant rice.'
    Grace-NEG plant rice

(153) Tchien Krahn
    kpee-a kpā nyunuū sɔ̄   'The raft cannot carry two children.'
    raft-NEG carry children two

(154) Wobé
    nynúū mēé a̍ na̍ nmɔ̄   'Little children don't drink wine.'
    children little NEG drink wine

In Nyabwa and Tchien Krahn, the same marker is used to negate imperatives. (Note that a supportive element, **lè**, occurs in Nyabwa.)

(155) Nyabwa
    àa̍ mū lè   'Don't go.'
    you:NEG go SUP

(156) Tchien Krahn
    aa zedaa nyɔglo   'Don't tell anyone.'
    you:NEG tell person

Apparently in most of these languages, the **a** suffix often assimilates to the vocalic quality of the final vowel of the subject when it is a pronoun (and sometimes when it is a full noun as well).

(157) Wobé
    ɔɔ̍ cē̄ āō   'He is not criticizing you.'
    he:NEG criticize you

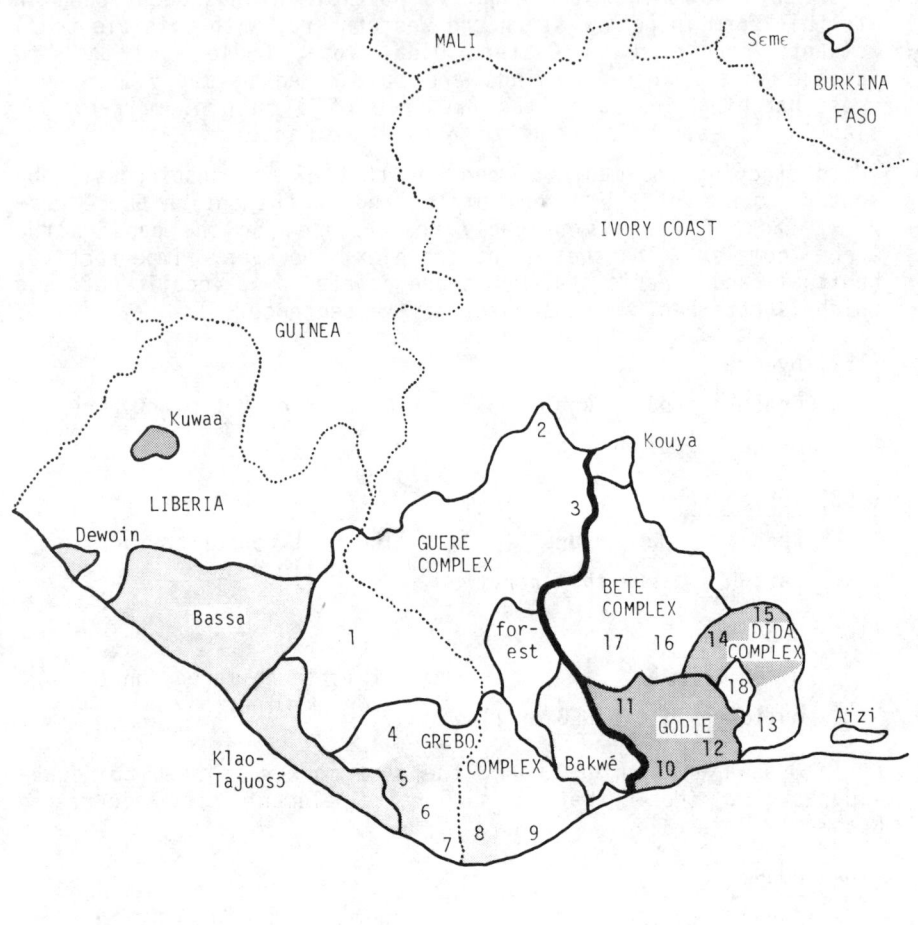

KRU LANGUAGE FAMILY
adapted from Marchese 1979

━━ division between Eastern and Western Kru

── division between complexes or unaffiliated languages

..... division between countries

▢ full form ní

▨ tonal remnant of ní

1. Krahn
2. Wobé
3. Nyabwa
4. Cedepo
5. Borobo
6. Nyabo
7. Grebo
8. Tepo
9. Bereby Kru
10. Neyo
11. Kwadia
12. Koyo
13. Lozoua Dida
14. Lakota Dida
15. Vata
16. Bété (Gagnoa)
17. Bété Soubré-Daloa-Guibéroua)
18. Ega (non-Kru)

Map 8. Distribution of ní

(158) Nyabwa

ɔ!ɔ́   ná   nmɔ   'He doesn't drink palm wine.'
he:NEG drink palm-wine

Tāpɛɛ!́ ná   nm   'Tapɛ doesn't drink
                          palm wine.'
Tapɛ:NEG drink palm-wine

(159) Tchien Krahn

kpàbɔɔ di kwɔ́nu   'The frog cannot eat leaves.'
frog:NEG eat leaves

It is interesting to note that except for tone, the negative particle **a** looks exactly like the imperfective marker **a** which is used extensively in the Guéré complex. The imperfective **a** occurs in exactly the same position as the negative marker **a**, that is, directly following the subject of the clause and in the same semantic environment (with imperfective and habitual actions). Except in Nyabwa, the **a** imperfective suffix usually occurs on mid tone. Since negative **ní** usually occurs on high tone and is often reduced to a high tone (as in Bété, Godié, etc.), it may be that the **a** negative particle is actually a coalescence of two morphemes—the imperfective nominal suffix **a** and a remnant of the high-tone negative particle **ní**.

     S-a   ní   V   O   ---->
     S-á!   ∅   V   O

Several cases of assimilation have been discussed. In particular, it has been seen that the fusion of subject pronouns and the negative particle **ní** is quite common, occurring in Eastern Godié, Bété, Lakota Dida, Western Bassa, and, if the hypothesis proposed above is correct, languages of the Guéré complex: Nyabwa, Wobé, and Tchien Krahn. The same type of fusion occurs in other African languages such as Hausa (J. Payne 1985) and Toura, a Mandé language (Bearth 1971:278).

(160) **mɔ́ɔ́**   ló   'I didn't go there.'
      I:NEG:ACC go

Thus, the coalescence of negative particles and pronouns is not unheard of in other languages, but it does seem to go against a basic tendency in language noted by J. Payne (1985): "In terms of position, negative particles are primarily associated with the verb or the verb phrase." Steele (1973) and Mulder (1978) both note that negatives tend to occur close to the verb (with preverbal position preferred) or early in the clause. Note that despite the attachment of **ní** to the subject, it is still close to the verb and early in the sentence. As the Kru examples show, through processes of assimilation and boundary shift, negative particles in

Kru may come to be primarily associated with the subject rather than the verb phrase of the clause. In the case of the string S **a** (imperfective marker) V O, the assimilation to S-SUF V O is understandable on phonological grounds since a single vocalic element rarely occurs as an independent morpheme in any but sentence-initial environment. This cannot, however, explain the assimilation and suffixation of a full CV morpheme like **nĭ**. Another possible explanation may be that as a modality marker, **nĭ** is "seeking" to cliticize onto some element. Since Kru languages are uniquely suffixing, the string S PART V O cannot possibly be reanalyzed as S PREFIX-V O, and the only other possibility is for it to attach itself onto the subject: S-SUF V O.

The association of sentential negation and subjects is certainly uncommon in languages of the world. Mulder (1978:85-86) puts forth the hypothesis that negative affixes tend to occur on verbs because their occurrence in other positions would cause "a confusion of scope." She notes: "In the case of a noun phrase, there would be ambiguity between noun phrase negation and sentence negation."

However, this is not the case in Kru, where negative affixes on the noun phrase do, in fact, indicate sentential negation. To my knowledge[14] they are not ambiguous and only indicate sentential negation.

The reduction of **nĭ** to a tone marked on the noun results in a state of affairs which also seems to run counter to one of J. Payne's basic claims about negation (1985):

> It seems that all languages use at least one of the three devices, negative verbs, negative particles and negative derivational morphemes, in order to effect standard negation. In a few cases, the use of one of these devices is accompanied by a secondary modification in the sentence to be negated. The modifications we have observed are: (a) a change in word-order, (b) a change in tone, (c) neutralization of tense distinctions, (d) the use of supporting verbs, and (e) a change in noun-case. Such modifications on their own, however, are not sufficient to negate any sentence type in any language. In this respect, negation contrasts with

---

14 Unfortunately, not much data is available on noun phrase or constituent negation in Kru. In the following example from Godié (kagbo), however, it can be seen that noun phrases may be negated by casting them in a topic-comment construction.

lìi   ì   6ʌ   lʌ   zəkpə kʊ́ nĭ   ì   plʌ   lʌ
things they leave LOC world up and they:REL enter there

nyʉkpɔ mlì   na, ıì   nyima wʊ̀ nyʉkpɔ
man   inside NF they:NEG spoil NEG man

'The things from this world that enter a man are not what defile him' or 'It is not the things of the world that enter a man and defile him' (Mark 7:15-16).

other features such as tense or mood, which may indeed be realized by such modifications alone.

Clearly, examples like those in 146-148 where tone is the sole indicator of negation are counterexamples to this claim.[15] It can be noted, however, that in some languages where tone alone indicates negation, these have begun to develop alternate signals of negation (see sect. 4.2). This would seem to indicate that Payne's claim should be modified to state that while tonal indicators of negation do exist, they are unfavored or unstable and tend to be accompanied by supporting elements which will eventually give rise to new negative morphemes.

4.1.2.4 Functions of nī in Proto-Kru. In both Eastern and Western Kru, nī and its remnants have been seen to occur. It has been shown in every language examined that nī and its remnants are used to negate habitual and generic statements, and also that nī may serve to negate imperfectives and imperatives. In Proto-Kru, then, nī must certainly have been the negator of habituals. It is possible that at some later stage the use of nī extended to imperfectives and imperatives. Since there is no other candidate for a Proto-Kru negative imperfective or imperative marker, it is likely that nī functioned as a negator for all three categories. As can be seen in the chart in section 4.1.2.1, there are some languages where nī is not now used to negate imperfectives or imperatives. However, the absence of nī can usually be explained by other changes which have affected the languages. In Dewoin and Bassa, nī is not used to negate imperatives, though it does negate habitual statements. In Dewoin, it was shown that the regular use of the nominal suffix **a** was lost as a marker of imperfective action and a periphrastic progressive construction took its place. This innovative construction is negated by a negative auxiliary, rather than a negative particle. Consequently, the use of nī as a negator of imperfective actions was lost. In Bassa as well, there is no trace of the typical Kru imperfective markers (the verbal suffix **e** or the nominal suffix **a**). The loss of such markers was certainly accompanied by the loss of nī (or in this case, nī) as the negator of imperfective clauses.

Likewise, several languages have innovated negative imperative auxiliaries. Presumably, these negative auxiliaries replaced nī in the innovating languages. This accounts for the absence of nī as a negative imperative marker in Bassa, Wobé, and Klao.

In conclusion, there is no doubt that a negative particle nī existed in Proto-Kru, and it seems likely that it functioned as a negator of imperfective, habitual, generic, and imperative clauses.

---

15 It may be argued that the lengthened vowels in 149-151 constitute part of the negative marker. However, in languages such as Godié, the long vowel can be interpreted as a single vowel with two tones (i.e., a vowel with two tones is realized as a long vowel).

4.2 Elaborative Innovation in the Negative System

Compared with negation systems in other Kru languages, the forms in certain dialects of Godié (notably kagbo and jlʉkɔ) are quite unique. It has been shown in previous sections that in Godié, there are remnants of both the **nī** nonauxiliary particle and the **nī** auxiliary. These can be seen in the jlʉlɔ dialect.

(161) remnant of the **nī** particle

 ɔ̄ɔ̄ lɨ̄ wʊ̀ sʉ̄kʌ́   'He's not eating rice' or
 he:NEG eat NEG rice   'He doesn't eat rice.'

(162) remnant of the **nī** auxiliary

 ʌ̄̄ n-ɔ́ wʊ̀ wā   'I don't like him.'
 I NEG-him NEG like

However, as these examples show, there is usually another element present in negative sentences, namely, the morpheme **wʊ̀**, which appears postverbally in sentences without an auxiliary (161), or following the tonal remnant or the combination n + object pronoun (as seen in 162). The Godié negative seems to be, then, a discontinuous morpheme **nī ... wʊ̀** or **⁻... wʊ̀**. With the possible exception of Sɛmɛ,[16] I have not found the morpheme **wʊ̀** in any other Kru language. Yet speakers of Godié recognize this morpheme as a signal of negation. How, then, is this form to be accounted for?

Givón (1975b:50) has noted that there are two basic motivating factors in syntactic change: simplification and elaboration. While negative constructions generally tend to be conservative, the language may innovate specific devices to "function as further elaborations of negative expressions." Negatives may be emphasized or receive specific time reference through the addition of morphemes. This may be done in English by adding words like 'ever', 'at all', 'yet', or 'damn' to already negative sentences. A good example of the effect of this elaborative mechanism on a negative system comes from French, where the present negation is a discontinuous morpheme which surrounds the verb or auxiliary.

Je **ne** parle **pas** anglais Je **ne** suis **pas** allé là-bas
I NEG speak NEG English I NEG be-AUX NEG go there
'I don't speak English.'   'I didn't go there.'

---

16 A particle wʊ̀ does occur in both affirmative and negative sentences in Sɛmɛ, a Kru isolate. Since Prost did not give a morpheme-by-morpheme translation, its gloss is unsure. However, it is possible that it is cognate with Godié wʊ̀.

 affirmative: n'a lu d'a **wo** bɛ
      I say he **WO** come 'I say he's coming.'

 negative: n **wo** le le bo 'I'm not eating.'
     I **WO** food eat NEG

Negation: Strategies and Innovations

It is well known (Givón 1975a; J. Payne 1985) that originally the negative in French was **ne**. Presumably, the morpheme **pas** (a noun meaning 'step') first functioned as the object of a verb.

Il ne marche pas   'He does not walk (a step).'
he NEG walk   step

Through time, **pas** came to be reanalyzed as part of the negative, giving rise to the discontinuous morpheme **ne...pas**. At the present time, the morpheme **pas** apparently has more functional load than **ne**. In colloquial French, the **ne** may be dropped in certain environments, as in the following sentence:

Je sais pas   'I don't know.'
I know NEG
[še pa]

Similarly, Munro (1973) notes that in Yuman languages, emphatic morphemes may be added to already negative sentences and may eventually be reanalyzed as part of the negative morpheme. This seems to have occurred in Mojave (p.12), where an emphatic **t** has combined with the original negative **mo** to give rise to a new negative morpheme **mot**. Parallel cases of reanalysis of emphasis morphemes have occurred in English (Givón 1975a; J. Payne 1985) and Welsh (J. Payne 1985). In Old English, the word **nawhiht** 'nothing' was reanalyzed as a negative marker. In Welsh, the word **ddim** 'thing' was originally added to negative statements for emphasis and was eventually reanalyzed as a mark of negation. Apparently the Godié negative marker **wʋ̀** has a similar origin.

As is commonly the case in other languages, in Kru, negatives may be modified by the addition of particles indicating specific time reference or emphasis.

(163) Vata
      nã̀ si   kã̀   'Don't laugh.'
      NEG laugh EMPH

(164) Dewoin
      ɔ sê ke ta   'He hasn't eaten yet.'
      he NEG yet eat

(165) Bassa (Clubvine:17)
      ɔ se naa   kua nyu   'He never works.'
      he NEG never work do

Note that these particles typically follow the main verb, or the auxiliary if one is present. This is precisely the distribution of **wʋ̀** in Godié.

(166) ɔ́ɔ   lɨ̅   **wʋ̀**   sʉkʌ̅   'He's not eating rice.'
      he:NEG eat NEG rice

(167) ɔ́ɔ   **wʋ̀**   sʉkʌ̅ lɨ̅   'He didn't eat rice.'
      he:NEG NEG rice eat

In the auxiliary construction, **wʋ̀** occurs after object clitics and tense markers.

(168) ʌ̃ n-ɔ́   **wʋ̀** yɨ̅   'I don't know him.'
      I NEG-him NEG know

(169) ʌ̃́   a   **wʋ̀**   lʊ   ɓʌlʌ   'I didn't kill anything.'
      I:NEG REC NEG thing kill

As a language learner, I consistently identified **wʋ̀** with negative sentences, and speakers often indicated to me that **wʋ̀** was the mark of negation. It was only after several years that I learned that **wʋ̀** may occur in affirmative clauses, meaning something like 'just'.

(170) **wlʋ̃** **wʋ̀** zʉkʌ ná yɛlɛ́ɛ   'Just look at me (I'm filthy).'
      lock EMPH today my skin-DEF

(171) **Naa, ŋwa-a wʋ̀ sa yã n kā wlʊ**
      I-say, put-it EMPH out and I VOL look
      'So, just lay it out (your arguments) and I'll consider (them).'

Thus the development of the negative in Godié is strikingly similar to cases of elaborative innovation in other languages. The original negative **nɨ́** was reinforced by an emphasis particle **wʋ̀**. The negative was then interpreted to be a discontinuous morpheme **nɨ́...wʋ̀**. It appears that **wʋ̀** is now gaining considerable ground as a mark of negation, and given the tendency of **nɨ́** to reduce phonologically, it would not be surprising if **wʋ̀** actually becomes the sole mark of negation (paralleling the growing dominance of **pas** in French). Though **wʋ̀** occurs in the overwhelming majority of clauses, it appears to be still optional in statements containing the negative auxiliary and stative or cognitive verbs.

(172) ʌ̃́   a   lɔ́   kʋ̀   'I was not there.'
      I:NEG REC there be

(173) ã̠   nyʉkpɔ kʌ̃   'I don't have anybody.'
      I:NEG man   have

The emergence of **wù** as a negative marker may provide some answers to a problem that has not yet been discussed. In a subset of Eastern languages (Koyo, Dida spoken in Lozoua, Yokouboué, Blé, and Guitry, and in some Godié dialects), the negative auxiliary is **tʌ** or **ta**, which has been shown to be derived from the verb 'leave' or 'let go'. What has not been mentioned is that in these same languages, the morpheme **ta** also occurs in postverbal position where it negates imperfective and habitual clauses.

(174) Koyo
      ɔ mʊ tā suklū   'He does not usually
      he go NEG school   go to school.'

(175) Godié (Sago)
      ɔ̄ yī tʌ̄   'He's not coming.'
      he come NEG

The distribution of **tā** is quite unusual. No other negative auxiliary in Kru appears in postverbal position. I believe that the use of **tā** as a postverbal imperfective negative marker is innovative in Southeastern Kru. First, in 175 it can be seen that there is a remnant of the **nī** imperfective marker. Presumably, as the **nī** reduced to a mere tonal marking, the signal of negation in the clause was weakened. At the same time, the **tā** negative auxiliary was moving away from its verbal origins to become a real mark of negation. Then, perhaps on the pattern of **wù** in dialects spoken no more than half an hour away, **ta** was inserted in postverbal position as a reinforcement of the imperfective negative. It will be recalled that **wù**, which comes from an emphasis particle, has exactly the same distribution as **tā**: in sentence-second position as an auxiliary and in postverbal position as an imperfective negative marker.

Another possible case of innovative elaboration occurs in the negative forms **nī...lV**. The morpheme **lV** found throughout Western and Eastern Kru (see 131-133; 149-150; 155) may be connected to a locative marker, possibly meaning 'there'. Compare the following forms from the kagbo dialect of Godié:

          NEG 'support'   lʌ
          Locative particle   lʌ

Lʌ could have been added onto negative statements much as **pas** was added to negative clauses in French, where it was eventually reanalyzed as part of the signal of negation.

Thus, it has been shown that the negative system has been a fruitful area for innovative elaboration in Kru, as it has been in languages all over the world.

4.3 Interaction of Negation with the Tense/Aspect System

The two negative strategies discussed in section 4.1 interact in various ways with other temporal and aspectual factors not yet mentioned. In this section, there will be brief discussions of the interaction of negative particles and auxiliaries with future, conditional, and progressive markers.

4.3.1 The negative future. Strategies for expressing the negative future differ considerably in Eastern and Western Kru. The discussion will begin with Western Kru since the formation of the negative future is more straightforward in this group.

4.3.1.1 Western Kru. Languages in Western Kru use mainly two strategies for negating future actions: (1) they combine the negative auxiliary **se** with a verb-related future construction, and (2) they combine the negative auxiliary **se** with future tense suffixes.

(1) **se** and the verb-related future. In languages where there is a 'go'-related future, the most common strategy for negation is simply to combine the construction with the negative auxiliary **se**. That is, where normally **mu** functions in auxiliary position, **se** "replaces" it, sending it to the end of the clause.

(176) Klao

    ɔɔ   mu dɛ cɛ   ɔ sē dɛ̄ cɛ́ mū
    he:INC FUT thing learn   he NEG thing learn FUT
    'He will learn.'   'He will not learn (anything).'

(177) Bassa

    ɔ mu kũã nyu-ɛ́   ɔ se kũã nyu-ɛ́ mu
    he FUT work do-NOM   he NEG work do-NOM FUT
    'He will work.'   'He will not work.'

(178) Gbaeson Krahn

    ɔ mu dbṳ̀ cɛ   ɔ se dbu cɛ ḿ
    he FUT rope cut   he NEG rope cut FUT
    'He will cut rope.'   'He will not cut rope.'

These structures are a direct result of the verb-like nature of both the negative auxiliary **se** and the future auxiliary **mu**. It can be noted that all verbs in Kru may embed in a similar fashion.

(179) Dewoin

    ɔ̃ nã̀ wūlī̃ɔ ghɔ́ɔ̃̄ 65   'He has stopped looking
    he PERF goat-D look-for stop   for the goat.'

Taking the above as the pattern, we can see that the negative future construction, such as in 177, has the following structure:

    ɔ se [[kùã nyu-ɛ́] mu]   'He will not work.'
    he NEG work do-NOM FUT
                            (go)

In this structure the complex complement of **se** is **kùã nyu-ɛ́ mu**, the complement of **mu** is **kùã nyu-ɛ́**, and the complement of **nyuɛ́** is **kùã**.

In chapter 3 it was shown that in some languages, the morpheme **i** or **yi** occurs in the same place as **mu** in the future negative.

(180) Wobé
    ɔ̄ sē̄ dɛ̄ di ī   'He will not eat.'
    he NEG thing eat FUT

(181) Tchien Krahn
    ɔ sèe plè i   'He will not run.'
    he NEG run FUT

(182) Nyabwa
    í sèe yli yī   'I will not steal.'
    I NEG steal FUT

(183) Dewoin
    ɔ se sayɛ̄ pi i   'He will not cook.'
    he NEG meat cook FUT

The structure of these sentences parallels the **mu** constructions (see Bassa example, 177).

    ɔ se kua nyuɛ mu   'He will not work.'
    he NEG work do FUT

It will be recalled that **i** is considered to be derived from the verb 'come'. Thus, both negative future constructions appear to come from structures meaning either 'I did not go to X' or 'I did not come to X'. With the shift of 'go' and 'come' to future modalities, the constructions were presumably reinterpreted to mean 'I will not X'.

(2) **se** and future suffixes. Another common strategy for expressing the negative future in Western Kru is to combine the

auxiliary **se** with future suffixes.[17] These suffixes are typically very specific in terms of time reference, referring to 'tomorrow', 'day after tomorrow', etc. As will be seen in chapter 5, these types of tense suffixes appear to be reduced forms of temporal adverbs.

(184) Klao

    dṍ <u>sē̄</u> <u>kā̄</u> dē   cē̄⁻   'Doe won't learn anything.'
    Doe <u>NEG</u> <u>FUT</u> thing learn

(185) Borobo

    ɔ <u>yè-à</u> kṳ̀à̀ nu   'He will not work tomorrow.'
    he <u>NEG-T</u> work do

4.3.1.2 Eastern Kru. In Eastern Kru the negative future is typically expressed by what appears to be a combination of the imperfective negative particle and the future auxiliary. This is the case in Neyo, where the negative marker **ne** precedes the future auxiliary **ka** (from Thomann).

(186) o <u>ne</u> <u>ka</u> gbo pla   'He will not enter the house.'
     he <u>NEG</u> <u>FUT</u> house enter

(187) o <u>nek'o</u>   ba   'She won't marry him.'
     she <u>NEG-FUT</u>-him marry

The basic word order is S NEG AUX O V, with the auxiliary **ka** taking both object clitics and tense suffixes. The **nıka** combination is used to negate both 'come'-related (**yi**) and 'have'-related (**ka**) futures.

(188) affirmative futures

    ɔ yi 6lı   ɔ ka 6lı
    he <u>AUX</u> sing   he <u>AUX</u> sing
    'He will sing.'   'He will/wants to sing.'

---

17 Not all negative futures fit the two patterns being discussed, though the majority do. In Tepo Kru the auxiliary **dé** combines with a supportive verb 'can' which takes a sentential complement (P. Thalmann, pers.com.).

    n dé lē̄ wɛ̀ b-ṍ yē̄ dɛ   'I will not see the
    I NEG PART can that-I see thing   thing.'

In Bakwé, there is a negative future auxiliary **nə̄mʎ** which may be followed by a tense marker.

    ɔ́ nə̄mʎ pē̄ brē̄ābré̄   'He won't sing tomorrow.'
    he NEG-FUT T sing-NOM

This form looks a great deal like an Eastern negative future, as seen in the next section.

Negation: Strategies and Innovations

(189) negative future

    ɔ nī ka   6lι   'He will not sing.'
    he NEG-FUT sing

In Lakota Dida, it will be recalled that the negative is expressed by a high tonal remnant of **nī** on the subject of negative sentences. The negative future in this language is made up simply of the future construction plus the tonal remnant: S-NEG **yi** (O) V.

(190) **Kūdu yi   ziki   sākā li**   'Kudu will eat rice
     Kudu AUX tomorrow rice eat   tomorrow.'

     Kudu ɔ́   yi ziki   sākā li   'Kudu will not eat
     Kudu he:NEG FUT tomorrow rice eat   rice tomorrow.'

Again, as in Neyo, it is the future auxiliary that hosts object clitics and tense suffixes.

(191) **waá   yi å   sa**   'They will not build it.'
     they:NEG FUT it build

(192) **ɔ́   yi wa   sākā 6lu**   'She shouldn't have
     she:NEG FUT PAST rice pound   pounded rice.'

The data underline certain characteristics about future auxiliary constructions. First, the data show that in these constructions, the auxiliary is being negated as a main verb (thus the order S NEG AUX O V coming from S NEG V_1 O V_2). This is in keeping with Givón's observation that negative structures are often syntactically conservative. Second, the data show the correlation between the imperfective aspect and the future--a correlation which was discussed at some length in chapter 3 (see sect. 3.5.4). It is the imperfective particle **nī**, not the auxiliary, which occurs here. If it were the auxiliary, the order would be S NEG O V_2 V_1.

The same combination of a future auxiliary and an imperfective negative particle can be seen in certain Southern Dida dialects, where the 'come'-related future combines with the imperfective postverbal negative marker **tā**. Recall that **tā** acts as a suffix and not as an auxiliary in imperfective contexts (see sect. 4.2).

(193) Lozoua Dida

    ɔ cι ta pàlṹ sla   'He will not build a house.'
    he FUT NEG house build

(194) Dida (from Guitry)

    ɔ cι tʌ̄ ci   'He will not come.'
    he FUT NEG come

Thus, the example from Lozoua Dida seems to be derived from a structure such as:

    ɔ   cɪ   tá [pàlʋ̀ sla]
    he come NEG house build
    S   V   NEG   O

'He is not coming to build a house', which is certainly reinterpreted as:

    ɔ cɪtá pàlʋ̀ sla   'He will not build a house.'
    he <u>NEG</u> house build
    S   <u>AUX</u> O   V

In Godié, the negative future is expressed by the auxiliary **náà**:

(195) ɔ **náà**   mɔ́   mʉ   'He won't go there.'
        he <u>NEG:FUT</u> there go

While this form is less transparent than the forms in the other Eastern languages, it is possible that it, too, is a combination of **nī + ka**. In support of this hypothesis is the fact that the full form **ka** and remnants of **nī** both appear as independent morphemes in the language (**nī** being the negative marker and **ka** the future marker). As was the case in Neyo, the auxiliary **náà** in Godié is the only strategy for negating future sentences.

(196) <u>affirmative futures</u>

    ɔ yi mʉ   ɔ kʌ́ mʉ
    he POT go   he VOL go
    'He will/can go.'   'He will/wants to go.'

(197) <u>negative future</u>

    ɔ **náà**   mʉ   'He won't go.' (also 'can't'/
    he <u>NEG:FUT</u> go   'doesn't want to')

In Vata, the negative future form is similar to the in Godié form **náà**, but the Vata form is much more problematic in terms of its behavior. This form (possibly a combination of **nī + waà**, a future marker) does not function as an auxiliary, as can be seen where the order is S NEG V O (from Koopman, pers.com.).

(198) ŋ́ **náà**   lē   sāká   'I won't eat rice.'
       I NEG:FUT eat:IMP rice
       S   NEG   V   O

Thus this future construction is negating like a simple imperfective sentence. Furthermore, unlike other examples from Eastern Kru seen here, the main verb **li** is overtly marked for the imperfective.

The negative future forms in Eastern Kru are even more diversified than what has been described so far. In Northwestern Dida (and more precisely in the villages of Niémélilié, Dogohiri, Gnahorêparêhouin, Zokolilié, and Guigédou) a negative auxiliary with the shape **zV** appears.

(199) Niémélilié

    ɔ   ze   yi   'He will not come.'
he NEG:FUT come

(200) Gnahorêparêhouin

    ɔ́   zʌ   yi   'He will not come.'
he:NEG FUT come

The origin of this auxiliary is not known. Some dialects (see 200) show a long-form pronoun probably indicating a remnant of high tone **nī**. If this is the case, **zV** may be an innovation as **wṹ** is in Godié (see sect. 4.2). The form could, in fact, be cognate with Godié **sêê** 'also' or 'either', which often appears in negative clauses.

The above discussion shows that there is much diversity in forms between Eastern and Western Kru, as well as within the two groups. In Western Kru, negative futures almost always contain the negative auxiliary **se** in combination with the verb 'go', with remnants of the verb 'come', or with the future suffixes. In Eastern Kru, on the other hand, negative futures often involve the imperfective negative marker **nī** or its remnants in combination with future auxiliaries.

4.3.2 Negative progressives. In section 2.3, it was shown that progressives in most Kru languages are expressed by a periphrastic construction involving the verb 'be at'. Because 'be at' is a stative verb, the progressive is negated, as is any other factative, by use of a negative auxiliary. Thus the negative construction used for the progressive looks very much like the negative future construction found in Western Kru.

    FUTURE: S NEG (O) V { **mu** (go) / **yi** (come) }
    PROG: S NEG (O) V be-at

Some examples of negative progressives are the following:

(201) Dewoin

    ɔ́ sē sāyɛ̄ pī   nǎ   nī   'he is not cooking meat.'
he NEG meat cook LOC BE

(202) Wobé

    ɔ̃ sẽ gbŭ pō á nẽ   'He is not building
    he NEG house build NOM BE   a house.'

(203) Bassa

    ɔ se kùã̀ nyū-ɛ̄ nĩ   'He is not working.'
    he NEG work do-NOM BE

(204) Nyabwa

    ī̀ se kɔbù po namʊ́ nĩ   'I am not planting rice.'
    I NEG rice plant NOM BE

(205) Kuwaa

    mă bɛ nu dè   'I am not going.'
    I:NEG go NOM BE

4.3.3 Negative conditionals. In chapter 3 it was shown that there are two basic strategies for expressing conditionals. In some languages, the antecedent contains a special conditional auxiliary (seen to be related to 'have' or 'come'). In others, the antecedent is marked by a special sentence-initial particle **bo**. Whatever the affirmative form, negative conditionals all have one characteristic in common: the antecedents contain auxiliaries and thus have the S AUX O V word order.

In languages of the Guéré and Grebo complexes, where the particle **bo** appears, the antecedent is negated by the addition of the regular negative auxiliary (**se** or its reflexes).

(206) Krahn

    pò ī̀ sé-ɛ́ nú   'If you don't do it, ...'
    COND you NEG-it do

(207) Wobé

    bò ɔ̃ sẽ dɛ̄ dī̀ ɛ̄   'If he doesn't eat, ...'
    COND he NEG thing eat SUB

(208) Tepo

    bɔ́ de le di   'If he doesn't come, ...'
    COND:he NEG LOC come

(209) Grebo

    bɛ yi nuíé   'If it isn't done, ...'
    COND:it NEG do-Passive

Negation: Strategies and Innovations   215

(210) Borobo
   bō   ē   gblā   fí   'If he doesn't cook rice, ...'
   COND:he NEG rice   cook

In other Western languages where auxiliaries express the conditional, the negative form also contains the negative auxiliary **se**. In Dewoin and Bassa the only difference between a negative factative clause and a negative conditional clause is that the conditional clause is dependent, being signalled by a subordinating morpheme.

(211) Dewoin
   ɔ   se   sayɛ̀   pi   nī   'If he doesn't cook meat, ...'
   he   NEG   meat   cook SUB

(212) Bassa (River Cess)
   ɔ   se   smi   kpɔ̄   nī   'If he doesn't catch fish, ...'
   he   NEG   fish   catch   SUB

In Klao and Sapo, it was shown that in the affirmative, the conditional is a 'come'-related auxiliary with special conditional markers which occur in the same position as regular tense markers. In the negative, the conditional markers cooccur with the regular negative auxiliary **se** (the presence of the markers distinguishes the clause from negative factative statements).

(213) Klao (Rickard)
   si-pa   klɔ   mú   'If you don't go to town, ...'
   NEG:you-COND:T   town   go

(214) Sapo
   ɔ   se-bɛ   kō   pí̀   'If he had not cooked rice, ...'
   he   NEG-COND:T   rice   cook

In Eastern Kru, where conditionals are also typically marked by auxiliary, the negated form usually contains the negative auxiliary **nī**.

(215) Bété (Guibéroua)
   ñ   nī   lū   kʌ̄ʌ̄   'If you don't have anything, ...'
   you NEG:COND   thing   have

(216) Lakota Dida
   ɔ   ne   bɔ   mlɛ   'If he doesn't go there, ...'
   he   NEG:COND   there   go

(217) Godié (ɟlʉkɔ)

ɔ	nʉ	wà	nʌ	'If he doesn't want to, ...'
he	NEG:COND	want	NF	

The negation of especially the auxiliary forms of the conditional seems to support the hypothesis that conditionals are merely dependent temporal clauses which serve as topics of a following comment (see sect. 3.8.3.3). This is borne out by the fact that in Dewoin, Bassa, Bété, and Lakota Dida, the antecedent in a negative conditional is virtually equivalent, except for marks of subordination, to a regular negative clause.

(218) Dewoin

ɔ́	se	sayɛ̀	pi	nī	cf.	ɔ́	se	sayɛ̀	pi
he	NEG	meat	cook	SUB		he	NEG	meat	cook

'If he doesn't cook meat, ...'   'He didn't cook meat ...'

In these languages, the negative conditional seems to come from a structure meaning:

Given: he didn't cook the meat

Consequent: we won't eat

The conditional forms reveal one interesting fact: where, in the same language, the **nī** may be reduced to a tone, in other negative forms conditionals often conserve the **nī** negative marker. In Bété, the full form **nī** appears when there is a full noun subject, but typically reduces with a pronoun subject. However, in the conditional form (215), the **nī** occurs even when the subject is a pronoun. In Lakota Dida, where **ne** never surfaces in any other negative (imperfective, factative, future), it does occur in its full form in the negative conditional (216). Thus, subordinate negative clauses are more conservative than main negative clauses. Again, this goes along with the general observation that subordinate clauses, which typically contain less new information, tend to be more conservative than main clauses (Givón 1975).

4.4 Conclusion

It has been shown that there are two principal negation strategies in Kru--negation by particle and negation by auxiliary. A particle **nī** was reconstructed as the negative marker of habitual and probably imperfective and imperative clauses. It was suggested that the postverbal particles sometimes accompanying **nī** or its remnants are innovative forms. Negative auxiliaries, whose primary function is to negate factative clauses, were shown to be derived from verbs meaning 'leave', 'let go', or 'lose'. Imperative negative auxiliaries may also develop from these verbs, though they apparently develop more commonly from the verb 'stop'. It was

claimed that negative auxiliaries arose from the complex structure
$$S\ V_1[(O)V_2\ {}_{nom}]_{COMP}$$
in essentially the same way as future auxiliaries. Finally, the interaction of the negation system and futures, progressives, and conditionals was briefly discussed.

The presence of the two negative strategies and their distribution based on aspectual factors confirm the claim made in chapter 2 that the imperfective/factative distinction is basic to the Kru family. As has been seen, this basic division permeates the Kru negation system.

5 EXBRACIATION: THE BREAKDOWN OF THE S AUX (O) V CONSTRUCTION

5.1 Introduction

In chapters 3 and 4, it was shown that a new syntactic pattern, S AUX (O) V, developed from S V_1 (O) $V_{2\text{ nom}}$ --the complex complement structure. Given that the unmarked order in sentences without auxiliaries is SVO (see sect. 1.4.2), the verb-final construction can be seen as being at odds with the existing order, and thus constituting an area of potential syntactic change. There is, in fact, evidence that the verb-final nature of the auxiliary construction is weakening. As a result, elements such as temporal and manner adverbs and oblique NPs designating reason and location --S AUX (O) V X--are appearing in postverbal position in several languages. In this chapter, this word order change will be examined in detail. Motivation for the change will be given and its gradual nature will be demonstrated. The discussion will begin with a presentation of variations in word order which occur within the family.

5.2 Synchronic Variation: Evidence for Historical Change

The basic pattern S AUX (O) V is presently attested in every Kru language examined for this study. Following linguists who have described the same phenomenon in other languages (Stockwell 1977; Vennemann, MS), the AUX...V construction will be referred to in this chapter as a verb brace since the elements AUX and V which make up the predicate surround the other nonsubjectival elements in the clause. This can be seen in Wobé and Godié.

(1) Wobé

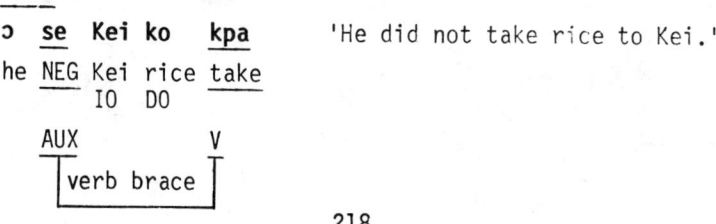

(2) Godié

    ɔ   yī   nŭgʌ̀sʌ   lɨ̃   'He will eat well.'
    he POT well   eat
                 ADV
        AUX   V
        ⌊___verb brace___⌋

Though the verb brace occurs in every Kru language, languages differ considerably as to what may or must occur within it. In some languages temporal adverbs may occur within it the brace, while in others, they would be ungrammatical in this position. Temporal and manner adverbs, reason phrases, and locative phrases are among the elements which may vary as to their position in the verb phrase. These will now be examined in turn.

5.2.1 Temporal adverbs. Cross-linguistically, temporal adverbs are very free in terms of position. In the Kru family, this is also true. Temporal adverbs may occur in sentence-initial position (where they are focussed) or in sentence-final position.

(3) Wobé

    sīã   ɔ   di-ɛ   ko   dé   dɔɔ
    today he eat-DEC rice LOC market
    'Today he ate rice at the market'   or
    'It's today he ate rice at the market.'

    ɔ   di-ɛ   ko   dé   dɔɔ   **sīã**
    he eat-DECL rice LOC market today
    'He ate rice at the market today.'

(4) Koyo

    pɔtɔ   ɔ   yī   ɓutu
    just-now he come:FACT house
    'Just now he came to the house'   or
    'It's just now that he came to the house.'

    ɔ   yī   ɓutu   **pɔtɔ**   'He just came to the house.'
    he come:FACT house just-now

While all Kru languages have the two orders shown above, they differ in restricting the occurrence of temporal adverbs within the verb brace. In Eastern Kru, temporal adverbs are commonly found within the verb brace, while in some Western languages like Wobé, they may never occur in this position.

Eastern Kru (temporal adverbs and phrases may occur within the verb brace)

(5) Godié (ɟlʉkɔ)

Ã̀ yÃ pʉ̀pɛ̀ sʉ̄kÃ bóō bīāà?
you PERF just-now rice bowl finish-Q
    AUX ADV   V

'Have you just finished (eating) the bowl of rice?'

(Kagbo)

Dali 6ɔ zemakō sakaa fι lɨ
Dali NEG day-before- rice-DEF all eat
         yesterday
      AUX ADV   V

'Dali didn't eat all the rice the day before yesterday.'

(6) Koyo

Dago ta yeka du mo   'Dago did not go to town today.'
Dago NEG today town go
     AUX ADV   V

(7) Lakota Dida

ɔ́ yi yré ta né yi   'He will not come in three days.'
he:NEG FUT days three in come
      AUX   ADV   V

Western Kru (examples from languages where temporal adverbs cannot occur within the verb brace)

(8) Gbaeson Krahn

ɔ mú dɛ́ dī sia   *ɔ mú sia dɛ́ dī
he FUT thing eat today
     AUX   V   ADV   AUX ADV   V

'He will eat today.'

(9) Péomé Wobé

ɔ mua dbo nua kã: *ɔ mua kã: dbo nua
he FUT work do right-now
                              AUX ADV   V

'He will work right now.'

(10) Nyabo

ɔ he kòã nu { kɛ́ɛte / pama }   *ɔ he { kɛ́ɛte / pama } kòã nu

he NEG work do { today / yesterday }   AUX ADV V

'He did not work { today / yesterday }.'

Manner adverbs have similar restrictions as to their occurrence within the verb brace.

5.2.2 Manner adverbs. In general, manner adverbs are more restricted in distribution than temporal adverbs. Unlike temporal adverbs, they usually cannot occur in sentence-initial position.

(11) Dewoin

ɔ nu-ó kua { fiofio / flo }   *{ fiofio / flo } ɔ nu-ó kua

he do-REC work { quickly / in vain }

'He did the work { quickly / in vain }.'

This generalization holds in most Kru languages. In terms of position within or without the verb brace, languages differ, however. As was the case with temporal adverbs, in Eastern Kru, manner adverbs readily occur within the verb brace.

(12) Koyo

Doñi yi kapakapasa lo6ee no
Doñi POT crazily work-DEF do
'Doñi will work in a haphazard way.'

(13) Godié

ɔ yi núgʌsʌ lɨ   'He will eat well.'
he POT well eat

(14) Lakota Dida

ɔ yia dʉgasa sákã li   'He will slowly eat rice.'
he FUT slowly rice eat

However, it many Western languages, this order is not allowed:

(15) Gbaeson Krahn
ɔ mú dɛ́ dī sùeī   'He will eat fast.'
he FUT thing eat fast
*ɔ mú sùeī dī dī

(16) Tao Wobé
ɔ se ko di pepe   'He didn't eat rice well.'
he NEG rice eat well
*ɔ se pepe ko di

(17) Borobo

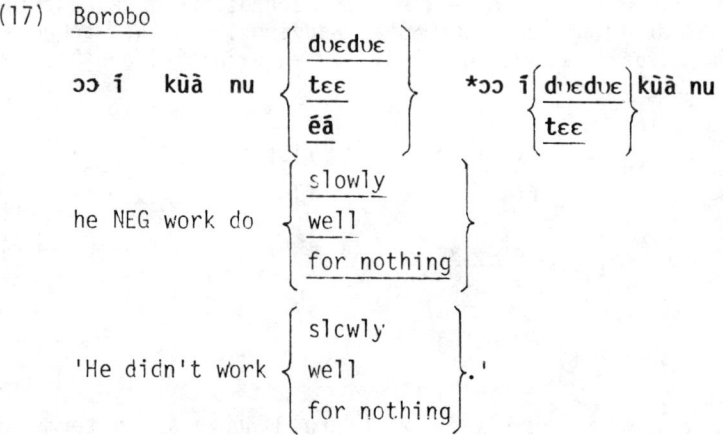

'He didn't work { slowly / well / for nothing }.'

These examples show that while manner adverbs may occur in sentence-final position in languages like Krahn, Wobé, and Borobo, they may never occur inside the verb brace. Similar restrictions seem to hold for reason clauses as well.

5.2.3 Reason phrases. The term **reason phrase** will be used in this study to refer to a noun phrase which supplies an answer to the question "Why did X do Y?" In Godié, such phrases are always made up of a possessor NP followed by the dependent noun zɛ. The NP itself may consist of a pronoun, a noun, or a full S.

(18) ī zɛ ʌ̃ yī   'It's for that I came.'
its sake I come:FACT

(19) ɔ yʌ yəku ɔ́ɔ́ lɨ́ wɯ̀ ī zɛ
he dry side he:NEG eat NEG its sake
'He's skinny because he doesn't eat.'

Exbraciation: The Breakdown of S AUX (O) V   223

Benefactives are expressed in the same way, as seen in Godié.[1]

(20) pıʌ nʊnʊ ɔ́ zɛ   'Buy this for him.'
     buy this his sake

(21) ɔ kíi   ná zɛ   'He's speaking for me (on
     he speak:IMP my sake   my behalf).'

Reason clauses such as these seen above are only loosely connected to the clause and can occur in sentence-initial position. Again, as was the case with adverbs, languages differ as to their restrictions on the placement of reason phrases when an auxiliary is present. Some languages allow reason phrases to occur within the verb brace, while others do not. In this case, however, there does not appear to be a clear East-West division.

Languages allowing reason phrases within the brace

(22) Dewoin (a Western language)
     í nà gēīpɔ́lɔ̄ sɛ̄ɛ̄   ní   ɔ̄ zē po
     I PERF God   thanks rain-DEF REAS PUT
     S AUX IO   DO   REASON   V
     'I have thanked God for (or because of) the rain.'

(23) Godié (an Eastern language)
     ɔ kʌ̄ dú   kòsùú   za   mʉ
                 gun-DEF
     he VOL village fire-DEF sake go
     'He will go to the village for the gun' or 'He
     will go to the village because of the fire.'

(These languages also allow reason clauses in sentence-final position.)

Languages which do not allow reason phrases within the verb brace
(Note that in some cases, reason clauses may be marked by two morphemes X NP Y.)

---

1 Note that in English, reason clauses and benefactives sometimes overlap in overt marking.

  Why did he win the medal?   For saving the man's life.
  What did he go to town for?   He went for the money.
  Who did he buy the dress for?   His wife.

(24) Klao
    dō a mu cɛ́ kó tʋ bò   'Doe will learn for Toe.'
    Doe IMP FUT learn REAS Toe REAS
    *dō a mu kó tʋ bò cɛ

(25) Péomé Wobé (Western Kru)
    ɔ se ko tɛ̏ de ɉunynɔ́kpao mú
    he NEG rice buy REAS woman REAS
    'He did not buy rice for the woman.'
    *ɔ se ko de ɉunynɔ́kpao ti mu tɛ̏

(26) Krahn (Western Kru)
    ă mú nyósúá tř͐ pő dŏ nĩ dbāā wé
    I:IMP FUT God thanks put REAS rain fall REAS
    'I will thank God for the rain' or 'I will thank
    God because of the rain.'
    *ă mú nyósúá tř͐ dŏ nĩ dbāā wé po

5.2.4 Locatives. Languages also differ as to the restrictions on the position of locatives. It was seen in chapter 3 that locative complements of verbs like 'go' and 'come' actually function as objects. As such, these locatives must occur within the verb brace.

(27) Godié
    ɔ kʌ́ dakpàdu mʉ   'He will go to Dakpadou.'
    he VOL Dakpadou go

(28) Wobé
    ɔ se (e) dɔɔ mu   'He didn't go to the market.'
    he NEG (LOC) market go
    *ɔ se mʉ (e) dɔɔ

However, there are other types of locatives which do not function as objects of the clause. These are called **nonterm** or **peripheral locatives** because they are not arguments of the predicate. Rather, they supply information about the location of the action. Again, languages differ in their restrictions on the occurrence of nonterm or peripheral locatives. In languages like Bassa and Dewoin, peripheral locatives may occur inside the brace.

(29) Bassa

<u>widi</u> na ma <u>de   ton</u> dyi vo
money PERF T <u>there beach</u> down^2 plenty
'Money has been plentiful at the beach.'

In other languages, like Wobé, peripheral locatives may never occur in this position:

(30) Wobé (Bearth)

ɔ se na <u>miabli</u>   'He didn't walk to Kouibly.'
he NEG walk <u>Kouibly</u>

*ɔ se <u>miabli</u> na

5.2.5 Summary of elements which vary with respect to their position within the verb brace. It has been shown that languages in the Kru family differ in regard to the placement of temporal and manner adverbs, reason phrases, and nonterm locatives within the verb brace. Some languages allow these items within the verb brace, while in other languages there are restrictions against this distribution. It can be noted that all the elements which vary as to their position within the brace are nonterms (they are not arguments of the predicate). Nonsubject terms such as direct objects, indirect objects, and term locatives, on the other hand, never show any variation in their position. In auxiliary constructions they occur <u>only</u> within the verb brace. This was seen in 28 and is also illustrated in 31.

(31) Wobé

ɔ se <u>kei ko</u> kpa   *ɔ se kei kpa <u>ko</u>
he NEG <u>Kei rice</u> take   *ɔ se kpa <u>kei ko</u>
S AUX IO   DO   V   *ɔ se <u>ko</u> kpa <u>kei</u>

'He didn't take rice to Kei.'

The noun phrases within the verb brace may be complex, consisting of conjoined or relativized nouns, or they may involve genitive constructions.

(32) Godié (genitive NP term locative)

nʉ́ wa yi <u>mɔ́   giyeé-nɛdɛ̀ nɛdɛ̀</u> mʉ
and they SEQ <u>there ocean:ASSOC-middle</u> go
    S   AUX   LOC   V

'And they went right into the middle of the ocean.'

---

2 **dyi** is a verbal particle accompanying the verb **vo** 'plenty'. See Marchese 1979:162-64 for more examples of particles in Kru.

(33) Klao (relativized object; example from Singler)
    na   mu kɔ́ né   Díba tè-a-ná   di
    I:IMP FUT rice that Diba buy-SUB-REL eat
    'I will eat the rice that Diba bought.'

(34) Dewoin (conjoined object)
    ɔ mu máyò   ní   pɛ̀ɛ   kè jɛ pá gí mu
    he FUT that-person water cold and thing white give FUT
    'He will give that person cold water and something white.'

These examples show that it is not the length or complexity of an NP which affects its position in the auxiliary construction, but its termhood. In all Kru languages, nonsubject terms occur within the verb brace, but nonterms such as reason phrases and peripheral locatives, as well as elements such as adverbs, show language-specific variation. That is, in some languages, these elements may occur within the verb brace, while in others such an occurrence would be ungrammatical.

5.2.6 Implications of the variation in word order. Within a given language, word order variation is often used for pragmatic reasons such as focussing or topicalization. Variations or differences in restrictions concerning word order within a language family, however, may suggest that some kind of historical change has occurred. It has been shown that in all Kru languages, the order S AUX O V is attested (as well as orders where terms such as indirect objects and term locatives appear within the verb brace). It was also shown that some languages allow nonterms and adverbs within the brace, while others do not. Thus two synchronic word orders are attested within the family: S AUX (O) V X and S AUX X (O) V, where X indicates nonterms and adverbs. This variation raises some important historical questions. Which of these two patterns is older? Is the occurrence of nonterms within the verb brace an innovation, or does it represent a more conservative order?

In the previous two chapters, it was shown that the construction S V_1 (O) $V_{2\;nom}$ gave rise to a new construction, S AUX O V. Thus, while the basic order in Kru is VO, another pattern has emerged where the object precedes the main verb. This new pattern can be seen as being at odds with the existing VO order. Migeod (1911:84) made the following observation: "In the Kroo languages or dialects apparently both practices [i.e., VO and OV word orders, L.M.] prevail, which, if correct, would point to two not yet reconciled influences being still at work."

If it is correct to assume that there is indeed a conflict between two basic word orders, then the variations in word order described above could be attributed to a process which is working to eliminate the conflict--namely, the process of exbraciation.

Exbraciation: The Breakdown of S AUX (O) V

"Exbraciation" is a term used by Vennemann (MS) and Stockwell (1977) to describe the movement of certain elements out of the verb brace v...V (corresponding to Kru AUX...V). In the case of English and German, it is claimed that there was a gradual rightward movement of elements out of the verb brace, beginning with nonterms and ending with objects. This movement is believed to be a major mechanism of word order change in languages moving from SOV to SVO. The synchronic data presented in the past sections may be interpreted in a similar manner. The facts show that two orders, S AUX X V and S AUX V X, exist. Since Kru is basically SVO, it may be that the family is undergoing exbraciation (movement of elements out of the verb brace) as a first step in eliminating the non-SVO S AUX O V word order. It must be noted that this is a change in progress since not all brace-internal elements (objects or terms of any kind) are moving out of the brace. In the remainder of this chapter, the process of exbraciation will be described in detail. First, motivation for such a development will be given. It will be seen that factors which motivate exbraciation in Kru coincide with those offered by Stockwell for a similar change in Old English. In a later section, an explanation of the actualization of the change will be given.

5.3 Factors Motivating Exbraciation

In languages where the phenomenon of exbraciation is attested, syntactic structures exist which set a pattern for the S AUX V X word order. In his discussion of exbraciation in Old English, Stockwell (1977:301) asks: "What are some of the patterns that led Old English speakers, increasingly as time went on, to believe that it was perfectly all right to put any object or adverbial constituent out to the right of the final verb, although this had earlier been rare and heavily constrained, or even totally ungrammatical?"

In answer to this question, Stockwell lists several facts about word order and rules in the language which establish an SvVX pattern or make the pattern acceptable. In brief, Stockwell (1977: 302-10) notes that as a result of certain rules, an SVX word order was established. Second, rightward movement rules such as relative clause, conjunct, and appositive extraposition, as well as afterthought, placed elements outside the verb brace, resulting in an SvVX order. Finally, sentential objects apparently always occurred in sentence-final position, again setting up an SvVX pattern. Similar types of arguments are offered by Aitchison for a parallel phenomenon in Greek: "a rightward operations conspiracy ... snowballed and destroyed an OV order" (D. Lightfoot 1979:393-95). The case in Kru is not exactly parallel, of course, since Kru is not at present undergoing the same SOV-->SVO shift. The change in Kru is restricted to the S AUX O V construction, since in sentences without auxiliaries, the basic order in all Kru languages is already SVO. However, the same motivating factors which Stockwell and Aitchison mention as playing a role in the exbraciation process in Old English and Greek can be found in Kru today.

5.3.1 Basic word order. Stockwell (1977:302-5) noted that though Old English was basically SXV, there was a verb-second rule which moved the finite verb into second position. When such sentences contained a simple verb, the resulting structure was SVX. This pattern led speakers to conclude that nominal and adverbial complements followed the main verb, leading eventually to the development of an SvVX construction. A similar motivation is present in Kru. In chapter 1, it was shown that in sentences without auxiliaries, the basic order is SVO or SVX. All elements, whether terms (direct objects, indirect objects, and locative objects) or nonterms (instrumentals, reason phrases and peripheral locatives) or elements like adverbs, normally occur in postverbal position.[3]

(35) Vata

ń	nɔ̀	nɔ́	gɔgɔ	lo6e	'My mother is always working.'
my	mother	do	always	work	
		V	ADV	DO	

(36) Godié

ɔ	fʌ	kĩfi	pʉtʉ	'He sent a package to the chief.'
he	send	chief	package	
	V	IO	DO	

(37) Wobé

ɔ	di-ɛ	kō	dè	dɔɔ	sĩã	'He ate rice at the market to-day.'
he	eat-DECL	rice	LOC	market	today	
	V	O		LOC	ADV	

Data of this type could lead speakers to make the following generalization: all nonsubjectival elements follow the main verb in the clause. This generalization would enhance the acceptability of the word order S AUX V X̲.

5.3.2 Rightward movement rules. Stockwell noted several rules in Old English including conjunct, appositive, and relative extraposition which moved elements into clause-final position. He also noted that afterthought had the result of also putting material in clause-final position. These rules and phenomena thus created a SvVX pattern, causing a breakdown in the verb-final nature of the V...V brace. (For examples, refer to Stockwell 1977:306-9.) Interestingly enough, parallel types of surface variation also

---

3 Postverbal elements such as those listed may also occur in sentence-initial position, but only when they are focussed. By focus, I refer to the form used when answering a specific question. For example, 'When did he go to the store?' 'It's t̲o̲d̲a̲y̲ (focus) he went to the store.' 'What did he buy?' 'It's b̲a̲n̲a̲n̲a̲s̲ (focus) he bought.'

Exbraciation: The Breakdown of S AUX (O) V

appear in Kru, and a similar S AUX V X pattern is established. Elements which occur in postverbal position include expanded subject or object NPs, conjoined NPs, afterthoughts, and various other items. These will now be described in detail.

5.3.2.1 Expanded NPs. There seems to be a general rule in Kru languages which permits the speaker to expand on something he has said by juxtaposing his comment at the end of the sentence. In the following Neyo example from a text transcribed by Thomann, the speaker "spells out," or gives examples of, the object 'all the animals of the forest floor'. The phenomenon could be viewed as a kind of verbal colon.

(38) ò ule kla zɔ̃ a mla fè <u>sie, kwale</u> ...
he call bush bottom ASSOC animals all <u>snails, turtles</u> ...
'He called all the animals living on the forest floor: snails, turtles ...'

The preceding sentence does not contain an auxiliary, but if one is present, as in the following Godié example, the verb no longer occurs in final position. Here the subject **wa** 'they' is expanded in postverbal position.

(39) ιyʌ̃ wa kʌ̃ sû nûu, <u>Kaadɛ, Papʊ, Gbɔklıŋwlɔ</u> ...
and they VOL also understand, <u>Carol, Lynell, Sue</u>
'So, Carol, Lynell, and Sue will understand too.'

As example 39 shows, this stylistic device of rightward movement provides an S AUX (O) V <u>X</u> pattern in the Kru family.

A similar device involves conjoined NPs. A pronoun subject may be expanded or added to in postverbal position through conjunction and the introduction of new participants. This can be seen in Nyabo and Bakwé.

(40) <u>Nyabo</u>

ɔ mi plïibo ɔ kɔ̃ ɔ yópli
he go:IMP Pleebo <u>he and his children</u>
'He and his children are going to Pleebo' or 'He's going to Pleebo, he and his children.'

(41) <u>Bakwé</u>

ɔ mʉ màkàtè klé ɔ nà wà jîkɔ̃ sɔ
he went market to <u>he and his children two</u>
'He went to the market, he and his children.'

When an auxiliary is present, the pattern S AUX (O) V X̱ occurs.

(42) Borobo

ɔ di trúbɔ́ mu-a ɔ yɔ́ jîoé
he AUX Monrovia go-NOM he and-his children
'He will go to Monrovia, he and his children.'

(43) Bété (Werle and Dagou 1976:199)

ń lǎgɔ́ yi-ɛ glɔ glɛ ɔ́ nyɛ̀ ɔ̀ jùə́ ā sɔ́
then God SEQ-NAR town arrive he and his children ASSOC two
'And God arrived at the village, along with his children.'

These cases seem to be examples of a certain stylistic variation which emphasizes or highlights some element. In Kru, new information typically occurs toward the end of the clause. It seems reasonable to assume that **lǎgɔ́** 'God' (a frequent character in folktales) is known information and thus occurs in subject position. 'His children' are undoubtedly new but secondary participants. Thus, this strategy is definitely not afterthought (the tacking on of forgotten elements, a strategy to be treated in the next section), but a way of introducing new, but secondary participants.

Welmers (pers.com.) notes a similar phenomenon in Kpelle, a Mandé language with a basic SOV word order. New information may be added following the final V.

Another type of expansion involves spelling out a pronoun referent which has occurred earlier in the clause. Syntactically this could be described as a kind of reverse topicalization, or comment-topic. In normal topic-comment constructions in Kru, topics precede the main clause and are recapitulated in the main clause by a pronoun (Marchese 1976, 1979).

(44) **tɛɛtɛɛ̀ jɛlɩɛ ɔ pʌ́ʌ̀ nʌ ɛ mɛ̀**
first arrow-DEF he throw NF, it go:FACT
'The first arrow that he shot, it went.'
‾‾‾‾‾‾‾‾‾‾‾‾‾‾‾‾‾‾‾‾‾‾‾ ‾‾‾‾‾‾‾‾‾
TOPIC COMMENT

In the following, the main clause contains a pronoun whose referent is named in sentence-final position. The following sentences were reported to occur in Koyo by Kokora (a speaker of Koyo) (1976:175). When I tried to elicit similar sentences in other languages, speakers only accepted them with the specification that the referent be in the presence of the speaker. In some languages, in fact, speakers were very dubious about sentences containing reverse topicalization. This seemed to be the case in the jlukɔ dialect of Godié.

?? ɔ́ dʌ kʌ, nyʉkpɔ nɔ
he-NEG place have man   DEN
'He's no good, this man.'

Note that each example contains a demonstrative, so it is safe to assume that this variation in word order serves a deictic function.

(45) Koyo
ɔ wɔtɔ pɨlɛ leyo nɔ   'He keeps cool, this king.'
he cool heart king this

(46) Nyabo
ɔ he koa-ko me yun   'He's no good, that man.'
he NEG be-good that man

(47) Kuwaa
we kãĩ de jiji dɔ̃ɔ   'He's not good, that man.'
he:NEG good BE man that

Thus these three expansion devices--(a) the listing of aforementioned material (examples 38 and 39), (b) the introduction of secondary participants through conjunction (examples 40-43), and (c) reverse topicalization (examples 45-47) all set up an S AUX (O) V X pattern--a pattern which plays a crucial role in exbraciation.

5.3.2.2 Afterthought is defined as the addition of forgotten elements to the end of a clause. Hyman (1975:126) first noted the possibility of afterthoughts occurring in Klao. In the example he cites, part of the object was forgotten and later added to the end of the clause.

(48) ɔ́ sɛ́ súa tè, táĩ kɔ̃   'He didn't buy fish...or rice.'
he NEG fish buy and/or rice

The same phenomenon occurs in several other Kru languages. In the following, part of the subject or object has been forgotten and tacked onto the end of the clause.

(49) Dewoin
ɔ nã̀ mɔ̃ɔ dɛ kè zimi   'He has bought rice... and fish.'
he PERF rice buy and fish
S AUX O V   part of O

(50) Bakwé

    ɔ nyá-ka kɔ́po suá <u>nyà srʉ̀</u>   'He will buy rice...and fish.'
    he FUT   rice buy <u>and fish</u>

Similar constructions could be cited from Borobo, Sapo, Nyabo, and Bété (from Guibéroua). However, in several Kru languages, afterthought is apparently not acceptable. Constructions such as those seen in 48-50 above were rejected by speakers of River Cess Bassa, Bereby Kru, and Godié.

(51)   Bereby Kru

    *ɛ ŋwɛmɔ́ kòò tɔ́ <u>kɔ́ hne kɔ̀ɔ</u>   'He will buy rice
    he FUT rice buy <u>and fish and</u>   and fish.'

(52)   Godié

    *ɔ yʌ sʉkʌ̀ pɩʌ <u>yʌ̀ zlɨ sɔ́</u>   'He has bought rice...
    he PERF rice buy <u>and fish two</u>   and fish.'

(53)   River Cess Bassa

    *ɔ mu mɔ́ dɔ̀ɔ́ <u>ke smi</u>   'He will buy rice...
    he FUT rice buy <u>and fish</u>   and fish.'

The River Cess speaker reacted to the above sentence in the following way: "You've got to finish saying all before you can say dɔ̀ɔ́," which is the main verb in sentence-final position.

   In fact, even in those languages where afterthought was acceptable, there is some question as to its actual usage. I have yet to actually <u>hear</u> an afterthought. In each case, I was forced to state the sent<u>ence</u> and ask: "Does that mean something? What?" Values for grammaticality were based on the speaker's response. Afterthought, then, is not as pervasive as other kinds of devices which allow elements to occur outside the verb brace, but it may be responsible for setting up an S AUX (O) V <u>X</u> pattern in some Kru languages.

5.3.3 Placement of sentential objects. In section 5.2.5 it was noted that nonsubjectival terms (direct and indirect objects as well as locative objects), no matter what their complexity, generally occur within the verb brace. There is, however, an exception to this general rule: sentential objects always occur in final position. This behavior is certainly due to the difficulty of processing sentence-medial clauses (Kuno 1974; Grosu and Thompson 1977). Thus, even in languages which are strictly SOV, sentential objects are often found following the final verb. Stockwell (1977) notes that in Old English sentential objects always occurred outside the verb brace. Again, this phenomenon in Kru and in Old English results in an S AUX V <u>X</u> word order which sets the pattern

Exbraciation: The Breakdown of S AUX (O) V   233

for exbraciation. The following from several Kru languages show the S AUX V X pattern:

(54) Dewoin

ɔ se kɔ ɔ mā zie pi 'She doesn't have to
she NEG have she HORT rice cook   cook rice.'

(55) Godié

wa kʉ kī mà wa yʌ wá lı gɨlɨ nʌ,...
they COND say that they PERF their things steal NF
'If they say that they have stolen their things, ...'

*wa kʉ ma wa yʌ wa lı gɨlɨ nʌ ki...

(56) Vata

ió káɔ́ iîmɛlɛ nà ɔ́ nɔ lɛ̄ mɔ̄
child VOL recognize that his mother is you
S   AUX V   sentential O
'The child will recognize that you are his mother.'

5.3.4 Auxiliary--verb "attraction." Finally, another factor may be playing a role in the breakdown of the verb-final construction in Kru. There is a general tendency (known as Bahagel's First Law) for the auxiliary and verb to unite, forming one constituent (Vennemann 1973; Hyman 1975). This would, of course, give rise to an S AUX V X structure. Though this kind of hypothesis is very difficult to prove, it can be pointed out that in Ivorian French, there is a strong tendency to do just this. The following was heard in a prayer:

Je vais servir   toi   'I will serve you.'
I go serve:INF you
S AUX V   O

Compare Parisian French:

Je vais te servir
I go you serve-INF

The clitic pronoun **te** is postposed and takes the independent form in the Ivorian example. Thus, the auxiliary verb 'go' is "united" with the main verb 'serve'. Again, this same pattern emerges when Godiēs speak French, even though they use the S AUX O V construction consistently when they are speaking Godié.

Parisian: Ivorian:

Je vais te frapper   **Je vais frapper toi**
I go you hit:INF   you (indep)
'I will hit you.'

Just how great a role this tendency is playing in the S AUX V X shift in Kru is hard to determine. Nevertheless, it may be a contributing factor.

5.3.5 Summary: Motivation for exbraciation.

It has been shown that there are several factors in Kru which tend to create the S AUX V X word order, consequently breaking down the verb-final nature of the auxiliary construction. These factors include:

(i) the basic SVX word order in clauses without auxiliaries

(ii) certain stylistic devices which allow elements to occur in postverbal position

(iii) the placement of sentential objects outside the verb brace

(iv) auxiliary--verb "attraction"[4]

There seem to be two different views as to the cause of exbraciation. With regard to word order change, Hyman (1975:119-20) tends to emphasize the importance of pragmatic considerations:

> One constantly present force in contributing to word order change is the conflict between syntax and pragmatics. That is, speakers, in the course of using a language, sometimes find it necessary to break the syntax and add elements in positions where they normally do not appear .... Once the speaker has put the verb down, it is no longer possible to add anything (in a strict SOV language). However, the speaker may forget to say something in the course of his utterance; or he may find it is necessary to add something, because his interlocutor has not understood .... In all these cases, ... he may wish to add something after the verb-final utterance ....

Afterthought, which Hyman claims to be one of the major mechanisms of word order change, certainly does play a role in word order change in Kru. In section 5.3.2, it was shown that omitted or forgotten elements may be tacked onto the end of a verb-final clause by means of conjunction. The evidence from Kru, however, suggests that afterthought is merely one of the many devices which

---

[4] Another factor in auxiliary-verb attraction may be the existence of the word order S PART V O. Note that negation and aspect may be expressed by particles occurring between the subject and the verb. Thus, the tendency for markers of modal or aspectual material to occur next to the predicate may have been established for some time.

Exbraciation: The Breakdown of S AUX (O) V

lead to the occurrence of material in postverbal position. Along these lines, Stockwell notes (1977:299):

> While the 'afterthought' notion draws some explanatory force from the plausible psychological motivation it suggests, I think there are a number of structural motivations within the syntax of OE that considerably strengthen the tendency to exbraciate, and in general I find more persuasive than psychological generalizations any explanation that depends on prior existence of syntactic patterns as a basis for analogical extension.

The Kru data appear to confirm Stockwell's basic approach since afterthought does not seem to be very common and is actually unacceptable to some Kru speakers. On the other hand, there are several devices (including afterthought) which allow material to occur outside the verb brace. It would appear that these devices, along with factors (i), (iii), and (iv), set up the surface order S AUX V X. This order, in turn, serves as a pattern for the process of exbraciation.

5.4 Actualization of the Change

Given that within the Kru family there are two variant word orders, namely, S AUX X V and S AUX V X (where X = reason phrases, nonterm locatives, and temporal and manner adverbs), and that there are patterns on which a movement outside the verb brace can be based, it is assumed that the historical change involves movement from within the verb brace to a position outside the verb brace: S AUX ⌈ V X⌉. Now the question arises as to how this change was actualized. In this section, it will be shown that elements move out of the verb brace in stages--they initially start in the brace, then they begin to move optionally. Eventually the position outside the brace becomes preferred, and finally obligatory. It will also be shown that factors such as transitivity have some effect on exbraciation. Later, the claim will be made that exbraciation first affects individual items of a lexical class and then eventually spreads through the class as a whole.

5.4.1 The stages of exbraciation: from optional to obligatory movement. From the examination of the synchronic evidence, it would appear that there are essentially three stages in the process of exbraciation:

(i) the element occurs obligatorily within the verb brace

(ii) the element occurs optionally outside the brace

(iii) the element occurs obligatorily outside the brace

Stage (ii) seems to be broken down into two substages. Throughout stage (ii), occurrence outside the brace is optional. At first, the inside is the preferred position, but eventually it is the outside. (The term "preferred" will be used to mean that the that the sentence is one offered by the speaker, while a sentence that is "OK" is acceptable to and translated by a speaker.)

Stages (i) to (iii) will now be illustrated by examples of exbraciation of temporal and manner adverbs as well as reason phrases and nonterm locatives.

5.4.1.1 Temporal adverbs. There are few examples of stage (i) exbraciation in the Kru group. In Godié, however, there are some temporal adverbs which occur within the verb brace and do not appear to be able to undergo exbraciation. This is the case with the Godié adverb sīsīō 'early' or 'soon'.

(57) ɔ yi sisiõ yi   ?/* ɔ yi yi sisio
      he FUT soon come
      'He will come soon.'

In most cases, there is a strong tendency for temporal adverbs to occur within the verb brace in Eastern Kru (including Godié).

(58) Neyo
     e i   zĕmle ku   'I'm going to die today.'
     I FUT today die

(59) Koyo
     Dago ta yeka du   mo   'Dago didn't go to town today.'
     Dago NEG today village go

(60) Lakota Dida
     nyũ yi pɔ̄tɔ̄ 6aa   'It's going to rain right now.'
     water FUT right-now fall

While the brace-internal position seems to be preferred, temporal adverbs may sometimes occur outside the brace. According to Vogler's description of Vata (1976) this is a kind of stylistic variation.

(61) Vata
     ǹ kā si   6ɛ̄tɛ́   'I will laugh right away.'
     I FUT laugh right-away

(62) Koyo
     Dago ta du mo yeka   'Dago didn't go to town today.'
     Dago NEG town go today

(63) Godié
     Dali wʋ̀ sākāa lɨ pɛ̄pɛ̄   'Dali didn't eat rice just now.'
     Dali NEG rice-D eat just-now

Exbraciation: The Breakdown of S AUX (O) V

Thus in most cases, the Eastern languages appear to be at the beginning of stage (ii), where temporal adverbs may occur inside or outside the verb brace, though the inside position seems to be favored. Borobo and Bassa also appear to be at stage (ii). Either position is acceptable.

(64) Borobo

ɔ í **dyīnōwānā** kōā nu   ɔ e⁵ kōā nu **dyīnōwānā**
he NEG today   work do   he NEG work do today
'He didn't work today.'

(65) Grand Bassa

ɔ se **pāniwá** kùā nyu   ɔ se kùā nyu **pāniwá**
he NEG yesterday work do
'He didn't work yesterday.'

Finally, in certain Western languages, stage (iii) has been reached: temporal adverbs occur obligatorily outside the verb brace.

(66) Tao Wobé

ɔ se ko di **sīā**   * ɔ se **sīā** ko di
he NEG rice eat today
'He didn't eat rice today.'

(67) Nyabo

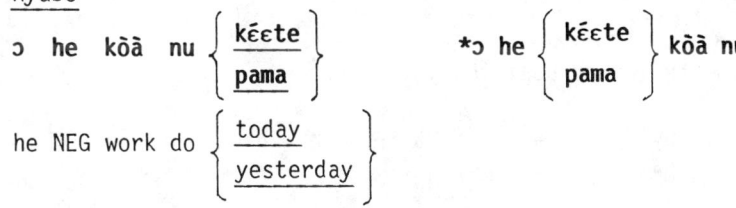

he NEG work do
'He did not work today.'

It has been seen that all three stages are attested synchronically in the Kru languages. In some cases, temporal adverbs occur obligatorily inside the brace. In some languages, temporal adverbs may occur either inside or outside the brace, while in others, they may occur only outside the brace. From the data available, it would appear that most languages are at stage (ii)--the stage of optionality. In the next section, it will be seen that manner adverbs are also at different stages in the exbraciation process.

---

5 Sometimes in my transcription, I wrote the negative as i, ɛ, or ye. There is probably no difference among them.

5.4.1.2 Manner adverbs. Basically, the same stages of development which were shown in regard to temporal adverbs also affect manner adverbs. Again, there is little synchronic evidence to justify stage (i). This is probably due to the fact that the elements under discussion are well on their way to an obligatory position outside the verb brace. However, there is an example of stage (i) in Tepo. Some adverbs such as **gbɛ́gbê** 'slowly' occur obligatorily inside the verb brace.

(68) ɔ dē <u>gbɛ́gbê</u> nâ   *ɔ dē nâ <u>gbɛ́gbê</u>
      he NEG <u>slowly</u> walk
      'He didn't walk slowly.'

Stage (ii) is seen in Eastern languages, where a brace-internal position is preferred, but a position outside the verb brace is possible.

(69) Koyo[6]
      **Doni yi <u>kapakapasa</u> lo6ee   no   Doni yi lo6e-e no
      <u>kapakapasa</u>**
      Doni FUT <u>crazily</u>   work-DEF do
      'Doni will work in a haphazard way.'

(70) Lakota Dida
      ɔ yia <u>dʉgasa</u> sākā li   ɔ yia sākā li <u>dʉgasa</u>
      he FUT <u>slowly</u> rice eat
      'He will eat rice slowly.'

In Bakwé, the second part of stage (ii) has been reached-- manner adverbs occur optionally inside or outside the verb brace, though the latter position is preferred.

(71) ɔ nyī ɟrópa a[7] fɛ <u>tàkàsīè</u>   'He didn't work slowly.'
      he NEG work ? do <u>slowly</u>
      ɔ nyī <u>tàkàsīè</u> ɟrópa a fɛ

Stage (iii) is attested in several Western languages where manner adverbs may never occur within the verb brace.

---

6 Kokora (1976) reports another sentence order: S AUX O <u>ADV</u> V.

  ɔ yi lo6e-e kapakapasa no   'He will do the job badly.'
  he POT work-DEF badly   do

7 In Bakwé and Tepo, a vocalic particle **a** occurs in some negative constructions. It could be the associative **a** occurring in a remnant of the O V nom construction, derived from something like 'he failed doing-<u>of</u>-work. This is very speculative, however.

Exbraciation: The Breakdown of S AUX (O) V

(72) Borobo

ɔɔ í kũã nu { dʋɛdʋɛ / tɛɛ / slowly / well }   *ɔɔ í { dʋɛdʋɛ / tɛɛ } kũã nu

he NEG work do { slowly / well }

'He didn't work slowly.'

(73) Gbaeson Krahn

ɔ mú dɛ́ dí sùeí   *ɔ mú sùeí dɛ́ dí

he FUT thing eat fast

'He will eat fast.'

(74) Tao Wobé

ɔ se ko di pepe   *ɔ se pepe ko di

he NEG rice eat well

'He didn't eat rice well.'

These data show that manner adverbs are attested synchronically in all of the stages proposed for exbraciation.

5.4.1.3 Reason phrases are not synchronically attested at stage (i) in any language examined in this study; that is, there is no language where reason phrases must occur within the verb phrase. This is probably because reason phrases are among the first elements to move out of the verb brace. However, stage (ii), where elements may optionally occur inside or outside the verb brace, is attested in Godié and Dewoin.

(75) Dewoin

í nà gɛ̃ĩpɔ́lɔ̃ sɛ̃ɛ̃ nĩ ɔ̃ zĩ po
I PERF God thanks rain-DEF REAS put
í nà gɛ̃ĩpɔ́lɔ̃ sɛ̃ɛ̃ po nĩɔ̃ zĩ

'I have thanked God for the rain' or
'I have thanked God because of the rain.'

(76) Godié

ɔ yi Dakpadou yi ɔ̃ zɛ
he POT Dakpadou come his sake
ɔ yi Dakpadou ɔ̃ zɛ yi

'He will come to Dakpadou for him.'

In many languages, however, exbraciation of reason phrases has become obligatory. This is case in Nyabo, Krahn, Klao, Péomē Wobē, and River Cess Bassa.

(77) Klao
dó-a   mu cɛ́   kó tʊ bò
Doe-IMP FUT learn REAS Toe REAS
*Dó a mu kó tʊ bò cɛ́
'Doe will learn for Toe.'

(78) Péomē Wobē
ɔ se ko tɛ̰̀ de ɉunynɔ́kpaó à tɪ mú
he NEG rice buy for woman ASSOC for
*ɔ se ko de ɉunynɔ́kpaó à tɪ mú tɛ̰̀
'Doe didn't buy rice for the woman.'

(79) Krahn
ă̰ mú nyósúá trɔ̃ pō dŏ nĭ dbáá wé
I:IMP FUT God thanks put REAS rain fall REAS
*ă̰ mú nyósúá trɔ̃ dŏ nĭ dbáá wé po

5.4.1.4 Locatives. As was shown in earlier parts of this study (see sect. 3.4.2), some locatives act as object NPs and, as such, always occur within the verb brace. The type of locative which occurs in a clause is essentially determined by the verb. Motion verbs like 'go', 'enter', 'arrive', 'come', and 'leave' are subcategorized to take locative complements.

(80) Tchien Krahn
ɔ̃ mū gw̃lɔ̃ mū   'He will go to town.'
he FUT town go

(81) Tepo
yruwle mʊ́ kayo gbo pa   'Chameleon is about to
chameleon FUT house under enter enter the house.'

(82) Bakwé
ɔ́ a bʌ̀tʌ̀ tɔ́   'He arrived at the
he PERF village arrive   village.'

(83) Godié
nĭ wa yi Dakpadu ɓà   'Then they left Dakpadou.'
then they SEQ Dakpadou leave

(84) Neyo

 balē a dē gbla   'A hippopotamus has climbed
 hippo PERF there climb   up there.'

Other verbs may be accompanied by locatives, but they are not subcategorized for these NPs. These nonterm locatives vary in position from language to language and thus show evidence of undergoing exbraciation. Nonterm locatives generally occur within the brace in Eastern languages such as Godié.

(85) ɔ yi mɔ́yι sʉkʌ̃ 6lɨ   'She will pound rice over
  she POT there rice pound   there.'

But even in this language, nonterm locatives sometimes occur outside the brace.

(86) ɔ yi sʉkʌ̃ 6lɨ mɔyι   'She will pound rice
  she POT rice pound over-there   over there.'

In Bassa, it is reported by Clubvine that peripheral locatives may occur inside or outside the verb brace.

(87) wiḍi na ma dyi vo ḍe ton   wiḍi na ma ḍe ton
 money PERF T down plenty there[8] beach   dyi vo
 S   AUX   V   LOC
 'Money is plentiful at the beach.'

(88) gaa dyu ni dyi pɛn ḍe gbun   gaa dyu ni ḍe gbun
 man child is down lie there house   dyi pɛn
 'The boy is sleeping in the house.'

Thus, though stage (i) is not attested, nonterm locatives do occur in the two substages of stage (ii) and in stage (iii).

In Nyabo, Kuwaa, and Dewoin, nonterm locatives may occur inside or outside the verb brace, but the outside position is preferred.

(89) Nyabo

 PREF: e mi nyawe cɛɛa yèlē Elizabeth ã ta
     I FUT Grebo learn there Elizabeth ASSOC house
     'I will learn Grebo at Elizabeth's house.'

 OK: e mi lē Elizabeth ta yō nyawe a cɛɛna

---

[8] In many Kru languages, a locative 'there' may precede a noun and act as a kind of demonstrative. The construction is probably genitive in nature: beach of there.

(90) Kuwaa
PREF: wɔ dḗ wá bɛni nṹ kulá no
she is rice carry NOM farm to
                              LOC
'She is carrying rice to the farm.'
OK: wɔ de wâ kulá no bɛni nṹ

(91) Dewoin
PREF: ɔ́ mu Zoú mu mu ɔ́ màa bláí
he FUT Zou go FUT his mother house
S AUX O   V   LOC
'He will go to his mother's house at Zou.'
OK: ɔ mu Zoú ɔ́ màa bláí mu mu
    S AUX O   LOC   V

In Wobé, stage (iii) has been reached. Nonterm locatives must occur outside the verb brace (Bearth, pers.com.):

(92) ɔ se na miabli   *ɔ se miabli na
     he NEG walk Kouibly
'He didn't walk to Kouibly.'

It has been proposed that nonterm NPs, like reason phrases, peripheral locatives, and elements such as manner and temporal adverbs, are undergoing, or have undergone, exbraciation in several Kru languages. This process appears to be taking place in three stages: (i) obligatory occurrence within the brace, (ii) optional occurrence inside or outside the verb brace, and (iii) obligatory occurrence outside the verb brace. In the next section, there will be a discussion of one factor which seems to be influencing exbraciation.

5.4.2 Valence as a determining factor in exbraciation. In the above discussion, it was noted that when verbs are subcategorized for a locative argument, this locative occurs within the verb brace. When the verb is not subcategorized for a locative complement, however, a nonterm locative may occur. Depending on the language, the peripheral locative will optionally occur inside or outside the brace, or obligatorily outside the brace (see 85-91). However, the situation is a little more complicated than stated above.

According to an analysis worked out by Bearth (pers.com.), each verb in Wobé has a restricted number of arguments for which there is a hierarchy: IO > DO > LOC (which he calls "destinaire," "patient," and "locatif" respectively). To determine whether a

Exbraciation: The Breakdown of S AUX (O) V

locative occurs inside or outside the brace, one has to know the valence of the verb and how many arguments there are. For example, 'go' has a valence of 1, so the locative will occur within the brace.

(93) ɔ   **se**   **(e)**   **dɔɔ**   **mu**   'He didn't go to the market.'
      he NEG   (LOC)   market   go
      S   AUX   LOC   V

The verb 'walk', on the other hand, has a valence of zero, so any locative occurring with this verb must occur outside the verb brace.

(94) ɔ   **se**   **na**   **miabli**   'He didn't walk to Kouibly.'
      he NEG   walk   Kouibly
      S   AUX   V   LOC

'Take' has a valence of 2, so when there are only two nonsubjectival arguments, the locative may occur within the brace.

(95) ɔ   **se**   **ko**   **(dé)**   **dɔɔ**   **kpa**   'He didn't take rice
      he NEG   rice   (LOC)   market   take   to the market.'
      S   AUX   O   LOC   V

But when a higher ranking argument is present (like an indirect object), the locative must occur outside the brace.

(96) ɔ   **se**   **kei**   **ko**   **kpa**   **dé**   **dɔɔ**   'He didn't bring rice to
      he NEG   Kei   rice   bring   LOC market   Kei at the market.'
      S   AUX   IO   DO   V   LOC

Evidently, purpose NPs are higher on the scale than normal locatives, since the presence of a purpose NP causes the locative to occur outside the verb brace.

(97) ɔ   **se**   **ko**   **ple-a**   **mu**   **de**   **dɔɔ**
      he NEG   rice   buy-NOM   go   LOC market
      S   AUX   LOC (PURP)   NP   V   LOC
      'He didn't go to buy rice at the market.'

Thus whether a locative occurs within or without the verb brace depends not only on whether the locative is a term or nonterm but also on the verb itself, its subcategorization, and the number of NPs which are to be incorporated into the clause. Bearth's analysis was restricted to Wobé, but the same kind of analysis could be applied in all Kru languages.

The same kind of phenomenon also appears to affect the exbraciation of nonterm elements. In Borobo and Sapo, manner adverbs differ as to their position inside or outside the verb brace, depending on the transitivity of the verb. With transitive verbs, manner adverbs must occur outside the brace.

(98) Borobo

ɔɔ ī kūā nu { dʋɛdʋɛ / tɛɛ }   *ɔɔ ī { dʋɛdʋɛ / tɛɛ } kūā nu

he NEG work do { slowly / well }

'He didn't work { slowly / well }.'

(99) Sapo

ɔ se kò di paapa   *ɔ se paapa kò di

he NEG rice eat fast

'He didn't eat rice fast.'

However, when the verb in the clause is intransitive, manner adverbs not only seem to occur within the verb brace but also are preferred within the brace.

(100) Borobo

PREF: ɔɔ ī dʋɛdʋɛ na   'He didn't walk slowly.'
      he NEG slowly walk

OK: ɔɔ ī na dʋɛdʋɛ

(101) Sapo

PREF: ɔ se { pɛpɛ / papa } na   'He didn't walk { slowly / fast }.'
      he NEG { slowly / fast } walk

OK: ɔ se na { pɛpɛ / papa }

It has been shown that one factor in exbraciation is the termhood of the element. Terms may never move out of the brace, while nonterms such as reason clauses and peripheral locatives and elements such as adverbs are showing signs of being exbraciated. The data from this section suggest that another factor that determines whether or not exbraciation takes place is the number of elements available at a given time. Exbraciation appears to be favored in some languages when there are several elements to be integrated into the clause. Thus, just one element may be tolerated (examples 98-101), but when there are two or more elements, the ones with lesser status (on a scale of termhood, as suggested by Bearth) will obligatorily be moved out. It must be noted that this phenomenon is language specific. It has been observed in three languages: Wobé, Borobo, and Sapo. It is not known if it occurs in other languages.

5.4.3 Exbraciation and individual lexical items. In the literature (D. Lightfoot 1979), it has been claimed that linguistic change may affect members of a lexical class one by one, until so many are affected that a new rule must emerge to maintain a certain degree of "transparency." In other words, exception features on lexical items eventually "overload" the system, resulting in the creation of new categories or changes in basic word order. Data from exbraciation in Kru confirm that change does affect individual members of a class, one by one. In this section, specific examples of this type of change will be given.

5.4.3.1 Manner adverbs in Tepo are a good example of how change affects individual members of a class. In Tepo, the stages which were seen to characterize different degrees of exbraciation can be seen to apply to individual lexical items. For example, the adverb 'slowly' occurs obligatorily within the verb brace (stage (i)).

(102) ɔ dé gbɛ́gbɛ̂ na   *ɔ de na gbɛ́gbɛ̂
      he NEG slowly walk
      'He didn't walk slowly.'

The adverb 'well', on the other hand, has begun to undergo exbraciation, and it occurs optionally inside or outside the verb brace (stage (ii)).

(103) ɔ dé ná tɛ̂   ɔ dé tɛ̂ ná
      he NEG walk well
      'He didn't walk well.'

The adverb 'quickly', however, has undergone stage (iii) exbraciation, and it must occur outside the verb brace.

(104) ɔ dé ná tátâ   *ɔ dé tátâ ná
      he NEG walk quickly
      'He didn't walk quickly.'

These data from Tepo show that change does affect individual members of a lexical class one by one. They also serve to confirm the stages of change by which exbraciation is carried out. An interesting question is why certain members of a class are affected before others. Is there any reason why **tátâ** 'quickly' should be exbraciated before **gbɛgbê** 'slowly'? For the moment, these questions remain unanswered.

5.4.3.2 The verb 'arrive'. Another case showing how exbraciation may be related to changes in individual lexical items involves the verb 'arrive'. The majority of Kru languages treat the verb 'arrive' as a potentially transitive verb; it is usually subcategorized as optionally taking a term locative as its complement. This can be seen where an attempt to move the locative out of the brace produced an ungrammatical sentence.

(105) Borobo
    ɔ di trubɔ   nynía   *ɔ di nynía trubɔ
    he FUT Monrovia arrive
    'He will arrive at Monrovia.'

(106) River Cess Bassa
    ɔ mu tùgbɔ̃   nyni glà   *ɔ mu nyni tùgbɔ̃ glà
    he FUT Monrovia arrive tomorrow
    'He will reach Monrovia tomorrow.'

(107) Kuwaa
    wɛ nɛ fɔdɛ́   tili   *wɔ nɛ tili fɔdɛ́
    he NEG Monrovia reach
    'He hasn't reached Monrovia.'

(108) Lakota Dida
    ɔ yi dãblé nẽ nyli   *ɔ yi nyli dãblé nẽ
    he FUT market at arrive
    'He will arrive at the market.'

However, in Dewoin, complements of the cognate verb appear both inside and outside the verb brace.

(109) outside
    ...í ji ŋini ná mǎ   gbo
      I SEQ reach my mother house
    'And then I arrived (or reached) my mother's house.'

(110) inside

    ...î ji mā̀ā̀ mú ŋini ínyà-sukpí-ínyà zi
    I SEQ person inside reach myself   REAS
    'And then I became of age' (literally: and then I
    reach the inside person for myself).

This proved to be the case in two other languages besides Dewoin: Grand Bassa and Vata. In Grand Bassa, locative arguments of other movement verbs like 'go' and 'leave' must occur within the verb brace.

(111) ɔ da gbɛ́ɛ̀zɔ̀ mu   *ɔ da mu gbɛ́ɛ̀zɔ̀
     he PERF Bassa go
     'He has gone to Bassa.'

But, with the verb 'arrive', the complement may occur inside or outside the verb brace.

(112) ɔ da gbɛ́ɛ̀zɔ̀ nyini   ɔ da nyini gbɛ́ɛ̀zɔ̀
     he PERF Bassa arrive
     'He has arrived at Bassa.'

In Vata, the complement of 'arrive' also occurs outside the brace. The following sentence was taken from a Vata text (Vogler 1976). It is not known, however, if there is a variant word order.

(113) ŋɔnɔ́ɔ́ nā́né uā̀ tɔ́: ɔ ká́ɔ́ nyli nà zalòkò
     woman-DEF walk long-time until she FUT arrive at Zaroko
     'The woman walked until she reached Zaroko.'

In a closely related language, Lakota Dida, a noncognate verb **wlʊ** 'arrive' or 'come out' shows similar behavior. The locative may occur inside or outside the verb brace.

(114) ɔ yi zaroko wlʊ   ɔ yi wlʊ zaroko
     he FUT Zaroko arrive
     'He will arrive at Zaroko.'

These data show that a verb can undergo a change in subcategorization. In the case of the verb 'arrive', the subcategorization has changed from being a transitive verb ([__ NP]) to being an intransitive verb ([- IP]). In other words, in the languages cited above, where 'arrive' used to take a term locative, it now takes a nonterm one. This change has resulted in a change in word order from the invariant:

        S AUX LOC (term) V

to two variant orders:

(i) S AUX LOC (nonterm) V

(ii) S AUX V LOC (nonterm)

While this change in subcategorization seems to have affected only one member of the class of motion verbs, it is conceivable that it could spread to other members of the same class. There is, in fact, some evidence that this is beginning to occur in Lakota Dida. In 114 it was shown that locative complements of the verb **wlʋ** 'arrive' or 'come out' may occur inside or outside the brace. However, the same speaker also accepted as grammatical sentences containing the verb 'come' with an exbraciated locative. According to the speaker who furnished these examples, the sentence with the complement outside the verb brace has a slightly different reading--namely, that the predicted event is not as likely to occur. Why this should be is not known.

(115)　ɔ　yi　zaroko yi　　　　　ɔ yi yi zaroko

　　　he FUT Zaroko come

　　　'He will come to Zaroko.'

This does not appear to be the case in other Kru languages. Within the same language, other members of the motion class do not show this behavior. Complements of such verbs may occur only within the brace.

(116) *ɔ yi { bɔ̃ / me } zaroko

　　　he FUT { come-back / go } zaroko

　　　'He will { come back from / go to } Zaroko.'

If the change continues to spread in this language, however, all motion verbs may eventually appear with their complements optionally outside the verb brace. Indeed, other Kru languages may eventually follow suit as well.

5.4.3.3 The locative la in Dewoin. It has been shown in previous sections that many motion verbs take what could be called "term locatives" as complements. Their status as terms is demonstrated by the fact that they occur within the verb brace. In Dewoin, there is an unusual case of exbraciation involving a locative. The locative **la** 'here' may appear outside the verb brace even when the verb in question usually takes a term locative complement. Two such verbs are **ji** 'come' and **mu** 'go'. Normally their complements occur within the verb brace.

Exbraciation: The Breakdown of S AUX (O) V

(117) ɔ nà zoú { ɟí / mu }   'He has { come / gone } to Zou.'
　　　he PERF Zou { come / go }

(118) í sè lè mu   'I didn't go there.'
　　　I NEG there go

However, the locative **la** 'here' may occur inside the brace (paralleling the examples seen above) or outside the brace.

(119) ɔ mu la ɟíí mu   ɔ mu ɟíí mu la
　　　he FUT here come-NOM FUT
　　　'He will come here.'

(120) ɛ sée là ɟi   'They haven't come here.'
　　　they NEG-PERF here come

(121) ná se ɟii là   'I will not come here.'
　　　I NEG come-FUT here

Other locatives like Zou (a town) and **le** ('there') never show this variation.

(122) *ɔ mu muû mu le   'He will go there.'
　　　He FUT go-NO MFUT there

(123) *ɔ mu muû mu Zou   'He will go to Zou.'
　　　he FUT go-NOM FUT Zou

There appears to be only one environment where **la** may not be exbraciated, and that is when it occurs with the perfect auxiliary **nà**.

(124) ɔ nà la ɟi   *ɔ nà ɟi la
　　　he PERF here come
　　　'He has come here.'

This case of exbraciation is very unusual. It looks as though the locative **la** is no longer being considered as a term locative. The factors motivating its exbraciation are not known, nor can the curious restriction on its internal position when the auxiliary **nà** is present be explained. Nevertheless, these data show how an individual member of a class (in this case locative nouns) may be individually affected by the process of exbraciation.

5.4.4 The hierarchy of exbraciated elements. It has been shown that in many languages elements such as nonterms and adverbs are undergoing, or have undergone, exbraciation. In contrast, nonsubjectival terms (including direct, indirect, and locative objects) maintain their position within the verb brace. This division is in keeping with what is known about exbraciation in other languages (Hyman 1975; Stockwell, pers.com.). Elements appear to be moving out of the verb brace according to some hierarchical scale, beginning with "lower status" elements like adverbs, and ending finally with object NPs. This results, of course, in the total breakdown of the verb brace construction.

It is interesting to note that there is some evidence that exbraciation is beginning to affect objects in the Kru family. In virtually all Kru languages, the verb 'finish' is a transitive verb, and it may take a simple NP as its complement, as seen in Godié.

(125) ɔ yʌ sʉkaá bóo 6ιʌ   'He has finished the
      he PERF rice:ASSOC bowl finish   bowl of rice.'

But often this verb takes a complex (verb-derived) complement:

(126) Godié
    wa 6ìλ̃   mʌlʌ lι   nʌ
    they finish drink-NOM NF
    'When they had finished drinking, ...'

(127) Dewoin
    ɔ́ gwɛ̀ 6í-ɔ́   6úlú   'He finished digging the
    he finish hole-DEF dig   hole.'

When there is an auxiliary, the complement of 'finish' normally occurs inside the verb brace (as any other object does).

(128) Godié
    wa   kʉ   mʌlʌ lι 6ιλ̃   nʌ
    they COND drink-NOM finish NF
    S   AUX   O   V

However, in Dewoin, such complex complements of the verb 'finish' occur obligatorily outside the verb brace.

(129) ɔ nã gwɛ̀ kwɔ̃ wɔlɔ̃
      he PERF finish clothes wash
      S AUX V   O
      'She has finished washing clothes.'

Exbraciation: The Breakdown of S AUX (O) V

(130) ɔ mu gwɛ̀ ɔ nù mu   'He will finish doing it.'
      he FUT finish it do FUT
      S AUX V   O

Yet, other Dewoin verbs which take nominalized verb phrases as complements maintain the expected word order S AUX O V.

(131) ɔ nã̀ kwiɛ wɔ́lɔ̃ 65   'He has stopped washing
      he PERF clothes wash stop   clothes.'
      S AUX   O   V

It appears, then, that the complex construction which is functioning as the object of 'finish' in examples 129 and 130 has been exbraciated. If object exbraciation is eventually to take place on a large scale within the Kru family, this is exactly how it would be expected to begin: by affecting one member of a lexical class (see sect. 5.4.3).

Constructions like those in 129 tend to suggest that the principle of auxiliary-verb attraction is at work here, since **nã̀** (PERF) and **gwɛ̀** 'finish' are united. A possible further development might be the reanalysis of this entire structure into the following simpler already existing pattern:

ɔ nã̀ + gwɛ̀ kwɔ̃ wɔlɔ̃
S   AUX   O   V

where **nã̀gwɛ̀** would function as a bimorphemic unit. It will be remembered that similar units have emerged as future auxiliaries (see sect. 3.8.2).

It is important to point out here that this is the only example in the entire Kru family found in the course of this study which shows an object being moved out of the verb brace. So, the basic generalization holds: nonterms (adverbs, peripheral locatives, and reason phrases) have been, or are on their way to being, exbraciated, while terms (direct and indirect objects) systematically resist being dislodged from the verb brace. Only the lonely case of Dewoin 'finish' may point the way to a complete breakdown of the S AUX (O) V construction.

5.5 Alternative Proposals

This chapter thus far has been devoted to showing how exbraciation has affected the Kru family. It seems only fair at this point to examine alternative proposals. If exbraciation is not a real process, there are two possible explanations of the data: one involving "inbraciation" (movement of elements into the verb brace, rather than out) and one involving the claim that there has been neither exbraciation nor inbraciation. These two hypotheses will now be discussed.

5.5.1 Proposal I: Inbraciation. One of the most obvious alternative explanations of the data in this chapter is that elements are moving into the verb brace, rather than out.

In chapter 1, it was stated that in this study, arguments would rely heavily on synchronic data from the Kru language family and a certain body of facts consisting of attested cases of linguistic change. To decide between the hypotheses of exbraciation and inbraciation, the attested cases of word order change must be reviewed. It was mentioned earlier that exbraciation is attested in at least two families where historical documentation is available: in the Germanic family (viz. English and German) and in the Hellenic family (Greek). It was shown that the motivation for exbraciation in Kru parallels, in many ways, arguments supplied by Stockwell (1977) and Aitchison (see sect. 5.3)--arguments that included the pressure of the VX order in noncomplex sentences and verb-auxiliary attraction, as well as the basic pattern
S AUX (O) V X,
which was established through the use of several stylistic devices. Thus there is motivation for exbraciation, and there are historical precedents for such types of changes.

To my knowledge, there is no precedent for inbraciation, i.e., movement of elements into the verb brace. Saeed Ali (pers.com.) has suggested that such a change occurred in Hindi. Unfortunately I have not been able to see his data. Hyman (forthcoming) does, however, note that in at least one Niger-Congo language, Aghem, there are the variant word orders S AUX V O X and S AUX O V X. He proposes that Aghem has a defocussing mechanism, whereby elements moved into the verb brace are defocussed. So far, my studies in Kru have not revealed any such defocussing mechanism. From my own intuitions in Godié, I would say, however, that in the sentences (a) ɔɔ́ wʋ̀ zʉkʌ sʉkʌ̄ lɨ (he-NEG NEG today rice eat) and (b) ɔɔ́ wʋ̀ sʉkʌ̄ lɨ zʉkʌ 'He didn't eat rice today.', there seems to be more emphasis on 'today' in (b). Otherwise, there appears to be no good reason why speakers would deliberately wish to interrupt an AUX-V sequence by the inbraciation of certain elements.

Thus, if motivation for a change is significant, the exbraciation theory seems more plausible than a scenario involving inbraciation.

5.5.2 Proposal II: No exbraciation nor inbraciation took place. The second alternative explanation would be that there has been neither exbraciation nor inbraciation. In chapters 3 and 4 it was claimed that the structure $S\ V_1\ (O)\ V_{2\ nom}$ gave rise to the present-day S AUX O V construction. One possible interpretation of the data as they have been presented is that nonterm elements and items such as adverbs always occurred after the object in the source structure. Schematically, then, this would give the following source structure:

$$S\ V_1\ O\ V_{2\ nom}\ X$$

Exbraciation: The Breakdown of S AUX (O) V

Upon reinterpretation, the following structure would be obtained:

$$S\ V_1\ O\ V_{2\ nom}\ X$$
$$S\ AUX\ O\ V\ \ \ \ \ X$$

If this scenario is accepted, it means that languages like Wobé (where the previous analysis suggested that all nonterm elements and adverbs have been exbraciated) have really undergone no change at all. The constructions in Eastern Kru (S AUX X O V) would have to be explained, however. This could be done by claiming that languages in the Eastern group followed a rule interchanging the object and elements like adverbs.

$$S\ V\ \underline{O}\ X\ \longrightarrow\ S\ V\ \underline{X}\ \underline{O}$$

When this rule is applied to the source construction, it yields the correct synchronic output.

(i) $S\ V_1\ OV_2\ X$
(ii) $S\ V_1\ X\ OV_2$ (word order shift)
(iii) $S\ AUX\ X\ OV$ (reinterpretation)

There are problems with this hypothesis, however. First, there is no motivation for the (i) --> (ii) word order shift. Second, even if the word order in Eastern Kru can be explained by this scenario, problems remain with the data from Western Kru. While languages in this group do conform to the S AUX O V X pattern, there are exceptions. In many languages there is at least one lexical item which disrupts the S AUX O V X pattern by occurring within the verb brace. In Borobo, time adverbs typically occur inside or outside the verb brace, but the adverb 'again' cannot occur outside the verb brace.

(132) ɔ í { dyīnòwànà / le } kòà nu   ɔ é koa nu <u>dyīnòwànà</u>

he NEG { today / again } work do   *ɔ é koa nu <u>le</u>

'He didn't work { today / again }.'

Similar data exist in Nyabo. Thus it would appear that there is evidence that, historically, elements moved out of the verb brace, leaving the adverb 'again' in its pre-exbraciation position. These exceptions considerably weaken the propositions that S AUX O V X was the original proto-order.

Thus, the alternatives to exbraciation (inbraciation or the S AUX O V X theory) are not motivated and do not conform to what is known about language change. In contrast, the exbraciation proposal is motivated by structural patterns existing in the family and is attested in other language families with more historical documentation. Furthermore, assuming that the process of exbraciation operates within the Kru family helps explain other historical processes, such as tense innovation.

5.6 Tense Innovation and Exbraciation

In the Kru family, most languages have a limited number of tense markers. In some Western languages, like Wobé and Krahn, there are apparently no tense markers at all. However, in others, especially those of the Grebo complex, there are many tense markers. In this section, it will be shown that temporal adverbs have been reduced and reanalyzed as tense markers. The data given will reinforce the scenario of exbraciation as it was presented in preceding sections of this chapter.

5.6.1 The data. In several Kru languages, there are two tense markers--one indicating recent past and one indicating remote past. This can be seen in Godié:

(133) ɔ lɨ a sʉkʌ 'He was eating rice (recently).'
      he eat-INC REC rice

(134) ɔ lɨ wʌ sʉk 'He was eating rice (a long time ago).'
      he eat-INC REM rice

There is a subset of Western languages, however, for which researchers have reported a large number of tense markers. Dawson (pers.com.) reports six in Tepo. There are at least four in Nyabo, and Innes (1966:55) indicates there are six tense distinctions in Grebo.

(135) unmarked
      nē dū blā   'I have pounded rice.'
      I pound rice

(136) **dà** 'day before yesterday'
      nē dū-da blā   'I pounded rice the day before yesterday.'

(137) **dɔ́** 'yesterday'
      nē dū-dɔ́ blā   'I pounded rice yesterday.'

(138) **ɛ́** 'today'
      nē dū-ɛ́ blā   'I pounded rice today' or 'I will pound rice today.'

(139) **á** 'tomorrow'
      nē dū-á blā   'I will pound rice tomorrow.'

Exbraciation: The Breakdown of S AUX (O) V

(140) dɔ́ 'day after tomorrow'
  nē dū-dɔ́ blā   'I shall pound rice the day after tomorrow.'

The examples just cited show that Grebo tenses are highly specific in meaning, and it is tempting to ask if these are not just time words ('yesterday', 'today', etc.), rather than true tense markers. In fact, upon examination, tense particles from many Kru languages show a striking resemblance to temporal adverbs and are obviously phonological reductions of them.[9]

The lists on the following pages show that tense markers are apparently derived from time adverbs. However, there is phonological and distributional evidence that tense markers no longer function as adverbs and in fact belong to a separate grammatical category. It will be claimed, therefore, that certain time adverbs have been reanalyzed as tense markers.

5.6.2 Arguments for a time adverb-->tense marker reanalysis. There are several reasons why the reduced particles listed above cannot possibly be analyzed as time adverbs. In this section, both phonological and distributional evidence will be given to show that there has, in fact, been a reanalysis and that time adverbs and adverb-related tense markers belong to separate grammatical categories.

5.6.2.1 Phonological evidence. Time adverbs and tense markers differ in the degree of their phonological dependence on the verb. In many languages, adverb-derived tense markers are phonologically bound to the verb stem and thus do not have the status of an independent time word. Many of the particles have the shape V.

e	'a long time ago'	Nyabo
a	'tomorrow'	Borobo
ε	'today'	Grebo

---

9 Exactly how the forms reduce cannot be predicted. In some cases, it is impossible to tell which syllable is reduced because the full form is reduplicated.

Tepo	ŋāŋā	ŋā	'tomorrow'

Sometimes the first syllable is retained.

Nyabo	kɛ́ɛ́te	kɛ́ɛ́	'today'
Tepo	kɛ́kɛ́gbō	kɛ́	'today'

However, in the majority of the cases in my corpus it is the final syllable which remains.

Nyabo	pāmā	mā	'yesterday'
Borobo	trṓto	to	'yesterday'
Cedepo	tōmɔ́tḗ	tḗ	'yesterday'
Bassa	ɓōzēe	zēe	'today'

Language	Time adverb		Tense marker
GREBO COMPLEX			
Nyabo	'today'	kɛ́ɛ́tḗ	kɛ̄ɛ̄
	'yesterday'	pàmā̃	mā̃
	'tomorrow'	?	a
	'a long time ago'	sēkèē̃(kḗ)	ē̃
Borobo	'yesterday'	trótʊ	to
	'tomorrow'	gââ	ā
Dyabo	'yesterday'	pama	ma
	'tomorrow'	?	kā̃
Cedepo	'yesterday'	tómɔ́tḗ	tḗ
	'day before yesterday'	ceneya	ya ~ ɗa ~ ã̄ ~ nã̄
	'tomorrow'	kã̀	kã̄
	'later today'	?	ā
Tepo	'today'	kɛ́kɛ́gbɔ̀	kɛ̀
	'yesterday'	tʊtʊtʊ	tʊ
	'tomorrow'	ŋàŋà	ŋà̃
	'earlier today'	?	wɛ̀
	?		lá̀ (far past)
	?		ò (past)
Grebo	'yesterday'	tédɔ́dɔ́	dɔ́
	'today'	tɛtinɛ́ɛ̀	ɛ́
	'day-before-yesterday'	?	dá
	'tomorrow'	?	à
	'day-after-tomorrow'	?	dɔ́
NOT IN GREBO COMPLEX			
Bassa River Cess	'yesterday'	pàniwá	wà
Grand Bassa	'yesterday'	ma6àa	maá
	'today'	6ɔ́zèe	zèe
Klao Talo	'one day removed'	pɛ́plaáka	aka (yesterday)
			kã́ (tomorrow)
			ka (discourse-related)
	'day-before-yesterday'	susumá	omá
	'today'	sɔnatí	front V (earlier today)
	'day after tomorrow'	?	lamá

Exbraciation: The Breakdown of S AUX (O) V   257

Language	Time adverb		Tense marker
Sɛttra	'one day removed'	poopraka	ka/aka
Gbuu	'yesterday'	pooplakana	ka
Neyo	'tomorrow'	kɛɛlɛ	lɛ
	'yesterday'	kaalaa	la
Bakwé	'tomorrow'	sremagbâpek	pe
	'long time ago'	yialewũlȅ	i

While the syllable structure V is certainly possible in Kru, it is generally restricted to two classes of morphemes: pronouns and suffixes of various types (plural, definite, associative, nominalizers, and aspectual markers). Thus, the reduced forms seem to occur as suffixes on the verb, rather than appear as full independent phonological words (like regular time adverbs).

Also, in some languages, adverb-derived tenses undergo phonological changes which typically are restricted to the phonological word. In Grebo (Innes 1966:55), tense markers are affixed to the verb stem, as seen in 135-140. Since they are suffixes, they assimilate to the nasal quality of the verb. In 141, the suffix **da** 'the day before yesterday' maintains its shape because the verb stem is oral.

(141) **nḗ dū́-dá̀ blȃ**   'I pounded rice the day
     I pound-T rice   before yesterday.'

However, in 142 the suffix changes shape because the stem is nasalized.

(142) **nḗ pĩ́-nà́ blȃ**   'I cooked rice the day
     I cook-T rice   before yesterday.'

In Talo Klao, the marker may assimilate to the vowel height of the verb stem or auxiliary (data from Singler).

(143) **sē̄tū̄ dī́-ūmā́   tī̄˜**   'Seto ate palm kernels the day
     Seto eat-DBY palm kernels   before yesterday.'

     sē̄tū̄ sē̄-ōmā́   tī̄˜   dī̀ 'Seto didn't eat palm
     Seto NEG-DBY palm kernels eat   kernels the day before yesterday.'

(144) **sē̄tū̄ dī́-ī́   tī̄˜**   'Seto ate palm kernels
     Seto eat-ET palm kernels   earlier today.'

     sē̄tū̄ sē̄-é̄   tī̄ˋ   dī̄ 'Seto didn't eat palm
     Seto NEG-ET palm kernels eat   kernels earlier today.'

These facts suggest that adverb-derived tense markers are part of the phonological verb word. Temporal adverbs, on the other hand, are independent words. Thus, temporal adverbs and their related particles exhibit very different phonological behavior.

5.6.2.2 Distributional evidence. From a distributional point of view, there are several reasons for considering that there has been reanalysis of time adverb as tense markers. First of all, reduced adverbs occur in exactly the same positions traditional tense markers do. (By traditional I refer to tense markers indicating recent and remote tense, which occur in many Kru languages and may not be related to time adverbs.) Traditional tense markers generally follow the main verb, but if an auxiliary is present, they follow that auxiliary instead, as seen in Dewoin (Welmers).

(145) ɔ pī $\left\{\begin{array}{c}\underline{\text{í}}\\\underline{\text{ō}}\end{array}\right\}$ sayɛ̄ 'He cooked meat $\left\{\begin{array}{c}\text{recently}\\\text{a long time ago}\end{array}\right\}$.'

    he cook $\left\{\begin{array}{c}\underline{\text{REC}}\\\underline{\text{REM}}\end{array}\right\}$ meat

(146) ɔ sē $\left\{\begin{array}{c}\underline{\text{í}}\\\underline{\text{ō}}\end{array}\right\}$ sayɛ̄ pi   'He didn't cook

                                   meat $\left\{\begin{array}{c}\text{recently}\\\text{a long time ago}\end{array}\right\}$.'

    he NEG $\left\{\begin{array}{c}\underline{\text{REC}}\\\underline{\text{REM}}\end{array}\right\}$ meat cook

The same is true of the reduced forms seen in Grebo.

(147) **ne mu-na-o**   'I went there the day
     I go-T-there   before yesterday.'

(148) **ne yi-da-o**   **mu**   'I didn't go there the day
     I AUX-T-there go   before yesterday.'

Thus, one argument in favor of a time adverb-->tense marker reanalysis is that the reduced time particles have exactly the same distribution as traditional tense markers.

   The second argument for reanalysis is that adverb-related tense markers often may not occur where temporal adverbs can. In section 5.2.1, it was shown that temporal adverbs are free in distribution. Sometimes the variation in word order is due to pragmatic factors. Focussed adverbs, for example, can occur in sentence-initial position. Reduced markers, however, never do. This can be seen in Talo Klao (Singler).

(149) **susumā̰ ɔ se-lá ɟi**   'He didn't come here the day
     <u>DBY</u>   he NEG-here come   before yesterday.'

Exbraciation: The Breakdown of S AUX (O) V

(150) ɔ se-omá-ná ɟi   *omá ɔ se-lá ɟi
he NEG-DBY-here come
'He didn't come here the day before yesterday.'

Furthermore, it has been seen that in many languages, temporal adverbs are undergoing, or have undergone, exbraciation. This means that they move optionally or obligatorily out of the verb brace. However, adverb-related particles do not undergo exbraciation. So, in Borobo, temporal adverbs can be optionally moved out of the verb brace, but reduced particles never can.

(151) ɔ í dyīnōwànà kùà nu   ɔ ye kùà nu dyīnōwànà
he NEG today work do
'He didn't work today.'

(152) ɔ ye tó kùà nu   *ɔ ye kùà nu tó
he NEG yesterday work do
'He didn't work yesterday.'

In Nyabo, time adverbs have undergone exbraciation--they occur obligatorily outside the brace. In contrast, reduced forms must occur within the brace.

(153) ɔ hé kùà nu { kɛ̀ɛtɛ́ / pàma }

he NEG work do { today / yesterday }

'He didn't work { today / yesterday } .'

(154) ɔ hé { kɛ̀ɛ / ma } kùà nu   *ɔ hé kua nu { kɛ̀ɛ / ma }

he NEG { today / yesterday } work do

'He didn't work { today / yesterday } .'

Another fact which indicates that time adverbs and their reduced forms no longer belong to the same grammatical category is that in many languages time adverbs and their related reduced forms cooccur.

(155) Tepo

  tōtútú ɔ di **tú** lé 'Yesterday he came.'
  <u>yesterday</u> he come <u>T</u> BE

  kɛ́kɛgbō n di **kɛ́** nē hṹíó 'Today I will rest.'
  <u>today</u> I AUX <u>T</u> BE rest

(156) Neyo (Grah)

  kɛɛlɛ e yi **lɛ** kɔkɔnese pi 'Tomorrow I'll cook snails.'
  <u>tomorrow</u> I FUT <u>T</u> snails cook

(157) Dyabo

  i di **ma** de **pama** 'I ate yesterday.'
  I eat <u>T</u> thing <u>yesterday</u>

 Thus in this section, three pieces of evidence have been given to show that time adverbs and their reduced forms do not belong to the same grammatical category (suggesting that reanalysis has taken place). This evidence is the following:

 (i) reduced forms have the same distribution as tense markers

 (ii) reduced forms do not have the freedom of distribution that time adverbs do

 (iii) in some languages, reduced forms and time adverbs cooccur.

5.6.2.3 A parallel case of tense innovation. It has been shown, then, that there are major phonological and distributional differences between time adverbs and their reduced counterparts--enough to warrant the claim that time adverbs have been reanalyzed as tense markers. It is well known (Givón 1976a) that the most common source of tense markers is verbs. We have shown in chapter 3 how 'go', 'come', and 'have' became future auxiliaries in Kru. In addition, Givón (1971, 1973) has shown how verbs like 'want' in Swahili and 'begin' in SiLuyana have turned into future markers. Also the verb 'finish' in Swahili has apparently given rise to three different past tense markers. According to Hyman (pers. com.), in Bamileke the verb 'return' has turned into a tense marker meaning 'later the same day'. It is also known that tense systems develop from aspectual ones. Such changes are attested in Luiseno (Jacobs 1975), French (Comrie 1976), and in Hebrew (Givón 1976; A. Gordon, MS), where the perfect has given rise to a past tense, the imperfect to a future tense, and a participial form to a present tense. But there are few documented cases in the literature of an adverb-->tense marker shift.

In 1968, Kiparsky claimed that tense in Proto-Indo-European should be considered as an adverbial constituent. (He notes that in 1880, Muller made a similar claim concerning tenses in Proto-Indo-European.) This proposal met with considerable opposition, however, because he had no real etymological evidence for linking tense markers with adverbs (Comrie, pers.com.). However, such a link has been established in an English-based pidgin, Neo-Melanesian. Labov (1971) claims that the future marker in Neo-Melanesian is derived from an adverbial marker 'by and by'. He gives the following four pieces of evidence in favor of this analysis (see also Sankoff and Laberge 1974):

(i) the future marker **bai** is a reduction of an adverbial expression **baimbai** ('by and by')

(ii) the particle has lost obligatory stress (suggesting it has changed from an independent word to a clitic)

(iii) it cooccurs with adverbs having a future reading:

<u>klostu</u> <u>bai</u> i dai

soon FUT he die

(iv) normally adverbs occur in sentence-initial position, but there is now a tendency for **bai** to occur between the subject and the main verb:

em <u>bai</u> kisim ples bilong John Tovue

he FUT

'He will come to take the place of John Tovue.'

Comparing the above developments with the adverb-->tense shift in Kru, one sees several similarities. First of all, tense markers in both Neo-Melanesian and Kru are reductions of full time adverbs. Second, the Neo-Melanesian particle **bai** loses stress. While there has been no systematic study of stress in the Kru group as a whole (an exception to this is Innes's (1966) and Luckau's (1975) studies of Grebo stress where it is claimed that stress in Grebo is contrastive), there is a parallel between loss of stress in Neo-Melanesian and the shift from independent word to verbal suffix in Kru. Third, as is the case in Neo-Melanesian, tense markers cooccur with time adverbs (emphasizing their separateness as a category).

The fourth point made by Labov involves the distribution of tense markers. In Neo-Melanesian there is evidently a change in progress concerning the position of the reduced particle **bai**. Originally **baimbai** occurred in sentence-initial position, but now the reduced form **bai** may occur in sentence-second position (between the subject and the verb). The change is not complete since **bai** occurs in this position only when the subject is a full noun or a third person pronoun. The shift seems significant, however, since cross-linguistically sentence-second position is the most likely position for modal elements (Steele 1973, 1975). Steele claims, in fact, that "since grammaticized elements tend to certain positions, their positions do not necessarily reflect pre-grammaticization word order." We have already seen that all tense markers in Kru (whether traditional or adverb-derived) are always attached to (or follow) the verb, or the auxiliary if one is present. It is interesting to note that in Kru these two elements are generally in sentence-second position. It is possible, then, following Steele's suggestion, that time adverbs in Kru originally occurred in sentence-initial or sentence-final position and, upon being reduced and grammaticized, became attached to the element in sentence-second position--that element being the verb or the auxiliary--thus paralleling the reduction and shift to second position of Neo-Melanesian **baimbai**.

In Kru, however, there is a much more plausible explanation. It has been claimed in preceding sections of this chapter that elements like time adverbs occur in postverbal or postauxiliary position, that is, within the verb brace. It was shown that this is the most common order in Eastern Kru at the present time (see examples 5-7). If these assumptions about word order are correct, then the reanalysis of time adverbs into tense markers took place without any shift in word order.

$$S \left\{ \begin{array}{c} V \\ AUX \end{array} \right\} ADV_{time} \left\{ \begin{array}{c} O \\ OV \end{array} \right\}$$
$$\downarrow \quad \downarrow \quad\quad \downarrow \quad\quad \downarrow$$
$$S \left\{ \begin{array}{c} V \\ AUX \end{array} \right\} tense \left\{ \begin{array}{c} O \\ OV \end{array} \right\}$$

Earlier in this discussion it was mentioned that the most common elements which become tense markers are verbs and aspect markers. However, Givón (1976:79) notes that while it is very plausible that time adverbs become tense markers, this does not occur very often because of the distribution of time adverbs within the clause. According to him, time adverbs normally occur in sentence-initial position. The word order as proposed above provides a reason for the unusual innovation of tense markers in Kru. Not only was there a semantic link between time adverbs and the category TENSE but also there was a favorable distribution of elements (time adverbs directly following verbs) for the reanalysis. Furthermore, there may have been a pattern for such reanalysis. If recent and remote past tense markers, as seen in Godié, Dewoin, Tepo, and Kuwaa, are actually reconstructable for Proto-Kru, they could have served as a pattern on which reduced time adverbs became reanalyzed as tense markers.

5.6.3 Proposed scenario for tense innovation. Given the phonological and distributional evidence for reanalysis and facts from a parallel case of tense development in Neo-Melanesian, the following scenario is proposed:

Exbraciation: The Breakdown of S AUX (O) V

Stage I. Time adverbs occur directly following the verb

As was seen above, this stage is still attested in many Eastern and Western languages. The following comes from Bassa:

(158) ɔ se pàniwá kùà nyu   'He didn't work yesterday.'
      he NEG yesterday work do

Stage II. Time adverbs are reduced

At this stage, time adverbs occur either in their reduced form or in their full form. The factors governing the occurrence of the form have not been studied, but it is assumed they are discourse-related. At this point, reduced particles are in complementary distribution with other time adverbs. (Just how this phenomenon would be handled in a synchronic grammar is not known. It is possible that **omá** in the Klao example would be treated as a proadverb.) Because the reduced forms have not yet been reanalyzed as tense markers, they may not cooccur with their related full forms. This stage is attested at the present time in Klao (Singler).

(159) **susumá** ɔ se-lá ɟi   'He didn't come here the day
      DBY   he NEG-here come   before yesterday.'

(160) ɔ se-**omá**-ná ɟi   'He didn't come here the day
      he NEG-DBY-here come   before yesterday.'

(161) ***susumá** ɔ se-omá-ná ɟi

Stage III. Reduced adverbs are reanalyzed as tense markers

Phonological properties (the suffix-like and dependent nature of the reduced particles) and the semantic correlation between time adverbs and tense markers allow for reanalysis. There are now two separate categories: time adverbs and tense markers. Since the reanalysis has taken place, the two may cooccur.

(162) Nyabo
      ɔ hé ma pama   koa nu   'He didn't work yesterday.'
      he NEG T yesterday work do

(163) Tepo
      ŋàŋà n di ŋà a koa nu   'I will work for him
      tomorrow I FUT T his work do   tomorrow.'

It is interesting to note that Talo Klao shows evidence of being at stage I and stage II. We have seen that the reduced form of the adverb **susumā** 'day before yesterday' has not yet been analyzed as a tense marker, while the reduced form of **pɛplaāka** 'yesterday' has. This again illustrates (see sect. 5.4.3) that members of a class are affected by reanalysis one at a time. In this case, different time adverbs within a given language are at different stages of reanalysis.

Stage IV. <u>Semantic shift</u>

Up to this point, reduced time adverbs (stage II) and reanalyzed adverbs (stage III) still carry a specific time reference. Stage IV, involving semantic shift, is attested in only a few languages, but it seems to be a potential area of syntactic change in any of the languages where tense has been innovated. At this stage, the specific tense marker is generalized to cover a larger semantic range. In two dialects of Bassa and in Neyo, the 'yesterday' tense has been generalized to cover all past actions. In River Cess Bassa, the past tense marker **wã** is apparently related to the time adverb **pàniwã** 'yesterday', but the marker may now refer to any past action. As a general past marker, it may cooccur with other time adverbs.

(164)　ɔ　kpɔ̃　wã̀　smi-ɔ̃　seèedɛ̀
　　　he catch <u>PAST</u> fish-DEF <u>a-long-time-ago</u>
　　　'He caught the fish a long time ago.'

The same phenomenon occurs in Grand Bassa, where the past tense marker is derived from 'yesterday' and cooccurs with adverbs with other time references.

(165)　ɔ　dɔ　maā　mɔ̀ɔ　kɔfɔ̃
　　　he buy <u>T</u>　rice <u>day-before-yesterday</u>
　　　'He bought rice the day before yesterday.'

In Neyo, both the yesterday-related and the tomorrow-related tense markers have been generalized to cover unspecified times in the past and the future. The marker **la**, coming from **kaalaa** 'yesterday', gives a general past reading, while the marker **lɛ**, derived from **kɛɛlɛ** 'tomorrow', has a general future reading. (The following examples are from Grah):

(166)　mà　6óyiée　6lá　**la**　mɔ́ɔ
　　　but foot　kill <u>PAST</u> me
　　　'But my foot was killing me.'

(167)　ē　yi　**lɛ**　saaa　nà　jɔ̃jóɔ　pi　wée
　　　I POT <u>FUT</u> also your corn-D fix exclamation
　　　'Later (in the day) I will cook your corn.'

Exbraciation: The Breakdown of S AUX (O) V

In fact, Thomann (1905) includes the tense markers as part of the verbal paradigm of Neyo, with no indication that they are derived from time adverbs or that they carry a specific time reference. In this paradigm, the tense markers **la** and **lē** are totally redundant since **a** already designates a past perfect action, and **i** and **ka** designate unrealized (future) actions.

(168) **passé proche** (recent past—no tense marker)

ō	a	li	'il vient de manger'
he	PERF	eat	'He just ate.'

passé absolu (absolute past)

ō	a	<u>la</u> li	'il a mangé'
he	PERF	<u>T</u> li	'He ate.'

(169) **futur** (future)

ō	i	<u>lē</u> li	'il mangera'
he	FUT	<u>T</u> eat	'He will eat.'

(170) **subjonctif futur** (future subjunctive)

ó	ka	<u>lē</u> li	'qu'il mange'
he	SUBJ	<u>T</u> eat	'He should eat.'

Another semantic shift may be possible, although thus far only one example has been found. In Klao (Talo dialect), the adverb **pɛplaāka** is used to refer to actions occurring one day removed from the time of speaking (yesterday or tomorrow). Normally, we would expect this to give rise to one tense marker to be used for both 'yesterday' and 'tomorrow'. This is apparently what occurred in the dialect of Klao described by Rickard (1970). The suffix **kã** refers to both 'yesterday' and 'tomorrow'. However, in the Talo dialect of Klao, there are three specific tense markers which could conceivably be derived from the same time adverb **pɛplaāka**.

aka	'yesterday'
kã	'tomorrow'
ka	'nonpresent (discourse-related)'

Though the tomorrow tense **ka** may be a borrowing (several Kru languages have the form **ka** meaning 'tomorrow'), it may be that one adverb has given rise to more than one tense marker (the reverse of the generalizing process seen in the preceding paragraphs).

5.6.4 The interaction between tense innovation and exbraciation.

In the preceding sections, it has been shown that tense markers have been innovated in several Kru languages through the reanalysis of temporal adverbs. It was suggested that the most plausible scenario for this reanalysis involves positing the following word order as the source construction:

$$S \begin{Bmatrix} V \\ AUX \end{Bmatrix} ADV_{time} \begin{Bmatrix} O \\ OV \end{Bmatrix}$$

This coincides with what has been proposed as the pre-exbraciation order S AUX X O V.

To summarize, then, there are two historic developments taking place:

(i) the reanalysis of time adverbs into tense markers

(ii) exbraciation of time adverbs (and other elements) out of the verb brace

These two processes are independent, but they do interact with each other. It can be noted that in some languages where exbraciation of temporal adverbs has been complete (Wobé and Krahn), no tense markers have developed. In these cases, it is temporal adverbs which seem to serve the function of tense markers. In Wobé, the following adverbs provide time reference for sentences (Egner, pers.com.).

-kwiie-	'yesterday'
-saan'	'day-before-yesterday --> two weeks ago'
sɔɔ-	'two weeks ago --> one year ago'
kpai	'one year ago --> many years ago'
sese	'very far in the past'

These words occur following objects in SVO sentences.

(171) ɔ mu-ɛ   -Bia'   -kwiie''-

he go-DECL Abidjan <u>yesterday</u>

'He went to Abidjan yesterday.'

These words also occur outside the verb brace. Like other temporal adverbs, they behave like nouns in that they can serve as the answer to WH questions and can occur in sentence-initial position when focussed. The most likely explanation is that exbraciation and possibly a rule of adverb shift (S V ADV O --> S V O ADV) moved these elements away from the verb and auxiliary, thus disrupting the environment for reanalysis. The result was that no tense markers were innovated in this language.[10]

---

10 It is not known if Wobé and Krahn ever had any tense markers. It is possible that there was a recent/remote past distinction before tense innovation began. Evidence for at least one tense marker--a remote *ó--does exist, as follows:

Western Kru		
	Dewoin	ó
	Klao (Rickard)	ó, ò, wo
	(Singler)	o
	Tepo Kru	o
Isolate		ó

Exbraciation: The Breakdown of S AUX (O) V

Another result of exbraciation is that it reinforces the distinction between time adverbs and their reduced forms. In a language like Nyabo, the reanalysis of reduced adverbs into tense markers had probably already begun when exbraciation occurred. The outcome of this sequence of events is that reduced particles stayed within the verb brace, while full time words were obligatorily moved out. The resulting distribution served to strengthen the adverb-->tense reanalysis, since the two categories came to occupy completely different positions. Thus, the interaction of tense innovation and exbraciation seems to have had a significant impact on the development of tense systems.

5.7 Conclusion

In this chapter, it has been proposed that the S AUX X V construction is being broken down by a process known as exbraciation --that is, movement of elements out of the verb brace. Exbraciation was described as a cross-linguistic phenomenon motivated by the basic SVX order in sentences which do not contain auxiliaries, by verb-auxiliary attraction, and by stylistic variations which establish an S AUX V X pattern. On the basis of such a pattern, elements have begun moving out of the verb brace, starting with elements of lesser status (nonterms and adverbs). It was shown that languages seem to pass through stages, where movement is first optional and then obligatory, and it was suggested that individual lexical items undergo the change one-by-one until a whole class is affected. Finally, it was shown that exbraciation may interact with the process of tense innovation and, in some cases, influence the development of tense systems.

Eastern Kru
    Godié   wʌ
    Neyo   wa, wɛ
    Vata   ʋā

(with Eastern Kru adding an extra low vowel o + Vowel). If the recent/remote distinction does go back to Proto-Kru, then this marker would have presumably been lost at some time in both Wobé and Krahn.

6 ON THE NATURE OF SYNTACTIC CHANGE: CONCLUDING REMARKS

This study has included a sketch of the Kru language family (chapter 1), a discussion of the basic aspectual distinctions in this group (chapter 2), a proposal for the development of the auxiliary construction S AUX O V (chapters 3 and 4), and a description of the breakdown of this construction (chapter 5). On the basis of this discussion, some observations can be made about the direction of change within the language family itself and about the nature of syntactic change in general. This brief chapter will contain two parts. In the first section, some implications of my findings concerning word order will be discussed. In section two, there will be a discussion of reanalysis and the role of variation in syntactic change. An attempt will be made to see how the facts presented in this study confirm or extend what is generally known about the nature of syntactic change.

6.1 Implications of This Study for Word Order in Proto-Kru

In chapter 1, it was pointed out that Kru languages have both OV and VO characteristics. This was explained by the fact that languages of the Niger-Congo family were presumably SOV at some protostage (Givón 1975b; Hyman 1975). As languages shifted from SOV to SVO, some OV characteristics were retained. The data presented in this study in no way refute this hypothesis, but they do indicate that at a very early stage, the Kru family had a basic SVO order. Evidence for this claim is given below.

In chapter 1, it was noted that there are two synchronically attested word orders in Kru: SVO and S AUX O V. However, it was shown in chapters 3 and 4 that the S AUX O V construction is not a direct remnant of an SOV order. Rather, it is claimed that this construction arose from an SVO construction:

$$S\ V_1\ [(O)\ V_{2\ nom}]$$
(i.e., S V O)

where OV_2 functioned as the complement of V_1. Thus, while the OV_2 nom word order is indeed a remnant of OV word order, the auxiliary

The Nature of Syntactic Change					269

construction itself has its roots in a basic SVO word order. This claim is borne out by the fact that the development of auxiliaries is an ongoing process in Kru at the present time and the source construction is the SVO main clause pattern noted above.

The second argument for a proto-SVO order is based on reconstruction. In chapters 2 and 4, it was shown that an aspectual marker ***a** and a negative marker **nī** can be reconstructed for Proto-Kru. Both of these elements occur in sentence-second position. This means that the order S PART V O is established as a proto order. The age of this construction is suggested at least by the great amount of assimilation which it has undergone. It was noted in both chapters 2 and 4 that PART often becomes a suffix on S, reduces to a tone, or even coalesces with pronouns, forming new pronoun sets. This phenomenon has led to a rather unusual development in Kru: the expression, in some cases, of both aspect and negation on the subject NP, rather than on the VP. Crucially, Steele (1975) found that the order S MOD V O (paralleling Kru S PART V O) exists only in languages with the basic order SVO. Thus, this evidence suggests that Kru languages have been SVO from a very early date.

It is worth noting that sentence-second particles are common in many Niger-Congo languages. For instance, Steele notes the order S MOD VO in Yoruba (from the Kwa group), Diola (from the West Atlantic group), and Gbaya (from the Adamawa group). This could be an indication that the switch from SOV to SVO occurred before Kru separated from other groups in Niger-Congo.

6.2 Observations on the Nature of Syntactic Change

Throughout this study there have been two predominant themes: (1) reanalysis and (2) the role of variation and coexistent systems in linguistic change. Both of these subjects will now be discussed.

6.2.1 Reanalysis
is essentially the reinterpretation of an element as another semantic or syntactic entity. Many cases of reanalysis have been described in this study. In chapter 2, it was proposed that a perfect suffix was reanalyzed as a factative marker. This reanalysis was basically semantic, i.e., one aspectual marker was reinterpreted as an indicator of a different aspect. Reanalysis may also involve shifting of grammatical categories. In an example in chapter 4, it was shown that an emphatic marker in Godié was reinterpreted as belonging to another category--the category signalling negation. Sometimes in the process of reanalysis a completely new grammatical category may emerge. This is the case with the verb-->auxiliary reanalysis described in chapters 3 and 4. Some of the basic characteristics of reanalysis will now be examined.

6.2.1.1 Universality of elements undergoing reanalysis.
The reanalyses described in chapters 2-5 for the most part have their

roots in widely attested semantic and syntactic shifts. For example, the shift of a perfect marker to a punctiliar aspect occurs in other languages of the world. Comrie (1976) notes that exactly the same shift occurred in French as the passé composé replaced the passé simple. The connection between 'go', 'come', and 'have' and future markers is also widely attested (chapter 3). The development of negative markers from verbs like 'stop' is attested in Welsh (J. Payne 1985), as is the development of emphatic markers into negative morphemes. On the whole, then, the reanalyses which have been described in this study are also attested in other language families.

One particularly interesting case of reanalysis involves the reinterpretation of time adverbs as tense markers. It is especially interesting because time adverbs have not been a recognized source of tense markers in natural languages. The shift from time adverbs to tense markers is found, however, in pidgins which are undergoing creolization (Labov 1971). The data from Kru show, then, that there is essentially no difference in the mechanisms of change between pidgins and nonpidgin languages, at least as far as tense development is concerned. This seems to parallel the claim made by Bickerton and Givón (1976:33) "that the two processes [pidginization and spontaneous diachronic change] are essentially similar and ... both are governed by possible universal linguistic principles ...."

6.2.1.2 Role of periphrasis and semantic ambiguity. That periphrastic constructions are often used to express aspectual and temporal notions is well known (Binnick 1976:43; Vroman 1977). In chapter 2, it was shown that the progressive aspect in Kru is expressed by a periphrastic locative construction with the following structure:

$$S\ V_1\ [(O)\ V_{2\ nom}]$$

For example, in almost all Kru languages, the construction

he be-at house-building
$$S\ V_1\ \ \ \ O\ \ \ \ V_{2\ nom}$$

means 'He is in the process of building a house'. Several constructions are patterned on the $S\ V_1\ O\ V_{2\ nom}$ construction. These include:

he goes house-building
he comes house-building
he has house-building
he stops house-building
he lets-go-of house-building

Many such constructions have or develop figurative meanings and thus express aspectual, temporal, or modal notions. For example, the construction 'he has house-building' does not refer to possession but rather to obligation (he must build a house). Other

The Nature of Syntactic Change

constructions develop semantic ambiguity. In some Kru languages, the expression 'he goes house-building' can have two meanings: 'he goes in order to build a house' or 'he will build a house'. These constructions may exist over long periods of time without undergoing any grammatical reanalysis. If reanalysis is to occur, another step is involved: the development of structural ambiguity, which is to be discussed in the next section.

6.2.1.3 The role of structural ambiguity. Structural ambiguity occurs when a given construction can be structurally interpreted in two different ways. As was pointed out in the last section, semantic ambiguity which has developed in a periphrastic construction may exist for a long time without any change in the structure of the construction. However, a certain change or combination of changes may occur which make a construction structurally ambiguous. This was seen in chapter 3, where the construction

$$S \ V_1 \ [(O) \ V_{2 \ nom}]$$

underwent two changes:

(i) V_1 was semantically bleached in line with certain universal tendencies

(ii) the nominalizer was phonologically reduced

This left the construction with the following shape:

$$S \ V_1 \ (O) \ V_2$$

This string is now structurally ambiguous. It could be interpreted, as it formerly was, with the OV_2 acting as the complement of V_1. Or, given the bleaching of V_1, it could be reanalyzed as the following:

$$S \ AUX \ (O) \ V$$

Indeed, this is precisely what occurred.

The same type of structural ambiguity arose with constructions containing adverbs. Due to the distribution of time adverbs in Kru (in direct postverbal position) and the semantic closeness between time adverbs and tense markers, the construction:

$$S \ \begin{Bmatrix} V \\ AUX \end{Bmatrix} \text{time-adverb} \begin{Bmatrix} O \\ OV \end{Bmatrix}$$

could also be interpreted as:

$$S \ \begin{Bmatrix} V \\ AUX \end{Bmatrix} \text{tense} \begin{Bmatrix} O \\ OV \end{Bmatrix}$$

These examples are classic cases of what is now recognized as a basic characteristic of syntactic reanalysis: "... a change in the structure of an expression or class of expressions that does not involve any immediate or intrinsic modification of its surface manifestation" (Langacker 1977:116. Compare also Andersen 1973; D. Lightfoot 1979).

6.2.1.4 Role of phonological change and reduction. In both of the cases outlined above, phonological reduction has played a role in the development of structural ambiguity. In the case of auxiliary development, the reduction and eventual disappearance of the nominalizer led directly to structural ambiguity. In chapter 3, it was pointed out that this phonological reduction may occur independently or may come about after the semantic shift of V_1. In the case of tense development, it must be remembered that it was the shortened variants of the time adverbs which were reanalyzed as tense markers. Thus, phonological reduction can play a major role in reanalysis if, in the process of reduction, structural ambiguity develops. It was also noted that once reanalysis has taken place, the reanalyzed elements are often susceptible to phonological change.

6.2.1.5 The possible result of reanalysis: complication in the grammar. As was stated earlier, sometimes reanalysis merely shifts elements from one grammatical category to another. This was the case in the reanalysis of an emphatic marker as a negative marker. In some cases, however, reanalysis may affect the grammar more profoundly by causing the creation of a new grammatical category. This occurred when main verbs such as 'go', 'come', and 'have' were reanalyzed as auxiliaries. From one point of view, reanalyses involving the verb-->auxiliary shift can be seen as the collapsing of complex structures into simplex ones. Thus, the complex construction

$$S\ V_1\ [(O)\ V_2\ {}_{nom}]$$

(which could be analyzed as having an embedded S) was reduced to a simplex (or in D. Lightfoot's terms "a more transparent") construction:

$$S\ AUX\ (O)\ V$$

It can be noted, however, that reanalysis has in this case introduced a new grammatical category AUX and has given rise to a new word order. Some linguists (such as Akmajian, Steele, and Wasow 1979) suggest that the category AUX may be a universal one. In this study, I have used the term AUX to refer to those modal elements which have been innovated in Kru. Within the framework of Akmajian et al., the emerging category would be M (modal). Reanalysis has, in a real sense, complicated the grammar considerably. The same can be said about the time adverb-->tense reanalysis. In languages where the category TENSE did not exist, the grammmar has become somewhat more complicated because of the reanalysis. Thus, it can be seen that reanalysis does not always lead to simplification in a grammar (Anderson 1973; D. Lightfoot 1979).

6.2.1.6 Reanalysis as an areal phenomenon. One question concerning reanalysis that has not been discussed in any detail is whether the proposed reanalyses are independent or not. To answer this question, each case of reanalysis needs to be treated separately.

In the case of the 'come'-related auxiliary, it was noted that the auxiliary or its remnants occur throughout the Kru family. Thus, the reanalysis of 'come' as an auxiliary probably occurred at a very early stage, before any major splits in the family. The 'go'-related auxiliary, on the other hand, is very recent. In chapter 3, it was noted that this reanalysis occurs primarily in Western Kru. It was also pointed out that languages are at different stages in the reanalysis. In Krahn, 'go' has developed into a full-fledged auxiliary, while in Wobé, 'go' (used as a future marker) still retains many of its verbal characteristics. These differences suggest that the reanalysis of 'go' to a future auxiliary is an independent innovation in each of the languages where it occurs. Nevertheless, it appears to be an areal phenomenon in that most of the languages in a given area have developed or are developing a 'go'-related future.

A related pattern can be seen in the reanalysis of time adverbs into tense markers. In chapter 5, it was shown that tense markers which emerge in a given language are specific to that language. Bassa has innovated two past tenses while Tepo has innovated at least four tenses (some past and some future). It is clear, then, that each language has independently undergone the time adverb--> tense marker reanalysis. Again, however, it is important to point out that the languages where reanalysis occurs are spoken in one geographic region--in this case, the region bordering the coast (see map 9).

These facts suggest that reanalysis may occur as an areal phenomenon, with languages situated closely together apparently influencing one another. Though many of the reanalyses in this study can be viewed as areal phenomena within the Kru group, nothing is known at this time about the possible influence of neighboring (but unrelated) languages in the cases of reanalysis described here.

To sum up, then, while reanalyses cannot be predicted the set of reanalyses which have been described in this study generally belong to a universal set of possible reinterpretations. It has been shown that reanalysis which involves a change in grammatical category is crucially dependent on structural ambiguity. It was also noted that reanalysis may result in a radical and profound change in the grammar by introducing new grammatical categories. Finally, since language consists of a set of interrelated systems, reanalysis may trigger further changes in the grammar. Bolinger (1968:128) notes that "languages are supersystems in which each sub-system is in barely stable equilibrium. Every time some accident unbalances the equilibrium at one point, the entire sub-system reacts to it." For example, the reanalysis of verbs into auxiliaries led to the new sentence order S AUX O V which is basically at odds with the SVO order. This structure is now being broken down, again causing new changes in the grammar. Thus reanalysis is itself a type of syntactic change and may set off one or a series of other changes in the grammar as a whole.

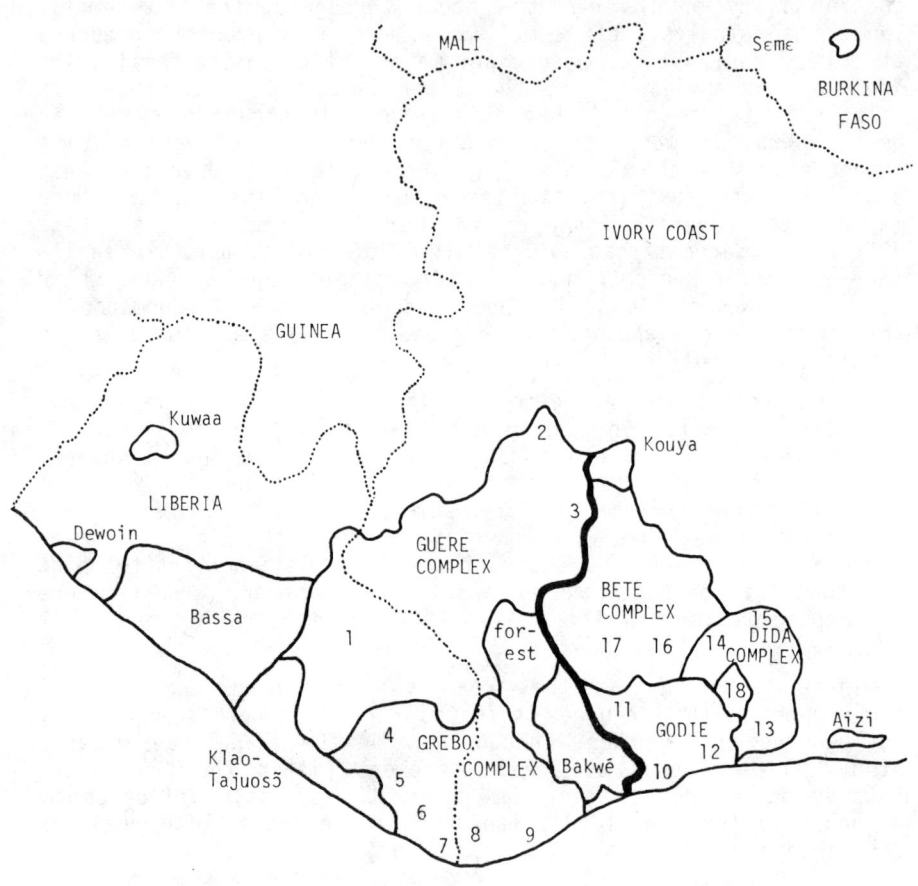

KRU LANGUAGE FAMILY
adapted from Marchese 1979

— division between Eastern and Western Kru

— division between complexes or unaffiliated languages

..... division between countries

☐ areas of tense innovation

1. Krahn
2. Wobé
3. Nyabwa
4. Cedepo
5. Borobo
6. Nyabo
7. Grebo
8. Tepo
9. Bereby Kru
10. Neyo
11. Kwadia
12. Koyo
13. Lozoua Dida
14. Lakota Dida
15. Vata
16. Bété (Gagnoa)
17. Bété Soubré-Daloa-Guibéroua)
18. Ega (non-Kru)

Map 9. Tense Innovation

The Nature of Syntactic Change

6.2.2 On the role of variation and competing systems. In the previous sections, various cases of reanalysis were reviewed and their common features were discussed. Along with reanalysis, another main theme of this study has been the role of variation and competing systems in language change. Many linguists (Anderson 1973; Labov 1971; Vroman 1976; Li and Thompson 1976, to name a few) have noted that in a given language two forms, or constructions, may emerge with essentially the same function. The forms coexist for a time until eventually one "wins out" over the other. Li and Thompson (1976) note that at one stage in its history, Chinese had one strategy for expressing causation, which they call a "non-compound" causative. As this causative began to decline, two new causative expressions emerged: a compound causative and a serial verb construction. These two forms competed over a period of time until the compound causative dominated and the serial causative disappeared. They note (p. 478) that "there is a period of competitive coexistence of the old and new until the former is eliminated."

There are many cases of such competitive coexistence in the Kru language family. The cases in Kru differ somewhat from the Chinese case in that sometimes when two forms are competing, one may be reanalyzed rather than completely eliminated. Below, several examples of competitive coexistence will be given, and it will be shown that the notion of competitive coexistence in Kru applies not only to replacement of one construction by another but also to cases of word order change.

The first case of competitive coexistence was seen in chapter 2, where it was suggested that a perfect suffix **a** was reanalyzed as factative aspect in several Eastern Kru languages. Leading up to this reanalysis, however, was the emergence of a perfect auxiliary which apparently coexisted with the perfect suffix over some period of time. Indeed, in several Bété dialects both markers appear to coexist at the present time. However, in most languages the auxiliary "won out" over the suffix. Rather than being eliminated (which apparently occurred in the Chinese case), the "losing" form was reanalyzed as a different aspect, the factative. In chapter 2, it was also claimed that at some stage of Proto-Kru, the imperfective aspect was signalled by two markers--a verbal suffix and a nominal suffix:

S-**a** V-**e** (O)

It was shown that these two forms were in competitive coexistence over a period of time. In some Western languages like Klao, the **a** form dominated and the **e** was reduced (and has ceased to be a mark of the imperfective). In many Eastern languages, the reverse is true. The **e** verbal suffix has dominated, and **a** has virtually disappeared (except for a remnant found in the forms of the third person plural subject pronouns). Most commonly, then, one of the forms has dominated, resulting in the elimination of the other form. However, in at least one language, Neyo, both forms have survived to the present; but there is some evidence that the **e**

suffix is beginning to gain ground. The form ɔ́ 6lī-ɛ̄ (without the
a suffix) may itself signal the incompletive.

5-3   6lī-ɛ̄   'He is in the process of singing.'
       he-IMP sing-IMP

(a in this case has assimilated to the vowel quality of the subject pronoun.)

Another case of competitive coexistence and eventual domination of one form over another involves the future auxiliaries in Western Kru. In chapter 3, it was noted that a 'go'-related future has developed in many Western languages. Yet there is evidence that an older 'come'-related future existed prior to this innovation. It is presumed that at one time 'come' was the main auxiliary used to express the future. Indeed, this is the state of affairs in Borobo. In many languages, however, the 'go' auxiliary future developed and coexisted with the 'come' auxiliary over a period of time. This is actually the case in Tepo at the present time. In the majority of Western languages, however, the 'come'-related future has definitely lost ground, while the 'go'-related future has dominated. So, in Krahn, Dewoin, and Bassa, the future is expressed by a 'go'-related auxiliary, but the 'come'-related future morpheme persists in the negative form in Krahn and Dewoin (thus confirming Givón's 1975 and 1979 claim that negative clauses are more conservative than affirmative ones). In Dewoin and Bassa, the older 'come'-related futures have been reanalyzed as conditional auxiliaries.

Yet another example of competitive coexistence involves the marking of negation in Godié. In chapter 4, it was shown that an emphatic particle wʊ̄ has been reanalyzed as a negative marker. Nevertheless, the older tonal remnant cooccurs with this morpheme:

ɔ́   wʊ   sʉkʌ̄ lɨ   'He didn't eat rice.'
he:NEG NEG rice eat

In this case, the coexistence of the forms persists. It seems likely, however, that one of the markers (probably the tonal one) will eventually be eliminated or reanalyzed.

Finally, in chapter 5 two more cases of coexisting constructions were described. In the case of tense innovation, it was suggested that time adverbs had both long and short variants. Sentences could contain one form or the other and were basically semantically equivalent. Due to several factors, the shortened forms were reanalyzed as tense markers. Again, this competition between two forms resulted not in the elimination of a set of forms, but in their reanalysis into another category.

Variation and competitive coexistence have also played an important role in word order change in Kru, as was seen in chapter 5. In the discussion on exbraciation, it was noted that as elements moved out of the brace, they seem to go through a stage of

The Nature of Syntactic Change

optional occurrence inside or outside the verb brace. This was seen to be an intermediate position between stage I, where elements occur obligatorily within the brace, and stage III, where elements occur obligatorily outside the brace. These findings are similar to claims made by Hawkins (MS) that as word order changes, there is a period of variation. He notes that if a language is going to undergo a change from the order N + GEN to GEN + N, there will be a stage of "modifier doubling" (both orders will be attested and vary over a period of time). Finally, "the new structure gains gradually in frequency until it eventually ousts the old structure entirely."

Similar stages of variation have been noted in the order of AUX and V in Old English. Traugott (1965:412) notes that for some time there were two orders, AUX + V and V + AUX, coexisting and competing until eventually the former "won out." The data from Kru, then, confirm the importance of the role of variation in word order change and emphasizes the gradual rate of change.

To summarize briefly, competitive coexistence plays a major role in several types of linguistic change: semantic and syntactic reanalysis, as well as basic word order changes.

6.3 Conclusion

In conclusion, this study has given a detailed account of certain aspects of the tense, aspect, modal, and negation systems in the Kru language family. As such, it makes a contribution to the mainstream of Kru studies--studies which all will admit are only in their beginning stages. Perhaps, more importantly, the study provides data and discussion of the general nature of syntactic change, with special emphasis on the universality of the changes described and the gradual rate at which they occur. Finally, it has been shown that considerable progress can be made in syntactic reconstruction and the tracing of historical developments in languages where little or no historical documentation is available.

REFERENCES

Akmajian, Adrian, Susan M. Steele, and Thomas Wasow. 1979. The category AUX in universal grammar. Linguistic Inquiry 10:1-64.

Andersen, Henning. 1973. Abductive and deductive change. Language 49:765-93.

Anderson, James N. 1973. Structural Aspects of Language Change. London: Longman.

Anderson, John M. and Charles Jones, eds. 1974. Historical Linguistics. (Proceedings of the First International Conference on Historical Linguistics) Amsterdam: North Holland.

Anttila, Raimo. 1972. An Introduction to Historical and Comparative Linguistics. New York: Macmillan.

Arvanites, Linda. n.d. Real and illusory patterns of discontinuous negation. MS.

Auer, B.J. 1870. Elements of the Gedebo Language. Stuttgart: P.E. Mission.

Awobuluyi, Oladele. 1974. Binary and non-binary aspects of transivity. (Paper presented at West African Linguistic Society, Yaoundé.) MS.

Bailard, Joelle. 1978. The subjunctive from Latin to Modern French: A study of semantic shift. (M.A. thesis, UCLA)

Bearth, Thomas. 1971. L'énoncé Toura. (Ph.D. dissertation. University of Geneva) Norman, OK: Summer Institute of Linguistics.

────── and Christa Link. 1978. Les tons du wobé: étude fonctionnelle. Annales 11:21-57.

────── and ──────. 1980. The tone puzzle of Wobé. Studies in African Linguistics 11:147-207.

Bennett, Patrick R. and Jan P. Sterk. 1977. South Central Niger-Congo: a reclassification. Studies in African Linguistics 8:241-73.

Bentinck, Julie. 1975. Le niaboua, langue sans consonnes nasales? Annales 8:5-14.

———. 1978. Etude phonologique du niaboua. Abidjan: Institut de Linguistique Appliquée and Société International de Linguistique.

———, C. Lesage, and Verena Hofer. 1974. Enquête dialectale des langues guéré, nyabwa, nyédebwa, kouya en relation complémentaire avec le wobé-tao. MS.

Bertkau, Jana S. 1975. A Phonology of Bassa. Monrovia: Peace Corps.

———, Gbadyu, Duitsman, and Mueller. 1974. A Survey of Bassa Dialects. Monrovia: The Ministry of Education and the Institute for Liberian Languages.

Benveniste, Emile. 1968. Mutations of linguistic categories. In Directions for Historical Linguistics, ed. by Winfred P. Lehmann, and Yakov Malkiel. Austin: Texas UP. pp. 81-94.

Bickerton, Derek and Talmy Givón. 1976. Pidginization and syntactic change: from SXV and VSX to SVX. In Papers from the Parasession on Diachronic Syntax, ed. by Sanford B. Steever, Carol A. Walker, and Salikoko S. Mufwene. Chicago: Chicago Linguistics Society. pp. 9-39.

Binnick, Robert I. 1971. Will and be going to. In Papers from the Seventh Regional Meeting of the Chicago Linguistic Society. Chicago: Chicago Linguistics Society. pp. 40-52.

———. 1972. Will and be going to II. In Papers from the Eighth Regional Meeting of the Chicago Linguistic Society, ed. by Paul M. Peranteau, Judith N. Levi, and Gloria C. Phares. Chicago: Chicago Linguistic Society. pp. 3-9.

———. 1976. How aspect languages get tense. In Papers from the Parasession on Diachronic Syntax, ed. by Sanford B. Steever, Carol A. Walker, and Salikoko S. Mufwene. Chicago: Chicago Linguistic Society. pp. 40-49.

Bolinger, Dwight. 1968. Aspects of Language. New York: Harcourt.

———. 1977. Another glance at main clause phenomena. Language 53:511-19.

Callow, Kathleen. 1974. Discourse Considerations in Translating the Word of God. Grand Rapids: Zondervan.

Canale, Michael. 1975. Implicational hierarchies of word order relationships. In Montreal Working Papers in Linguistics, ed. by David Lightfoot et al.

Catholic Sisters at Grand Cess. n.d. Kru Sentences. MS.

Chung, Sandra. 1970. Negative verbs in Polynesian. (Harvard University senior honors thesis)

———. 1976. Case marking and grammatical relations in Polynesian. (Ph.D. dissertation, Harvard University)

——— and Alan Timberlake. 1985. Tense, aspect, and mood. In Language Typology and Syntactic Description, vol. 3 ed. by Timothy Shopen. Cambridge: UP. pp. 202-58.

Clubvine, Percy E. n.d. Bassa Grammar. MS.

Comrie, Bernard. 1976. Aspect. Cambridge: UP.

Crocker, W.G. 1844. Grammatical Observations on the Bassa Language. Edina, Liberia.

Dalgish, Gerard M. 1976. Locative NP's, locative suffixes, and grammatical relations. In Proceedings of the Second Meeting of the Berkeley Linguistic Society. Berkeley, CA. pp. 139-148.

Dawson, Keith. 1973. Remarks on negation in Tepo Kru. Language Data 21. Dallas: Summer Institute of Linguistics.

———. 1975. L'accord vocalique en tépo. Annales 8:15-26.

———. 1975. Tépo clause types. MS.

———. 1975. The Kru dialect cluster. MS.

Decamp, David and Ian F. Hancock, eds. 1974. Pidgins and Creoles: Current Trends and Prospects. Washington, D.C.: Georgetown UP.

Delafosse, M. 1904. Vocabulaires comparatifs de plus de 60 langues ou dialectes parés a la Côte-d'Ivoire. Paris.

Devlin, E., M. Thurber, K. Knight, and A. McCormick. n.d. Beginning Kru. (Liberian Language Development Project) San Francisco, CA.: San Francisco State College.

Duitsman, John. n.d. Phonology of Krahn. Institute of Liberian Languages. MS.

———, N. Campbell, and N. Kwejige. 1972. A survey of the Guéré dialects in the Ivory Coast. Institute of Liberian Languages. MS.

Egner, Ingeborg and Verena Hofer. 1978. Information marquée dans la proposition wobé. Annales 11:10-19.

Fauquenoy, Marguerite Saint-Jacques. 1974. Guyanese: a French creole. In Pidgins and Creoles: Current Trends and Prospects, ed. by David DeCamp and Ian F. Hancock. Washington, D.C.: Georgetown UP. pp. 27-37.

Friedrich, Paul. 1974. On aspect theory and Homeric aspect. (IJAL Memoir 28) Chicago: UP.

Givón, Talmy. 1971a. Historical syntax and synchronic morphology: an archeologist's field trip. In Papers from the Seventh Regional Meeting of the Chicago Linguistic Society. Chicago: Chicago Linguistic Society. pp. 394-415.

———. 1971b. On the verbal origin of Bantu verbal suffixes. Studies in African Linguistics 2:145-64.

———. 1972. Studies in ChiBemba and Bantu grammar. (Studies in African Linguistics, Supplement 3) Los Angeles: UCLA Press.

———. 1973. The time-axis phenomenon. Language 49:890-925.

———. 1975a. Negation in languages: pragmatics, function, ontology. In Stanford Working Papers in Universals 18:59-116.

———. 1975b. Serial verbs and syntactic change: Niger Congo. In Word Order and Word Order Change, ed. by Charles N. Li. Austin: Texas UP. pp. 49-112.

———. 1976a. On the SOV reconstruction of Southern Nilotic: Internal evidence from Toposa. In Papers in Honor of William E. Welmers, ed. by Larry M. Hyman, Leon C. Jacobson, and Russell G. Schuh. (Studies in African Linguistics, Supplement 6.) Los Angeles: Department of Linguistics, UCLA. pp. 73-93.

———. 1976b. On VS word order in Israeli Hebrew: Pragmatics and typological change. In Papers in Hebrew Syntax, ed. by Peter Cole. Amsterdam: North Holland.

———. 1979. On Understanding Grammar. New York: Academic Press.

———. 1982. Tense-aspect modality: The Creole prototype and beyond. In Tense-Aspect: Between Semantics and Pragmatics, ed. by Paul J. Hopper. Amsterdam: John Benjamin. pp. 115-163.

Gordon, Amnon. 1983. Aspects in Hebrew. MS.

Gratrix, Carol. 1975. Morphotonologie du godié. Annales 1:62-69.

——— and Lynell Marchese. 1974. Enquête dialectale dida, godié, et neyo. MS.

Greenberg, Joseph H. 1963. Some universals of grammar with particular reference to the order of meaningful elements. In Universals of Language, ed. by Joseph H. Greenberg. Cambridge, Mass.: M.I.T. Press.

———. 1966. The Languages of Africa. Bloomington: Indiana UP.

Grimes, Joseph E., ed. 1978. Papers on Discourse. 1978. Dallas: Summer Institute of Linguistics.

Grosu, Alexander and Sandra A. Thompson. 1977. Constraints on the distribution of NP clauses. Language 53:104-151.

Haiman, John. 1974. Targets and Syntactic Change. The Hague: Mouton.

———. 1978. Conditionals are topics. Language 54:564-89.

Hansell, J. n.d. Tchien study. Monrovia: Assemblies of God. MS.

Hawkins, John. n.d. On the nature of word order change: Evidence from Germanic. MS.

Heine, Bernd. 1975. The study of word order in African languages. In Proceedings of the Sixth Conference on African Linguistics, ed. by Robert K. Herbert. Columbus, OH: Department of Linguistics, Ohio State University. pp. 161-83.

Herault, G. 1970. L'Aïzi. In Atlas Linguistique de Côte d'Ivoire 11.

References

———. 1971. L'Aïzi: Esquisse phonologique et enquête lexicale. Abidjan: Institut de Linguistique Appliquée.

Herskovitz, Melville J. and Si Tagbe. 1930. Kru proverbs. Journal of American Folklore 43:169.

Hobley, June. 1964. A preliminary tonal analysis of the Bassa language. Journal of West African Languages 1.2:51-57.

———. 1965. Bassa verbal formations. Journal of West African Languages 2.2:39-50.

Hofer, Verena. 1968. Types et séquences de propositions en wobé. In Papers on Discourse, ed. by Joseph E. Grimes. Dallas: Summer Institute of Linguistics. pp 324-30.

———. n.d. Structure de l'information en discours wobé. MS.

——— and Thomas Bearth. 1975. Système vocalique et sandhi vocalique en wobé. Annales 8:135-58.

Hopper, Paul J. and Sandra A. Thompson. 1980. Transitivity in grammar and discourse. Language 56:251-99.

Hudson, Richard A. 1976. Arguments for a Non-Transformational Grammar. Chicago: UP.

Hyman, Larry M. 1971. Consecutivization in Fe'Fe'. Journal of West African Languages 10.2:29-43.

———. 1975. On the change from SOV to SVO: Evidence from Niger-Congo. In Word Order and Word Order Change, ed. by Charles N Li. Austin: Texas UP. pp. 115-47.

———. 1977. Focus prominence in African Languages. In Proceedings of the Tenth Annual Conference on African Linguistics.

Ingemann, Frances. 1978. A bibliography of Liberian languages. Anthropological Linguistics 20:64-76.

———. 1972. Kruan languages of Liberia. Liberian Studies Journal.

——— and John Duitsman. 1977. A survey of Grebo dialects in Liberia. Liberian Studies Journal 7:121-31.

———, ———, and W. Doe. n.d. A survey of the Krahn dialects in Liberia. (Paper read at the Tenth Meeting of the West African Linguistic Society.) MS.

——— and R. Thompson. 1973. A Kuwaa (Belle) word list. Liberian Studies Journal 5:17-23.

Innes, Gordon. 1966. An Introduction to Grebo. London: Luzac.

———. 1967. A Grebo-English Dictionary. West African Language Monograph No. 6. Cambridge: UP.

Jacobs, Roderick A. 1975. Syntactic Change: a Cupan (Uto-Aztecan) Case Study. Berkeley: UP.

———. 1976. Syntactic Reconstruction and the Comparative Method:

a Uto-Aztecan Case Study. In Linguistic and literary studies in honor of Archibald A. Hill, ed. by Mohammad Jazayery, Edgar E. Polomé, and Werner Winter. Lisse, Netherlands: Ridder. pp. 165-74

Kaye, Jonathan, Hilda Koopman, and Dominique Sportiche. 1982. Projet sur les Langues Kru: Premier Rapport. Montreal: University of Quebec.

King, Robert D. 1969. Historical Linguistics and Generative Grammar. Englewood Cliffs, NJ: Prentice-Hall.

Kiparsky, Paul. 1968. Tense and mood in Indo-European Syntax. Foundations of Language 4:30-57.

Koelle, S.W. 1854 (reprinted in 1963). Polyglotta Africana. Grax, Austria: Akademische Druck.

Kokora, Pascal. 1970. Aperçu grammatical du koyo. Annales 1:97-103.

———. 1976. Studies in the grammar of Koyo. (Ph.D. dissertation, Indiana University) Ann Arbor, Michigan: University Microfilm.

———. 1979. Esquisse phonogique du koyo. In Cahiers Ivoriens de Recherche Linguistique. Abidjan: Institut de Linguistique Appliquée.

Kuno, Susumi. 1973. Constraints on internal clauses and sentential subjects. Linguistic Inquiry 4:363-85.

Labov, William. 1971. On the adequacy of natural languages I: the development of tense. University of Pennsylvania. MS.

Laesch, James and Gary Oltoff. n.d. A preliminary comparison of Ivorian Tepo Krou with some Liberian Grebo dialects. Institute of Liberian Languages. MS.

Lakoff, Robin. 1972. Another look at drift. In Linguistic Change and Generative Theory (Essays from the UCLA Conference on Historical Linguistics in the Perspective of Transformational Theory), ed. by Robert P. Stockwell and Ronald K. S. Macaulay. Bloomington: Indiana UP. pp. 512-38.

Langacker, Ronald W. 1976. Non-distinct Arguments in Uto-Aztecan. Berkeley: UP.

———. 1977. Syntactic reanalysis. In Mechanisms of Syntactic Change, ed. by Charles N. Li. Austin: Texas UP. pp. 57-139.

Lehmann, Winfred P. and Yakov Malkiel, eds. 1968. Directions for Historical Linguistics. Austin: Texas UP.

Li, Charles, N. 1975. Word Order and Word Order Change. Austin: Texas UP.

———. 1977. Mechanisms of Syntactic Change. Austin: Texas UP.

——— and Sandra A. Thompson. 1974. An explanation of word order change: SVO—SOV. Foundations of Language 12:201-14.

References

———— and ————. 1974. Historical change of word order: a case-study of Chinese and its implications. In Historical Linguistics I: Syntax, Morphology, Internal and Comparative Reconstruction (Proceedings of the First International Conference on Historical Linguistics), ed. by John M. Anderson and Charles Jones. Amsterdam: North Holland. pp. 200-17.

Link, Christa. 1975. L'interprétation de la consonne médiane dans la structure syllabique CCV en wobé. Annales 8:205-13.

Lightfoot, David. 1974. The diachronic analysis of English modals. In Historical Linguistics I: Syntax, Morphology, Internal and Comparative Reconstruction (Proceedings of the First International Conference on Historical Linguistics), ed. by John M. Anderson and Charles Jones. Amsterdam: North Holland. pp. 219-49.

————. 1979. Principles of Diachronic Syntax. Cambridge: UP.

Lightfoot, Nancy. 1974. Tones on Kru monosyllables. Anthropological Linguistics 16:425-41.

Lord, Carol. 1973. Serial verbs in transition. Studies in African Linguistics 4:269-96.

————. 1975. Igbo verb compounds and the lexicon. Studies in African Linguistics 6:23-48.

————. 1976. Evidence for syntactic reanalysis: from verb to complementizer in Kwa. In Papers from the Parasession on Diachronic Syntax, ed. by Stanford B. Steever, Carol A. Walker, and Salikoko S. Mufwene. Chicago: Chicago Linguistic Society. pp. 179-91.

————. 1977. How Igbo got from SOV serializing to SVO compounding. In Papers from the Eighth Conference on African Linguistics, ed. by Martin Mould and Thomas J. Hinnebusch. (Studies in African Linguistics, Supplement 7) Los Angeles: Department of Linguistics and African Studies Center. pp. 145-55.

Lukau, S. 1975. A Tonal Analysis of Gebo and Jabo. (Ph.D. dissertation, Stanford University).

Maire, John and P. Thalmann. 1980. Enquête dialectale kroumen. (Série conjointe, no. 5.) Abidjan: Institut de Linguistique Applique and Société International de Linguistique.

Marchese, Lynell. 1975. Morphonologie du verbe godié. Annales 8:215-39.

————. 1976. Subordination in Godié. (M.A. thesis, University of California at Los Angeles).

————. 1977. Subordinate clauses as topics in Godié. In Papers from the Eighth Conference on African Linguistics, ed. by Martin Mould and Thomas J. Hinnebusch. (Studies in African Linguistics, Supplement 7). Los Angeles: Department of Linguistics and African Studies Center, UCLA. pp. 157-64.

―――. 1978a. Time reference in Godié. In Papers on Discourse, ed. by Joseph E. Grimes. Dallas: Summer Institute of Linguistics. pp. 63-75.

―――. 1978b. La Subordination en Godié. (Publications conjointes 4) Abidjan: Institut de Linguistique Appliquée and Société International de Linguistique.

―――. 1978c. Le développement des auxiliaires dans les langues kru. Annales 11:121-31.

―――. 1979. Atlas linguistique kru: essai de typologie. (Linguistique africaine 73) Abidjan: Institut de Linguistique Appliquée.

―――. 1979. Tense-Aspect and the development of auxiliaries in the Kru language family. (Ph.D. dissertation, University of California in Los Angeles) Ann Arbor: University Microfilms.

―――. 1980. Les types de négation dans la famille kru et une particularité du système godié. Cahiers Ivoriens de Recherche Linguistique 6:90-101.

―――. 1982a. Basic aspectual categories of Proto-Kru. Journal of West African Languages 12:3-23.

――― and Ann Hook. 1982b. Enquête dialectale en pais aïzi. In Atlas des langues kwa de Côte d'Ivoire, ed. by Georges Hérault. Abidjan: University of Abidjan. pp. 173-79.

―――. 1983b. Assertive focus and the inherent focus nature of negatives and imperatives: evidence from Kru. Journal of African Languages and Linguistics 5:115-29.

―――. 1977. A reconstruction of Proto-Kru initial consonants. MS.

―――. n.d. Ega MS.

――― and Ann Hook. n.d. The Kru language family. (To appear in Current Trends in Linguistics.)

Migeod, Frederick W.H. 1911. The Languages of West Africa. Vol. 1. London: Keagan-Paul.

Monu, Augustus. n.d. Kru tone patterns. Monrovia: United Methodist Church.

Mortvedt. n.d. Dewoin verb, clause, and sentence structure. MS.

Mulder, Jean. 1978. Universal grammar and diachronic syntax: The case of the Finnish negative. (M.A. thesis, UCLA).

Munro, Pamela. 1973. Reanalysis and elaboration in Yuman negatives. Linguistic Notes from La Jolla 5:36-62.

―――. 1976. On the form of negative sentences in Kawaiisu. Proceedings of the Berkeley Linguistic Society 2:308-18. Berkeley: University of California.

References

Muysken, Pieter. 1977. Syntactic Developments in the Verb Phrase of Ecuadorian Quechua. Lisse, Netherlands: Ridder.

Payne, J. 1860. A Dictionary of the Grebo Language. New York: Edward O. Jenkins.

———. 1864. Grebo Grammar. New York: The Mission.

———. 1867. A Dictionary of the Grebo Language. Philadelphia: Kind and Baird.

Payne, John R. 1985. Negation. In Language Typology and Syntactic Description, vol. 1, ed. by Timothy Shopen. Cambridge: UP. pp. 197-242.

———. n.d. The similarities between sentence-initial subordinate clauses and topics. MS.

Person, Yves. 1966. Des Kru en Haute-Volta. BIFAN 28:485-91.

Pike, Kenneth L. 1970. Tagmemic and Matrix Linguistics Applied to Selected African Languages. Norman, OK: Summer Institute of Linguistics.

Prost, André. 1964. Seme. In Contribution a l'étude des langues voltaïques. Dakar: IFAN.

Pullum, Geoffrey and Deirdre Wilson. 1977. Autonomous syntax and the analysis of auxiliaries. Language 53:741-88.

Rickard, T. 1970. Kru Grammar. Monrovia: United Methodist Church.

Ross J. 1967. Auxiliaries as Main Verbs. In Studies in Philosophical Linguistics. Series 1, ed. by W. Todd. Great Expectations Press.

Sankoff, Gillian and Suzanne Laberge. 1974. Acquisition of native speakers by a language. In Pidgins and Creoles, ed. by David De Camp and Ian F. Hancock. Washington, D.C.: Georgetown UP. pp. 73-84.

Sapir, Edward. 1931. Notes on the Gweabo language of Liberia. Language 7:3-41.

Schachter, P. 1985. Parts-of-speech systems. In Language Typology and Syntactic Description, vol. 1, ed. by Timothy Shopen. Cambridge: UP. pp. 3-61

Shapira, Rina. n.d. Where do tense and aspect come from? MS.

Sherzer, Joel. 1976. An Areal-Typological Study of American Indian Languages North of Mexico. New York: American Elsevier.

Shopen, Timothy, ed. 1985. Language Typology and Syntactic Description, vols. 1-3. Cambridge: UP.

Singler, John. 1979. The segmental phonology of verb suffixes in Talo Klao (Kru). (M.A. thesis, University of California in Los Angeles).

Steele, Susan. 1973. The potential tendencies of model elements and their theoretical implications. (Ph.D. dissertation, University of California at San Diego).

———. 1975. On some factors that affect and effect word order. In Word Order and Word Order Change, ed. by Charles N. Li. Austin: Texas UP. pp. 199-268.

———. 1978. The category AUX as a language universal. In Universals of Human Language 3, ed. by Joseph H. Greenberg, Charles A. Ferguson, and Edith A. Moravcsik. Stanford: UP. pp. 7-45.

Stockwell, Robert P. 1977. Motivation for exbraciation in Old English. In Mechanisms of Syntactic Change, ed. by Charles N. Li. Austin: Texas UP. pp. 291-314.

Stucky, Susan. Locative phrases and alternative concord in Tschiluba. Studies in African Linguistics 9:107-19.

Sylla, Yero. 1977. Perfect and imperfect verbs in Fula: their forms and functions. (M.A. thesis, University of California at Los Angeles).

Thomann, G. 1905. Essai de manuel de la langue néoulé. Paris.

Thompson, Richard. 1976. A phonology of Kuwaa. (M.A. thesis, San Jose State University).

Timberlake, Alan. 1977. Reanalysis and actualization in syntactic change. In Mechanisms of Syntactic Change, ed. by Charles N. Li. Austin: Texas UP.

Traugott, Elizabeth C. 1965. Diachronic syntax and generative grammar. Language 41:402-15.

———. 1978. On the expression of spatio-temporal relations in language. In Universals of Human Language 3, ed. by Joseph H. Greenberg, Charles A. Ferguson and Edith A. Moravcsik. pp. 369-400.

Van Leynseele, Helene. 1978. Restrictions on serial verbs in Anyi: A working paper on the transitivizing function of serial verb construction. (Paper presented at West African Linguistic Society, Freetown, Sierra Leone.) MS.

Vennemann, Theo. 1974. Topics, subjects, and word order: from SXV to SVX via TVX. Historical Linguistics I: Syntax, Morphology, Internal and Comparative Reconstruction (Proceedings of the First International Conference of Historical Linguistics), ed. by John M. Anderson and Charles Jones. Amsterdam: North Holland. pp. 339-76.

———. n.d. Exbraciation as a mechanism of word order change. MS.

Vogler, P. 1974. Le problème linguistique kru: éléments de comparaison. Journal de la Société des Africanistes 44:147-76.

———. 1976. Description synchronique d'un parler kru: le vata. Thèse d'Etat. Paris.

References

Vroman, William. 1977. Predicating raising and the syntax-morphology-semantics cycle: Latin and Portuguese. (Ph.D. dissertation, University of Michigan).

Wald, Benjamin. 1973. Variation in the system of tense markers of Mombasa Swahili. (Ph.D. dissertation, Columbia University).

Walker, K., D. Smith, and M. Budd. n.d. Beginning Dyabo. (Liberian Research Project) San Francisco, CA: San Francisco State College.

Welmers, Beatrice and William E. Welmers. 1968. Igbo, a Learner's Manual. Los Angeles: African Studies Center, UCLA.

Welmers, William E. 1963. Associative a and ka in Niger-Congo. Language 39:432-47.

———. 1968. Efik. (Occasional Publication, No. 11) Ibadan: Institute of African Studies, University of Ibadan.

———. 1973. African Language Structures. Berkeley: UP.

———. 1977a. The Kru languages: a progress report. In Language and Linguistic Problems in Africa: Proceedings of the Seventh Conference on African Linguistics, ed. by Paul F.A. Kotey and Haig Der-Houssikian. Columbia, SC: Hornbeam. pp. 353-62.

———.1977b. Mood in Dewoin. In Language and Linguistic Problems in Africa: Proceedings of the Seventh Conference on African Linguistics, ed. by Paul F.A. Kotey and Haig Der-Houssikian. Columbia, SC: Hornbeam. pp. 344-50.

Werle, J.M. and J. Gbalehi. 1976. In Phonologie et morphologie du bété de la région de Gibéroua. (Publications Conjointes 2) Abidjan: Institut de Linguistique Appliquée.

———, Raymond Zogbo, and Ann Hook. 1977. Enquête dialectale du bété. (Linguistique Africaine 60) Abidjan: Institut de Linguistique Appliquée.

Westermann, Diedrich and Margaret A. Bryan. 1952. Languages of West Africa. London: Oxford UP.

Wilson, John L. 1838. A Brief Grammatical Analysis of the Grebo Language.

———. 1839. Dictionary of the Grebo Language.

———. 1849. Comparative Vocabularies of Some Dialects.

Zogbo, Georges. 1975. Analysis phonologique du bété. (M.A. thesis, Université d'Abidjan).

———. 1981. Description d'un parler bété (Daloa): morpho-syntaxe et lexicologie. Thèse pour le doctorat de 3e cycle.

INDEX

Included in this Index are names of authors and languages, and where they appear in the text; not given are all the occurrences of their use in identifying material in examples. Likewise, only a selected few of the key words and phrases helpful to the reader are to be found here, with some glossary items quoted from the text.

action, potential 104
action, sequential 163-65
adjunct 90-91
adverb shift 266
adverb reanalysis 255-60
adverbs 250-255, 261
  focussed 258, 266
  manner 221-22, 238-39, 244, 245
  temporal 219-21, 225, 236-37, 255-60, 262
  temporal, reanalyzed 254, 272
  time, reduced 254-62, 263-65, 267
  (see also particle, adverb-related)
adverbs (derived tense markers) 255-60
adverb vs. tense marker 255-60
  reanalyzed 260
afterthought ('the addition of forgotten elements onto the end of a clause', 231) 227, 229, 231, 234-35
affirmative factative (completive) 59
affirmative future 129, 210
Aghem 252
agreement (see vowel harmony)

Aïzi 9, 10, 19, 65 (see also isolates, Kru)
Akan 123
Akmajian, A. 272
ambiguity 101, 109
  loss of 101-4
  semantic 270-71
  structural 271, 273
American Indian 1
Andersen, H. 115-16, 271
Anderson, J.N. 160, 272
────── and C. Jones 160
Antilla, R. 123
Anyi (see Kwa)
appositive 228
Arabic, Palestinian 99
Aranda and Walbiri (Australian) 117
aspect ('different ways of viewing internal temporal constituency of a situation' 25) 20, 25, 29-71 (see factative, imperfective, perfect, perfective, progressive)
assimilation 43-44, 195, 201
associative marker 18-19
Auer, B.J. 11, 41, 44
auxiliary 26, 72, 78
  and aspect 80

and full verbs 73-83
and phonological change 141-42
and serialization 83-89, 92
-to-verb "attraction" 233-34, 251
double 146-147
Awobuluyi 90
Aymara 189
Bahagel's First Law ('the general tendency for the auxiliary and the verb to unite forming one constituent', 233)
Bai Boikai 131
Bailard, J. 262
Bakwē 7, 9, 14, 42
Bambara 166, 170
Bamileke 260
Bantu 149
  ChiBemba 181
  Grassfields 111
Bariba Gur 170
Bassa (Grand and River Cess) 14, 57, 131, 136, 196, 264, 273
  Western 201
BE 52, 58, 175, 188-89, 194
Bearth, T. 13, 201
───── and C. Link 16
'be at' 63, 64-67, 188, 213
Belle (see Kuwaa)
benefactive/dative inflectional suffix 20, 86, 233
  (see also: derivational suffix, postposition, and serialization)
Bennet, P.R. and J.P. Sterk 3
Bentinck, J. 11
Benue-Congo 138
Benveniste, E. 38, 81, 111, 138
Bereby Kru (see Kru)
Bété 35-37, 38, 45-46, 51, 104-5, 144, 185, 275
  complex 10
  Daloa 10, 161, 195
  Gagnoa 10
  Gbadie/Gbadi 1, 35
  Guibéroua 176
  Kosseoa 10, 35
  Soubre 35
Bétés 2-4, 5, 7
Betu (see Klao)
Bickerton, D. and T. Givón 270

bimorphemic auxiliaries (see double auxiliaries)
Binnick, R.I. 103, 270
bleach (-ed, -ing) 102, 119, 271
  semantic 103-4
Bolinger, D. 151, 273
Borobo 167, 244-45, 253, 259, 276
Bua 9
Callow, K. 145
Camerounian Pidgin (see Pidgin, Camerounian)
Canale, M. 22
causative (see derivational suffixes)
Central Guéré (see Guéré)
chain, dialect 7, 9
change, phonological 108, 109-11, 114, 127
  and semantic shift 109, 115
  syntactic 204
ChiBemba (see Bantu)
Chichewa 89
Chinese 88
Chukchi 188
Chung, S. 1, 27, 170
───── and A. Timberlake 27, 170
clause, purpose 145-46
clause, reason 223 (see also phrase, reason)
clause, sentence-initial 145
clause, sequential 144-45
clause, temporal 145
clauses, conjoined 87
clitic, tonal 106
Clubvine, P.E. 196, 241
cluster ('groups of mutually related languages', 5) 9 (see also complex)
coalescence 201
coexistence 131, 276
  competitive 130-32, 275-77
coexistent systems 131-32
comitative 87 (see also serialization)
comparatives 86 (see also serialization)
competing systems 275-77
  and word order change 276-77
complex ('a group of related languages', 5: see also cluster)

Bété complex 5
Dida complex 5
Grebo complex 9
Guéré complex 9
complex complement 94, 98
complex future auxiliary 146, 147 (see also double auxiliary)
compound(s) 19, 94
compound, verbal (see verbal compound)
Comrie, B. 26, 33, 39, 63, 66, 68, 70, 270
concomitive 87
conditional 83-86
conditional auxiliary 156-58
 and full verbs 158
 'come'-related 162
 development of 160-63
conditional conjunction 153-54, 162
conditional pronouns (see pronouns, conditional)
conjunct 228
conjunction 87, 153
consonants 13
cooccurrence 101-2
copula 21, 149, 187
Creole, Hatian 111
Creoles and Pidgins 111, 124
creolization 270
Crioula of Guinea 145
Crocker, W.G. 11
customary action 141
Dalgish, G.M. 89
Daloa Bété (see Bété)
Dawson, K. 11, 167
────── and P. Thalmann 11
defocussing mechanism 252
Delafosse, M. 3, 11
deletion 89 (see also serialization)
derivational suffixes 20 (see also suffixes)
Devlin, E. 195
Dewoin 9, 14, 53-54, 57, 106, 117-18, 131, 162, 215, 246, 248, 250-51
dialect chain ('where a series of speech forms are intercomprehensible along a continuum, with speech at the ends of the continuum being quite divergent', 5)
Dida 5, 173, 179
 Eastern 199
 Guitry 173, 179
 Lakota 7, 35, 197, 198, 211
 Lozoua 5, 11, 35, 43, 70, 127, 146, 152
 Northwestern 213
 Southern 184, 211
 Yokoboué 5, 11, 35, 146, 179
Dida complex 5, 10
Diè (Ega) 5
Diola (West Atlantic group) 269
direct and indirect object 225, 251 (see also nonterm)
directionals 108
directions 18
discourse functions 142, 145 (see also innovated future auxiliary)
distribution 258-67 passim
 of auxiliaries 81
 of auxiliaries and full verbs 78
 of focussed adverbs 258-60
 of temporal adverbs 258
Dorobo 9
double auxiliaries (bimorphemic) 146-53 (see also complex future auxiliary)
double future auxiliary 146
double reanalysis 117, 119 (see also reanalysis)
Dougbo 9
Duitsman, J. 9, 11
Dyabo 21
Eastern Dida (see Dida)
Eastern Godié (see Godié)
Eastern Kru (see Kru)
East Ostyak (Ural Altaic) 117
Ecuadorian Quechua (see Quechua, Ecuadorian)
Efic 119, 140
Egner, I. 11, 22
elaborative innovation 204-7 (see also change, syntactic)
emphasis 205-7
English 103, 113, 142, 151, 204-5, 223
 Liberian 124
 Old 33, 205, 227, 228, 232, 277

EQUI-NP 150
Ewe 119, 140
exbraciated locative (see locative)
exbraciation ('the breakdown of the S AUX (0) V construction', 218) 226-27, 233
  and individual lexical items 245-49
  cause of 234
  factors in (see valence)
  of temporal and manner adverbs 236-39
  stages of 235-42
expansion devices 231
factative aspect ('past time for verbs expressing action; present undefined time for verbs expressing state or situation', 31) 30-39
  and semantic overlap 70
  and tone 61, 80
  contrasted with imperfective 39-63 passim
Fante/Fanti (see Kwa)
Fe'Fe' 102
Figian 188
Finnish 123
Finno-Urgric 123
focus ('used in answer to specific questions or to correct a false impression', 79) 226, 228
  effect on word order 79-80
  focussed adverbs 258, 266
focussing 226 (see variations in word order)
Fopo 9
French 37, 70, 124, 160, 270
  Ivorian 233
  Parisian 233
Friedrich, P. 63
Fula 179
  Funta Tooro, dialect of 181
full verbs 73
  and future auxiliaries 73-77, 79-83
  and tone 80
  become auxiliaries 82
fusion (see coalescence)
future auxiliaries (see chapter 3)
  derived from full verbs 82 (see also serialization)
  'come'-related 120-32
  'go'-related 96-120 passim
  'have'-related 120-323
future auxiliary, modals 26, 72, 78
  and aspect 80
  and change, tonal 94
  and conditional 153-63
  and focus 79, 80
  and negative 79
  and obligation 76
  and volitive future 27
  as verbs, full 73, 78, 79, 80-82
  as verbs, main 77
  complex 146, 147 (see also auxiliary, double)
  grammatical category 82
  in temporal clauses 145
  relative age of 127
  status of 77
  syntactic class 83
future, negative 208
future, perifrastic 72
future suffixes 72
Gã 158
Ganoa Bétē (see Bétē)
Gbaeson (see Krahn)
Gbalehi 14, 197
Gbaya (Adamawa) 46, 461
Gbe 11
Gbepo 9
Gbolo 9
Gbuu 257
Gebedo 9
genitive 17
Gérē complex 9, 214 (see also (Krahn))
  Central 9
  Eastern 9
Glio, Oubi 8
German 77
Givón, T. 23, 63, 96, 99, 106, 124, 131, 180, 198, 204, 260, 262
Glebo 8, 9
Godié 7, 45, 78, 140, 151, 204, 212, 236 (see also Jlʉkɔ, Kagbo)
  Eastern 7, 201

Sago 179
Southern 184
Gordon, A. 111
Gouro 7
Grah C. 11
Grand Bassa 9, 104, 105, 264, 273
Grassfields (see Bantu)
Gratrix, C. 11, 127
────── and L. Marchese 5
Grebo 9, 91, 153, 166
  Gweabo 180
  moods in 27
Grebo complex 7, 9, 180
Greek 252
Greenberg, J. 3, 22 (see also universals, Greenberg's)
Grosu, A. and S.A. Thompson 398
Guéré 88, 112, 317, 331, 336, 338-39, 361, 367
  complex 3, 7, 153, 214
Guérés 3
Guibéroua 176 (see also Bété)
Guitry (see Dida)
Gur 170
Gwari 69
Gweabo (see Grebo)
habituals 170, 197, 207
  and imperative 170
  and imperfective 55
  negated 169-70
  negative 216
  past habitual 192
Haiman, J. 161
Hansel, J. 121
'have' auxiliaries 131-37
  and semantic shift 140
Hawkins, J. 23, 277
Hebrew 145, 260
Heine, B. 23
Herault, G. 183
hierarchical scale 250 (see also exbraciation)
Hobley, J. 57, 136
Hofer, V. 22
Hopper, P. and S. Thompson 92
hortative 170
  imperative 180, 192
  negated 170
  obligatory 104, 126, 170
Hyman, L.M. 23, 85, 88-89, 102, 231

Hyman's proposal 83
Igbo 31, 102, 113, 192
Ijo (Kalabari) 84, 88
imperative 28, 180, 216
  hortative 192
  negated 169-70
imperative auxiliary 185
imperative negative auxiliary 169, 184, 216
imperfective aspect ('indicates durative or ongoing action and is often used to indicate action' 29: see aspect) 32, 70, 108, 125, 197, 207
  in Proto-Kru 55-62
  versus perfective 30
  versus progressive 66-67
imperfective nominal suffix 52-55
imperfective verbal suffix 40-52
inbraciation ('movement of elements into the verb brace rather than out', 251) 251-54
indirect object 21, 225 (see also nonterms)
Indo-European 110, 123, 137
inflectional suffixes 20
Ingemann, F. and J. Duitsman 9
Innes, G. 11, 27, 90, 103, 175
innovated future auxiliary 142
innovated negative marker 177
innovation
  elaborative 206-7
  tense 254, 260-7
innovative go-related future negative 132
innovative meaning 109
inchoative derivational suffixes 21
instrumental derivational suffixes 21, 84
instrumentals 86
intension/intent 99, 100
  intension, loss of 98, 100
  (see also shift, semantic)
isolates, Kru 9, 65 (see also Aīzi, jlʉkɔ, sɛmɛ)
  (non-Kru: Ega/Diès) 5
Ivorian French (see French, Ivorian)
Jabo 5
Jacobs, B. 118, 260

jlʉkɔ 7, 176, 184, 185, 204 (see also Godié)
Jukun 123
Kagbo 7, 176, 190, 204
Kalabari (see Ijo)
Kaye, J. 5
Kiparsky, P. 261
Kishamba 111
Kitiapo 9
Klao 10, 46, 49, 84-5, 106, 231
  Betu 9
  Nifu 9, 10, 134
  Settra 9
  Talo 256, 263, 265
Klepo 9
Koelle 11
Kokora, D.P. 7, 13, 40, 59, 77
Kosseoa (see Bêtê)
Kouyas 7
Koyo 7, 10, 59, 77, 184
Kpelle (see Mandé)
Kplebo 9
Krahn 9, 46-7, 49, 61, 100, 107, 253
  Gbaeson 9, 47, 49, 61, 115, 125, 161
  Konobo 166
  Tchien 9, 61, 134, 179
Krio 111
Kru (classification) 2-10
  Bereby (Piê) Kru 9
  Eastern 5-7
  history of 23
  isolates (see Aīzi, Kuwaa, sɛmɛ) 9, 10, 65
  Modern Eastern 37
  Proto-Eastern 37
  Proto-Kru 35, 36, 38, 55, 62, 68, 70, 117, 166, 196, 203, 262, 267, 269, 275
  Proto-Western 55, 174
  Settra (Setra) 9
  Southeastern 207
  Tepo 9, 53, 107, 109, 113, 117, 142, 174, 190, 245, 273, 276
  Western 7-9, 13, 120
Kuno 232
Kuwaa 14, 38, 57, 65, 155, 177
  Belle 9
Kuwaiisu 188
Kwa 67, 84-87, 109, 119

Anyi 85
Ewe 67
Igbo 31, 102, 113, 170
Fante 86
Gã 158
Twi 109, 158
Kwadia 7
Kwejige 9
Labov, W. 113, 131, 261, 270
Laesch, J. 11, 72
Lafage, P. 3
Lakota (see also Dida) 7, 35, 197, 198
Langacker, R.W. 1, 271
Langdon, 23
Latin 38, 111, 138
LeSaout 13
Li, C.N. and S.A. Thompson 116
Liberian Engish (see English, Liberian)
Lightfoot, D. 1, 33, 82
Lightfoot, N. 47, 106
Link, C. 11, 13, 185
linguistic change 418
locative
  complement 92, 240, 246, 248
  exbraciated 248
  nonterm (nonargument, peripheral) 90-92, 224, 225, 240-42, 247, 251
  noun 249
  particle 207, 224
  phrase 219, 224
  term 91, 243, 246-48
locatives 240, 247
  and adjuncts 91
  and progressives 67
  exbraciation of 249
  nonterm/nonargument 91
  positions of 224, 247
Lord, C. 1, 113, 119, 140
Lozoua (see Dida)
Luganda 124, 149
Luiseno (Azteco-Tanoan) 117, 260
Mahibouo 105
Maidu (Pentutian) 105
Maire, J. and P. Thalmann 9
Malinke (see Mandé)
Mandé 10, 62, 123
  Kpelle 67, 170, 230
  Malinke 123
  Toura 189, 201

Index

Vai 123
manner adverbs (see adverbs, manner)
Marchese, Lynell 3, 13-14, 51, 118, 151, 197
────── and A. Hook 9
────── and C. Gratrix 67
Migeod, F.W.H. 83, 158, 226
mixed system ('word order both OV and VO', 16) 16-22
 implications of 22-23
modals 26 (see also future auxiliary)
Modern Eastern Kru (see Kru)
modifier doubling ('both orders will be attested and vary over a period of time', 277: see also coexistence, competitive)
Mohave 205
mood ('has to do with the actuality of an event, subject involvement, evidence of reliability', 27)
moods in Grebo 27
Mortvedt 120, 131, 182
Mulder, J. 193, 201
Munro, P. 188, 205
Muysken, P. 111, 138
negation 27, 42, 273, 301, 311, 462, 475
 and elaborative innovation 204-7
 and tense/aspect 208
 by negative imperative auxiliary 180, 184
 by negative factative auxiliary 167-70, 170-79
 by negative particle 193-203 passim
 interaction of with the tense/aspect system 208-13
negative conditional 214-16
negative factative auxiliary 171-79
 development of 189-93
 forms and distribution of 171-79
 reconstruction of 193-203
 verbal origin of 180-89
negative future 208-13
negative imperative auxiliary 180, 184-87
negative particles 168, 193-203
negative progressive 213-14
Neo-Melanesian 261
neutralization 61
Neyo 32, 89, 140, 151, 264, 275
Niaboua 187
Nifu (see Klao)
Niger-Congo 1, 23, 62, 83, 123, 138
Niger-Kordofanian 1
Nitiabo 9
nominalized verbs 94
nominalized particle 104
 loss of 104-7
nonargument 91
nonsubjectival terms 224, 250
nonterm locatives (see locatives, nonterm)
nonterm peripheral locatives ('supply information about the location of the action', 224) 224, 228
nonterm ('not arguments of the predicate', 224) 224-25, 251, 253 (see also adjunct)
Northwestern Dida (see Dida)
noun phrase 19
 expanded 229-31
noun, conjoined or relativized 225-26
noun, locative (see locative noun)
Nyabo 9, 259, 267
Nyabwa 9, 14, 53, 64, 136
Nyenebo 9
object
 direct 225, 251
 exbraciation of 251
 indirect 225, 251
 sentencial 232 (see also nonterms)
obligation 104, 126, 137-40, 165
Old English (see English, Old)
OluLuyia 89
order, word (see word order)
Oubi 9, 174
OV characteristics
 of noun phrase 16-19
 of verb phrase 20-21
overlap, semantic 66, 70
Palipo 9

Parisian French (see French, Parisian)
particle
  adverb-related 255-59
  locative 207, 224
  negative 167-70, 180, 187, 193-203, 216
  nominalizing 112
  reduced 258-60
  sentence-second 24, 27, 155-56, 269
'passé accompli pontuel' 35, 37
passive (see suffixes, derivational)
past auxiliary 125
past tense marker 264
Payne, J. (1864) 11, 58
Payne, J. 58, 170, 187, 188, 192, 201, 270
Payne, T. 176
Péomē Wobé (see Wobé, Péomē)
perfect aspect ('refers to a past action whose result is still relevant at the time of speaking', 29) 68-70, 275
perfect auxiliaries 68-70, 275
perfective/factative ('designates punctiliar action', 30) 29-32
perfective/imperfective 29-30 (see also Comrie 33)
peripheral locative, nonterm (see locative)
periphrasis 72
  and future tense 72
  and semantic ambiguity 270
periphrastic
  locative 270
  perfect 30, 63-66
  progressive 54, 57, 63-68
  verbal construction 25
'permansif' 35-7, 69
Person, Y. 10
Peterson, T. 111
phonological change 42, 104-9, 141, 42
  and vowel harmony 113
  in auxiliary 141-42
  in shape of verb stem 108-9
  interaction with semantic shift 109-14
  with 'come' 211

  with 'go' 104-14
  with 'have' 141-42
phonological reduction 43, 109, 126, 255, 271
phonological systems overview 12-16
phrase, locative 219, 224
phrase, noun 19, 225
  expanded 229-31
  purpose 243
phrase, reason (see reason phrase)
phrase, verb 20-22
Pidgin, Camerounian 113
Pidgins + Creoles 111, 124, 270
Pike, K.L. 96
Plapo 9, 109
Portuguese 66, 131
possession 134, 138
postposition 86
potential 104, 126
  'come'-related 126
  'go'-related 104
potential future 27 (see future auxiliary)
prediction 149 (see also volition)
progressive aspect ('expresses ongoing action', 29)
progressive construction (relative age of) 68
  locative progressive 67
  periphrastic progressive 54, 57, 63-66, 68
progressive vs. imperfective 66, 67
prohibitive auxiliary 180
pronoun
  conditional 151-55
  imperfective 108
  presumptive 108
Prost, R.P.A. 51
Proto-Indo-European 170, 261
Proto-Eastern-Kru 36, 37
Proto-Kru 35, 36, 38, 55, 62, 68, 70, 117, 166, 196, 202, 262, 267, 269, 275
Proto-Niger-Kordofanian 88
Proto-Uto-Aztecan 189
Proto-Western-Kru 55, 174
punctiliar action (perfective) 29

Index

purpose clauses 143-45, 150, 163-65
purpose NP 243
Quechua, Ecuadorian 111, 138
reanalized adverbs (temporal) 254, 272
reanalysis ('essentially the reinterpretation of an element as another semantic or syntactic entity', 269) 30, 127, 141, 142, 258 (see also shift, semantic)
  affects one verb at a time 119
  as an areal phenomenon 272
  complete 141
  double 117-19
  of adverbs 255-60, 265-66
  of emphatic marker 272
  of future auxiliaries 146
  of perfect auxiliary 70
  of time adverbs 258
  tone accompanying 109, 141
reason clause 223
reason phrase ('supplies an answer to the question "why did X do Y?"', 222) 223, 225, 239
reconstruction 186
  of the factative marker 33-38
reduced adverbs 258-60, 267
reduced particles 254-60
reduced time particles 258
reduction, phonological 30
  and structural ambiguity 271-72
  of nominalizer 109, 126, 271
  of nominalizing particle 104-5
reinterpretation (see reanalysis)
relative extraposition 228
relativized nouns 225
remnants of a particle 196-99
  of noun class suffixes 17
  tonal 47, 199, 204, 213
  vocalic 46
retracted vowels ('vowels pronounced with the tongue root retracted and the neck muscles tightened', 14-15) 108-9
Rickard, T. 106, 265
rightward movement 227
  rules of 228
River Cess Bassa 9

Romance (Sursilvan Rhetian, see Indo-European) 123, 137
Ross, J. 77
Sabo 9
Sago (see Godié)
Sankoff, G. and S. Laberge 261
Sapir, E. 180, 190
Sapo 9, 93, 146, 191, 215, 244-45
Sardinian 139
Schachter, P. 23, 25, 85
Scottish 67
semantic ambiguity 270-71
  bleaching 103, 104, 117 (see also shift, semantic)
  extension 104, 126, 139
  overlap 66, 70
  reanalysis (see reanalysis)
  shift (see shift, semantic)
Sεmε (Siamou) 9-10, 14
sentence-final suffix 22
sentence-initial marker 24 (see also word order)
sentence-second particle 24, 27
  and auxiliaries 24
sentence-second position 78, 81
sentencial object (see object)
sequential action 163, 165
sequential auxiliary 85, 144-45
serialization hypothesis ('cases where two verbs occur within one sentence, but do not enter into any of the coordinate or subordinate relationships defined elsewhere in the language', 85) 83-89
  objection to 84-89
Setra (Settra) (see Kru)
Shapira, R. 111
shift, adverb 266
shift, semantic 30, 36, 98-99, 103, 110-15, 264-65, 270
  and phonological reduction 109-10
  complete 103-4
  with 'come' future 120-26
  with 'have' 137-41
shift, syntactic 264, 269
SiLuyana 260
simplification ('a motivating factor in syntactic change', 204)

simultaneity 164-65
Singler, J. 11, 257
Soubre (see Bété, Soubre)
SOV 83, 84, 88-9, 109, 227, 230, 232, 268
Spanish 137
stages of exbraciation (see exbraciation)
Steele, S. 117, 201, 262, 269
Stockwell, R.P. 227-29, 232, 235
Stucky, S. 89
subcategorization 247
suffixes 23
  benefactive 20, 86, 223
  causitive 20
  derivational 20
  future 72, 209-10
  inchoative 20
  inflectional 20
  instrumental 21, 84, 86
  perfect 29, 68, 275
  passive 20
  verbal 40, 86
SVO 83-84, 109, 193, 227, 266, 268, 273
Swahili 84, 88, 92, 99, 145, 260
synchronic analysis 120
  variation 2, 218
syntactic change, nature of 268
syntactic reanalysis ('a change in the structure of an expression that does not involve any immediate or intrinsic modification of its surface manifestation', 271) 115, 277
syntactic reconstruction 277
Tagoura 105
Talo Klao (see Kru)
Tchien (see Krahn)
temporal adverb (see adverbs)
  reduced and reanalyzed 254-62 passim
  exbraciation of 236
tense: innovation and exbraciation of 254-60, 263-6, 276
tense marker (see also time adverb) 254, 258, 263-65, 270, 272-74
  past tense 264
tense ('relating the time of the situation referred to to some other time ... the time of speaking', 26) 254, 260, 263 and mood 26
Tepo (see Kru)
term 91, 228, 244
termhood 226, 244
term locative (see locative, term)
Thalmann, P. 9, 11, 154
Thoman, G. 11, 75, 229, 265
Thompson, R. 9
Tiempo 9
time adverb (see adverbs)
  differs from tense marker 255-60
Tisher, H. 11, 61
Tiv (Arvanites) 189
tone (contour, modulated, register) 16, 175, 185, 189, 194, 198, 210, 202, 269
topicalization, reverse 230
topic-comment 198
Toura (see Mandé)
Traugott, E. 23, 110, 277
transparency 114, 245
  transparent structure 117, 272
Trembo 9
Trepo 9
Tschiluba 89
Tuobo 9
Twi 109 (see Kwa)
universality 277
  of locative-progressive connection 67
  of elements undergoing reanalysis 269
universals, Greenberg's 16
  and time reference 110
Uto-Aztecan 188-89
Vai (see Mandé)
valence 242, 243
  as a determining factor in exbraciation 242
Van Leynseele, H. 275
variation 2
  and competing systems 275-77
  synchronic 2, 218
variations in word order 218-26
  of locatives 224-25
  of manner adverbs 221
  of reason phrases 222
  of temporal adverbs 219

Vata 34, 43, 51, 135, 148, 212
Venneman, T. 23, 109, 227
verbal compound 113
verbal particle 196, 225
verbal suffix 36
verb-auxiliary attraction 233
verb-auxiliary continuum 157, 171, 190, 200
verb-auxiliary shift 117
verb brace 218, 225
verb categories 23, 25, 36, 39
verb-derived future auxiliary 142, 153
verb, full 73, 77-83
  and negative auxiliary 180-89, 189-93
verb, nominalized 94
verb phrase 20-22
verb-second rule ('moved the finite verb into second position', 228)
Vogler, P. 3, 34, 43, 51, 149, 236
VO characteristics 16
  of noun phrases 19
  of verb phrases 21
volition 140, 149
volitive future 27
Voltaic (Gur) 3
vowel harmony 14, 15, 16, 23, 113, 123
vowels
  advanced 14, 15
  central 5, 14
  high-back 108
  nasalized 147
  nonretracted 108
  retracted 14
  rounded/unrounded agreement 123
Vroman, W. 66
Walbiri (Australia) 117
Wald, B. 99
Walker, K. 21
Wapa 123
Webo 9
Wedebo and Kplebo 9
Welmers, B. and W.E. Welmers 85
Welmers, W.E. 3, 18, 31, 33, 39, 62, 67, 89, 127, 131, 145, 170
Welsh 67, 192, 270
Werle, J.M. 11, 14, 161
———— and Dagao 176
———— and J. Gbalehi 14, 197
Westerman, D. and M. Bryan 3
Williamson 84
Wobé 9, 13, 16, 58, 85, 91, 114, 185, 192, 245, 266
  Péomé 224, 240
  Tao 237, 239
word order 16, 225
  and focussed adverbs 258, 266
  basic 228
  placement of sentencial objects 232
  rules of 228-31
  sentence-initial markers 24
  variations in 226
yes-no questions 22
Yoruba (Kwa group) 90, 269
Yuman 205
Zogbo, G. 161
Zogbo, R. 195, 196

Summer Institute of Linguistics
Publications in Linguistics

(* = in microfiche only   ** = also in microfiche)

1. **Comanche Texts** by E. Canonge (1958) *
2. **Pocomchi Texts** by M. Mayers (1958) *
3. **Mixteco Texts** by A. Dyk (1959) *
4. **A Synopsis of English Syntax** by E. A. Nida (1960) *
5. **Mayan Studies I** by W. C. Townsend et al. (1960) *
6. **Sayula Popoluca Texts, with Grammatical Outline** by L. Clark (1961) *
7. **Studies in Ecuadorian Indian Languages I** by C. Peeke et al. (1962) *
8. **Totontepec Mixe Phonotagmemics** by J. C. Crawford (1963) *
9. **Studies in Peruvian Indian Languages I** by M. Larson et al. (1963) *
10. **Verb Studies in Five New Guinea Languages** by A. Pence et al. (1964) **
11. **Some Aspects of the Lexical Structure of a Mazatec Historical Text** by G. M. Cowan (1965) *
12. **Chatino Syntax** by K. Pride (1965) *
13. **Chol Texts on the Supernatural** by V. Warkentin (1965) *
14. **Phonemic Systems of Colombian Languages** by V. G. Waterhouse et al. (1967) *
15. **Bolivian Indian Tribes: Classification, Bibliography and Map of Present Language Distribution** by H. and M. Key (1967) **
16. **Bolivian Indian Grammars I and II** by E. Matteson et al. (1967) *
17. **Totonac: from Clause to Discourse** by A. Reid et al. (1968) *
18. **Tzotzil Grammar** by M. M. Cowan (1969) **
19. **Aztec Studies I: Phonological and Grammatical Studies in Modern Nahuatl Dialects** by D. F. Robinson et al. (1969) **
20. **The Phonology of Capanahua and its Grammatical Basis** by E. E. Loos (1969) **
21. **Philippine Languages: Discourse, Paragraph and Sentence Structure** by R. E. Longacre (1970) **
22. **Aztec Studies II: Sierra Nahuat Word Structure** by D. F. Robinson (1970) **
23. **Tagmemic and Matrix Linguistics Applied to Selected African Languages** by K. L. Pike (1970) **
24. **A Grammar of Lamani** by R. L. Trail (1970) **
25. **A Linguistic Sketch of Jicaltepec Mixtec** by H. C. Bradley (1970) **
26. **Major Grammatical Patterns of Western Bukidnon Manobo** by R. E. Elkins (1970) **
27. **Central Bontoc: Sentence, Paragraph and Discourse** by L. A. Reid (1970) **
28. **Identification of Participants in Discourse: A Study of Aspects of Form and Meaning in Nomatsiguenga** by M. R. Wise (1971) **
29. **Tupi Studies I** by D. Bendor-Samuel et al. (1971) **
30. **L'Enonce Toura (Côte d'Ivoire)** by R. Bearth (1971) **
31. **Instrumental Articulartory Phonetics: An Introduction to Techniques and Results** by K. C. Keller (1971) *
32. **According to Our Ancestors: Folk Texts from Guatemala and Honduras** by M. Shaw et al. (1971) *
33. **Two Studies of the Lacandones of Mexico** by P. Baer and W. R. Merrifield (1971) **
34. **Toward a Generative Grammar of Blackfoot** by D. G. Frantz (1971) *
35. **Languages of the Guianas** by J. E. Grimes et al. (1972) *
36. **Tagmeme Sequences in the English Noun Phrase** by P. Fries (1972) **
37. **Hierarchical Structures in Guajajara** by D. Bendor-Samuel (1972) **
38. **Dialect Intelligibility Testing** by E. Casad (1974) **
39. **Preliminary Grammar of Auca** by M. C. Peeke (1973) **

40. **Clause, Sentence, and Discourse Patterns in Selected Languages of Nepal**, parts I, II, III, IV by A. Hale et al. (1973) **
41. **Patterns in Clause, Sentence, and Discourse in Selected Languages of India and Nepal**, parts I, II, III, IV by R. L. Trail et al. (1973) **
42. **A Generative Syntax of Peñoles Mixtec** by J. Daly (1973) **
43. **Daga Grammar** by E. Murane (1974) **
44. **A Hierarchical Sketch of Mixe** as spoken in San José El Paraíso by W. and J. Van Haitsma (1976) **
45. **Network Grammars** by J. E. Grimes et al. (1975) *
46. **A Description of Hiligaynon Syntax** by E. Wolfenden **
47. **A Grammar of Izi**, an Igbo Language by P. and I. Meier and J. Bendor-Samuel (1975) **
48. **Semantic Relationships of Gahuku Verbs** by E. Deibler (1976) **
49. **Sememic and Grammatical Structures in Gurung** by W. Glover (1974) **
50. **Korean Clause Structure** by Shin Ja Joo Hwang (1976) **
51. **Papers on Discourse** by J. E. Grimes et al. (1978) **
52. **Discourse Grammar: Studies in Indigenous Languages of Colombia, Panama, and Ecuador**, parts I, II, III by R. E. Longacre et al. (1976-77) **
53. **Grammatical Analysis** by K. L. and E. G. Pike (1980; revised 1982) **Instructor's Guide for** <u>Grammatical</u> <u>Analysis</u> by K. L. and E. G. Pike (1976) **
54. **Studies in Otomanguean Phonology** by W. R. Merrifield et al. (1977) **
55. **Two Studies in Middle American Comparative Linguistics** by D. Oltrogge and C. Rensch (1977) **
56. **Studies in Uto-Aztecan Grammar**, parts I, II, III, IV by R. W. Langacker et al. (1977-84) **
57. **The Deep Structure of the Sentence in Sara-Ngambay Dialogues** by J. E. Thayer (1978) **
58. **Discourse Studies in Mesoamerican Languages**, parts I and II by L. K. Jones et al. (1979) **
59. **The Functions of Reported Speech in Discourse** by M. L. Larson (1978) **
60. **A Grammatical Description of the Engenni Language** by E. Thomas (1978) **
61. **Predicate and Argument in Rengao Grammar** by K. Gregerson (1979) **
62. **Nung Grammar** by J. E. Saul and N. F. Wilson (1980) **
63. **Discourse Grammar in Ga'dang** by M. R. Walrod (1979) **
64. **A Framework for Discourse Analysis** by W. Pickering (1980) **
65. **A Generative Grammar of Afar** by L. Bliese (1981) **
66. **The Phonology and Morphology of Axininca Campa** by D. L. Payne (1981) **
67. **Pragmatic Aspects of English Text Structure** by L. B. Jones (1983) **
68. **Syntactic Change and Syntactic Reconstruction** by J. R. Costello (1983)**
69. **Affix Positions and Cooccurrences** by J. E. Grimes (1983) **
70. **Babine and Carrier Phonology**: A Historically Oriented Study by G. Story (1984) **
71. **Workbook for Historical Linguistics** by W. P. Lehmann (1984) **
72. **Senoufo Phonology, Discourse to Syllable** by E. Mills (1984) **
73. **Pragmatics in Non-Western Perspective** by G. L. Huttar and K. J. Gregerson (1986) **
74. **English Phonetic Transcription** by Ch.-J. N. Bailey (1985) **
75. **Sentence-initial Devices** by J. E. Grimes (in preparation)
76. **Hixkaryana and Linguistic Typology** by D. C. Derbyshire (1985) **
77. **Discourse Features of Korean Narration** by S. J. Hwang (in preparation)
78. **Tense/Aspect and the Development of Auxiliaries in Kru Languages** by L. Marchese (1986)**

For further information or a catalog of all S.I.L. publications write to:

        Bookstore
        Summer Institute of Linguistics
        7500 W. Camp Wisdom Rd.
        Dallas, TX 75236